WORLD® AIR POWER JOURNAL

Aerospace Publishing Ltd
AIRtime Publishing Inc.

Published quarterly by
Aerospace Publishing Ltd
179 Dalling Road
London W6 0ES
UK

ISSN 0959-7050
Aerospace ISBN 1 874023 85 9 (softback)
1 874023 86 7 (hardback)
Airtime ISBN 1-880588-07-2 (hardback)

Published under licence in USA and Canada by AIRtime Publishing Inc., USA

Editorial Offices:
WORLD AIR POWER JOURNAL
Aerospace Publishing Ltd
3A Brackenbury Road
London W6 0BE UK

Publisher: Stan Morse
Managing Editor: David Donald

Editors: Robert Hewson
David Donald

Sub Editor: Karen Leverington

Editorial Assistant: Tim Senior

Origination by Chroma Graphics
Printed in Italy by Officine Grafiche de Agostini

Correspondents:
General military: Jon Lake
USA Washington: Robert F. Dorr
USA Southwest: Randy Jolly
Europe: John Fricker
Russia/CIS: Yefim Gordon
Asia: Pushpindar Singh
Canada: Jeff Rankin-Lowe
Argentina: Jorge Nunez Padin
Chile: Patrick Laureau

The publishers gratefully acknowledge the assistance given by the following people:

Squadron Leaders Jim Rankin and Paul Harrison, RNZAF, for their help with the Airtrainer briefing.

Vance Vasquez, NAWC/WPNS PAO Point Mugu for the MA-31 target information.

All those, both named and unnamed, who provided material for the *Executive Outcomes* feature.

Denny Lombard at Lockheed Martin Skunk Works for their invaluable assistance with the U-2 article.

Tim Lewis and Chris Shepherd at PRO Strike Command, Wing Commander Squelch (station commander), Squadron Leader Cookson and the personnel of RAF(U) Goose Bay, Wing Commander James Kirkpatrick (OC) and all the personnel of No. 17 Squadron for their assistance with the *Western Vortex* report.

The editors of *WORLD AIR POWER JOURNAL* welcome photographs for possible publication, but cannot accept any responsibility for loss or damage to unsolicited material.

World Air Power Journal is a registered trademark in the United States of America of AIRtime Publishing Inc.

World Air Power Journal is published quarterly and is available by subscription and from many fine book and hobby stores.

SUBSCRIPTION AND BACK NUMBERS:

UK and World (except USA and Canada) write to:
Aerospace Publishing Ltd
FREEPOST
PO Box 2822
London
W6 0BR
UK

(No stamp required if posted in the UK)

USA and Canada, write to:
AIRtime Publishing Inc.
Subscription Dept
10 Bay Street
Westport
CT 06880, USA
(203) 838-7979
Toll-free order number in USA:
1 800 359-3003

Prevailing subscription rates are as follows:
Softbound edition for 1 year: $58.00
Softbound edition for 2 years: $108.00
Softbound back numbers (subject to availability) are $19.00 each. All rates are for delivery within mainland USA, Alaska and Hawaii. Canadian and overseas prices available upon request. American Express, Discover Card, MasterCard and Visa accepted. When ordering please include your card number, expiration date and signature.

U.S. Publisher:
Mel Williams
Subscriptions Director:
Linda DeAngelis
Charter Member Services Manager:
Joanne Harding
Retail Sales Director: Jill Brooks
Shipping Manager: E. Rex Anku

WORLD®
AIR POWER
JOURNAL

CONTENTS

Volume 28 Spring 1997

Military Aviation Review

International

Eurofighter progress and problems

Agreement between the Eurofighter partners earlier in 1996 on work-shares and procurement totals encouraged the UK government to lead the way during the Farnborough air show in announcing its decision to support the £26 billion production investment phase. This was due to be authorised by all four governments concerned before the end of 1996, and Deputy Prime Minister Michael Heseltine said that there was no doubt that the remaining partners would follow Britain's lead. Spain, however, has been experiencing problems in funding its requirement for 87 EF 2000s.

In its most recent report on arms programmes' cost escalation, the UK National Audit Office noted a further increase in the British share of Eurofighter R&D of £1.25 billion, against original projections of £2.88 billion, to a new total of £4.13 billion, or £124 million above inflation. It brings the overall UK Eurofighter programme cost to £15.4 billion ($23.86 billion), apparently including R&D and the production of 232 EF 2000s, plus options for 65 more, resulting in a new overall cost per aircraft of around £66.38 million ($102.86 million). The first of these, says the NAO, will not enter RAF service before late 2001, three years later than originally planned and 43 per cent over budget.

Although more problems are anticipated from continued defence budget reductions planned in Germany, as well as in the UK, it now seems that Luftwaffe Eurofighters will be to a standard similar to those of the other partners, rather than the downgraded and cheaper versions originally demanded by German Defence Minister Volker Ruehe. While the German government is formally committed to completing its share of the £9 billion Eurofighter development programme, revised 1997 German defence budget plans presented last July, which reduced planned expenditure from DM48.4 billion ($32.5 billion) to DM46.6 billion ($31.2 billion), contained no funding for several major military programmes, including the EF 2000. Current Luftwaffe commitments are for 180 Eurofighters, including 40 ground-attack versions, with requirements for at least 20 more; Italy is initially buying 121, with another nine options, making an overall programme total of 620.

By the time of the Farnborough air show, the three Eurofighter prototypes had accumulated around 240 sorties totalling 215 hours in the hands of 15 pilots. They were joined on 31 August in Spain by CASA-built and EJ200-powered DA.6, the first two-seat EF 2000. DA.4, the second two-seat version, was due to follow soon afterwards from Warton. As the fire-control radar testbed, the DASA-built DA.5 was due to start flying with an ECR-90C installed in November, and Alenia's DA.7 was planned to complete the EF 2000 flight-development fleet before the end of 1996.

Prior to the Farnborough show, Warton's DA.2 development leader had reached Mach 1.8 and over 700 kt (1290 km/h) CAS, turns of 6.2 *g*, and 20° angle of attack in 132 sorties on Phase 1 flight-control system software. New Release 2A standard digital FCS software was scheduled to allow Mach 2, 20° AoA and carefree handling to be achieved in Germany's DA.1 in the following weeks, while the next Release 2B issue would extend this coverage with external stores and autopilot inputs. Release 3 will cover the full operational FCS spectrum by late 1997.

Europe

BOSNIA:

US military aid proposals

A $100 million military aid programme has been announced by the US government to train and equip the armed forces of the recently-formed Bosnian Federation. This country is also receiving $140 million in training aid from several Moslem countries in the Middle and Far East. The US aid package will reportedly include 15 surplus Bell UH-1 utility helicopters, as well as 45 tanks and 80 armoured personnel carriers.

Croatia has also been negotiating with Turkey for the purchase of three CN.235M tactical transports from 50 built for the THK by Turkish Aerospace.

CZECH REPUBLIC:

Combat aircraft dilemma

The Czech Defence Minister in Prague said in August that massive defence budget cuts would not allow acquisition of new types at this stage. Czech air force pilots, plus those from Hungary and Poland, had made several evaluation flights in F-16Ds in the US and in a leased US Marine Corps F/A-18D in Europe as part of the proposed combat aircraft re-equipment plans. Defence Minister Miroslav Vyborny said that he saw no alternative to reviving earlier proposals to upgrade the Czech air force's MiG-21s – a plan previously strongly opposed by parliament as a waste of money.

Pressure to change these policies was being exerted by Aero Vodochody, which was negotiating component production agreements with Lockheed Martin and MDC, and by other Czech aerospace companies, to persuade the government to release combat aircraft re-equipment funds. Similar budget pressures in Hungary resulted in the deferment of a decision on new combat aircraft procurement until the spring or summer of 1997.

FRANCE:

Five-year defence programme

France's slimmed-down *loi de programmation*, which allocates Fr1,111 billion ($214.8 billion) for defence spending including Fr516 billion ($100 billion) for arms and equipment between 1997 and 2002, sets out new procurement totals and timescales for most major programmes. In most cases, they are both stretched and cut. Following strong German pressure, the French government has confirmed its intention of buying the Future Large Aircraft and of taking up its full original commitment for 215 Tiger helicopters.

The French Defence Ministry was apparently prepared to place firm orders for 52 FLAs between 2004-15 and allocate Fr650 million in initial funding, although it still refuses to get involved in financing the development phase. It claims that its guaranteed orders would allow French industry to raise the necessary R&D capital on a commercial basis, and it appears that Germany is prepared to adopt similar policies for its 75 FLAs required between 2008-2016.

Following the French example, Germany also withdrew FLA funding allocations from its 1997 military budget. Both countries were expected to become signatories to a revised European Staff Requirement for the $6 billion development phase for the new transport, put forward on 24 July 1996. European FLA requirements were then still quoted as about 293 aircraft, each with a programme price of $75 million (about $55 million), fly-away. The source of FLA funding is still unclear, but the UK has a particular problem in requiring replacements for its second batch of 30 C-130Ks from about 2003.

So far as France's joint helicopter programmes are concerned, Germany will have to accept that the new funding plans will allow only the first 25 French Tigers to be ordered in 2000-2002, for initial deliveries stretched by about two years to 2003. France also planned to cut its naval NH-90 helicopter order from 60 to 27 and stretch deliveries to 2005, followed by only 68 of the battlefield version from 2011. It later raised its overall NH-90 procurement target to 160, compared with its original 220.

Among other major programmes,

The Bulgarian air force operates four specially-marked Aero L-29 Delfins at Shtarkelovo for air show appearances. Delfins are also assigned to several fast-jet bases for training and weather checks.

The Austrian air force's 4th Squadron celebrated 20 years and 50,000 hours flying the Pilatus PC-6 with this colourful scheme. The squadron emblem is the 'Blaue Elise', the blue ant-eater from the* Pink Panther *movies.

Further equipment for the HZS (Croatian air force) has recently arrived in the form of the Pilatus PC-9, of which at least two have been delivered.

This specially-marked Mirage IVP commemorated EB 2/91's 32 years operating the supersonic strategic bomber.

service entry of the first of 60 (not 86) Rafale Ms into the French navy is now planned for 2002, when the first two Rafale Cs will be delivered to the Armée de l'Air, for operation by 2005. The navy will now also receive only three instead of four Grumman E-2C Hawkeyes, with no funding for a second aircraft-carrier, and the air force only three instead of five extra Boeing C-135FR tankers from 1997. AA combat aircraft will decrease from 405 today to 360 in 2002 and 300 in 2015, including 41 Mirage 2000Ds and 37 upgraded Mirage 2000-5s delivered between 1997-2002. In the same period, army helicopter strength will decrease from 340 to 168.

More aircraft retirements

Other recent AA aircraft withdrawals have included the last of five remaining Sud SE.210 Caravelle jet transports from nine originally delivered from 1963. The Aéronavale also retired its last Breguet 1150 Atlantic on 31 August from Flottille 22 at Nîmes-Garons, leaving three squadrons operating replacement Dassault Atlantique ATL.2s in maritime patrol roles.

HORIZON deliveries begin

French Army Aviation (ALAT) took formal delivery at Phalsbourg on 24 June of its first HORIZON battlefield surveillance system. This comprises two Eurocopter AS 532UL Mk 1 Cougar transport helicopters, equipped with a rear-mounted Thomson-CSF radar which can be extended below the fuselage for airborne operations, and a mobile ground-processing station. Most data processing, for surveillance over a 108-nm (200-km) radius, is done on the ground, although each Cougar also has an operator's console. Operational trials by the first unit at Phalsbourg will precede delivery of two more HORIZON-equipped AS 532ULs for a second similar system, due in mid-1997.

GERMANY:

Defence budget economies affect aircraft programmes

Cuts of DM1.25 billion ($786 million) imposed by the Federal German government on the 1996/97 defence budget, to a revised total of DM47.1 billion ($30.85 billion), is resulting in deferral of several Luftwaffe transport aircraft procurement plans. In late May, Defence Minister Volker Ruehe was proposing to delete all funding in the current year for the Luftwaffe's proposed acquisition of a second pair of ex-airline Airbus A310-300s as Boeing 707-320 replacements, to supplement two already in service, as well as for the planned conversion of all four as tanker/transports. Also affected is the proposed Luftwaffe purchase of two more Canadair Challenger 601 executive jets and four Eurocopter AS 332 Super Puma transport helicopters for VIP and government official use.

No cuts in operational equipment are planned in the current budget, but further economies proposed in the coming year could present further threats to the Eurofighter and similar programmes for first-line systems. The German navy was expecting funding in June for seven new Westland Super Lynx ASW helicopters for its new frigate fleet, but the accompanying upgrade of its 17 existing Lynx Mk 88s to Super Lynx standards has apparently been postponed as part of the economies.

GREECE:

More F-16s sought

Following deliveries from late 1988 of 34 new-build Block 30 Lockheed Martin F-16Cs and six two-seat F-16Ds, and orders for another 40 Block 50 F-16C/Ds due next year, the Greek air force (EPA) has reportedly completed negotiations for 80 earlier F-16A/Bs from USAF surplus stocks. They are expected to undergo some refurbishment and upgrading before delivery, but the EPA has a further requirement for 40 more new F-16/Ds, for which negotiations are being finalised.

HUNGARY:

Combat aircraft procurement postponed

Hungarian air force interest in 36 JAS 39 Gripens or other new or surplus advanced fighter aircraft is being maintained, as indicated by requests for proposals issued last July, although a decision has now been ruled out until some time in 1997. This will allow more time for evaluation and cost considerations of the various submissions, which also include surplus or new F-16s and F/A-18s from the US, and for assessment of Hungary's proposed NATO membership.

NORWAY:

Sea King deliveries

The first of two Sea King Mk 43Bs ordered from a £15 million contract in November 1993 for SAR roles, and delivered to the Royal Norwegian air force last May, was the 330th built by Westland since 1969, and one of the last from Yeovil. Sea King production is now being transferred to Weston-Super-Mare to free Yeovil for AH-64D Apache manufacture. The RNoAF is increasing its Sea King fleet to 12 aircraft, and is planning to buy up to 20 attack helicopters at the turn of the century.

P-3C upgrade contract

Loral Defense Systems, now taken over as Lockheed Martin Tactical Systems, has been awarded a $65 million contract for an avionics upgrade of the four Lockheed P-3C Orions of the Royal Norwegian air force. These are being fitted with satellite and secure communications equipment, as well as new missile-warning systems.

ROMANIA:

MiG-21 upgrade programme begins

From the first major MiG-21 upgrade contract yet placed, worth around $300 million, Romanian Aerostar (Bacau) and Elbit Defence Systems will shortly deliver to the Romanian air force the first of about 100 reworked aircraft, including 10 two-seat MiG-21UM combat trainers. These ageing MiG-21M/MFs, now known as Lancers, will receive extensive avionics and systems modernisation in Romania by a combined Aerostar/Elbit team. Twenty-five of the single-seat Tumanskii R-13-powered MiG-21s will be equipped for both interception and ground-attack roles, while the remainder will have only Elta EL/M-2001-B ranging radar for dedicated close-support operations.

Elbit has undertaken prototype design, including a comprehensive infrastructure upgrading of Aerostar's Bacau facility, and installation of the Israeli Cimatron CAD/CAM system. Working in close conjunction with Aerostar, Elbit has integrated several advanced Israeli systems into the MiG-21, including the Elta EL/M-2032 radar with a new radome, used in the Lancer's air-to-air versions.

Improved avionics are provided in modular blocks, and are integrated with new and boosted electrical systems to provide for the increased power and cooling requirements. New systems also include an Elbit multi-role mission computer, single or twin Elbit cockpit displays and El-Op HUD, cockpit TV, Mason HOTAS, and a GMAv air data computer unit. Among other new items are IMI/TAAS chaff/flare dispensers scabbed to each side of the rear fuselage, Litton Italy navigation systems that use a GPS-updated gyro platform, Elbit DASH helmet-mounted sight, plus stores management, integrated communications, missile control, Elisra passive

Seen on an MFG 2 Tornado are two examples of the Aramis missile, a European weapon being developed by Daimler-Benz and Aérospatiale. It has a dual IR/anti-radar seeker and ramjet motor.

German army Hueys have been deployed to former Yugoslavia in support of IFOR operations. This is a UH-1D of Heeresfliegerregiment 10 from Fassberg, wearing the white scheme worn for such work.

radar warning, and datalink systems.

A major design objective was to allow the upgraded MiG-21 to operate not only with Romania's standard Russian weapons, but also new-generation precision-guided or smart weapons and off-boresight AAMs from both East and West. The Lancer is touted as the first aircraft to achieve this aim, with the help of five new universal pylons incorporating digitised 1553 datalinks. Its versatility was demonstrated by the mixed weapon load of the close-support variant at the 1996 Farnborough air show, comprising a Russian UB-32 rocket pod and an Israeli Rafael Python 3 AAM on the port underwing pylons; a Russian R-73E (AA-11 'Archer') and Elbit Opher ASM with infra-red target-matching homing to starboard; and a large bomb or drop tank on the fuselage centre-line station. The belly-mounted 23-mm GSh-23 twin-barrelled cannon remains unchanged.

Following contract signature in November 1993, the first single-seat prototype made its maiden flight on 23 August 1995, two months ahead of schedule, and was followed by a two-seater MiG-21UM prototype on 8 May 1996. Test flying by Israeli and Romanian pilots is now nearing completion at Bacau, and deliveries started last October, for completion in 1999. Elbit and Aerostar are looking for further MiG-21 upgrade opportunities, since more than 5,000 of these ageing fighter are still thought to remain in operation.

Romanian Cobra production approved

Plans for IAR to assemble Bell AH-1F attack helicopters under licence to meet national requirements for up 100 have now received US State Department approval. The future of this potentially $1 billion Bell Textron/IAR co-production programme apparently depends on financing it from additional Romanian HueyCobra sales to other countries in Central Europe and elsewhere.

One of the most elaborate special schemes of recent years was worn by this JG 72 F-4F in commemoration of the unit's 35th anniversary in 1995. The aircraft made only one flight in these colours – to Manching for ICE conversion.

RUSSIA:

MiG-MAPO reorganised

The former MiG-MAPO group has formed the nucleus of a new state-controlled military-orientated aerospace enterprise combining the assets and resources of a dozen airframe, engine, avionics and equipment designers, manufacturers and support organisations, plus the Moscow-based joint-stock commercial Aviabank. Formed in May 1996, the new Military Industrial Group/Moscow Aircraft Production Organisation (now MIG – rather than MiG – MAPO) also incorporates the Kamov helicopter design bureau, although none of that group's associated production centres are listed among the factories in the new consortium.

This also comprises the Klimov engine design group and its associated Chernychev RD-33 production facility; the Ryazan radar and electronics group; and several avionics, accessories, repair and equipment factories in Moscow, St Petersburg and Rostov-on-Don. Initial aircraft development, production and marketing will include the new MiG 1.42 multi-role fighter, MiG-29, MiG AT advanced trainer, the Kamov Ka-32, Ka-50 and Ka-52 helicopters, and the Ilyushin Il-103 lightplane.

Over 400 of 1,300 or so MiG-29s built to date have gone to 22 foreign customers, including other deliveries of more than 80 worth over $2 billion between 1993-95 to Hungary (28 in all), India (10), Iran, Malaysia (18), Romania (six) and Slovakia (18). Other MiG-29 operators are listed by MIG-MAPO as Bulgaria, Belarus, Cuba, Germany, India, Iraq, Iran, Kazakhstan, Moldova, North Korea, Poland, Russia, Syria, Ukraine, Uzbekistan, Turkmenistan, Yemen and Yugoslavia. Production is continuing of the air defence MiG-29SE and multi-role MiG-29SM for unspecified customers, alongside development of the upgraded fly-by-wire MiG-29M (MiG-33 for export), and the thrust-vectored MiG-35.

MiG 1.42 existence confirmed

Farnborough marked the official Russian release, after many years of secrecy, of the MiG 1.42 designation, previously known by that name only in the West. In Russia, this F-22 equivalent has been referred to merely as the fifth-generation MFI (multi-function interceptor), and MIG MAPO has been allowed to confirm only its "development and experimental production", and that it is still undergoing (ground) tests. The prototype is known to have been hangared at the Zhukhovskii flight-research institute for several years, but Russian defence budget cuts have delayed its completion and first flight schedules. Funding shortages are also considered likely to limit its future development and production.

MiG AT/Yak-130 update

The MiG AT is competing with the Yakovlev Yak-130 for a potentially large Russian air forces order, and for export. Making its UK debut at Farnborough, the MiG AT advanced trainer arrived there for its 100th flight, with a total of about 55 hours, having made its official first flight only on 21 March 1996. This was at the Gromov flight research institute at Zhukhovskii in the hands of MIG MAPO chief test pilot Roman Taskaev, who also flew the AT in the Farnborough show. Slight changes have been made during initial flight development to the leading-edge flap sections, which now end outboard of the recessed engine intakes in a pronounced dog-tooth. Elevator span has also been reduced, and is now inset within the tailplane.

Powered by two SNECMA Larzac 04R20 turbofans, the MiG AT had then exceeded 400 kt (740 km/h), 40,000 ft (12190 m), 5 *g* and 18° Alpha in its flight development programme. The type is being offered for export, especially to India, and for light ground-attack as the single-seat MiG-AC and two-seat ATC. Two more MiG AT prototypes had been completed, and were awaiting their electronic flight instrumentation and associated systems from Sextant Avionique in France in September, to join the flight-test programme at Zhukhovskii.

Yakovlev's Yak-130 advanced trainer demonstrator followed its MiG AT competitor into the air within just over a month, with a formal initial flight of 35 minutes at Zhukhovskii on 25 April 1996, after an earlier brief hop along its 5.5-km (3-nm) runway. Flown by Yakovlev chief test pilot Andrei Sinitsyn, the Yak-130 weighed 6600 kg (14,550 lb) at take-off, including 1000 kg (2,204 lb) of fuel, and is to be followed from 1997 by three other flight prototypes, plus two for static testing. Yakovlev test pilot Oleg Kononenko is also assisting with the 200 sorties planned for the flight development programme. After a few initial sorties, the Yak-130's distinctive winglets were removed because of aeroelasticity problems, and may be stiffened on the scaled-down second prototype.

Partnering Yakovlev in joint development and marketing of the slightly smaller Yak/AEM-130 production version, Aermacchi has confirmed receipt of the first R&D funds for this programme from the Russian government. Although limited, these funds are claimed by Aermacchi to have been accompanied by a government pledge to buy 150-200 of the definitive Yak/AEM-130 for the Russian air forces, "despite the announced fly-off between this aircraft and the MiG AT."

This appears to confirm other reports that small orders will be placed for both types by the Russian air forces (VVS). A mock-up of the smaller definitive production aircraft, with other modifications to meet the needs of potential export customers, has been completed at the Yakovlev plant. The Nizhni Novgorod production factory has also launched the first phase of the Yak/AEM-130 industrialisation programme at its own risk, pending some government funding.

In Slovakia, Povazske Strojarnye, manufacturers with Progress in Moscow of the Yak/AEM-130's planned new DV-2S or RD-35 turbofan powerplant, are similarly awaiting the release of Sk266 million ($8.8 million) in promised government finance for its R&D. RD-35 interest is also reported by Aermacchi from "a large Western engine manufacturing group", which is now negotiating a collaborative agreement. Aermacchi, which owns all industrial and commercial rights to the Yak/AEM-130 outside the former USSR area, maintains that the new aircraft will set the standard against which all future advanced trainers will be matched.

SPAIN:

Spanish navy gets Harrier II Plus

9ª Escuadrilla of the Spanish fleet air arm is in the process of receiving eight Harier II Plus aircraft assembled under licence by CASA at its facility in San Pablo, Seville. Delivery schedule is as follows:

	BuNo.	Delivery date
01-914	165028	31/01/96
01-915	165029	29/03/96
01-916	165030	24/05/96
01-917	165031	18/07/96
01-918	165032	31/10/96
01-919	165033	31/01/97
01-920	165034	31/03/97
01-921	165035	31/07/97

These aircraft will complement the unit's 10 AV-8B Harrier IIs which operate in the day fighter/attack role. The AV-8Bs are scheduled to be upgaraded to Plus standards by CASA from late 1997 or early 1998. If funds allow it, one or two AV-8B twin-stickers

Two Italian 'specials' are this F-104S (above) of the 21º Gruppo, 53º Stormo at Cameri marked for the 1996 Tiger Meet, and Piaggio-Douglas PD.808RM (right) of the 14º Stormo at Pratica di Mare.

will be purchased in 1998.

8ª Escuadrilla disbanded on 16 August 1996 and its seven AV-8Ss and two TAV-8Ss were transferred to the Royal Thai navy, for its 105 Squadron. Four 8ª Esc pilots have been posted to 9ª Esc, and on 17 August the remaining six formed the Thai Training Team. They will train the eight Thai pilots who are undergoing the Strike Fighter pilot syllabus with the US Navy. Training at Rota started in late August 1996 and will conclude in July 1997. 105 Sqn and its nine Harriers will then embark on the new carrier *Chakri Naruebet*, and will sail to Thailand accompanied by two Spanish pilots.

SWEDEN:

Re-engined Sk 60W deliveries begin

Saab Military Aircraft began redelivery to the Swedish air force last September of the first nine of 96 Saab Sk 60W basic jet trainers re-engined with Williams/Rolls-Royce FJ44 turbofans in place of their original Turboméca Aubisque units. Some delays had resulted from air intake modification requirements, but the remaining Sk 60s in the upgrade programme are being similarly modified at F5 Wing, or SAF Flight Academy, at Ljungbyhed, where they will remain in service until at least 2010.

TURKEY:

Second-batch F-16 production

Delivery took place on 19 July 1996 from Turkish Aerospace Industries (TAI) of the first of a second batch of 68 Lockheed Martin Block 50 F-16Cs and 12 two-seat F-16D-50s for the Turkish air force (THK) through the $2.5 billion Peace Onyx II programme. Earlier, TAI had completed 152 Block 30/40 F-16C/Ds for the THK (which also received eight directly from GD), plus 34 F-16C-40s and 12 F-16D-40s for the Egyptian air force.

UKRAINE:

Strategic nuclear weapons finally returned to Russia

Prolonged negotiations and political arguments finally resulted in the return by the Ukraine government at the beginning of June of the last Russian strategic nuclear weapons in its custody. These comprised the 19 mainly unserviceable Tupolev Tu-160 'Blackjack' Mach 2 variable-geometry strike aircraft of the 184th Heavy Bomber Regiment at Priluki, and 24 Tupolev Tu-95MS 'Bear-H' turboprop bombers, together with 372 nuclear cruise missiles. Also returned to Russia were 176 SS-18 'Satan' and SS-22 ICBMs, plus 1,240 nuclear warheads.

UNITED KINGDOM:

BAe wins Nimrod 2000 and CASOM contracts

Last-minute delays in long-awaited MoD procurement decisions following Cabinet disputes on public-spending cuts between the Treasury and Defence ministers were finally resolved only hours before the summer UK Parliamentary recess began on 25 July 1996. It took the intervention of Deputy Prime Minister Michael Heseltine in support of Defence Secretary Michael Portillo to prevail over Chancellor Kenneth Clarke for agreement to be reached to go ahead with the three most urgent MoD programmes, worth nearly £4 billion. These comprised the SR(A) 420 Nimrod replacement requirement; a new conventionally-armed stand-off missile (CASOM) for the SR(A) 1236 requirement; and a new air-launched anti-armour weapons system (AAWS) for SR(A) 1238.

There was little surprise at British Aerospace being selected as prime contractor for two of the three programmes. This included a potential £2 billion order for 21 Nimrod 2000 replacement maritime patrol aircraft (subject to final contract negotiations), reduced from the 25 originally planned as a concession to the Treasury. With MATRA in France, BAe Dynamics' Storm Shadow submission was also selected to fulfil the CASOM requirement. The British industry hat-trick was completed by the planned award to the GEC-Marconi Dynamics' team of a contract for its Brimstone anti-armour weapons for the AAWS programme.

The emphasis on British industry predominance in these projects was further accentuated in the Nimrod 2000 programme by selection of the 17,750-lb (78.96-kN) Rolls-Royce BR710 as its new turbofan powerplants, in preference to the GE CF34-8C, and of Racal Thorn Defence Systems' Searchwater 2000MR main surveillance radar instead of the cheaper Elta EL/M-2022A.

As prime contractor, BAe will be wholly responsible for systems integration and for the airframe, which will include a completely new carry-through lower centre-fuselage fuel tank box and inner wing-sections to be built at Chadderton for the bigger engines. Boeing will continue to supply the central tactical system, although the MoD announced a "new strategic partnership" from contractual negotiations between the US company and GEC-Marconi Avionics to provide key elements of the mission systems equipment. GMAv was previously associated with Lockheed Martin for the latter's Orion 2000 bid for the RMPA programme.

The MoD said that British companies would receive work to the full value of the contract, which also involves FR Aviation, Shorts, Smiths Industries, Lucas Aerospace, Messier-Dowty, and Normalair-Garrett, providing 2,600 jobs in the national defence industry. A contributory factor in Nimrod 2000 selection was the decision by Boeing Defense and Space Group and McDonnell Douglas Aerospace to join BAe in planning to relaunch production of the only turbofan maritime patrol aircraft so far developed. The estimated market would be up to 650 new MPA, worth more than $14 billion, over the next 30 years. They would have Boeing/GMAv's new digital mission systems avionics (MSA), based on the P-3 Update IV package which was cancelled by the US Navy, and on the three Boeing 737-2X9 Surveillers sold to Indonesia. MDC involvement would cover airframe and overall weapon system aspects.

As the MoD pointed out, selection of the Storm Shadow development of the APACHE "would cement the recently-announced merger of the missile businesses of British Aerospace and MATRA, thus strengthening BAe's ability to play a leading role in a restructured European industry." Although it shares a similar low-observable airframe and turbojet propulsion system with the Franco/German APACHE EG, the Storm Shadow's unitary warhead, extra fuel cell that increases its range up to 324 nm (600 km) (unofficial report), and INS/GPS/terrain-reference (TERPROM) navigation/targeting system will all be of UK origin. A GEC-Marconi Avionics imaging infrared seeker will be used in the terminal engagement phase for target recognition and acquisition.

In its final Storm Shadow proposals, BAeD was reportedly able to offer the RAF significantly more missiles, believed to be up to about a 1,000, still within its earlier programme costs; this was on the basis of collaborative procurement with the French and German air forces. Approximately 1,600 UK employees in BAeD's Bristol, Lostock and Stevenage factories will be involved in the £650 million Storm Shadow programme, which will also result in 100 per cent contract returns to British industry.

Storm Shadow will employ the 1,080-lb (490-kg) BROACH kinetic energy penetrator warhead on which BAeD's Royal Ordnance subsidiary has been working for the past five years. BROACH is designed to penetrate several metres of reinforced concrete or other hardened targets by the use of tandem explosive charges, the first being shaped to focus a gas jet and create a large funnel-shaped hole. The second, comprising a conventional HE bomb, passes through the hole and detonates within the target. BAe claims that this technology doubles the destructive efficiency of the warhead over conventional types, and, coupled with the precision-guidance systems and high delivery speeds from opti-

The Dutch Tactishe Helikopter Groep (THG) officially received the Eurocopter AS 535U2 Cougar on 31 May 1996. Seventeen are on order, for service with 300 Squadron.

Kamov has revealed the almost complete Ka-52, a two-seat derivative of the Ka-50 'Hokum'. The prototype consists of a new cockpit section grafted on to a Ka-50 airframe.

mum dive angles, ensures the destruction of hardened aircraft shelters, command and control bunkers, missile launch sites, and similar targets.

The RAF's single-seat Harrier GR.Mk 7s and EF 2000s can each carry two Storm Shadows, while the two-crew Tornado GR.Mk 4s have provision for four. The basic APACHE is entering French service using sub-munitions for runway-denial roles, and BAeD has been talking to several NATO countries about possible Storm Shadow procurement. Among these was Germany, which has since abandoned its APACHE stand-off missile procurement plans in favour of developing DASA/Bofors's similar KEPD 350 Taurus weapon system.

After surviving Treasury attempts for its cancellation in the public spending battle, the GEC-Marconi Dynamics/Rockwell Brimstone was selected by the MoD as the UK's new £725 million anti-armour weapons system. This finally showed a clear preference for individual homing missiles with a limited stand-off capability of up to about 17 nm (32 km), rather than longer-range sub-munition dispensers. In this respect, Brimstone was competing only against BAeD's Typhoon development of ASRAAM, although it was also challenged by three contending dispenser systems: the Hunting/DASA SWAARM 2000, the Texas Instruments/Shorts Griffin-38, and Thomson/Thorn's TAAWS.

The Brimstone is a fire-and-forget development of the Rockwell AGM-114F Hellfire Optimised ATM with GEC-Marconi Avionics millimetric-wave radar homing and a unitary or tandem HEAT warhead, and has an overall weight of about 110 lb (50 kg). The missile employs a digital autopilot coupled with a miniaturised INS and launch platform information to orbit the target until identification and lock-on. A small precursor charge counters reactive armour, after which a crush fuse detonates the main warhead, generating a highly penetrative Mach 6 plasma jet.

Tornado GR.Mk 1 MLU

British Aerospace at Warton received the first of an initial batch of 80 RAF Tornado GR.Mk 1s on 1 April 1996 for incorporation of mid-life upgrades to GR.Mk 4 standard. The first of two RAF Tornado development aircraft (ZD708) started flight trials with some of the MLU modifications as long ago as 29 May 1993, but shrinking procurement budgets have delayed implementation of the programme, as well as reducing its scope. Major casualties of the MLU were its originally-planned GEC-Marconi Avionics SPARTAN terrain-referenced navigation and -following system, associated radar altimeter, and modified intakes with reduced radar cross-sections for covert low-level attacks.

GMAv is supplying a variety of other sensors and displays, including new pilot's head-up and multi-function displays, cockpit symbol generator, digital map database and display, computer loading system, video recorder, and enhanced Mil Std 1760 II stores management systems for future advanced weapons. It will also integrate its night-vision goggles and forward-looking infra-red equipment in the GR.Mk 4, together with onboard defence systems, GPS and TIALD compatibility. Initial release to service, originally planned for February 1998, may now be delayed, and funding is still being sought to upgrade a second batch of 62 RAF Tornado GR.Mk 1s to GR.Mk 4 standard.

RAF Jaguar upgrade plans

Delays through defence economies in planned deliveries of the Eurofighter, of which the RAF is expecting its first two production examples in 2001, have brought a requirement for further life extensions of the UK's three squadrons of 42 Jaguar strike/reconnaissance aircraft. Twelve of these were hurriedly upgraded to GR.Mk 1B/T.Mk 2B standards through an Urgent Operational Requirement (41/94) for the1994 Bosnian campaign, mainly to operate with GEC-Marconi's Thermal Imaging Airborne Laser Designator (TIALD) pod for use with precision-guided munitions.

New systems for the Jaguar GR.Mk 1B, linked by a Mil Std 1553B digital databus, included a high-resolution wide-angle 1:1 ratio head-up display and colour multi-function cockpit display, plus computer symbol and digital generators, a modified 1064C inertial navigation system with integrated GPS, and hands on throttle and stick (HOTAS) capability. The first Jaguar GR.Mk 1Bs were available to take part in the UN's Operation Deliberate Force in Bosnia from August 1995, in which they provided TIALD laser designation and target marking for nearly 50 Paveway II LGBs dropped by RAF Harriers.

Similar, although simplified, upgrades are now being applied to the rest of the RAF Jaguars through a two-phase Jaguar 96 and 97 programme. Its most significant addition is that of TERPROM ground proximity warning systems, for which BAe Systems and Equipment Ltd (BASE) has received a £3 million MoD contract after successful flight trials in a Jaguar at Boscombe Down. TERPROM uses stored digital terrain elevation and obstacle data in conjunction with aircraft navigation inputs to correlate aircraft position with stored data, to fly at minimum heights without external navaids or telltale forward emissions. It also combines terrain following, ground proximity and obstacle warning with passive target ranging in a single unit.

Other upgrade additions include night-vision goggle cockpit capability and improved air-to-air missile aiming. For the longer-term, consideration is also being given to rectifying Jaguar power limitations from installation of an Adour 811 compressor module on the current Adour 104s, and increasing turbine operating temperatures to provide thrust increases of up to 25 per cent. Compatibility with ASRAAM and ALARM missiles, as well as helmet-mounted sights, is also being studied, for service until at least 2008.

RAF helicopter retirements

The venerable Westland Wessex twin-turboshaft helicopter was due to end its mainland UK Royal Air Force search and rescue career in June, when the last pair of HC.Mk 2s of C Flight, No. 22 Sqn, were to be replaced at RAF Valley by Westland Sea King HAR.Mk 3s. However, problems with the Sea King HAR.Mk 3A meant that the Wessex had to continue in the role for several months longer. Although the Wessex will no longer be involved in mainland UK SAR operations, it will continue to equip the SAR Training Unit at Valley until spring 1997. It will also maintain its previous roles for some time with No. 72 Sqn in Northern Ireland, No. 28 Sqn in Hong Kong (until 1997), and No. 84 Sqn in Cyprus, as well as transport duties with No. 32 (The Royal) Sqn at Northolt. About 50 new medium transport helicopters will be sought by the RAF to replace its remaining Wessexes from around 1998.

Naval Apache proposals

The Royal Navy's No. 847 Sqn at Yeovilton, responsible for support of No. 3 Commando Brigade of the Royal Marines, is considering replacing its current TOW-armed Lynx AH.Mk 7s with eight of the 64 MDH AH-64D Longbow Apache attack helicopters on order for the Army Air Corps. They are expected to be armed with the GEC-Marconi Avionics Brimstone development of the Rockwell Hellfire, but those for the Royal Marine unit would need to be navalised in terms of extra corrosion-proofing and other protection for shipboard operation.

Middle East

IRAQ:

US missile attacks resumed

Twenty-seven US cruise missiles were launched in the early hours of 3 September in response to Iraq army attacks on northern Kurdish towns. The missiles included 13 Boeing AGM-86Cs from Guam-based Boeing B-52Hs of the 2nd Bomb Wing at Barksdale, CA, plus 14 BGM-109 Block 3 Tomahawks from American warships in the Persian Gulf. The US missiles were targeted against southern Iraqi air defence command posts and SAM sites, following northerly extension by the Western coalition of the No-Fly Zone in that area from the 32nd to the 33rd Parallel, almost to the outskirts of Baghdad.

An additional 17 Tomahawks were fired from US warships in the Gulf on the following day against four of the same targets which had not been completely destroyed. A HARM was also launched from a patrolling USAF F-16C in the No-Fly Zone against an

Rarely seen outside its native land is this SOKO G-4 Super Galeb of the Serbian air force. It was visiting Aviano AB in Italy.

Above: 60072 is the prototype of the re-engined Saab Sk 60W. The aircraft is powered by a Williams/Rolls FJ44-1C turbofan.

Right: Seen during fit check on a Tornado GR.Mk 1 is the Rockwell/GEC-Marconi Brimstone anti-tank weapon for the RAF.

SA-8 site which was tracking it. More Iraqi SAMs were later launched unsuccessfully against other F-16s, resulting in US promises of further retribution and the transfer of eight Lockheed F-117s to bases in Kuwait.

JORDAN:

F-16 lease agreement

The Royal Jordanian air force has recently concluded a $220 million five-year lease agreement with the American government. It will cover 12 ex-USAF Lockheed F-16As and four two-seat F-16Bs including structural and engine upgrades before delivery in late 1997, to double their service lives to 8,000 flying hours. The F-16s are expected to re-equip the RJAF's No. 25 Sqn, currently operating Mirage F1C interceptors at Azraq air base. Another two similar F-16 batches are also planned by Jordan, for the total re-equipment of three RJAF fighter squadrons.

QATAR:

British equipment procurement plans

According to unofficial press reports during the Farnborough air show, Qatar is negotiating with the UK to buy a $1.6 billion arms package. This would mainly comprise a dozen BAe Hawk 100/200 light fighter/trainers, but could also include air defence equipment, notably Shorts Starburst surface-to-air missiles.

SAUDI ARABIA:

Cougar helicopter order

Twelve Eurocopter AS 532A2 Cougar armed versions of the Super Puma Mk 2 have been ordered by the Royal Saudi air force in a Fr3 billion ($593 million) contract for combat SAR roles. These are mainly concerned with the recovery of shot-down aircrew, for which the Cougars may be armed with 20-mm cannon, 12.7-mm machine-guns and rockets.

UNITED ARAB EMIRATES:

New combat aircraft short-list

The Dassault Rafale and Lockheed Martin F-16 were short-listed in late August 1996 by the UAE for its long-standing requirement for up to 80 new multi-role combat aircraft. Other contenders included the Mirage 2000-5, Panavia Tornado, Eurofighter, JAS 39, MDC F-15, MiG-29 and Su-35/37. Further evaluation is planned by the UAE of the two finalists, before contract signature expected some time in 1997.

Ten former Ukrainian air force Aero L-39s have appeared on the civil register for onward sale. This example was seen at Chernigov.

Far East

CHINA:

New F-7 variants from Chengdu

A new lease of life from Chengdu's long-established MiG-21 development was expected from details revealed at the 1996 Farnborough air show of further design improvements, resulting in the J-7E and its export equivalent, the F-7MG. These aircraft incorporate airframe, engine and equipment upgrades, the main external changes concerning increased wing area to improve combat agility by a claimed 45 per cent, together with gains in take-off, climb, ceiling and landing performance.

Although the central portion of the original MiG-21's 57° clipped delta wing has been retained unchanged, new tapered outer panels have been added from about half-way out, increasing the overall span by 3.83 ft (1.17 m) to 27.3 ft (8.32 m), and the wing area by 8.17 per cent or 20.2 sq ft (1.88 m²), to 267.8 sq ft (24.88 m²). The new cranked leading-edges have only 42° of sweep on the outboard sections, which also feature manoeuvring slats supplemented by combat flap settings. With the Guizhou WP-13F twin-spool turbojet developing 14,815 lb (65.9 kN) thrust, the extra wing area reduces normal take-off and landing field performance to about 600-700 m (1,968-2,297 ft).

The upgraded F-7MG retains the twin underfuselage 30-mm cannon of earlier F-7s, plus provision for five external weapons stations. GEC's original Type 226 Skyranger range-only radar has been replaced by the GEC-Marconi Avionics Super Skyranger, described as a full-function radar using coherent technology to achieve scan, look-down and shoot-down capabilities. Upgrades have also been made in the F-7's original nav/attack equipment, which included GMAv's Type 956 HUD/WAC, Type 3400 UHF/VHF, TACAN, VOR/DME/ILS, EFIS, ECM and stores management systems.

A prototype F-7MG was scheduled to make its debut at China's first international air show in Zhuhai in November 1996.

Sukhoi production deal criticised in Russia

Some criticism has emerged in Russia of China's $1.2 billion licensed production agreement for the Sukhoi Su-27, according to ITAR-TASS agency reports. This agreement limits China to producing a maximum of 200 Su-27s at the rate of no more than 50 per year. There are fears in Russia that, after three or four years, the Chinese could make minor changes in the Su-27 design and build it as an indigenous type, as they have done with the MiG-21, and then compete in domestic and foreign markets against the original Sukhoi product.

Following earlier deliveries of 26 single- and two-seat Su-27s, the AF/PLA reportedly received 11 of a second batch of 24, including three two-seat Su-27UBs, to Suixiu air base on 25 July 1996. Like Wuhu, where the first batch of the AF/PLA Su-27s is reportedly based, Suixiu is protected by some of China's three batteries of Antey S-300 Patriot-type air defence missiles purchased from Russia.

Among recent deliveries form British Aerospace at Warton have been the Hawk Mk 203s for the Royal Air Force of Oman (above), now in service with No. 6 Squadron, and the Tornado IDS aircraft for the Royal Saudi Air Force's second batch (left). The third Saudi squadron will be No. 75, joining Nos 7 and 66.

helicopters, and a Fuji/Bell AH-1S Cobra gunship.

F-2 developments

Progress with the JASDF's Mitsubishi F-2 fighter programme included the first flight on 24 May 1996 at Nagoya of the fourth and last development prototype, and its delivery to join the other three at the Air Development and Proving Command centre at Gifu. The fourth XF-2 was the first to incorporate a co-cured composite wing manufactured by Lockheed Martin from the transfer of Japanese technology with this technique, which was part of the original joint US/Japanese FS-X agreement.

This involves bonding composite components to dispense with metal structural joints, and is a key feature of the US company's 40 per cent share of production for the 130 aircraft on order. General Electric will undertake about 60 per cent of the production of the F-2's F110-129 turbofan, the remainder being done in Japan by Ishikawajima Harima (IHI), including assembly and testing. F-2 work will be worth around $3.7 billion to US industry.

Shenyang F-8 IIM flies

Flight development of the Shenyang F-8 IIM twin-jet heavy all-weather fighter began with a successful initial prototype flight on 31 March. The aircraft has been upgraded with new avionics that include an advanced pulse-Doppler radar, with look-up/look-down capabilities and BVR air-to-air missiles.

Following cancellation by the US government in mid-1989 of an F-8 II upgrade contract with Grumman through the Peace Pearl programme, the F-8 IIM was taken over as a joint project by the Shenyang Aircraft Industrial Company, Shenyang Aircraft Research Institute and the China National Aero-Technology Import & Export Corporation (CATIC). An Israeli industrial mission is believed to have assisted with systems design and development of the F-8 IIM – which appears to be aimed mainly at export markets – and is thought to have contributed some items of equipment.

INDONESIA:

Ex-Pakistani F-16 purchase deferred

Negotiations with the US in late 1996 to acquire nine of the 28 new GD Block 15 F-16A/Bs bought earlier by Pakistan for $658 million, and subsequently embargoed by Congress, were postponed until FY 1997 following further Congressional objections to Indonesia's human rights record. Final terms involved the cost of pre-delivery upgrades for the F-16s, stored in the US since their completion in 1991-92. Having originally cost Pakistan $23.5 million each, the F-16s were reportedly marketed by the US for about half that price. Indonesia was apparently prepared to offer only $9 million per aircraft, however, and also demanded 30 per cent in offset returns.

Pakistan received its first F-16 repayments of $124 million from the US on 23 April 1996, with another $160 million in FMS credits due in June. Following initial deliveries of 12 Fighting Falcons, Indonesian air force chief of staff Air Vice-Marshal Sutria Tubagus said that the TNI/AU needed four F-16 squadrons, each of 16 aircraft, plus 20 more BAe Hawks. In late 1996, however, the ex-Pakistani F-16s were being offered to the Philippines by the US.

More BAe Hawk orders

Sales of the BAe Hawk to Indonesia originally comprised 20 Mk 53 advanced trainers in 1980, followed by eight Mk 109 two-seat lead-in fighter trainers and 16 single-seat Mk 209 light multi-role fighters, which are now being delivered. They are being further boosted by a second similar batch of Mk 209s from accompanying options. This will allow the TNI/AU to operate two fighter/ground-attack squadrons, each with 16 Hawk 200s and four Hawk 100s, and to use the remaining 14 Hawk 53s for advanced training.

CASA C.212 contract

Recent aircraft orders for the Indonesian defence forces placed with IPTN have included a $107 million contract for another six licence-built CASA CN.212 light turboprop transports and three MBB NBO 105CB light helicopters. They will increase overall IPTN output of these types to 100 and 118, respectively, while an additional $4.2 million Indonesian naval order for an NBell 412 helicopter brings the licence-built total of this type to 25. Another new IPTN contract worth over $150 million and now being finalised will involve initial orders for five twin-turboprop CN.235MPA maritime patrol aircraft, plus a single transport version for both TNI/AU and naval use.

JAPAN:

Self-Defence Force budget proposals

Cuts in Japan's 1995 defence budget will result in the disbandment of one of the JASDF's 13 fighter squadrons, as well as the transfer to reserve status of about 20 of the JMSDF's 101 Lockheed/Kawasaki P-3C Orion maritime patrol aircraft, plus completion of JGSDF Fuji/Bell AH-1S attack helicopter procurement with the 85th aircraft. The 301st Hikotai of the 5th Air Wing at Nyutabaru, currently operating MDC/Mitsubishi F-4EJ Kai Phantoms and Kawasaki T-4 advanced trainers, is expected to be the disbanded JASDF squadron.

Japanese FY 1997 military budget requests in August 1996 totalled 4.99 trillion yen ($46.13 billion), or only 2.88 per cent more than in the previous year. Proposed JASDF aircraft procurement includes another nine Mitsubishi F-2 support fighters, compared with 11 ordered in the current year, and follows six prototypes. JASDF funding was also sought for two of four Boeing E-767 AWACS aircraft, four Raytheon Beech U-125A SAR light jets, three Mitsubishi/Sikorsky UH-60J SAR helicopters, and three Gulfstream IV (U-4) transport aircraft.

JMSDF FY97 aircraft requests included seven Mitsubishi/Sikorsky SH-60J ASW helicopters, plus two UH-60Js for SAR. The JGSDF wants funding for five Kawasaki OH-X recce helicopters, three next-generation LH-X liaison and reconnaissance aircraft, six Fuji/Bell UH-1J and UH-60 utility helicopters, two Boeing CH-47J cargo helicopters, and a Fuji/Bell AH-1S Cobra gunship.

First flights for new types

Recent significant first flights for the JSDF have included the first of four Boeing 767-200 transports modified for AWACS roles, on 9 August from Everett, WA. Powered by two 61,500-lb (273.56-kN) General Electric CF6-80C2B6FA turbofans, the 767 AWACS has a dorsal radome and missions systems avionics similar to that of the original Boeing E-3s, with overall performance improvements. The first JASDF delivery is planned in 1998.

The JGSDF's prototype Kawasaki OH-X scout helicopter took to the air at Nagoya on 6 August. The wholly-indigenous 3.5-tonne tandem-seat sensor-equipped OH-X is intended to replace the JGSDF's 193 Kawasaki/Hughes OH-6J/D LOHs. Designed in conjunction with the JDA's Technical R&D Institute (TRDI), and powered by two 885-shp (660-kW) Mitsubishi TS1-10 turboshafts, the helicopter is unarmed apart from four Toshiba Type 91 defensive AAMs. The four flight and two ground prototypes will be followed by 200 or more production OH-Xs costing $1.2 billion.

US-1A upgrade plans

Seven remaining ShinMaywa US-1A turboprop-powered sea-going SAR amphibians of the Japanese Maritime Self-Defence Force are to undergo a major $470 million five-year upgrade by their original manufacturers to improve their performance and extend their useful operating lives. Major changes will include replacement of the original IHI-built GE T64 turboprops by Allison AE2100 powerplants, and the provision of pressurisation; new avionics and fly-by-wire control systems will also be installed. Funding is being sought for ShinMaywa to build three new US-1As to similar standards, which include an extension in operating range to around 2,700 nm (5000 km).

SOUTH KOREA:

Special mission Raytheon Hawker 800 order

Ten Hawker 800XP special mission derivations of the original HS 125 have been ordered by the Republic of Korea air force (RoKAF) from Raytheon at a cost of $460 million. They are powered by twin TFE731-5BR turbofans and fitted with special E-Systems remote control surveillance signals intelligence avionics installations and other surveillance sensors, including Loral advanced imaging radar (LAIRS). Delivery is scheduled from 1999, and the aircraft are intended to help monitor North Korean military activity.

More US weapons ordered

The US Pentagon has notified Congress of FMS contracts for the supply to South Korea of 46 MDC AGM-84 Harpoon anti-ship missiles costing $90 million, and 45 RIM-7P Sea Sparrow ShAMs worth $19 million for its new KDX-1 destroyers.

F-6 pilot defection

A Shenyang F-6 (MiG-19) of the Korean People's Army Air Force (KPAAF) landed safely at South Korea's Suwon military air base, near Seoul, on 23 May 1996 in the hands of its defecting pilot, with an escort of six RoKAF F-16s. Captain Lee Chol-su, aged 30, was the first KPAAF pilot to defect from North Korea since 1983, despite the $300,000 standing reward offered by the Seoul government as an encouragement. Captain Lee was given political asylum in South Korea, where his F-6 was apparently retained.

MYANMAR (BURMA):

More Mil helicopters acquired

Five more Mil Mi-171 twin-turboshaft transport helicopters recently ordered by Myanmar's military government will increase its air force total of this type to 12. They will supplement 12 PZL Swidnik W-3U Sokol helicopters delivered earlier from Poland, and 10 Mil Mi-2 'Hoplite' gunships received from Eastern Europe.

PHILIPPINES:

New combat aircraft plans

Although the ambitious armed forces 15-year modernisation programme budget has been almost halved by President Ramos to Ps170 billion ($6.49 billion), Ps50 billion ($1.908 billion) has been allocated to buy up to 18 new combat aircraft, weapons and associated equipment over the next five years. The air force is evaluating the main international contenders, including the Dassault Mirage 2000-5, MDD F/A-18, Kfir and MiG-29, and 18 zero-time ex-Pakistani F-16A/Bs are also being offered by the US for only $240 million – a unit cost of a mere $13.3 million. Five-year PhilAF procurement plans also include a dozen SAR helicopters and six new air defence radars.

SINGAPORE:

KC-135 tanker acquisition

Requirements for two tanker/transports, plus another two boom and hose-reel kits for local conversion of the selected type, are being met by Singapore government orders for four surplus Boeing KC-135As from the US government. This decision followed evaluations of such projects as the Airbus A310 MRTT, Boeing's projected 767-200ER tanker, IAI's Boeing 707 conversions, and the MDD KDC-10-30.

The KC-135s will be upgraded from competitive tenders with new CFM56-2 turbofans and systems to KC-135R standards. They will also be fitted with underwing Flight Refuelling Ltd Mk 32B hose-reel pods in addition to the original F-16-compatible refuelling boom, through a $280 million FMS contract.

TAIWAN:

Mirage 2000 deliveries

Formal delivery of the first of its 60 Mirage 2000-5 multi-role fighters to the Republic of China air force (RoCAF) took place at Dassault's Bordeaux-Merignac factory on 7 May 1996. Also included in the RoCAF's Mirage order are 1,500 MICA active radar-guided BVR AAMs, close-range Magic 2 AAMs, and precision-guided weapons. The Mirages are initially planned to start replacing the ageing Lockheed F-104 Starfighters of the RoCAF's 2nd Tactical Fighter Wing at Hsinchu from early 1997.

Shown at Indonesia's air show in 1996 were the specially-painted F-16s of the 'Elang Biru' aerobatic team (above), formed with assistance from the 'Thunderbirds'. Below is one of the TNI-AU's new Hawk Mk 209s, part of a batch of 16 destined for 12 Skwadron (which is transitioning from the A-4). A second 16-aircraft Mk 209 order has been announced for a second unit.

New aircraft negotiations in progress

An FMS contract worth $53 million is being discussed with the US to acquire 30 Bell Textron TH-67 JetRanger training helicopters, each equipped with AN/AVS-6(V)1 night-vision goggles. Taiwan is also negotiating with Lockheed Martin to buy the last four C-130H-30 Hercules off the Marietta line, as a follow-on to its four C-130Hs delivered in 1993-94. Negotiations are being finalised by the Taiwanese navy for a second batch of 11 Sikorsky S-70C Thunder Hawk ASW helicopters costing around $400 million. These will supplement the nine remaining S-70Cs from 10 delivered to Taiwan in 1990.

THAILAND:

Hornet contract signed

A $578 million FMS contract was signed with the US by the Thai government for four McDonnell Douglas F/A-18Cs and four two-seat F/A-18Ds, plus associated weapons and equipment, including MDC AGM-84 Harpoon AShMs. This package is expected to include Hughes AIM-120 AMRAAMs at a later stage. The Royal Thai air force is expected to receive its first Hornets in October 1999.

Further F-5 upgrades planned

Following completion of an earlier USAF limited upgrade of its 35 or so Northrop F-5E/Fs with a Litton LN-39 INS, mission computer and a GEC-Marconi HUD, the Royal Thai air force is evaluating more extensive

Photographed departing on a Mitsubishi test flight from Nagoya prior to delivery ot the JASDF/TRDI is the first XF-2B. Four F-2s (two XF-2As and two XF-2Bs) are with the TRDI for development trials. The two-seater is fully combat-capable.

Nine Beechjet T400s have been ordered by the JASDF, and these now serve as multi-engined trainers like the similar T-1 Jayhawk. The T400s serve with the 41st Hikotai at Miho.

modifications. They would include a new lightweight pulse-Doppler radar such as the Elta 2034, FIAR Grifo, Lockheed Martin APG-67 or Westinghouse APG-66, and new structural components to extend the aircraft's fatigue lives.

Turboprop DC-3s ordered

Three Basler Turbo 67s, which are veteran Douglas DC-3s re-engined with Pratt & Whitney PT6A-67 turboprops, have been ordered by the Thai government for RTAF operation in cloud-seeding roles.

Southern Asia

AFGHANISTAN:

Taliban defection

Following recent defeats suffered by rebel Taliban Islamic fundamentalist forces by Afghan government troops, a MiG-21 pilot from the TIFF defected with his aircraft into Bagram air base in mid-July. Taliban forces operating from the rebel-held areas of Ghazni and Kandahar in southern Afghanistan are estimated by US intelligence to operate up to 100 aircraft, which also include MiG-23s, Sukhoi Su-22s, various transports and 20 Mil helicopters, as well as about 900 Soviet-era tanks and a similar number of artillery pieces, plus large numbers of FROG-type rockets. At least 40 aircraft and large stockpiles of ammunition were acquired when Taliban forces captured Herat air base in August 1995.

INDIA:

Su-30MK contract finalised

The IAF's long-planned acquisition of the canard-equipped Sukhoi Su-30MK two-seat advanced multi-role fighter went ahead in July with an initial Rs60,142 million ($1.68 billion) order to Russia for 40 examples, for delivery between 1997-2001. They are being acquired mainly for combat control roles, and negotiations are apparently continuing for associated smart weapons and armament, plus a production licence for Hindustan Aircraft, to meet an IAF requirement for about 60 more. Thrust-vectoring is reportedly planned for the last 22 of India's initial Su-30MKs from 1999. Earlier allegations by parliamentary opposition members of kick-backs demanded by Indian officials concerned with placing the contract have not so far been pursued.

Deliveries of the basic two-seat Sukhoi Su-30 fighter-controller version from the Irkutsk Aviation Production Association (IAPO) have reportedly already started to the Russian air force (VVS), although flight-development of a prototype Su-30MK with canards (Su-30I) was not expected to start at Irkutsk until early 1997. A joint IAF/Defence Research and Development Organisation evaluation committee recommended Su-30MK procurement in preference to the Dassault Mirage 2000-5, although some Indian defence elements continue to press the merits of the French fighter, in which Pakistan is also interested but has so far been unable to afford.

August was an important month for the Japanese military. On the 9 August the first Boeing E-767 AWACS (above) aircraft flew, while three days earlier Kawasaki had flown the first example of its OH-X scout helicopter (below).

Fighter avionics upgrades planned

Planned avionics upgrades of more than 100 Indian air force MiG-27Ms and 36 Dassault Mirage 2000H fighters have resulted in RFPs being extended to the Tamam Division of Israel Aircraft Industries for trial installations of that company's TN-90 Q/G integrated tactical GPS and air combat manoeuvring instrumentation system (ACMIS). They will be evaluated on a competitive basis with similar Western equipment before contract finalisation.

Harrier attrition replacements sought

Having lost two of its four Harrier T.Mk 60 two-seat V/STOL trainers through accident attrition, Indian naval aviation has been discussing the possibility of acquiring up to five ex-USMC TAV-8A Harrier trainers long withdrawn from service, or similar aircraft now being replaced in the RAF by Harrier T.Mk 10s. INA is also continuing negotiations with British and Israeli companies for the upgrade of its remaining 23 Sea Harrier FRS.Mk 51s to a similar standard to the RN's Sea Harrier FA.2s, with Blue Vixen or Elta EM/2032 pulse-Doppler radar, BVR AAMs, and new defensive aids sub-systems, to extend their service to 2010.

Special mission Astra order

Although unannounced, the Indian government is understood to have signed a contract for six AlliedSignal-engined TFE731-engined IAI Astra SPX light business jets for its Defence Aviation Research Centre. They will be in a special mission configuration with extensive electronics sensors, and will supplement three similarly-equipped Gulfstream GIIIs, two Learjet 35s and two ex-Air India E-Systems-equipped Boeing 707s in an IAF-operated unit in the Delhi area for electronic intelligence roles.

PAKISTAN:

Upgraded Mirage IIIs bought from France

Financial negotiations with France for the FFr12 billion ($2.32 billion) purchase of 26 to 32 Mirage 2000-5s and associated weapons to replace Pakistan's embargoed US F-16s have been continuing with apparently little prospect of success, because of budget limitations in Islamabad. That Pakistan is hedging its bets is evidenced by the Fr500 million ($96.7 million) contract award to the French SAGEM group for the supply of 40 upgraded older Mirage IIIEs. These may include ex-French air force aircraft withdrawn from the AA inventory in 1994, plus 17 Mirage IIIEEs and five two-seat IIIDEs taken over from Spain, although the PAF is also reported to have bought nine low-houred similar aircraft from Lebanon. All 40 are to be refurbished and upgraded by for a total cost of Fr500 million ($96.7 million), before entering PAF service over the next two years.

SAGEM had received a similar upgrade contract in 1992 for 15 PAF Mirage IIIEs, and the follow-on order is expected to include virtually the same MAESTRO modular avionics and nav/attack systems package. This includes Uliss INS/GPS and possible TERCOR contour-matching, wide-angle HUD, HOTAS, IRIS FLIR and improved ECM; 35 FIAR Grifo M I-band fire-control radars have also been ordered by the PAF. Pakistan has already returned to service about half the surplus 50 Mirage IIIOs bought in 1994 from Australia, in addition to acquiring 22 Mirage IIIEs and two-seat IIIDEs from Spain.

More aircraft deliveries

Having operated a dozen or so Mil Mi-8s since 1969, Pakistan army aviation is now doubling its 'Hip' complement with current deliveries from the CIS of 12 of the later upgraded Mi-17 variants. French offers in late 1994 to the Pakistan navy of a second batch of three ex-Aéronavale Dassault-Breguet Atlantic ASW/patrol aircraft, ostensibly as spares back-ups for three similar aircraft operated by No. 29 Sqn, have apparently only recently been fulfilled. The first two of the second batch flew into Sharea Faisal air base in June 1996.

Taiwan has begun to receive its batch of 120 F-16As and 30 F-16Bs (illustrated). These are to Block 20 standard with colour displays.

SRI LANKA:

More aircraft deliveries

Recent equipment deliveries have been made to the Sri Lankan air force for continued operations against Tamil Tiger guerrillas. They include another four Antonov An-32 'Cline' turboprop transports from Ukraine, five ex-IDF/AF Kfir C-2 fighter-bombers and a Kfir TC-2 combat trainer from Israel to equip No. 10 Sqn at Katunayake, and three Mil Mi-24D 'Hind-D' helicopter gunships for No. 9 Sqn. The An-32s supplement a single aircraft of this type remaining from three delivered to the SLAF in 1994, and four leased An-24s.

Australasia

AUSTRALIA:

Caribou replacements

Spain's CASA group is being joined by Air New Zealand in a bid to replace the Royal Australian Air Force's 21 de Havilland Canada DHC-4 Caribou piston-engined STOL transports with 14-18 new CN.235M-9 turboprop successors. Air New Zealand Engineering Services, which already undertakes heavy maintenance for the RAAF's Lockheed C-130s and the GE F404 turbofans of its F/A-18 Hornets, is offering lifetime technical support for the CN.235s. These aircraft are competing with the IPTN-built CN.235 Phoenix and Alenia G.222s for this Australian Defence Project Air 5109 contract within the RAAF's Light Tactical Airlift Capability programme.

Advanced trainers short-listed

Proposals from McDonnell Douglas for the RAAF's $A1 billion ($807.4 million) Project Air 5367 requirement for 40 new lead-in fighter trainers were rejected in a down-selection by the Australian Defence Ministry in September. MDD had offered the T-45A Goshawk with either a Rolls-Royce Adour or AlliedSignal/AIDC ITEC F124 turbofan. Aermacchi's MB.339FD and BAe's Hawk 100 have now been short-listed as final contenders for the requirement, on which a decision was expected by late 1996 or early 1997.

Popeye 2 order confirmed

Rafael's 2,500-lb (1134-kg) Popeye 2 long-range precision-guided ASM has been ordered for the RAAF's F-111 fleet in a recent contract worth about $40 million. A joint company known as Precision Guided Systems US has been formed by Rafael and Lockheed Martin for the collaborative production and marketing of the Popeye missile family.

NEW ZEALAND:

Super Lynx selected?

Although no announcement was expected until after the October elections, the RNZ Navy was understood to have selected before that date the Westland Super Lynx in preference to the Kaman SH-2G for its Westland Wasp shipborne ASW helicopter replacement. The RNZN requirement was for six ASW helicopters to operate from its 'ANZAC'-class frigates, for which its Super Lynx 200s would be re-engined with ITEC T800 turboshafts offering up to 30 per cent more power, in place of its current Rolls-Royce Gem 42s. Earlier, NZ Defence Minister Paul East had said that New Zealand wanted to ensure that its new helicopters would be compatible with those required by Australia, through a collaborative programme. The RAN wanted 14 frigate-operated ASW types, plus options on nine more, to meet its Project Air 1411/1427 specifications. A joint announcement on the final choice was expected in November.

Eighteen of Australia's 19-strong P-3C Update II/W Update II.5 fleet serving with Nos 10 and 11 Sqns are being upgraded to AP-3C standard. The first will re-enter service in 1997. All now wear this low-visibility scheme. The fleet is being augmented by three P-3Bs for training and support.

Africa

BOTSWANA:

First combat aircraft acquired

Ten ex-Canadian Forces Canadair/Northrop CF-5A fighters and three two-seat CF-5D combat trainers from 60 surplus examples are being acquired by the Air Arm of the Botswana Defence Force in Central Africa. They are offered for sale through Bristol Aerospace at an overall cost of $50 million, including flight and technical training. These aircraft are apparently some of the 24 CF-5s upgraded by Bristol with CF-18 avionics as lead-in fighter trainers, giving them advanced combat capabilities, prior to their withdrawal from Canadian service due to defence economies. Other than new radios and IFF equipment, they will require little in the way of further refurbishment by Bristol as part of its 20 per cent share of the contract to give the AABDF a new level of combat capability. The BDF is also receiving two ex-USAF Lockheed C-130Bs from a US FMS contract.

SOUTH AFRICA:

US C-130B transfers

No. 28 Sqn has operated seven Lockheed C-130B Hercules since late 1962 without loss and with no external technical support. The aircraft have recently been supplemented by the donation of five similar examples from the US under Foreign Military Sales auspices, from AMARC storage. Others are going to Ethiopia and Romania. The C-130Bs undergo basic refurbishment before despatch, but their supply does not include free spares and crew training.

South America

ARGENTINA:

Super Etendard loss

Dassault Super Etendard 3-A-203 was destroyed in a crash on 30 May 1996. It was one of the Argentine navy's most famous aircraft, having launched the AM-38 Exocet anti-ship missiles which sank the British cruiser HMS *Sheffield* and the transport vessel *Atlantic Conveyer* during the 1982 Falklands War. The aircraft struck a fuel bowser during a low-level pass at Punto del Indo naval air base, south of Buenos Aires, killing its pilot Lieutenant Sergio Ruben Marquez from the 3rd Attack Wing.

BRAZIL:

New fighters sought

The Brazilian government has allocated $5.2 billion in long-term funding for up to 72 replacements for its Mirage IIIEs and Northrop F-5E/F fighters for delivery from about 2005. The FAB is evaluating leading international combat aircraft for this FX requirement, including the Dassault Mirage 2000-5, Rafale, Saab JAS 39 Gripen and contemporary Russian fighters. Approval for FAB requests for information on US F-16s and F/A-18s awaits a reversal by President Clinton of the current State Department arms veto applied to Latin America, which the Republican opposition in Washington is committed to ending. In the meantime, Lockheed Martin has been talking with EMBRAER about the possibility of an F-16 licensed production programme for the FAB and other Latin American air forces.

PERU:

Russian reinforcements?

According to Latin American press reports, more than 50 ex-Soviet combat aircraft were delivered in mid-1966 to Peru from Belarus, including some 28 MiG-29s and at least 20 unspecified Sukhoi types. Peru has operated Su-22s and other former Soviet aircraft with low attrition rates for many years, and may have taken the opportunity to increase its air force inventory at advantageous prices. If these reports were true, Peru may have acquired some Su-25s, since these were the only tactical ground-attack aircraft operated by Belarus.

This CF-18 wears special markings for 3 Wing, consisting of a giant maple leaf in planform. The aircraft also has the lark badge 425 'Alouette' Squadron on the fuselage.

North America

CANADA:

Lockheed L-100 purchase

Two unsold civil-equipped L-100-30 freighters from Lockheed Martin's now-closed Hercules I production line at Marietta have been bought by the Canadian Forces for a reported $78 million. The aircraft are intended to supplement the CF's 30 or so remaining CC-130H Hercules.

UNITED STATES:

Hercules II joins flight test programme

Following the successful maiden flight of the prototype C-130J (actually a -30 which will eventually join the RAF) at the beginning of April, the second aircraft joined the flight test programme in May. The aircraft concerned was a standard-length C-130J (94-3026), which will be the first for the US Air Force. It undertook its maiden flight on 4 June with Lockheed Martin test pilot Lyle Schaefer at the controls, and lasted six hours and 14 minutes.

During the flight the aircraft achieved an altitude of 35,000 ft (10668 m), and was reported to have handled similarly to a conventional C-130, but was more powerful and much quieter. The third and fifth examples will also be for the RAF, while the fourth will be 94-3027 for the USAF. These will be evaluated by Lockheed Martin as well as by the Air Force Flight Test Center at Edwards AFB, CA. The manufacturer anticipates the C-130J receiving certification by the FAA in May 1997.

The US Air Force has placed an order for a single WC-130J version with FY 1996 funding, which is planned for delivery in August 1997. Production C-130J orders consist of two from FY96 which will be delivered in October 1997, followed by 10 additional aircraft reserved for funding from FY97. This is at variance to the details initially made available, which indicated the FY 1997 budget request contained only one C-130J. Lockheed had planned to terminate C-130H production once the C-130J order book began to increase, but the USAF has continued to fund the C-130H for the Reserves. The 731st AS at Peterson AFB, CO will receive aircraft from 1993 and 1994 orders, followed by the 167th AS, WV ANG which has acquired examples from 1994 and 1995 production. Additional orders have been placed for C-130Hs, including two from FY95 due for delivery in May 1996, six FY 1996 to be delivered between June and August 1996, and four FY 1996 for delivery between October and December 1996.

New tailcode allocations

A number of new tailcodes have been applied in recent months as Reservist units have re-equipped. At Boise Air Terminal, ID the 190th Fighter Squadron applied tailcode 'ID' to their first OA-10A (81-0995) which had entered service by 20 April. The co-located 189th Airlift Squadron had received its first C-130E (63-7849) by the same date, although this was still displaying 'LK' from its former operator, the 314th AW at Little Rock AFB, AR. The 190th FS had used tailcode 'WW' on its F-4Gs, with this code being transferred to the 35th FW at Misawa AB, Japan in June. The 35th was allocated 'WW' while stationed at George AFB, CA and operated the F-4G earlier in the decade. The 192nd Airlift Squadron was officially redesignated from a reconnaissance squadron on 19 April, with its C-130E carrying tailcode 'NV'. C-130E 62-1858 was present for the official ceremony with the new tailcode, and sported a white fin band containing the legend 'High Rollers'. Two other uncoded C-130Es were also present, although the pair of 'Pacer Coin' C-130Es, which was loaned by the 24th Wing for crew training, had returned to Howard AFB, Panama. It is not known if these aircraft will join the unit at a later date, as the squadron was due to have operated them in a dedicated reconnaissance role.

First Air Force One retired

Former 89th Airlift Wing C-137B 58-6970, nicknamed 'Queenie', was finally retired from service on 17 June and flown from Andrews AFB, MD to Seattle, WA to join the Museum of Flight. The aircraft was one of three VIP-configured C-137s ordered in 1958 as presidential transports, and was the first jet-powered Air Force One. Designated as a VC-137A initially, 86970 was delivered to the 1254th Air Transport Wing at Andrews AFB, MD on 4 May 1959. Later in its career the aircraft was re-engined with TF33s and was redesignated as a VC-137B. The aircraft joined the 89th MAW in January 1966 when the unit was formed to replace the 1254th ATW. The VIP prefix was removed from all such aircraft under the Presidency of Jimmy Carter, with 86970 becoming a C-137B.

Beaufort applies tailcode

A retrograde step has taken place at Marine Corps Air Station Beaufort, SC where the commander of Marine Air Group 31 (MAG-31) has decreed that all the resident aircraft will have tailcode 'BM' for Beaufort Marines. By May 1996 the code had begun to appear on F/A-18Cs including those of VMFA-251. F/A-18Ds of VMFA(AW)-332 were deployed to Aviano AB, Italy to perform patrols over Bosnia as part of Operation Joint Endeavour, and had begun to adopt the new tailcode during June. The application of tailcodes applied at station level is not seen as being popular, and will probably be abandoned once the MAG-31 commander is replaced.

C-27 Spartans grounded

The 12 Alenia C-27A Spartans assigned to the 310th AS, 24th Wing at Howard AFB, Panama were grounded for two weeks from 15 May while inspections were carried out following the discovery of cracks in the horizontal stabiliser attachments of one aircraft. The squadron is due to lose six of its 18 C-27A crews, with a corresponding reduction in flying hours of one-third from October 1996, due to budget constraints. The Air Force has tried unsuccessfully for the last four years to eliminate the C-27A from the inventory, as the type is not popular. The C-27 is primarily employed to provide rapid response delivery of cargo and personnel to remote locations in Central America that have short, unprepared landing surfaces. The wing also operates the C-21A and C-130H, with the majority of resupply missions being performed by the latter while the C-27s were grounded.

F-16 reconnaissance optical pod deployed

The 149th FS at Richmond/Byrd Field, VA became the first F-16C squadron to deploy with the Lockheed Martin reconnaissance optical digital reconnaissance pod when five aircraft flew to Aviano AB, Italy on 30 May for Operation Joint Endeavour. The pod is mounted on the centreline hardpoint, and will enable the Air Force to resume tactical reconnaissance operations for the first time since the RF-4C was retired from service earlier in the decade. The Air National Guard requires another 16 pods which will enable additional squadrons to perform tactical reconnaissance missions. Among those which may receive these pods are the 107th FS at Selfridge ARB, MI, 113th FS at Hulman Field, Terre Haute, IN, 121st FS (DC ANG) at Andrews AFB, MD, and the 175th FS at Joe Foss Field, Sioux Falls, SD.

On 24 April 1996 the ACTIVE (advanced control technology for integrated vehicles) F-15 testbed flew for the first time using pitch/yaw thrust-vectoring in supersonic flight. ACTIVE is a joint USAF/NASA/McDonnell Douglas/ Pratt & Whitney project.

Marine Corps Osprey plans

The Marine Corps has commenced planning for the delivery of the initial operational examples of the Bell-Boeing MV-22A Osprey, following the placing of a $404 million order for the first four aircraft on 7 June. The aircraft should begin delivery later in the decade, with the final example expected to be received by December 1999. The Marine Corps has a requirement for 425 MV-22s to replace both the CH-46 Sea Knight and CH-53 Sea Stallion.

The first unit earmarked to receive the Osprey is Marine Helicopter Training Squadron 204 (HMT-204), which will be redesignated as VHMT-204, with initial operating capability due in 2001. The unit is currently stationed at MCAS New River, NC where it undertakes aircrew conversion with the CH-46E and CH-53D/E. The first operational MV-22A squadron will be VHMM-264, which is currently designated HMM-264 and operates the CH-46E, and is also based at MCAS New River under the Fleet Marine Force Atlantic (FMFLANT). The squadron will be the first deployable Osprey unit, and will spearhead the introduction of the type into operational service.

New Stratotanker designation announced

The US Air Force recently announced a new designation for the C-135 Stratojet series: WC-135W, which has been applied to three former WC-135Bs which are associated with test and evaluation of systems and training of aircrew for the strategic reconnaissance role. The new suffix 'W' to the WC-135 has been allocated primarily because there is a need to revise the flight manuals following the deletion of the flight engineer's position from the aircraft. Therefore, the manuals for the WC-135W will differ from other aircraft in the C-135W series. The three aircraft include 61-2666, which has been assigned to Detachment 2 of the 645th Materiel Squadron of Air Force Materiel Command (AFMC) for many years as a testbed for reconnaissance systems. The aircraft is stationed at Greenville, TX, the main operating base of E-Systems Inc., which is one of the major corporations involved in the development and installation of airborne reconnaissance and electronic equipment. The other two aircraft are 61-2665, which was a WC-135B assigned to the 55th Wing to train crews flying the OC-135B Open Skies aircraft, and 61-2667, which also served with the 55th Wing as a TC-135B. The 55th Wing is located at Offutt AFB, NE and is the sole operator of the RC-135 fleet within the US Air Force.

61-2666 visited Mildenhall and Souda Bay, Crete in June 1992 in the same basic mid-grey scheme applied when the aircraft was assigned to MAC's Air Weather Service as a WC-135B. In place of the inscription 'Weather' in the MAC band, was 'DET 2'. At the time the aircraft showed no external modifications, although the air scoops located on the side of the fuselage to help cool internal weather monitoring equipment had been removed and the ducting faired over. The aircraft is reported to have changed appearance recently to resemble an RC-135W.

Wearing temporary civil registration N130JC, this is the second C-130J to fly and the first to be built for the USAF. The first US aircraft will reportedly be delivered either as WC-130s for weather reconnaissance or as EC-130s for the Rivet Rider programme.

AV-8B remanufacture programme to be terminated?

The programme to remanufacture 73 US Marine Corps AV-8B Harrier IIs to night-attack radar-equipped configuration as the Harrier II Plus has been recommended for termination by the US General Accounting Office (GAO). A study by the GAO has suggested that the $2.2 billion programme could be completed for a considerably reduced sum of money through the purchase of new AV-8Bs. The Marine Corps estimates the individual cost of remanufacturing each AV-8 to be between $23 and $30 million, whereas a new Harrier II Plus could be procured at a cost of $30 million. However, the GAO has estimated the individual cost of the new AV-8B to be only $24 million. The GAO also believes the Naval Air Depot (NADEP) at Cherry Point, NC will find it difficult to meet production targets within budget. The programme began in August 1994, with the first conversion, 165305 (previously AV-8B 162728), being completed and returned to the Marine Corps by January 1996. The aircraft is currently under evaluation with VX-9 at NAWC China Lake, CA. The next two conversions are with McDonnell Douglas at St Louis, while the remaining five of the initial order for eight are with the NADEP at Cherry Point.

Last F-4Gs retired from Boise and Nellis

The final examples of the F-4G Wild Weasel version of the Phantom were retired from service with the 190th Fighter Squadron at Boise Air Terminal, ID recently. The final four aircraft left Boise for the last time on 20 April, destined for storage with AMARC at Davis-Monthan AFB, AZ. The distinction of being the last of the four to land at Davis-Monthan fell to 69-7291 'WW', which touched down around 3 p.m. A small ceremony was held on the arrivals ramp to commemorate this significant event. The 190th FS had applied sharkmouths to some of its F-4Gs for the last few missions.

The 561st FS retired its last F-4Gs on 26 March 1996 at Nellis AFB, NV. The occasion was marked by the squadron commander's aircraft (69-7295) receiving appropriate artwork, including '1963 PHAREWELL 1996' along the spine. The nose was repainted with a sharkmouth for the occasion. The squadron is scheduled for inactivation during the summer.

The phasing out of the F-4G does not completely end the career of the Phantom in USAF service, for the F-4E remains active with the 20th FS, 49th FW at Holloman AFB, NM. They are operated to train German air force crews and will continue in service until the autumn, by which time the Luftwaffe will have its own Tornados and F-4Fs in residence. The Germans formed the Taktische

The tempo of the competition for the JSF (Joint Strike Fighter) is increasing. This is an impression of Northrop Grumman/McDonnell Douglas/BAe design in STOVL form for the Royal Navy. The aircraft has widely splayed YF-23-style tail fins.

Two ANG F-16 units celebrating their 50th anniversaries in 1996 are the 134th Fighter Squadron, Vermont ANG (above) and the 174th FS, South Dakota ANG (below).

Ausbildungseinheit (Tactical Training Centre) on 1 May to operate the aircraft, although day-to-day flying duties will be co-ordinated by the 49th FW. The initial complement of Tornados will be 12 aircraft, eventually rising to 42 by 1999, operating alongside 24 F-4Fs. The first five Tornados were ferried from Jever AB to Holloman during April, and batches of F-4Fs followed. Initial instruction training is due to start in July, with the first aircrew receiving tuition from October.

The Germans have trained their pilots in the US since 1955 with T-37Bs and T-38As at Sheppard AFB, TX. By 2000 the pilot training programme will be performed exclusively in the US. Initial flying training will be conducted on Beech Bonanzas at Goodyear, AZ, followed by fast jet tuition at Sheppard AFB, prior to pilots and navigators receiving operational conversion at Holloman AFB.

Additional Strike Eagles for the Air Force

The Air Force has confirmed it will be acquiring another 18 F-15E Strike Eagles as attrition replacements in a multi-year procurement. The previous order book closed in July 1994 when the last examples, which were funded in 1992, were delivered to the 48th FW at RAF Lakenheath and the 57th Wing at Nellis AFB, NV. The first six of the new contract were ordered on 13 May with FY 1996 funding, and will be followed by the remaining 12, to be purchased from the 1997 and 1998 budgets. The six aircraft from FY 1996 will begin construction in October, but will not be delivered until November 1998. The reason for the protracted delay is unknown. Production of the 12 F-15Es from FY 1997 and 1998 will be completed by 1999. They will be constructed at the McDonnell Douglas facility at St Louis, MO alongside existing orders for the F-15I for Israel and the F-15S for Saudi Arabia.

Composite wings reorganised

Air Combat Command is to reorganise its composite units. The 74th FS, 23rd Wing at Pope AFB, NC due to transfer its F-16Cs to the 20th FW at Shaw AFB, SC; in exchange, the 55th FS at Shaw AFB will transfer its OA/A-10As to Pope AFB. At Seymour Johnson AFB, NC the completion of the transfer of KC-10As from the 4th Wing to Air Mobility Command has enabled the unit to be redesignated as a fighter wing. The 366th Wing at Mountain Home AFB, ID is to consolidate its assets at home base with the transfer of the B-1Bs of the 34th BS from Ellsworth AFB, SD by mid-1997, which is slightly later than originally planned. Finally, the 347th Wing at Moody AFB, GA will add a combat rescue element to the unit's mission upon the activation of a squadron operating the HC-130N/P and HH-60G.

MC-130P designation update

Updating the previous report in *World Air Power Journal* Volume 27 that Air Force Special Operations Command (AFSOC) had redesignated its HC-130N/P models as MC-130s, both versions are now designated as MC-130Ps. The Air Force announced the change on 15 February 1996. Twenty-eight aircraft are involved, assigned to the 5th SOS, 919th SOW at Duke Field, FL (AFRes); 9th SOS, 16th SOW at Eglin AFB, FL, 17th SOS, 353rd SOG at Kadena AB, Okinawa, and 67th SOS, 352nd SOG at RAF Mildenhall, UK (all AFSOC); and 550th SOS, 58th SOW at Kirtland AFB, NM (AETC). The last unit is responsible for training personnel destined for operational service with AFSOC.

Unit news

AETC has activated the 48th FTS flying the T-1A at Columbus AFB, MS under the 14th FTW. At Randolph AFB, TX the 562nd TFS has replaced the 558th FTS operating the T-43A with the 12th FTW.

The 43rd ARG at Malmstrom AFB, MT is to relocate to MacDill AFB, FL in October 1996, with the latter facility passing from Air Combat Command to AMC. The 43rd operates a dozen KC-135Rs under the 91st ARS.

The 19th ARW at Robins AFB, GA is to be downgraded to group status at the end of FY96 following the reduction in the number of KC-135Rs assigned. The unit is being reduced in size primarily to make additional ramp space available for the E-8Cs of the 93rd ACW and the B-1Bs of the 128th BS, Georgia ANG. The latter unit received its first B-1B on 1 April. The unit had tailcode 'GA' applied when it flew the F-15A/B at Dobbins AFB, although the two-letter identifier has more recently been assigned to the C-130Hs of the 158th AS at Savannah.

Air Mobility Command inactivated the 18th Airlift Squadron at McGuire AFB, NJ on 1 July 1995; its C-141Bs were redistributed or retired.

The 452nd Air Mobility Wing became the host unit at March AFB, CA on 23 March, and the facility was redesignated as an Air Reserve Base. The wing has the 336th ARS operating the KC-135E, alongside the 729th and 730th AS flying the C-141B.

C-9A 71-0876, which is operated in the VIP role by Det 1, 75th AAS at Chièvres AB, Belgium for the Commander in Chief of SHAPE, returned from major overhaul in the US. The aircraft was recently repainted in a blue, white and gold colour scheme similar to that of the fleet assigned to the 89th AW at Andrews AFB, MD.

The Army has announced that the 1st Battalion, 227th Aviation Company at Fort Hood, TX will be the first fully equipped unit to operate the AH-64A Longbow, with deliveries due to begin by September 1997.

At Tinker AFB, OK the 552nd Air Control Wing has operated a pair of TC-18E trainers with civilian identities assigned. These were former civilian Boeing 707s obtained to perform the training and proficiency role for E-3 Sentry crews with the 966th AACTS. More recently, they have adopted the military serials 84-1398 and 84-1399. Tinker also has the Navy's Sea Control Wing One (SCW-1) in residence operating the E-6A/B Mercury, and a single TC-18F 165343 performing a similar role to the Air Force's TC-18Es. The Navy unit has a support UC-12B 161327 coded 'VQ', as the wing is divided into VQ-3 and VQ-4 although aircraft are operated on a pooled basis.

USAF C-12Fs transferred to the Army

The Companion Trainer Program, which was used for proficiency training by airlift and tankers units, has been terminated completely by Air Mobility Command and the 12 C-12Fs have been transferred to the US Army. The final six examples had left the 3rd Wing at Elmendorf AFB, AK and the 51st FW at Osan AB, RoK by the summer of 1996. The CTP role was seen as a cost-effective method of permitting aircrew to remain proficient at routine flying without using expensive KC-135s and KC-10s. Air Combat Command has also gradually phased out the programme from its bomber units, except for the 9th RW at Beale AFB, CA and the 509th BW at Whiteman AFB, MO, which have retained the T-38A. Approximately a dozen of the displaced C-12Fs were assigned to Europe for Army service in Germany, Italy and Turkey, to replace the C-12C. Others have been flown to Far East units, and the remainder have been stationed in the USA.

HQ 17th Air Force reorganised

The Headquarters 17th Air Force is to be inactivated on 30 September 1996, with its assets redistributed between the 3rd and 16th Air Forces. The 17th AF has its headquarters at Sembach AB, Germany, and is responsible for two major flying units: the 52nd Fighter Wing at Spangdahlem AB and the 86th Airlift Wing at Ramstein AB, both in Germany. These wings will join the 3rd Air Force, headquartered at RAF Mildenhall. Basically, assets of the 17th AF located north of the Alps will become part of the 3rd AF, while those south of the Alps will be administered by the16th Air Force from Aviano AB, Italy.

The reorganisation will enable a streamlining of the USAFE command structure, for three regional support groups will inactivate at the same time as does the 17th Air Force. The 603rd, 616th and 617th RSG at Mildenhall, Aviano and Sembach currently supervise the smaller, non-flying facilities within their area of responsibility. These locations now will report to the nearest major unit: the 603rd RSG in the UK and Norway will be accountable to the 100th ARW at Mildenhall, while some of the responsibilities of the 616th RSG at Aviano will become part of the 31st FW. The obligations of the 617th RSG will probably become part of the 86th AW. Among the smaller units are air base squadrons, comms sites, and munitions squadrons.

FY 1997 budget

The Department of Defense has revealed its list of requirements for purchase during FY 1997. In the face of lower-than-anticipated inflation, the DoD has additional funds in the budget for procurement. Among the items for consideration were eight C-17A Globemaster IIIs, a single C-130J, two E-8C Joint STARS, four F-15Es, four F-16Cs, and 12 Raytheon Beech Mk II trainers. Details have since changed and the number of F-15Es and C-130s have been amended. The C-17 purchase is part of acquisition reform measures which it is estimated could save the military more than $13 billion, thereby providing funds for modernisation programmes and other requirements. The Air Force has instigated a seven-year C-17 purchase which could save $900 million if fully approved by Congress. The House and Senate defence appropriations committees have agreed with the multi-year scheme. The Air Force expects other large-scale multi-year orders to reap large financial rewards, such as the Joint Direct Attack Munition (JDAM) programme. If implemented, the cost of development of JDAM could save almost $2.9 billion, while the unit cost is likely to shrink from $40,000 to $14,000 per item. The F-15Es and F-16Cs are attrition replacements required to prevent a short-fall in combat capability early in the next decade.

The Navy request for itself and the Marine Corps will include the first 12 production F/A-18E Hornets, two E-2Cs, a dozen T-45As, four V-22 Ospreys, and the remanufacture of another 10 AV-8B Harrier IIs. The Navy also has an interest in a multi-year acquisition of aircraft, with 150 F/A-18E/F models required between FY 1998 and 2001, while the number of V-22s in the same period has been established at 31. Rotary-winged requirements include four Navy versions of the UH-60 in FY99, although the exact version has not been determined, followed by eight in FY 2000 and nine in FY 2001 as replacements for the CH-46D fleet. The Navy has approximately 72 CH- and UH-46s performing the VertRep role aboard its vessels. Other requirements are for 100 UH-1Ns and 180 AH-1Ws of the US Marine Corps to be refitted with four-bladed rotor systems.

The Army is seeking an extension of the H-60 Black Hawk production and has a requirement for 180 between FY 1997 and 2001. Army assignment is 172, and the remaining eight (as HH-60Gs) are for the Air Force.

The Air Force has issued a request for proposals for the development of an airborne laser system, with an anticipation of a service entry by 2006. The Boeing 747 is considered as the most appropriate aircraft type to house the system, and three are being modified. The primary mission of the airborne laser will be to defend the US and its allies against attack by ballistic missiles in either the United States or an overseas combat theatre.

The Air Force will be seeking funding to enable upgrades to its fleet of fighter and attack aircraft to ensure their effectiveness into the next century. Among the types which may receive enhancements are the A-10, F-15, F-16 and F-117. The proposals will include a new, smaller LANTIRN system and a datalink for the F-15 and F-16 to quicken their response during combat.

Miramar to become MCAS by October 1997

NAS Miramar, CA will become a Marine Corps Air Station on 1 October 1997, with the name possibly being changed to MCAS San Diego. The final two squadrons to move to Miramar are VMGR-352 with the KC-130F/R and VMFAT-101 with the F/A-18A/B/C/D; they will remain at MCAS El Toro until new infrastructure has been completed either in 1997 or 1998. Meanwhile, the move by the Marine Corps helicopters from MCAS Tustin to El Toro is to be accelerated with completion due by 1997 instead of 1999.

Development of the second-generation Hornet continues apace. F/A-18E4 (above) is now flying as the high angle-of-attack test-ship, painted in high-visibility orange and white to allow tracking by ground-based cameras. The aircraft has a spin chute fitted. On 6 August 1996 the 'Superbug' undertook its first catapult launch (below) when F/A-18F1 launched from Patuxent River's test catapult, piloted by Commander (Selectee) Tom Gurney.

VF-2 officially moved with its F-14 Tomcats from NAS Miramar to NAS Oceana, VA during April 1996 as part of the ongoing transfer of Navy assets away from the base. The Tomcat community is to vacate NAS Miramar by October 1996 and VF-213 will be one of the last squadrons to leave. The transfer of all Navy equipment from the base should be completed by the middle of 1997.

The Navy is to establish the Naval Strike and Air Warfare Center (NSAWC) at NAS Fallon, NV, which will integrate the Naval Fighter Weapons School (NFWS) with the Carrier Airborne Early Warning Weapons School (CAEWWS). Both units were located at NAS Miramar, although the aircraft of the NFWS flew to their new home at NAS Fallon on 29 May. The amalgamation will enable the NSAWC to conduct courses for all categories of carrierborne, fixed-winged aircraft types.

F-111F retired from service

The final examples of the F-111F in operational service were retired by the 27th FW at Cannon AFB, NM on 29 July. The 524th FS had the honour of the being the last F-111F operator, hosting a Vark Farewell Reunion at Fort Worth between 26 and 28 July which was attended by former 'Aardvark' personnel. The retirement effectively ended the operational career of the F-111 in the US Air Force in all but its electronic jamming role.

US reduces force level on Okinawa

The US government is to reduce its presence on the Japanese island of Okinawa during the next eight years, with the return of 20 per cent of the land currently occupied by the military. The Marine Corps facility at Futenma will close and the KC-130Fs of VMGR-152 will move to MCAS Iwakuni, Japan. To make room for the Hercules, Iwakuni will reduce its complement of a dozen AV-8Bs deployed from the US for six-month rotations.

Surplus KC-135s for Singapore

More of the stored KC-135As in storage with AMARC at Davis-Monthan AFB, AZ are to be supplied to overseas

The 24th Wing at Howard is flying its Chrysler/Alenia C-27s again after a grounding following the discovery of cracks. All now wear the 'proud grey' scheme. The wing is to lose six of its 18 C-27s.

customers. The latest air arm to express an interest is the Singapore air force, which is considering acquiring four tankers that will be re-engined and completely refurbished if a satisfactory price can be negotiated.

B-2 news

The Pentagon announced on 21 March that the President had authorised the funding to enable the prototype B-2 flight test airframe 82-1066 (designated Air Vehicle 1 or AV-1) to be upgraded to full operational standard. This will use $493 million which Congress added to the FY 1996 defence budget for the 'Stealth Bomber' programme. The upgrade will increase the B-2 inventory to 21 aircraft and will extend the production line to July 2000. The exact cost involved was under negotiation between the Air Force and Northrop Grumman, although there is confidence the cost could be contained within the allocated sum. Funding has already been made available for another test aircraft, AV-2, to be upgraded. AV-1 has less capable low-observability characteristics, which will be improved, with the aircraft having the same capabilities as those from Block 30 production. During its test phase AV-1 was used to evaluate the flying qualities of the design, and to verify the low observability of Block 10 production.

Although the US administration has repeatedly stated that it does not intend to extend production of the B-2 beyond present levels, a Heavy Bomber Industrial Capabilities Study has recommended that Northrop Grumman maintains and preserves the long-lead items such as planning and tooling. This action would greatly reduce costs in the event of a need to restart production at a later date. The White House has also stated that it sees the purchase of additional precision-guided munitions as being more cost-effective than buying additional B-2s.

Operational B-2s continue with long-distance flights to participate briefly at air shows. On 9 March 1996 the sixth production B-2A (89-0127 'Spirit of Kansas') of the 509th Bomb Wing flew from Whiteman AFB, MO to the Ferie Internacional del Aire y del Espacio (FIDAE) at Santiago, Chile. The aircraft departed Whiteman AFB and flew non-stop to Santiago with the aid of two air refuelling hook-ups. The aircraft overflew the air show before returning to its home base to record a 24½-hour non-stop round trip. This was the longest flight of the B-2 to date. Previously, a B-2 had flown from Whiteman AFB to the Asian Aerospace Show in Singapore where the aircraft landed briefly, as it did at last year's Paris air show.

The 509th BW received its 11th B-2A on 15 May, the third to enter operational service in 1996. The aircraft in question was also the first Block 20 example and features the most up-to-date technology installed. Following the completion of the current order for 20 production aircraft, the earlier examples will be reworked to Block 30 configuration. On 27 May, B-2A 90-0041 was officially named 'Spirit of Hawaii' in ceremonies at Hickam AFB, HI. This aircraft was the ninth example to enter service with the 509th BW and was delivered to the unit on 11 January 1996.

The operational B-2A fleet was grounded for a week from 10 May while the engine exhaust systems were inspected following two inflight failures of the clamp which secures the exhaust duct to the engine. Subsequently, an unidentified B-2A was grounded for a short period after sustaining external damage and paint discoloration to its wing surfaces after suffering a lightning strike while on a training sortie from Whiteman AFB on 24 May.

C-17 multi-year purchase contract completed

The Air Force has completed a multi-year contract with McDonnell Douglas for the purchase of 80 C-17A Globemaster IIIs at a cost of $16.2 billion. The order is the largest multi-year contract ever placed by the US government for military equipment. It will ultimately save the Department of Defense an estimated $1 billion for McDonnell Douglas, the prime contractor, and the numerous sub-contractors will be able to obtain materials in huge bulk purchase at discounted prices. The order includes 350 Pratt & Whitney F-117 turbofan engines worth $1.7 billion, which is the single largest contract for powerplants in the company's history. The contract enables the Air Force to plan for operations with the full requirement of 120 C-17As assigned to Air Mobility Command, Air Education and Training Command and the Air National Guard. Deliveries are scheduled for completion in November 2004.

AETC has formed the 58th Airlift Squadron (previously at Ramstein AB, Germany) under the 97th Air Mobility Wing at Altus AFB, OK as the training unit for the C-17A. The squadron received its first Globemaster III on 23 March, which marks the initial entry into service for the C-17A with AETC. The unit joins the 55th ARS, 56th AS and 57th AS operating the KC-135R, C-5A and C-141B, respectively.

The completion of the evaluation programme at Edwards AFB in 1994 has enabled the majority of test C-17s to be reworked to operational standard with deliveries to the 437th AW at Charleston AFB, SC. The Air Force has indicated that the C-17 could remain in production for many years past the planned termination date early in the next decade, as McDonnell Douglas is studying the possibility of adding a fuselage extension of between 20 and 40 ft (6.1 to 12.2 m). The modified C-17 could be ordered as a replacement for the C-5 Galaxy, although the short-field characteristics of the Globemaster would be severely curtailed.

JSF news

The proposed Joint Strike Fighter (JSF) is gathering momentum, and is currently being considered for service after the F-22 Rapier. The JSF will replace the F-16 in USAF service, although it may also be obtained by the Navy and Marine Corps. The Air Force has a requirement for 2,036, enabling deployment to Air Combat Command as well as to PACAF and USAFE. The Navy has suggested a need for 300 and the Marine Corps requires 642 as replacements for the F/A-18. The British Fleet Air Arm has an interest in obtaining 60 as replacements for its Sea Harriers, with a possibility of sub-contracting taking place in the UK.

F-22 and JSF for USAFE

The Air Force has confirmed its ongoing commitment to the maintenance of forces in the United Kingdom well into the next decade. The 48th FW at RAF Lakenheath is to receive the F-22A and later the new Joint Strike Fighter (JSF). The F-22A will replace the existing F-15C/Ds of the 493rd FS, possibly as early as 2005, and will

On 19 August 1996 McDonnell Douglas undertook the first launch of the MA-31 aerial target from a QF-4 at NAWC-WD Point Mugu. The MA-31 is a version of the Russian-built Zvezda-Strela Kh-31, deployed by the Russians as an anti-radar and anti-ship weapon. The MA-31 will be used to simulate high-speed anti-ship missiles. Four test launches are planned prior to procurement.

retain one squadron of F-15Es to be operated alongside the JSF.

YC-15 to fly again

The McDonnell Douglas YC-15 is being refurbished to fly again after more than 15 years in storage in the Arizona desert. The aircraft will be bailed to the manufacturer as a testbed for advanced technologies, and will operate from McDonnell Douglas facilities in Long Beach, CA.

As a company demonstrator, the YC-15 is expected to help McDonnell Douglas explore technologies for a civilian version of the C-17, called the MD-17. The MD-17 is aimed in part at the market for outsized cargo carriers, now dominated by Antonov aircraft. The company is also working on an Advanced Theater Transport (ATT) design which combines features of the YC-15 with a four-engined, tilt-rotor concept. Funds are available to refurbish and fly the first YC-15 but McDonnell Douglas also hopes eventually to fly the second. The YC-15 was powered by four Pratt & Whitney JT8D-17 turbofan engines rated at 16,000 lb (71.17 kN) thrust. The first aircraft also flew with a 22,000-lb (97.86-kN) thrust General Electric/ SNECMA CFM56 turbofan in the port outboard nacelle, and the second aircraft was fitted with an 18,000-lb (80.07-kN) thrust Pratt & Whitney JT8D-209 turbofan in the same location.

JPATS squadron

As the US Air Force proceeds with the Raytheon PC.9 Mk II JPATS (Joint Primary Aircraft Trainer System), the service has decided that the first operational squadron will be the 559th Flying Training Squadron at Randolph AFB, TX. First deliveries are scheduled for 1999.

RAH-66 Comanche resumes flying

The US Army's Boeing-Sikorsky RAH-66 Comanche helicopter (94-0327) made its second flight on 24 August 1996, more than seven months after the first following a pause caused by mechanical problems. The 54-minute flight at West Palm Beach, FL, by Sikorsky's Rus Stiles and Boeing's Reggie Murrell was the first for the Comanche since 4 January 1996.

The Army cleared the Comanche to return to flight after the manufacturers identified the resonance problem that caused a gear in the Comanche propulsion system testbed transmission to fail in mid-1996.

USAF orders Israeli executive jet

The US Air Force in August 1996 issued a $20.8 million contract for two Astra SPX executive jets to replace C-21A Learjets currently in the USAF inventory. With a range of 3,025 miles (4868 km), the SPX has considerably longer legs than the C-21A, as well as a larger cabin. The aircraft will be designated C-38A.

Boeing 757 VIP transport order

Boeing will supply up to four leased VIP 757-200 narrow-body twin jetliners to the 89th Airlift Wing at Andrews AFB, MD after winning a $365.5 million VC-X contract to replace the Boeing VC-137B. The military Boeing 757s will be designated C-32A. The USAF wants the aircraft in service by February 1998. Apart from secure communications, they will be nearly off-the-shelf standard, with a three-class cabin and first-class sleeper seats in the distinguished visitor area.

The same manufacturer had also submitted the Boeing 767-200ER as a VC-X candidate, referred to in manufacturer's literature as the C-32A. McDonnell Douglas has submitted a version of the MD-11 which was initially deemed suitable but lost favour when Air Force officials decided they wanted a somewhat smaller aircraft.

In late July 1996 this F-111F visited the Lockheed Martin works at Fort Worth as part of the retirement ceremonies for the 'Aardvark'. The aircraft was painted with nose markings commemorating the F-111's battle honours, together with the tailcodes of the major units which flew the type.

T-38C Talon upgrade

McDonnell Douglas won a US Air Force competition to build two prototype T-38C Talon trainers, develop ground training simulators, and upgrade 425 current T-38As to T-38C standard.

The USAF is expected to keep upgraded Talons in service as advanced trainers until 2020. The T-38C will provide both advanced flight training and lead-in fighter training. By taking the lead toward upgrading the USAF's entire Talon fleet (originally manufactured by Northrop), the McDonnell Douglas team also stands an excellent prospect of foreign sales of T-38/F-5 variants to Germany, Taiwan, Turkey, and other nations.

The T-38C will be modified with an inertial navigation system with an imbedded GPS, head-up display, cockpit multi-function displays, HOTAS (hands on throttle and stick) technology, EFIS (electronic flight instrumentation system), and a collision avoidance system.

A T-38C prototype first flight in June 1998 is to be followed by 18 months of flight evaluations. In April 2000, MDC will begin six years of production conversions at its plant in St Louis, MO.

Boeing 767 for Japan

The Boeing 767-200 AWACS (Airborne Warning and Control System) for Japan was rolled out at Boeing International Field, Seattle, WA and made its first flight on 9 August 1996, piloted by Charles Gebhardt and Gerald White. The Japanese 767s are powered by two General Electric CF6-80C2B6FA turbofan engines each producing 61,500 lb (124.09 kN) of thrust.

E-8C production

The Pentagon has approved full-rate production of the Boeing/Northrop Grumman E-8C J-STARS (Joint Surveillance Target Attack Radar System), a move that will ultimately give the US Air Force a fleet of 20 aircraft. 'Production' of new E-8Cs is accomplished by modifying Boeing 707-320C airliners. The USAF now operates two E-8As and one E-8C, but none is in final configuration. The two E-8As will be brought up to E-8C standard, and at least one E-8C will remain as a test asset. Six 707s are being modified to J-STARS configuration, which will raise the number to 16.

JSOW weapon tests

An F-16D Fighting Falcon dropped the first AGM-154B version of the JSOW (Joint Stand-Off Weapon) on 28 July 1996 at the Eglin AFB, FL range. Lockheed Martin is developing a flight test software package that integrates JSOW, JDAM (the Joint Direct Attack Munition), and the Wind Corrected Munitions Dispenser with the F-16. The US Navy was scheduled to complete first-phase operational tests of its AGM-154A variant, compatible with the F/A-18C/D Hornet, in October 1996.

The USN has recently formed the NSAWC (Naval Strike and Air Warfare Center) at NAS Fallon, integrating the work of FWS ('Topgun') and NSWC ('Strike U'). Among the equipment is this adversary-painted SH-60F.

Hawaii Air National Guard

Defenders of paradise

At a time when US policy in the Pacific is critical, the Hawaii Air National Guard is caught in an era of change. Until the 1990s, Hawaii's air guard was known as a fighter squadron that also flew a single transport aircraft. Today, the 154th Wing at Hickam Air Force Base near Honolulu is one of the largest Air National Guard (ANG) establishments. The Hawaii guard is graphic evidence of the extent to which the US relies on the reserve component of its armed forces. Except for a few Army helicopters, the 'HANG' operates all US combat aircraft in the Hawaiian Islands. The Hawaii guard is noteworthy for another reason: it is pioneering the use of night-vision goggles (NVGs) in air-to-air fighter tactics.

The HANG's 154th Wing today boasts three flying squadrons. The 199th Fighter Squadron operates McDonnell Douglas F-15A/B Eagle fighters. These are the oldest Eagles in inventory but have been upgraded with a multi-stage improvement programme (MSIP). Four have been modified to accommodate NVGs. The 203rd Air Refueling Squadron flies the Boeing KC-135R Stratotanker, and the 204th Airlift Squadron operates the Lockheed C-130H Hercules.

The USAF calls the 154th a 'combined' wing (different aircraft for different missions) rather than a 'composite' wing (different aircraft performing the same mission). A 154th Wing milestone came in May 1996 when the 199th became the first USAF fighter squadron to sit active defence alert using night-vision goggles. It would be a mistake, today, to view the Hawaii Air National Guard as a fighter outfit.

The 199th and its F-15A/B MSIP Eagles are charged with defending Hawaii. This is where a surprise Japanese attack befell Pearl Harbor on 7 December 1941, and memories linger of the strike by carrier warplanes that crippled the US fleet, razed installations like Hickam, and sank or seriously damaged 19 warships, destroyed 239 aircraft and killed 2,300 Americans. The attackers lost only 23 aircraft. Today, the ANG's Eagle squadron provides the only defence of the 50th US state. While standing alert and pioneering night-fighting tactics, the 199th also must devote resources to traditional problems: in 1994-95, they deployed to Incirlik, Turkey to enforce a 'No Fly' sanction against Iraq, and to Howard AFB, Panama for drug interdiction operations.

Hawaii's F-15 pilots use ITT-manufactured Model F4949 NVGs, also identified by the generic term ANVIS (Aviator's Night Vision Imaging System). They have long been used by US Army helicopter crews for air-to-ground work. The NVGs amplify existing white light from stars, the moon, radiated light from the bottoms of clouds – whatever is available – and use infra-red technology to function like a television camera to create an image. "When you're wearing them, it's like looking down a soda straw," says Captain Stan Hong of the 199th FS. US doctrine now relies on fighting at night and Hong says that NVGs "bring ass kickage to a whole new level."

According to officers in Hawaii, no other F-15 unit was willing to devote the time and resources to night air combat tactics. F4949s had been employed on a limited basis during drug interdiction missions but not for the full range of air-to-air combat actions. Now, F-15 pilots can intercept bombers or cruise missiles during the nocturnal hours, make 'blind' passes on wayward aircraft without having to reveal themselves with a telltale searchlight, and even carry out a dogfight in total darkness.

Shortly after the Hawaii ANG made its first flight with NVGs in February 1994, the 199th deployed to Gulfport, Mississippi (in April 1994) for a realistic test of F-15 versus F-15, with and without the new technology. Subsequently, Hawaii guard fliers used night-vision goggles on an anti-drug deployment to Panama (October-December 1995). In April-May 1996, two 199th FS pilots were sent to Kadena Air Base, Okinawa to pass along their knowledge of night-fighting to a core of pilots in the USAF's 44th Fighter Squadron, the 'Bats', who fly F-15Cs – a rare instance of the Air National Guard showing the way for the regulars.

Fifty-one thousand man-hours went into the 199th's NVG effort. Nonetheless, when the 199th took the task of becoming the USAF's premier NVG F-15 unit, the commander was warned that other priorities could not be set aside. The squadron deployed to Incirlik AB, Turkey on 3 December 1994 to take over the Provide Comfort II

***Left:** The 204th Airlift Squadron has five C-130Hs on charge, used for general transport and for para-dropping support of the 25th Infantry Division.*

***Below:** The 199th FS operates the F-15A MSIP. In addition to local air defence responsibilities, the squadron is also occasionally tasked with overseas deployments.*

***Above:** Since 1994 the 199th FS has been equipped with ANVIS night-vision goggles. The squadron has been instrumental in developing the art of night dogfighting using the equipment.*

KC-135Rs from the 203rd ARS provide tanking support for the air defence Eagles. They, too, play their part in American global policing duties.

commitment aimed at denying flight to Iraqi forces in Kurd-occupied north of Iraq. For a period in late 1994 and early 1995, the 199th FS was patrolling Iraq (with four of its own aircraft plus others borrowed from other units), standing alert at Hickam, and working up in NVGs, all at once.

The 199th FS celebrated its 50th anniversary on 16 November 1996. The squadron has flown P-47N, F-86E, F-86D, F-102A, F-4C and F-15 fighters. Today's fighter force consists of 15 F-15A MSIP fighters with a PAA (primary aircraft authorised) figure of 15.

The 203rd Airlift Squadron operates nine KC-135R Stratotankers, with a PAA figure of eight. The tankers are gradually being painted with a new yellow-bordered tail flash and bear distinctive Hawaiian names.

The tanker squadron received its first aircraft on 4 December 1992 when 64-14832 was delivered. The squadron's first major deployment was to Pisa, Italy on 14 October 1995 in support of Operation Deny Flight. The unit has sent aircraft to 45 locations including Guam, Thailand, Korea, Australia, Iceland, Japan, and Singapore. Recently, the 203rd supported B-52H Stratofortress deployments to Diego Garcia in connection with US operations against Iraq.

The 204th Airlift Squadron operates five Lockheed C-130H Hercules transports, with a PAA figure of four. The squadron was activated on 1 October 1994. Previously, the Hawaii guard had operated a single C-130A and, before 1984, a single de Havilland C-7A Caribou.

Unlike some transport units that merely haul cargo, the 204th is trained in operations, to support the US Army's Hawaii-based 25th Infantry Division 'Tropic Lightning'. The squadron made the first airdrop in Hawaii on 13 February 1995 and its first night airdrop on 2 July 1995. **Robert F. Dorr**

Aircraft of the 154th Wing

McDonnell Douglas F-15A MSIP: 76-0032, 76-0062, 76-0063, 76-0064; 76-0068, 76-0103, 76-0113, 76-0114; 76-0018, 76-0019, 76-0120; 77-0074, 77-0077, 77-0078, 77-0079
McDonnell Douglas F-15B MSIP: 74-0149, 75-0081
Boeing KC-135R: 57-1508 *Hoku-Kea* (Southern Cross), 59-1472 *Maka-'lo LANI* (Eye of the Hawk), 60-0318 *Hina-Li'i* (Sea of the Chiefs), 60-0323 *Makali'i* (Pleiades), 60-0329 *Kape'a* (also, Southern Cross), 60-8030 *Makaha* (a star near Aldebaran), 61-0290 *Hoku Lele* (Meteor), 62-3514 *Hoku Lea* (the Clear Star), 64-14832 *Hoku Pa'a* (Polaris)
Lockheed C-130H Hercules: 79-0475, 79-0478, 79-0479, 93-2041, 93-2042

Aerospace CT-4/B Airtrainer

New colours for the 'Plastic Rat'

The Royal New Zealand Air Force has recently made a decision on a new colour scheme for its NZ Aerospace CT-4/B Airtrainers, used by the Pilot Training Squadron at RNZAF Base Ohakea. The need for a higher-visibility colour scheme was determined after a period of operations from Ohakea (also home to the A-4K Skyhawks of Nos 2 and 75 Squadrons and the MB.339CBs of No. 14 Sqn) after the PTS moved to Ohakea from Wigram in 1991. In the new environment, students and instructors have to contend with camouflaged fast jets in the circuit as well as reduced airspace for their own training manoeuvres. This latter aspect was seen as the most pressing reason for higher visibility, as the Airtrainer is fairly low powered and aerobatic manoeuvres always result in height loss, with the possibility that an aircraft might find itself descending onto another which had not been spotted against the terrain.

The gull grey and red colours worn by the Airtrainer fleet since introduction in 1976 were an adaptation of the final scheme worn by the Harvards previously used for initial instruction. The Airtrainer fleet was due for a repaint, the task having last been done 11 years ago, and the decision was made to evaluate the current scheme against three possible alternatives, namely overall black, yellow and white. Two-tone schemes were discounted on grounds of painting cost and because they tend to break up the outline of small aircraft, giving a camouflage effect. Accordingly, three aircraft were painted and evaluated in the working environment of the PTS and in specially flown trials against a variety of backdrops. During the painting process each aircraft acquired a piece of 'under-tail art' depicting a cartoon rat (in reference to the CT-4's 'Plastic Rat' nickname) and a name. The aircraft were: NZ1937 (white) *Casper*, NZ1938 (yellow) *Nana*; and NZ1941 (black) *Stealth*. A further aircraft, NZ1939, was painted yellow later in the trials.

The visibility trials programme, instigated and undertaken by

The Airtrainer colour schemes trialled by the RNZAF Pilot Training Squadron are seen here, with the old scheme on NZ 1943. The black CT-4 was least visible over forest.

The colour scheme chosen at the end of the trials was yellow with black control surfaces. The 'Red Checkers' aerobatic team may have to consider a change of name.

Squadron Leader Jim Rankin of the PTS, was conducted in several ways: a photographic sortie; intercept sorties, opportunity evaluations (pilots reporting at what distance they spotted other aircraft during normal operations); and a pilot survey. Photographs of the four aircraft together taken against a variety of backdrops produced some interesting results. The black aircraft stood out best against cloud and blue sky, but worst against dark water, farmland and forest. The white aircraft was easily visible against dark water, farmland and forest, but less so against light-coloured water, blue sky and urban areas, and almost invisible against cloud. The yellow Airtrainer stood out well against all trial backgrounds, with cloud and light water being its weakest areas.

Other considerations were cost (which required a single fuselage colour), maintainability (including stain resistance, corrosion monitoring and the detection of working rivets), operational factors, and aesthetic and historical considerations. During a period when the black aircraft was down for maintenance, it was decided to try that aircraft's control surfaces on the yellow aircraft. As these parts could be painted separtely without masking and were relatively small, the disadvantages of a full two-tone scheme were overcome.

On the basis of the trials, which were ongoing for more than a year, the yellow scheme with black control surfaces was favoured by pilots and operational staff, not least for its attractiveness and historical connection with RNZAF trainers of the past. This scheme was recommended to the Defence Department and approval was given in August 1996. Repainting of the 18-aircraft fleet was expected to be completed during 1997.

The RAF has completed a similar evaluation in recent years and has standardised on an overall black scheme for its Bulldog, Tucano, Hawk, Jetstream and Dominie aircraft. Black was rejected in the RNZAF trials partly due to different operational conditions (dark pasture and forest terrain), and yellow (with black) was deemed the most suitable for a small, slow-moving trainer. In order to further enhance the visibility of the CT-4s and reduce 'late sightings' around Ohakea, a programme to evaluate High-Intensity Strobe Lights has been undertaken in conjunction with the colour scheme trials and is still continuing. **Jim Winchester**

Tupolev Tu-142MR

Submarine communications

The Tu-142 'Bear-F' is the Russian navy's standard long-range maritime patrol platform, operating in several sub-variants. In 1986, a new variant was identified by the West, dubbed 'Bear-J', an equivalent of the US Navy's TACAMO aircraft (Lockheed EC-130Q/Boeing E-6A). The antenna fit differed considerably from the ASW aircraft, and its role was obviously that of long-range communications between SLBM-armed submarines on patrol and the national command authorities.

In addition to the Tu-142MR, the Kipelovo regiment flies Tu-142Ms for maritime patrol work. This is a 'Bear-F Mod 3'.

Production of the small number of these Tu-142MRs was begun in 1982 at the Taganrog plant. A prototype was produced which appeared to be based on the original Tu-142 'Bear-F' airframe, probably by conversion. It retained the glazed nose and undernose radar of the first ASW variant, but had the TWA, fin-tip aerial, satnav bulge and underfuselage blade aerials as described later.

Production aircraft were based on the Tu-142M-Z ('Bear-F Mod 2' and 'Mod 4') airframe with angled-down refuelling probe, raised cockpit and interior redesign. Internally the Tu-142MR was configured to carry large amounts of communications

A Tu-142MR of the Kipelovo regiment lands at its base. The 'Bear-J' has an aft-facing antenna on the tip of the fin, similar to that fitted to the Tu-95MS 'Bear-H'.

A close-up of a Kipelovo-based Tu-142MR reveals the large ventral fairing for the TWA, complete with a weighted drogue on the end. The external ducting provides power and cooling to the forward sensors from equipment in the rear fuselage.

equipment, as befitted its role.

Some of the equipment is common to the Tu-142M-Z 'Bear-F Mod 4', including the undernose fairing housing various sensors, linked to generator and ancillary equipment in the rear fuselage by a long external duct. The 'Mod 4's' passive warning receivers are also fitted under the rear fuselage. The long ADF blade aerial on the forward fuselage is also carried, but the Tu-142MR also has two additional HF blade aerials under the rear fuselage. The nose dispenses with the Tu-142M-Z's glazed tip with small thimble radome in favour of a much larger dielectric 'pimple' fairing, with additional receivers either side. On the spine above the central fuselage is a large bulge for the Glonass satellite navigation equipment.

The primary mission equipment is located in the former weapons bay, and consists of a TWA (trailing wire antenna) of about 8000 m (26,250 ft) length. This is deployed from a large fairing which is mounted below the central fuselage. Like the E-6, the Tu-142MR deploys the TWA while flying a tight orbit, the weight on the end of the aerial pulling it to an almost vertical position. With the TWA at its fullest extent, the Tu-142MR can undertake VLF (Very Low Frequency) communications with submerged submarines.

A variety of systems can be used for transmitting and receiving messages from surface sources, the most distinctive being the HF antenna mounted in a spike fairing ahead of the fin tip. Satellite communications is possible through the domew antenna behind the flight deck.

It is thought that 10 Tu-142MRs were produced at Taganrog, and they are divided between the Russian navy fleets. They have been seen operating together with Tu-142M-Zs, and operate with 'Bear-F'-equipped regiments.

David Donald

Zvezda/McDonnell Douglas MA-31

US Navy fires Russian missile

The Threat/Targeting Systems department of the Naval Air Warfare Center Weapons Division (NAWC/WD) at Point Mugu has now completed initial flight testing of the target known as the MA-31, based on the Russian Kh-31 (AS-17) anti-ship missile built by Zvezda and normally employed by the MiG-27, MiG-29, Su-17, Su-24 and Su-27. At Point Mugu the launch platform was a piloted McDonnell Douglas QF-4N.

The Navy programme began in 1993 with a concept exploration and definition phase for a cost-effective SSST (Supersonic Sea Skimming Target) to provide realistic training for the Navy. McDonnell Douglas acts as prime contractor.

The tests began with ground trials of the booster at China Lake, and jettison tests over a pit. Captive-carry tests were performed using the Russian-built AKU-58 launcher rail, followed by an inert-body drop to assess separation characteristics.

Live trials began with a launch from 3,000 ft (914 m) altitude, after which the MA-31 descended to 1,000 ft (454 m), performed a 10*g* weave manoeuvre and flew at Mach 2.5 for 17 nm (19.5 miles; 31 km). The second test followed a similar pattern before descending to 30 ft (9 m) for its final flight. The third test descended directly to 30 ft, performed its weave manoeuvre and flew at low altitude for 20 nm (23 miles; 37 km). During the second test the Russian General Klishen flew in the rear seat of the QF-4N.

In late November 1996 an MA-31 will be included in the missile qualification shoot of the destroyer USS *Gonzalez*, and future plans for the target include extending the range to 45 nm (52 miles; 83 km) and fitting a home-on beacon system. An purchasing option exists for a further 20 missiles. As Mike Gorman, MA-31 Flight Test System engineer, succintly puts it: "If you can't replicate the threat, you might as well buy it."

David Donald

The MA-31 is a version of the Kh-31A anti-ship missile which has inertial mid-course/terminal radar guidance system, and usually has a 90-kg (198-lb) HE blast frag warhead. The Kh-31 is available in two body lengths (with differing ranges), and in a passive guidance anti-radar version (Kh-31P). It is carried on an AKU-58 launcher.

Indonesia

Tentara Nasional Indonesia-Angkatan Udara – TNI-AU (Indonesian National Army-Air Force)

Commander (from 18 March 1996)
Marsekal Madya TNI Sutria Tubagus

All the air force squadrons were concentrated into two operational commands on 1 April 1985: Komando Operasi Angkatan Udara (KOOPSAU) I in Jakarta, for the western part of Indonesia, and KOOPSAU II in Ujung Pandang, for the eastern part of Indonesia.

Fighter force

Over the past years, the air force has repeatedly expressed its need for additional fighter aircraft in order to protect the archipelago, comparing its small force with those of Singapore and Malaysia.

The current major upgrade programme involves the eight F-5Es and four F-5Fs of SkU.14. On 8 June 1995 a $40 million contract was signed with SABCA of Belgium. The programme is called MACAN (Indonesian for 'tiger'), which stands for Modernisation of Avionics Capabilities for Armament and Navigation. It includes a radar upgrade, Litton INS, GEC Marconi Avionics Sky Guardian RWR and HUD/WAC, HOTAS controls and a Mil Std 1553B databus. The first two aircraft, F-5E TS-0501 and F-5F TL-0516, arrived at Gosselies on 31 May 1995 for a period of 18 months. The remainder of the TNI-AU's F-5s will be upgraded in Indonesia with SABCA support, all to act as F-16 lead-in trainers.

With the delivery on 11 December 1989 of the first of eight F-16As and four F-16Bs, ordered in August 1986, Indonesia started preparing its forces for the 21st century. The aircraft replaced the OV-10F in SkU.3, the premier fighter squadron. The Broncos were used to reactivate SkU.1, a former light bomber unit.

In November 1995, the air force expressed a total requirement for 64 F-16s to equip four squadrons, and showed interest in the (28) Pakistan air force F-16s stored at the AMARC facility in the US. Following an unsolicited US offer, the TNI-AU announced the purchase of eight F-16As and one F-16B on 26 April 1996, for a total cost of $110 million. All the aircraft will be updated to Indonesian standard and include a drag-chute housing, ILS, software update and AGM-65 Maverick capability. Funding for the purchase of all (28) of the PAF F-16s is not yet available. The TNI-AU will now have a total of 16 F-16As and four F-16Bs, as F-16B TS-1604 had crashed by 1994. It has not been decided yet if they will equip a second squadron (probably SkU.11), although this seems unlikely.

At time of writing the supply of the F-16s had stalled after the US Congress expressed dissatisfaction at Indonesia's human rights record. The Indonesian Foreign Minister, Ali Alatas, was quoted as responding "...we never asked for the fighter planes, and we don't need them." He went on to say, "If the original offer still stands, we will buy them. In any case, we can find other places to buy fighter planes, if we really need them." President Suharto had originally refused the offer of the F-16s, in 1995, on the grounds that they were not a priority.

Display team

Reviving a tradition, in 1995 the TNI-AU formed a new demonstration team known as 'Elang Biru' ('Blue Falcon') with F-16s from SkU.3. Its first public display was on 5 October 1995 at Halim-Perdanakusuma, celebrating the 50th anniversary of the Armed Forces (ABRI). The first of eight aircraft in a special blue/yellow scheme was F-16A TS-1607, which made its first flight on 29 December 1995. The second display was on 9 April 1996, also at Halim, celebrating the 50th anniversary of the TNI-AU.

Attack force

A total of 32 former Israeli DF/AF A-4Es and TA-4Hs were delivered between 1980 and 1982, forming SkU.11 and SkU.12 in the tactical fighter role. After 14 years of intense (combat) use, the A-4s of SkU.12 were grounded in late 1995, and the best aircraft from approximately 27 survivors are now concentrated in SkU.11. The OV-10Fs, delivered in 1976/77 and now part of SkU.1, were withdrawn from service during 1996. The 12 remaining examples are veterans of numerous operations in East Timor and Irian Jaya, but were also used as IPTN chase planes.

In June 1993, the TNI-AU ordered eight Hawk Mk 109s and 16 Hawk Mk 209s for £500 million. The total requirement for the next 25 years is 96 armed Hawks in eight squadrons. In order to accommodate the new Hawks, the air base at Pekanbaru, home of SkU.12, was upgraded from 1993 and received a new hangar, aircraft shelters, workshops, simulator and housing for the RAF instructor pilots. The first five TNI-AU pilots were sent to England in late 1995, and two returned to Pekanbaru on 17 May 1996, together with the first three Mk 109s for SkU.12.

The second delivery was planned for 27 May 1996, and included the first three Hawk Mk 109s for SkU.1. The last of these 24 Hawks should have been delivered by 13 January 1997. In FY 1996/97, $676 million has been reserved for a second batch of Hawks, and in June 1996 an option for 16 Hawk Mk 209s was exercised by the TNI-AU. SkU.1 is intended to relocate to Pontianak, West Kalimantan, by 1999 thus extending the TNI-AU's combat reach to the widely-disputed Spratley Islands.

Transport fleet

On the transport front, the six remaining F27-400Ms of SkU.2 have been supplemented by IPTN-produced CN.235M-100s. The first two paratroop variants arrived on 12 January 1993, followed by two LAPES (low-altitude parachute extraction system) aircraft in 1993 and two medevac aircraft in 1994. Three additional CN.235-MPAs are part of a $151 million joint TNI-AU and TNI-AL order, revealed in June

TNI-AU order of battle (October 1996)

KOOPSAU I

Skwadron Udara 2
Lanuma Halim-Perdanakusuma, Jakarta
Fokker F27-400M *(6)*
Airtech (IPTN) CN.235M-100 *(6)*

Skwadron Udara 6
Lanuma Atang Senjaya, Bogor
Sikorsky S-58T *(approx. 10)*
IPTN (MBB) NBO 105CB *(2), SAR duties for Badan SAR Nasional (BASARNAS)*

Skwadron Udara 7
Lanud Kalijati, Subang
Bell 47G *(approx. 11)*
Hughes 500C *(sold?)*
Bell Model 204B *(2?)*

Skwadron Udara 8
Lanuma Atang Senjaya, Bogor
IPTN (Aérospatiale) NAS 330L *(1?)*
Aérospatiale SA 330J *(approx. 7)*

Skwadron Udara 12
Lanud Pekanbaru, Pekanbaru
British Aerospace Hawk Mk 109 *(4*)*
British Aerospace Hawk Mk 209 *(8*)*

Skwadron Udara 17
Lanuma Halim-Perdanakusuma, Jakarta
Boeing 707-3M1C *(1)*
Aérospatiale SA 330L *(1?)*
Fokker F27-400M *(1)*
Fokker F28-3000/-3000R*(1)*/*(1)*
Lockheed C-130H-30 *(1)*
Lockheed L-100-30 *(3)*
IPTN (Aérospatiale) NAS 332L1 *(2)*

Skwadron Udara 31
Lanuma Halim-Perdanakusuma, Jakarta
Lockheed C-130H-30 *(6)*

KOOPSAU II

Skwadron Udara 1
Lanuma Abdulrachman Saleh, Malang
Rockwell OV-10F *(12)*
British Aerospace Hawk Mk 109 *(4*)*
British Aerospace Hawk Mk 209 *(8*)*
**on order*

Skwadron Udara 3
Lanuma Iswahyudi, Madiun
Lockheed Martin F-16A *(8)*
Lockheed Martin F-16B *(3)*

Skwadron Udara 4
Lanuma Abdulrachman Saleh, Malang
Cessna 401 *(5)*
Cessna 402 *(2)*
IPTN (CASA) NC.212M-200 *(4)*
Piper PA-34? *(2?)*

Skwadron Udara 5
Lanud Hasanuddin, Ujung Pandang
Boeing 737-2X9 *(3)*

Skwadron Udara 11
Lanud Hasanuddin, Ujung Pandang
McDonnell Douglas A-4E *(approx. 25)*
McDonnell Douglas TA-4H *(2)*

Skwadron Udara 14
Lanuma Iswahyudi, Madiun
Northrop F-5E *(8)*
Northrop F-5F *(4)*

Skwadron Udara 15
Lanuma Abdulrachman Saleh, Malang
Hawk Mk 53 *(14 from SkaDik.103)*

Skwadron Udara 32
Lanuma Iswahyudi, Madiun
Lockheed C-130B *(8)*
Lockheed KC-130B *(2)*
Lockheed C-130H *(2)*

Wing Pendidikan 1/Sekolah Penerbang (Pilot School)
Lanuma Adisucipto, Yogyakarta

Skwadron Pendidikan 101
Lanud Adisumarmo, Surakarta
ASA AS 202 *(max 38)*
Cessna T-41D *(12?)*

Skwadron Pendidikan 102
Lanuma Adisucipto, Yogyakarta
Beechcraft T-34C *(max 20)*

Skwadron Pendidikan 103
Lanuma Iswahyudi, Madiun
British Aerospace Hawk Mk 53 *(14)*

Satuan Udara Pertanian
Lanuma Halim-Perdanakusuma, Jakarta
Pilatus PC-6B *(5), agricultural use*

Akademi ABRI Bagian Udara (Air Force Academy)
Lanuma Adisucipto, Yogyakarta
Cessna 172 *(2), from 1984*
Cessna T-41D *(?), communications*
PZL-104 *(1) from 1984, target tug*

ɓove: The A-4E Skyhawks of ʞU.11 are all refurbished ‹-IDF/AF aircraft.

Right: Indonesia has a single squadron of 11 F-16s (SkU.3) which may soon be augmented.

Above: The F-5Es of SkU.13 are undergoing a major upgrade under the joint IPTN/SABCA MACAN programme.

Below: Twenty Hawk Mk 53s were delivered between 1980 and 1984. They serve with W.P.1/SkaDik. 103 in a TWU/operational attack role.

ɓove: Some SkU.11 A-4Es have a ·anked refuelling probe – to avoid fuel ·gestion after cut-off from the tanker.

Below: A line-up of BAe Hawk Mk 53s from SkaDik. 103, seen at Halim-Perdanakusma, after the ABRI 50th anniversary flypast.

ɔ96. The VIP unit SkU.17 has also added a number f aircraft to its fleet. Two IPTN NAS 332L1s /VIP models) were delivered on 22 February ɔ93, followed by two ex-Garuda F28-3000Rs uring December 1994. Finally, the two ex-Ierpati L-100-30s were passed on to SkU.17 by ugust 1995, after overhaul at Bandung.

SkU.4 has passed on six of its 10 NC.212s to ther branches of the armed forces. The police ·ceived the two old NC.212M-100s on 1 July ɔ95, while PENERBAD (the army) and ISNERBAL (the navy) were each to receive two ʼC.212M-200s.

ɩirborne radar modernisation

The 1990s will witness a steady upgrading and xpansion. In 1989 a $117 million contract was gned with Boeing to upgrade the three 737-2X9s ı use with SkU.5. The modifications included an ɒdate of the Motorola SLAMMR (side-looking rborne modular multi-mission radar), a new nose ıdar, infra-red detection system, GPS, IFF and nproved data processing and displays. Aircraft ıI-7301 was modified by Boeing and delivered by October 1993. The remaining two (AI-7302 and AI-7303) were modified by IPTN at the Air Force Maintenance Depot 010 at Bandung. AI-7302 was completed by April 1994, and AI-7303 by late 1994.

Not every branch of the air force is expanding. The Department of Forestry (Dep. Kehutanan) had sold all its remaining NBO 105CB helicopters by December 1990, and they were not replaced. Several T-34Cs from the air force's training wing, W.P.1, have found their way to the US, as well as the first H500Cs from SkU.7 (by February 1996).

Pilot training programme

Would-be officers enter the Air Force Academy for a period of three years, during which they receive basic military training and undertake studies. They receive their first flying lessons on gliders and in the AS 202. Basic technical knowledge is acquired with the Ground School, SkaDik. 104. Those who pass start their Elementary Training (Latih Mula, LM) with SkaDik. 101 at Adisumarmo, Surakarta. Here they undertake 40 hours' flying in the AS 202 Bravo (60 hours for pilots destined for the Naval Aviation and Police Services).

Students then return to Adisucipto for 110 hours of Basic Training (Latih Dasar, LD), with SkaDik. 102 on the T-34C Turbo Mentor. Finally, they move to the large air base of Iswahyudi, Madiun, where they join SkaDik. 103 for 90 hours of Advanced Training (Latih Lanjut, LL) on the BAe Hawk Mk 53.

Those students who successfully complete the course become pilot officers and are divided into three groups: fighter, transport and helicopter pilots. Fighter pilots undergo conversion at their assigned squadron (but SkU.11 is the dedicated A-4 conversion squadron). Transport pilots generally begin with SkU.4, and helicopter pilots all go to SkU.7 for their transition and training on the Bell 47G and H500.

The TNI-AU has strong ties with civil aviation in Indonesia. Before students graduate from the academy, they all have the chance to take the Commercial Pilot Licence Course at Curug. Many Garuda and Merpati airline pilots are from the TNI-AU, and they also act as instructors with several civil pilot schools (PLP at Curug, JFS at Surabaya and DFS at Halim) in Java. **Marco Pennings**

Dinas Penerbangan Angkatan Laut – DISNERBAL (Naval Aviation Service)

Commander (1996) KADISNERBAL Laksamana Pertama TNI Setio Rahardjo

On 8 March 1996, the Chief of Staff of the Naval Aviation Service announced the planned purchase of the IPTN CN.235-MPA (maritime patrol), NC.212 (light transport) and GAF N22 Nomad (tactical maritime patrol). The CN.235s are part of a $151 million joint TNI-AU and TNI-AL order revealed in June 1996, for five CN.235-MPAs including three for the TNI-AU and two for DISNERBAL, plus one CN.235M-100 (paratroop) for DISNERBAL. The Nomads will be ex-Australian army aircraft grounded in 1995.

The late 1994 programme named On Top II was intended to add six NC.212s and three NBO 105s to the service's strength; after some delay, a $107 million contract with IPTN was confirmed in June 1996. The NC.212s are to replace old Nomads with RON 800, and aircraft destined for navy use (six NC.212-MPAs) were still unmarked and with IPTN in October 1995. The first NC.212-MPA in RON 800 markings was seen in June 1996. Two former TNI-AU NC.212M-200 transports were delivered to RON 600 in early 1996, but delivery of IPTN NBO 105s was delayed into 1996

The DHC-5 Buffalo transport will soon be entering service. Two examples from five ex-UAE air force aircraft are presently being overhauled by IPTN at Bandung, for delivery in August 1996. They will replace RON 600's C-47s, which were withdrawn from use and have been stored since 1988/89, although one was probably still operational in December 1993. On 26 June 1996, GKN Westland confirmed UK government approval for the sale of six Sea Lynx and Super Lynx ASW helicopters to the Indonesian navy, to be operated from four new naval vessels. They would replace the 10 HAS.Mk 1 Wasps with RON 400, four of which are thought to remain airworthy, and will operate next to six IPTN NB-412S helicopters delivered in 1989/90. A $4.2 million order for an additional NB-412 was revealed in June 1996.

Pilot training programme

The Akademi TNI-AL (AAL) at Morokrembangan (Bumi Moro), Surabaya, also houses the Sekolah Penerbang TNI-AL (SENERBANG), or Pilot School. Students first enter Ground School, and fixed-wing pilots then continue with RON 200. Here they receive 80 hours of elementary training on the DC-100 and F-33A, and 40 hours of basic training on the PA-38. Advanced training is type related, and takes place with one of the other fixed-wing squadrons. There, they start as co-pilots, and after a minimum of 700 hours qualify as captains. Helicopter pilots receive all their training with RON 400.

DISNERBAL order of battle

(October 1996)

Skwadron Udara (RON) 200/Latih
Lanudal Juanda, Surabaya
Rockwell DC-100 Lark Commander *(4)*
Beechcraft F-33A Bonanza *(2)*
SOCATA TB-9 Tampico
Piper PA-38 Tomahawk

Skwadron Udara (RON) 400/Heli
Lanudal Juanda, Surabaya
Sud Alouette II *(2?)*
IPTN (MBB) NBO 105CB *(4)*
Westland Wasp HAS.Mk 1 *(4)*
IPTN (Aérospatiale) NAS 332F *(max 4)*
IPTN (Bell) NB-412S *(max. 6)*

Skwadron Udara (RON) 600/Angkut
Lanudal Juanda, Surabaya
IPTN (CASA) NC.212M-200 *(max 10)*

Skwadron Udara (RON) 800/Patroli Maritim
Lanudal Juanda, Surabaya
GAF N22B *(max 11)*
GAF N22SL *(max 6)*

Dinas Penerbangan Angkatan Darat – PENERBAD (Army Aviation Service)

Commander (1995) KADISPENERBAD Brigjen. TNI Djoko S. Martono

Over the past 10 years, PENERBAD has primarily focused on expanding its helicopter fleet. On 8 September 1988, four IPTN NB-412Ss were delivered to PENERBAD's attack helicopter squadron, Skuad.1, supplemented in 1995 by three IPTN NB-412HP (High Performance) models. Also delivered to Skuad.1 were six IPTN NBO 105CB-4 attack helicopters, between 1990 and 1994. PENERBAD plans to purchase 20 Bell 205s on the US civil market and convert them for military use, starting in 1996.

The remaining three (of five) ex-UAE air force DHC-5 Buffalos delivered to IPTN in September 1995 were to be transferred to the general support squadron, Skuad.2, in March 1996. They replace the service's DC-3s withdrawn from use by October 1995. Early in 1996, PENERBAD's Skuad.2 also received two NC.212M-200s from the TNI-AU.

Since 1977, PENERBAD has seen many periods of combat against guerrillas in East Timor (Fretilin) and Irian Jaya. On 8 January 1996, several foreigners were taken hostage by members of the Organisasi Papua Merdeka (OPM), the Papua Liberation Organisation in Irian Jaya. They were rescued by the ABRI on 15 May 1996 with the help of PENERBAD Bell 205s and NB-412s, and after the arrival of Israeli UAV recce-drones in the area. Most of the action took place near Mapnduma in the Jayawijaya mountains. On 10 May 1996 an unknown (possibly PENERBAD) ABRI helicopter crashed in Irian Jaya, killing five and injuring seven. A technical problem in bad weather forced the helicopter down near an OPM hideout, where it crashed in the jungle.

Pilot training programme

Pilot training starts with 90 hours of combined primary and basic training on the H300C. Those students who are to become fixed-wing pilots go to the civil Juanda Flying School (JFS) in Surabaya. After their course there, they return to SEBANG for 70 hours of advanced training on the CN.212, BN-2A (wfu?), Grand- or Turbo Commander. Helicopter pilots receive 70 hours of advanced training on the Bell 206, NBO 105 or Bell 205. After graduation, they all begin as co-pilots. They will need 450 flying hours (including 350 hours type-rated) to qualify for the captain-pilot course. This course includes another 60 hours of flying training.

PENERBAD order of battle

(May 1996)

Sekolah Penerbang – SEBANG TNI-AD (Semarang Pilot School)
Lanumad Achmad Yani
Bell 206
Hughes 300C *(max 17)*
NBO 105CB *(max 13 including those in Skuad.1/2)*
Bell 205A-1 *(min 7 including those in Skuad.1)*

Skwadron Udara Angkatan Darat (Skuad) 1/Heli Serbu (Attack Helicopter Squadron)
Lanumad Achmad Yani, Semarang
IPTN (MBB) NBO 105CB/CB-4 *air attack*
IPTN (Bell) NB-412S *(max 4)* *air mobility*
IPTN (Bell) NB-412HP *(3)* *air mobility*
Sud SE 3160
Bell 205A-1 *air mobility*

Skwadron Udara Angkatan Darat (Skuad) 2/Bantuan Umum (General Support Squadron)
Lanud Pondok Cabe, Jakarta
Rockwell Aero Commander 680FL *(3)*
IPTN (CASA) NC.212M-200 *(6)*
de Havilland Canada DHC-5 Buffalo *(3)*
IPTN (MBB) NBO 105CB

Subdirektorat Polisi Udara (Police Air Service)

Commander (1996) KASUBDIT Polisi Udara Kolonel (Pol.) Frans Wenas

The service's main tasks are SAR, medevac and air detection. The police received two old NC.212M-100s from the TNI-AU on 1 July 1995,becoming operational on 13 October. Its sole Piper PA-31T (P-2005) crashed on 29 September 1995, during a rehearsal for the armed force's 50th anniversary flypast. The service has expressed interest in NB-412s, although production had to be halted due to quality problems.

Polisi Udara order of battle

(October 1996)

Subdir. Polisi Udara
Lanud Pondok Cabe, Jakarta
Cessna U206 *(1)*
Bell 206B *(1)*
IPTN (MBB) NBO 105CB *(21)*
IPTN (CASA) NC.212M-100 *(2)*

*his VIP-scheme **L-100-30 Hercules** of **SkU.17** (above) – note the cabin 'indows – contrasts with the new low-visibility camouflage seen on a '-130H (right) of the same unit, seen at **Husein-Sastranegara** air base.*

*bove: **IPTN** has supplied **CN.235M-100s** to **SkU.2** s much-needed tactical transports. **CN.235M** 'eliveries have been slow from **IPTN**.*

*Above: **Fokker F27-400M** Troopships serve with **SkU.2**. The Troopship can carry up to 46 fully-equipped paratroops.*

*Above: **Skuad.2, PENERBAD**, flies **IPTN**-built **NC.212M-200s**, along with all its other fixed-wing types from **Pondok Cabe** air base, Jakarta.*

***Left:** Students who complete their primary pilot training on the **AS 202** transition on to the **T-34Cs** of **SkaDik.102**.*

***Right:** An **Sku.8 SA 330J** in the newly-adopted 'low-vis' colours. Note the second Puma in the old scheme.*

*bove: Indonesia traded **CN.235s** for **DHC-5s** to vin an order for **IPTN** from the **UAE** air force. The)HC-5 Buffalos obtained in exchange are now in ervice with **PENERBAD** and **DISNERBAL** units.*

*Above: This **IPTN**-built **NBO 105CB-4** is seen at **IPTN**'s Bandung flight test facility before delivery to **PENERBAD**'s **Skuad.1**. Note its emergency flotation gear and **NB-412s** on the production line.*

*Above: **IPTN** has produced a mix of **NBO 105CBs** and 'hot-and-high' **NBO 105CB-4s** for the Indonesian armed forces. This **NBO 105CB** (note the weapons pylon) is a **PENERBAD** aircraft.*

*'he locally-assembled **NAS 332Fs** of **RON 400/Heli** ıre shore-based at **Lanudal Juanda**, Surabaya, and ·an be armed with **Exocet** missiles for anti-hipping missions.*

***PENERBAD**'s declining fleet of **Bell 205A-1s** is now divided between the army's pilot school and the operational attack helicopter squadron (**Skuad.1**), both based at **Lanumad Achmad Yani**.*

*Air mobility for the army is increasingly the task of **IPTN**-built **NB-412s**. **Skuad.1** has both the **NB-412S** (seen here) and **NB-412HP** – with higher operating weights and improved transmission – in service.*

The Iceland Defence Force

at Naval Air Station Keflavik

In Cold War days Iceland was a strategic NATO outpost, the scene of 'Bear' hunts and epic ASW sorties. The end of that era threatened, briefly, to bring to an end Iceland's military importance. Here, *World Air Power Journal* reports on how the NATO forces deployed to Iceland have adapted to the changing times.

Like the rest of the world, Keflavik has changed its nature since the demise of the Communist regime in the Soviet Union. The traffic of Russian 'Bears' (and the occasional 'Badger' and 'Bison') has completely ceased, and that of Russian submarines through the Greenland-Iceland-UK (GIUK) gap has diminished a great deal. Operational tactics and the composition of forces based in Iceland reflect this new world order, and both have changed considerably, as have the complement and types of aircraft.

Most visibly, the 57th Fighter Squadron (previously a fighter interceptor squadron) – or 'The Black Knights of Keflavik' as it became known – was disbanded on 2 March 1995. Its operational duties were taken over by a series of deployments of units from the continental United States. The number of aircraft deployed is bound by an agreement from 4 January 1994, reaffirmed in April 1996, between the US and the Icelandic governments.

This agreement, also referred to as an 'agreed minute', was signed after more than a year and a half of bilateral consultations between the US and Iceland. It reaffirms the commitment of both nations to the 1951 Defence Agreement: that US forces should remain in Iceland; that Iceland will provide mutually agreed necessary facilities in Iceland; that the US will continue to make arrangements for the defence of Iceland; that both nations will adjust to a changed state of world affairs; and that both nations will make their best efforts to reduce the cost of operations at Keflavik.

The agreed minute was signed by the then-US Deputy Secretary of Defense, William J. Perry, and the Foreign Minister of Iceland, Jón Baldvin Hannibalsson. In the document, the two governments also agreed on the following points:

To reduce the number of US Air Force fighter aircraft operating permanently at NAS Keflavik from its current number of 12 (at the time assigned to the 57th FS) to a minimum of four (from 1 April 1994), in order to retain active air defence capability in Iceland;

To maintain at Keflavik the capability and infrastructure for the operation of fighter aircraft;

To maintain the search and rescue squadron (now the 56th RQS);

To maintain US Naval Air Station Keflavik;

To maintain the Iceland Air Defence System;

To continue the biennial Northern Viking series of exercises;

To discontinue operations of two communication facilities.

The implementation of the first point took a year to reach fruition, the first of the Stateside units to take up the watch being the 1st Wing from Langley AFB in January 1995.

Most observers seem to agree that the wishes of the US Air Force and the US Navy did not go hand in hand when the reduction of forces in Iceland was being negotiated. The Air Force wanted to withdraw all its fighters and the rescue squadron, and in fact had made the necessary budgetary arrangements and notified the relevant NATO agencies. The Navy wanted to keep its facilities in Iceland active and continue to base its maritime patrol aircraft there. The Icelandic daily newspaper *Morgunbladid* reported on 6 January 1994 that the USAF had wanted to recall all its F-15s and over 900 military personnel on 1 January 1994. This constituted over a third of the military personnel at Keflavik.

It was only after consultation and participation of high government officials, including a meeting between Vice President Al Gore and Prime Minister Davíð Oddsson, and another between Foreign Secretaries Warren Christopher and Jón Baldvin Hannibalsson that a common basis was agreed upon.

Earlier, the changes to the structure of the Defence Force were: in 1990 the one remaining USAF Boeing E-3 Sentry (AWACS) at Keflavik was redeployed to support Desert Storm and a NATO E-3 took over its duties until March 1992; in July 1991 the 57th FS was reduced in strength from 18 to 12 F-15 Eagles (10 C models and two D models); in January 1992, the 57th's alert posture changed from 10 minutes to one hour; in June 1992 the permanent E-3 deployment was ended.

Today, after almost two years' implementation of the agreement, the deployments have consisted of four to six F-15s at any one time. In July 1997 Keflavik is going to see F-16s take part in the deployments. This will bring new operational problems, for the pilots of the 85th Operations Squadron (the successor to the

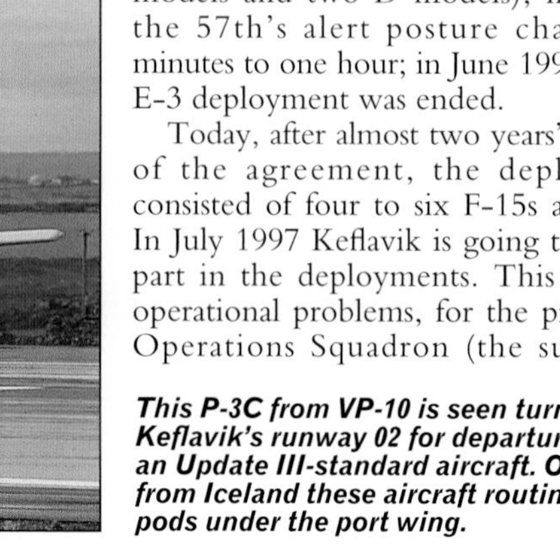

This P-3C from VP-10 is seen turning on to Keflavik's runway 02 for departure. This Orion is an Update III-standard aircraft. On operations from Iceland these aircraft routinely carry ESM pods under the port wing.

Iceland no longer has the 'Black Knights' to defend it, but relies instead on rotational deployments of F-15s from the continental United States. This pair of 'TDYed' Eagles belongs to the Eglin-based 59th FS/33rd FW.

57th FS) are F-15 qualified. The most likely solution is that extra F-16 pilots will be brought in, with the stationed pilots going TDY to keep current while the F-16s are here.

Under the system that was devised for the rotation, the 1st Fighter Wing from Langley AFB in Virginia stood the watch from January to March 1994. The 1st Wing sent aircraft and pilots from all three squadrons of the wing (27th, 71st and 94th). All deployments until October 1996 are listed elsewhere. The pilots usually stay for two weeks – the ground crews staying longer. A kernel of assigned personnel, both pilots and maintenance people, provide continuity. They belong to the 85th OS 'White Knights', which was formed on the day the 57th disbanded. It acts as an umbrella unit for these deployments and controls the operations of both the fighters and the tanker flight. For about two years, the latter has consisted of one KC-135 deploying to Keflavik for two weeks.

The tanker flight also consists of one K(or H) C-130 of various marks coming from six AFRes, ANG and USMC units supporting the 56th Rescue Squadron with its HH-60G Pave Hawks. These units rotate every week.

The command structure at Keflavik

The Iceland Defence Force (IDF) is a joint service organisation that controls and supervises all aspects of the operations at Keflavik. It is commanded by a Navy rear admiral, who usually has a P-3 background. He is also the Commander, Iceland Defence Force, the Commander, Fleet Air Keflavik, the Island Commander Iceland, and the Commander, Iceland Anti-Submarine Warfare Group (CTG84.1). IDF has the following main components: 85th Group/Air Forces Iceland; Naval Air Station Keflavik; Iceland Sector Anti-submarine Warfare Group – Fleet Air Keflavik; Army Forces Iceland. Of these components, the only one that does not have permanent units at Keflavik is the Army, but Army officers serve on the joint IDF staff.

RAF Nimrods from the Kinloss Wing – the octopus badge marks this example as a No. 206 Sqn aircraft – are still regular visitors to Keflavik. The waters of the GIUK gap were the Nimrod's regular Cold War hunting ground.

85th Group

For many years the USAF parent organisation at the base was known as Air Forces Iceland (AFI). On 31 May 1993 AFI was inactivated, and the 35th Wing was activated in its place, assuming the same function. This was part of the Air Force's 'objective wing' plan, intended to carry on the history of famous World War II flying units. On 1 October 1994 the 35th Wing was transferred to Misawa, Japan, the 35th having been a Pacific/West Coast unit for most of its life, and the unit activated in its place at Keflavik was the 85th Wing. This wing is a combination of the lineage and history of the 85th Tactical Fighter Training Wing and the former AFI. Commensurate with the drawdown in fighter strength at Keflavik, the wing was redesignated the 85th Group 'The Guardians of the North'. Interestingly, its insignia carries no number.

The 85th Group is made up of the 85th Operations Squadron, 85th Logistics Squadron, 56th Rescue Squadron, 85th Civil Engineering Squadron, 85th Mission Support Squadron, 85th Security Police Squadron, and 932nd Air Control Squadron. Of these, the 56th RQS is the only one with its own assigned aircraft: it has had four HH-60G Pave Hawk helicopters since September 1991.

Fighter operations

The F-15s operate daily training flights, usually with a flight of four in the morning and a two-ship in the afternoon. In the morning, the aircraft generally get the support of the deployed KC-135 to extend their endurance and to practise refuelling. The most common operational configuration of the Keflavik-based F-15s is two underwing tanks instead of the single fuselage tank. This gives the aircraft slightly more than twice the additional range due to better aerodynamics. The only exception to this was the first deployment by the 1st Wing, when all five aircraft used three tanks, and two aircraft of this year's 'Cape Cod' 101st FS, Massachussetts ANG, deployment which flew with the centreline tank only.

Currently, there are no live intercepts, the last having taken place on 10 September 1991. This brought to a close an era during which the 57th Fighter Squadron had made over 3,000 intercepts. That figure does not imply that over 3,000 different Soviet reconnaissance aircraft were intercepted from the year 1962. For example, when a 'Bear' flew around the island inside the MADIZ (Military Air Defence Identification Zone), the 57th often sent relays of F-102As and later F-4s to escort the aircraft until it left the MADIZ, and such flights are reported to have counted as a number of intercepts. A correct count of aircraft intercepted has not come to light.

A pair of E-3s, one NATO and one USAF, was deployed to Keflavik to provide AEW support for Operation Northern Viking 95. The USAF Sentry (the original prototype E-3A) carries the colours of all the 552nd ACW's squadrons in its finstripe.

There are no real divert fields in Iceland for the F-15s; Reykjavïk has the longest runway, at 5,300 ft (1615 m). An agreement has been negotiated with the IDF that the runways at Akureyri in the north and Egilsstadir in the east be available as emergency fields for P-3s. However, they have no arrest facilities and only few facilities for servicing fighters, and the Air Force does not want to use them as they are. Therefore, the nearest actual fighter divert fields are in Scotland, Norway and Greenland. When the five units were in Iceland, it was a rule to fly to Leuchars in Scotland with two aircraft and a tanker on the first Wednesday of each month, weather and other commitments permitting. Landings were not planned, but two or three approaches were made followed by a return with the tanker, refuelling both ways. This practice has been discontinued.

Additionally, the occasional trip to Leuchars and Lakenheath is undertaken to honour the contact with NATO's British partners and fellow F-15 operators in Europe.

To provide added training, the 85th Group has made arrangements with a number of units to engage in dissimilar air combat training (DACT). The Tornado F.Mk 3s from Leuchars came to work with the 1st Wing in March 1996. Norwegian F-16s are a common sight, with two to four aircraft usually staying two or three days. There has also been the occasional Danish F-16. Although Belgian and Netherlands F-16s do often transit on their way to and from Canada and the US, they have not done any training with the Iceland-based units.

On 8 July 1996, a composite flight from four Norwegian squadrons – 331 Skv, 332 Skv, 334 Skv and 338 Skv – came to Keflavik for two weeks of DACT training. The flight consisted of eight F-16As and one F-16B. They practised with the five F-15Cs from the 59th FS, which arrived on 3 July to replace the 101st FS. On their first day, four F-15s and four F-16s practised defending the local tanker from four attacking F-16s. The Norwegian F-16 pilots get a good opportunity to practise air refuelling at a time like this.

On 23 August 1996 two ET-133 (T-33A) Silver Stars from Canada's 434 (CS) Sqn ('Bluenose Squadron') at Greenwood, Nova Scotia arrived at Keflavik in the company of one Canadair CE-144 Challenger of the same unit. They stayed at Keflavik for a week and practised with the F-15s. The 'T-Birds' carried the Ericsson Erijammer A100 jamming pod on its

Above: Flown by Lt Col Bob Donze, the first commander of the 85th Operations Squadron, this F-15 is one of those deployed to Iceland by the Oregon Air Guard's 123rd FS/142nd FG between March and May 1996. A small number of F-15-rated pilots are permanently assigned to the 85th Group 'White Knights' to provide some operational continuity for the constantly changing Eagle deployments.

Left: Canada's CP-140 Auroras are regular visitors to Keflavik. This example wears the winged trident badge of 407 Squadron, normally based at Comox in British Columbia.

first visit to Europe. 434 (CS) Sqn and 414 (CS) Sqn at Comox, British Columbia are (at the time of writing) the only North America-based units using the A100 pod. It differs from, for example, the ALQ-188 jamming pod in that it provides its operator with feedback on actions taken by the 'adversary' radar and weapon system. The EWO can assess and critique the techniques employed by his opponent. Using this type of modern equipment, the Canadian air force is planning to use its 'T-Birds' in the ECM training role until at least 2015.

On the morning of 29 August, the 85th OS plus the 434 Sqn detachment's ET-133s simulated bombers attacking a submarine base. The Challenger supported them with ECM, and two of the escorting F-15s simulated Sukhoi Su-27 'Flankers' of an unidentified nation. The two other F-15s defended the target. The Challenger is stressed for *g* loads between 2.58 and -1.0: on this mission, it was operated to the limit!

The Canadians then went on to Norway to take part in Exercise Northern Lights/Bright Horizon. They intend to return to Europe regularly to work with other NATO forces on realistic electronic warfare exercises.

All of this illustrates how the 85th OS provides realistic training for its people in the minimalist setting of Keflavik.

Exercises

Exercises are undertaken which, at least in previous years, often involved elements from abroad like the Norwegians with their F-16s and the RAF with Tornados and Jaguars. One of these is the regular series of Viking Thunder exercises, which are held when training needs dictate and take place approximately twice a year. The major exercise, Northern Viking, is held every second year as detailed in the agreed minute. The purpose of Northern Viking is threefold:

To practise and test the logistics of moving everything needed for a large force to Iceland on time;

To see how the units assigned and the Stateside-based augmentation units perform under simulated combat conditions;

To give those same units a chance to practise working together, improving co-ordination, communications, and to introduce them to the Icelandic terrain, weather and local conditions.

Northern Viking 1995

Northern Viking was last held in 1995. This was in a way significant, because it was the first time that the defence of Iceland had been practised after the 57th FS was disbanded and the number of based fighters reduced. To augment the stationed force of five F-15Cs from the 59th FS, 33rd FW, five F-15Cs and one F-15D from the 58th FS, 33rd FW deployed to Keflavik for the duration of the exercise.

The arctic beauty, and austerity, of Keflavik and its surrounds must come as a surprise to those units arriving there from less hostile climes. This KNL Block 15 F-16A from 331 Skv was part of the regular Norwegian fighter deployment in 1996.

Another first was the use of B-1Bs from the 7th BW at Dyess and B-52Hs from the 5th BW at Minot. They practised simulated attacks in the Low-Level Manoeuvring Area in the middle of the desolate highlands. This occasion marked the first time that B-1s or B-52s had ever landed at Keflavik. On the first day of the exercise, on 17 July, two B-52s landed after their manoeuvres and were then based at Keflavik for the duration of the exercise. This created some problems on the ground, because no taxiway was really wide enough to take both of a B-52's outrigger wheels. Some perimeter lights had to be removed on the edge of taxiways to allow those same wheels to run in the mud, so to speak, just to get the aircraft off the runway and onto the ramp area. Therefore, they had to taxi in position on the runways, which were wide enough for even for a B-52 to turn around on the end. There was no such problem for the 7th BW's B-1Bs.

The three-tank configuration shows that this is an F-15C returning home from a three-month stint in Iceland. Operational Eagle sorties from Keflavik are routinely flown with just two fuel tanks, as KC-135 tanker support is invariably available.

A 338 Skv F-16A seen landing on runway 29 after a DACT sortie. The Norwegian Falcons not only take advantage of the Keflavik Eagles for ACM training but also of the KC-135s, whenever possible, for much-appreciated IFR practice.

The four days of the exercise saw the B-1s and B-52s simulate attacks at least twice each day, flying over the base at ever-lower altitudes and increasing speeds. Some of the participating F-15 pilots stated that the B-1s were "moving at quite a clip" when they flew inland from the south coast towards Keflavik. The F-15 force was given the assignment to protect both the bombers and the island. Thus they participated in both the blue and the red forces.

Other aircraft at the exercise were three RAF Tornado GR.Mk 1s (13 Sqn), a USAF EC-130H (43rd ECS at Davis-Monthan AFB), an E-3A from NATO and another from the 552nd ACW at Tinker AFB. Additionally, two Learjets of Phoenix Air served as ECM training aids. The US Army contingent also brought two Chinooks for various heavylift support. The Chinook crews have a good time in Iceland: one of their duties is performing various lifting operations for Icelandic civil authorities, such as replacing a helo pad in the famous volcanic island of Surtsey, which gives them the opportunity to really experience the country.

The alert hangar at Keflavik was in constant use from the time it was built in 1955 until early May 1996. Then IDF stopped using it for alert aircraft in view of the alert status being degraded to a couple of hours.

The alert 'barn' is now in use as a spare hangar, and when the nine Norwegian F-16s arrived on 8 July four of them were sheltered there; the other five were in the hardened shelters, which now house the alert aircraft. No pilots or aircraft now stand a quick-reaction alert at Keflavik. All alert missions are flown from the hardened shelters, and airborne aircraft are considered to be part of the alert force.

The 56th Rescue Squadron

The rescue unit at Keflavik is among the best in the world, and is now equipped with four HH-60G Pave Hawks. Its primary mission is to rescue downed US pilots, but it is also available to the Icelandic authorities in case of need. This has often been the case, especially before the Icelandic coast guard received its Super Puma TF-LIF. Since that aircraft has no inflight-refuelling capabilities, the assistance of the 56th is still sometimes necessary.

The rescue mission previously was performed by a variety of aircraft: USAF SB-17G Flying Fortress belonging to a unit called the 'Iceland Air Rescue Unit', and then the 53rd Rescue Squadron with Grumman SA-16A Albatrosses, Douglas SC-47s and SC-54s, and Sikorsky H-19s. When the US Navy took over the operations of the station and it became Naval Air Station Keflavik in 1961, the two H-19s were transferred to Navy control, together with two DHC L-20 Beavers and four Douglas C-47s. All of these received BuNos, the C-47s in the range 150187-150190, the L-20s 150191 and 192, and the H-19s 150193 and 150194.

The Navy rescue unit received a number of Sikorsky H-34s, but two of these crashed in the 1960s. When the Air Force again took over the rescue mission in 1971, it brought HH-3As, and HC-130s began to be rotated from Woodbridge, England to support them.

Gruelling rescue

On 10 January 1994 two of the 56th's HH-60Gs performed a particularly difficult and heroic rescue when a tugboat with seven crew members sank upright and very quickly in heavy surf off the east coast of Iceland at about 6:00 a.m. Heavy breakers kept the crew from getting into lifeboats or even calling for help on the radio. Their only chance was to lash themselves to the mast on top of the bridge, and hope that a helicopter would retrieve them. The HH-60 crews had to fly without inflight refuelling because the KC-130 broke down. The Icelandic coast guard's Dauphin had to turn back because of the weather. It was an extremely bad flight; hazardous, with turbulence so severe that on more than one occasion the HH-60s were almost thrown upside down, and visibility most of the way was practically nil. After one ground refuelling at the town of Höfn in Hornafjörður on the southeast coast, they arrived over the boat, sent two para-rescue men

Left: Dutch P-3Cs maintain a permanent presence at NAS Keflavik, including one example (312) that has never been permanently based in the Nertherlands, since its acquisition in 1985, to avoid paying import duty.

Left: The HH-60Gs of the 56th RS are the only permanent USAF presence on the island. The continued availability of their vital SAR cover is seen as essential by the Icelandic government.

Above: The US Navy maintains this UP-3A as the Keflavik 'station flight'. This aircraft is named Valkyrja and carries 'fin art' of a Valkyrie's head.

After ACM training sorties the F-15s head for the refuelling tracks to top up with fuel and derive full training benefit from the mission.

down to the six surviving sailors and hauled them off the boat in stages about 10 hours after it sank. Needless to say, the survivors had lost all hope of rescue.

Afterwards, the HH-60s were unable to fly back to Keflavik because of the atrocious weather and almost zero visibility. They landed in the fishing village of Neskaupstaður on the east coast, in a parking lot which happened to be deserted because of the heavy snowfall. This village has long been nicknamed 'Little Moscow' due to the Leftist predominance in town politics. On this night the rescue crews were the heroes of the town and, in fact, of the whole country. In May 1995, the command pilot of the lead HH-60, Captain John Blumentritt, received the Aviator Valor Award and the two para-rescue men who went down to the boat received the Cheney Award. All the crew members of both helicopters received the MacKay Trophy for this rescue, as well as Icelandic decorations for valour.

The Navy and the P-3 at Keflavik

The US Navy is the host service at Keflavik, which is both a naval air station and Keflavik International Airport. The station used to be one of the most important in the world for anti-submarine operations because of its position in the middle of the GIUK gap. It often

Eagle Sortie

A typical F-15 training scenario at Keflavik involves four F-15s in two-on-two air combat training. This permits the F-15s to operate in the smallest and most basic of acceptable fighting formations: the two-ship element. The standard war-fighting formation of the F-15 is a four-ship, but, because of limited aircraft availability, F-15s in Iceland practise two-ship training the majority of times.

A routine mission in Iceland starts with a briefing two hours before take-off. The briefing consists of administrative details and then the scenario and special instructions. The scenario may be as complex as a transition-to-war defensive counter air (DCA) mission with complex identification criteria, or it may be a simple offensive counter air (OCA) mission escorting strikers against a simulated target. These parameters are chosen by the flight lead based on training needs of the flight and training asset availability. No matter what the mission, F-15 basics do not change: solid radar work plus excellent visual mutual support, radar warning awareness and 100 per cent valid weapons execution. Typically, the F-15s will be controlled by the 932nd Air Control Squadron (LOKI) for the entire mission. LOKI obtains clearance from the ICAA for the fighters and tanker to use airspace northwest of Keflavik. The airspace extends from 28 to 160 nm (52 to 296 km) away from Keflavik. Although this seems large, aircraft travelling faster than the speed of sound do not take long to traverse the entire area.

An air combat training sortie generally has two blue air forces attempting to identify and destroy two or more red air forces. All aircraft use a training mode which displays simulated missile fly-out in the cockpit, affording the pilots real time assessment of the reliability and validity of their weapons employment. The aircraft generally start 60 nm (110 km) apart, confer to make sure that both sides are ready, and then call 'fight's on'. The blue air force will then perform whatever function they were assigned that day, be it OCA or DCA. The differences are dramatic, but the basic execution remains the same. The F-15s first identify an aircraft which meets their commit criteria and merits investigation. They commit to the target (bogey), attempt to identify the bogey with the help of LOKI and then determine what to do. If the target is hostile, the F-15s attempt to employ weapons before red air starts shooting at them. It requires a very quick cross-check and situational awareness for a pilot to run his radar, fly the jet, keep track of his wingman, know if the enemy is targeting him, identify the target and finally employ the correct weapon. Considering that both aircraft are often flying towards each other at near the speed of sound, a 60-nm set-up takes three minutes. It demands training and solid preparation.

Air training today is very complex, involving beyond-visual-range weapons, electronic countermeasures and supersonic aircraft. However, the fundamentals of mutual support between wingmen, smart tactics, and driving the fight by shooting first, stay the same. These are the fundamentals upon which aircrew build when they get into more complex scenarios, which include not four aircraft but 40, and not two red air bandits but 25. The basics stay the same, and that is what they practise, so they can go anywhere in the world and project US air power by gaining air supremacy.

Assembled on the ramp for KEFTACEX 1/96 are MPAs from 601 Esq (P-3P), 30º Stormo (Atlantic), 333 Skv (P-3C), 23F (Atlantique II), Detachment Keflavik/Marine Luchtvaardienst (P-3C), MFG 3 (Atlantic), VP-26 (P-3C), No. 206 Sqn (Nimrod MR.Mk 2P) and VP-16 (P-3C).

went by the nickname of 'Anti-submarine Capital of the World'. It was one of the first stations outside the continental US to host a P-3A Orion squadron, in 1964, this being VP-8 'Tigers'. A P-3C squadron, VP-49 'Woodpeckers', deployed here as early as 1969. Over the years the most modern versions of the Orion have been based at Keflavik. As relations have eased between East and West, the number of deployed aircraft has diminished, and only four US Navy P-3Cs are now based. This is in accordance with the current USN practice to split-deploy its anti-submarine squadrons, e.g. to Keflavik and Roosevelt Roads. Also, the number of active squadrons has decreased considerably over the past four years, with just 13 left and one more to be disbanded in 1997.

The P-3C squadrons originally seen at Keflavik were the Jacksonville-based squadrons, VP-5, VP-16, VP-24, VP-45, VP-49 and VP-56. When the Update II model of Orion was introduced to Brunswick in 1979, those squadrons began to be deployed to Keflavik. VP-44 was the first, followed by VP-23, VP-11, VP-10, VP-8 and VP-26, and then again VP-16 with what was sometimes known as the Update II.5. The original aircraft now mostly belong to VP-68. Operational considerations occasionally disturbed this system, as when the Moffett-based VP-46, VP-9 and VP-40 were deployed. Right after VP-40 left Keflavik in the summer of 1985, the toning-down of the USN's P-3 fleet started. All identifying markings were quickly removed from the entire active fleet, and then in 1991-92 the wholesale repainting in the current matte grey tactical finish started.

In 1992 the deployed squadrons began to bring older airframes which had been upgraded to the Update IIIR version with electronic kits. The squadrons deploying with this version were again the Jacksonville squadrons, VP-5, VP-10, VP-16, VP-24 and VP-45. This update did not include the Sonobuoy Reference System (SRS) which, on the Update II and new-build Update III, can be recognised by the 10 large blade antennas distributed around the fuselage and on the horizontal stabilisers. The ESM pod traditionally seen under the left wing between the fuselage and the inner engine has disappeared from the Update IIIs, being replaced by wingtip sensors.

Navy Reserve deployments

During 1996 Reserve squadrons have been very much in evidence at Keflavik, with two to three aircraft from a Reserve unit being present most of the time. The period of deployment is six weeks for each squadron, with the actual crews spending two weeks on station. The crew rotations overlap, so that there is a new crew every week. The period of February to September of 1996 was devoted to deploying to Keflavik. The units participating in this programme are detailed belows.

Reserve squadrons are sending aircraft and crews to Keflavik for a number of reasons. 1) The diminishing number of active squadrons means that the Reserves have pledged to supply two aircrews to the east coast active squadrons

On 17 July 1995 the B-1 made its first appearance at Keflavik. At that time two B-1Bs from the 7th Bomb Wing, Dyess AFB, deployed for Operation Northern Viking 95 alongside a much increased contingent of 11 F-15s.

Two B-52Hs also took part in Northern Viking 95. Like the B-1s, this was the first time 'Buffs' had ever landed on Iceland. The sheer size of the B-52s caused major headaches when it came to ground manoeuvring.

Recent (standing) US deployments

USAF F-15 Eagle Units

UNIT	*HOME BASE*	*DEPLOYMENT*
1st Wing	Langley AFB	17 Jan/3 March 1995 (all three squadrons)
101st FS/102nd FG	Otis AFB	2 March/17 May
123rd FS/142nd FG	Portland IAP	15 May/1 July
59th FS/33rd FW	Eglin AFB	30 June/3 Oct
60th FS/33rd FW	Eglin AFB	2 Oct/3 Jan 1996
1st Wing	Langley AFB	2 Jan/1 April 1996
123rd FS/142nd FG	Portland IAP	30 March/17 May
101st FS/102nd FG	Otis AFB	16 May/6 July
59th FS/33rd FW	Eglin AFB	3 July/(3) Oct

US ANG and AFRes KC-135 units

UNIT	*HOME BASE*	*DEPLOYMENT*
141st ARW	Fairchild AFB, WA (ANG)	1/16 Jul 1995
155th ARW	Lincoln MAP, NE (ANG)	15/30 Jul
121st ARW (ANG)	Rickenbacker ANGB, OH	28/13 Aug
434th ARW	Grissom ARB, IN (AFRes)	12/27 Aug
507th ARW	Tinker AFB, OK (AFRes)	26/10 Sep
117th ARW	Birmingham IAP, AL (ANG)	09/24 Sep
108th ARW	McGuire AFB, NJ (ANG)	22/08 Oct
157th ARW	Pease ANGB, NH (ANG)	07/22 Oct
452nd AMW	March AFB, CA (AFRes)	21/05 Nov
141st ARW	Fairchild AFB, WA (ANG)	04/19 Nov
101st ARW	Bangor IAP, ME (ANG)	17 Nov/03 Dec
168th ARW	Eielson AFB, AK (ANG)	02 Dec/17 Dec
507th ARW	Tinker AFB, OK (AFRes)	16 Dec/31 Dec
161st ARW	Phoenix, AZ (ANG)	30 Dec/14 Jan 96
190th ARW	Forbes Field, KS (ANG)	13 Jan/28 Jan
940th ARW (AFRes)	McClellan AFB, CA	27 Jan/12 Feb
107th ARW (ANG)	Niagara Falls IAP, NY	10 Feb/25 Feb
171st ARW (ANG)	Pittsburgh IAP, PA	24 Feb/10 Mar
117th ARW (ANG)	Birmingham IAP, AL	09 Mar/24 Mar
126th ARW	O'Hare IAP, IL (ANG)	23 Mar/07 Apr
100th ARW (Active)	Mildenhall AB, UK	06 Apr/23 Apr
108th ARW (ANG)	McGuire AFB, NJ	19 Apr/04 May
203rd ARS	Hickam AFB, HI (ANG)	04 May/18 May
128th ARW (ANG)	Mitchell ANGB, WI	18 May/02 Jun
121st ARW (ANG)	Rickenbacker ANGB	31May/16 Jun
151st ARW	Salt Lake City IAP, UT (ANG)	15 Jun/30 Jun
171st ARW	Pittsburgh IAP, PA (ANG)	29 Jun/14 Jul
155th ARW	Lincoln MAP, NE (ANG)	13 Jul/28 Jul
452nd AMW	March AFB, CA (AFRes)	26 Jul/11 Aug
186th ARW (ANG)	Key Fd, Meridian, MS	09 Aug/25 Aug
434th ARW	Grissom ARB, IN (AFRes)	23 Aug/08 Sep
121st ARW	Rickenbacker IAP, OH (ANG)	06 Sep/22 Sep

US ANG, AFRes and USMC HC/KC-I3O units

UNIT	*HOME BASE*
210th RQS	Kulis ANGB, Anchorage, AK (ANG)
129th RQS	Moffet Field, CA (ANG)
102nd RQS	F. S. Gabreski, NY (ANG)
301st RQS	Patrick AFB, FL (AFRes)
304th RQS	Portland IAP, OR (AFRes)
2nd MAW	MCAS Cherry Point, NC (Active/USMC)

(These six HC/KC-130 units take turns in providing one aircraft each on a weekly rotation)

USN Reserve P-3 Orion units

UNIT	*DEPLOYMENT PERIOD*
VP-64	3 February/23 March 1996
VP-66	16 March/4 May 1996
VP-62	27 April/29 June 1996
VP-92	27 June/early August 1996
VP-68	Late July/14 September 1996

VP-68 'Blackhawks', was stood down at the end of September 1996, and had only three to four aircraft on strength at the time of writing

Above: The 'Bluenoses' of 434 Sqn are Canada's ECM aggressors and their lovingly maintained ET-133 Silver Stars partner CE-144 Challengers in this role. In August 1996 the 'T-birds' deployed to Keflavik to exercise with the Eagles of the 59th FS/33rd FW.

Right: Based in Cartersville, Georgia, Phoenix Air provides a fleet of special mission Learjets for (chiefly) US military contract duties. This Learjet 36A was providing threat simulation during Northern Viking 95.

the whole year round. 2) The Reserve squadrons are implementing a new programme of combining active duty with familiarisation of the operational areas in which personnel would have to perform if they were called up. This entails using the two-week annual training period of each crew to the full extent, operating out of Keflavik, Roosevelt Roads or Sigonella, Sicily. The crews have been well prepared for their duties on their weekend stints and come fully prepared for procedures peculiar to the area. They have undergone exhaustive simulator training, and when they arrive they share the full duties of the active squadrons. This means not only aircrew but also maintenance personnel, who go into the maintenance shops without regard to their unit and mix with the active crews. 3) The policy of the Department of Defense is to have the Reserves use the same type of equipment as the active units and to be fully mission-capable, thus being a realistic Reserve force in case of need.

The mainstay, or anchor unit, is still the active-duty squadron. This has been VP-26 since August 1996, and now that the Reserve participation is over VP-16 from Jacksonville is also deploying with two aircraft to Keflavik for six months. The strength of the PatronKef is still five aircraft: four active and one Dutch.

The active-duty squadrons at Keflavik are mostly equipped with the older P-3Cs updated to IIIR standards, compared to the newer aircraft equipping the Reserve units, which in many cases are new-build Update III aircraft. When asked about the differences in operating these aircraft, the pilots answer that they are all the same, except that the older aircraft are older, but the equipment operators see the newer computers as a real benefit.

NATO ASW force

The aircraft operate in the conventional patrol role of surface and sub-surface search and surveillance. With Russian submarines becoming more scarce in these waters, the crews practise instead with NATO surface ships and submarines. The older crew members complain that the younger generation has too seldom had the opportunity to listen to and track real Russian submarines and that therefore there has been a degradation in the detection and tracking capabilities of the whole ASW force, regardless of the newer equipment.

The Royal Netherlands navy has had one P-3C (312) stationed at NAS Keflavik since

In 1996 434 Sqn introduced its new Ericsson-supplied Erijammer A100 EW pods into service. After a debut at Maple Flag, in which the new system outshone all other comparable EW simulators, the A100 came to Iceland in August.

1985. This particular P-3 is a permanent presence at Keflavik because the Netherlands navy has not paid its import duties, and therefore it cannot be based in the Netherlands. It does go there for maintenance and overhaul, however. This accounts for the presence of other P-3Cs of the Royal Netherlands at Keflavik.

The Canadians are frequent visitors with their CP-140 Auroras. Also seen are the Atlantics (and Atlantiques) of the French, German and Italian navies, plus the Nimrods of the RAF.

From 16-26 October 1996 an ASW exercise, KefTacEx (Keflavik Tactical Exchange), was held at NAS Keflavik. Patrol aircraft from nine different countries participatied, including the United States Navy, the Netherlands, Great Britain, Canada, France, Germany, Italy, Norway and Portugal.

NAS Keflavik used to have its own station aircraft for local transport. These originally were Douglas C-47Js taken over from the USAF, and later C-117Ds. One of the latter, BuNo. 17191, is now a part of the collection of gate guardians outside the headquarters of the 85th Group and the naval station. They were used for transport and commuting inside Iceland, e.g. to the radar stations originally situated on each corner of the island and operated by military personnel.

The naval station has also had its own aircraft for international commuting, originally consisting of a Lockheed C-121C Super Constellation and then Douglas C-118s. Since August 1984 this duty has been fulfilled by the UP-3A station aircraft, BuNo. 150495, which, although it carries no titles or national markings, has its tail marked with a Valkyrie's head and goes by the name *Valkyrja*. The aircraft is used for orientation and practice flights for naval station personnel and for general-purpose commuting.

Orion Mission

The pre-flight starts three hours before the assigned take-off time, and begins with a briefing for the tactical co-ordinator (Tacco), patrol plane commander (PPC), second pilot, navigator/communicator, non-acoustic sensor operator and the two acoustic operators. This 30-minute briefing will detail the mission's operating area, other traffic, communication plan and the intelligence picture. After the brief, the nav/comm and the third pilot (3P) obtain the cryptology equipment necessary for secure communications. Meanwhile, the two flight engineers and the inflight technician (IFT) prepare the aircraft.

The next two and a half hours take the crew through pre-flights of the respective equipment, reporting 'gripes' to the mission commander. The pilots check for the safety of flight hardware, the Tacco checks his training equipment, and the nav/comm checks the comms fit and GPS/Omega/INS for accuracy. The acoustic operators (SS1 and SS2) check their ability to detect and track acoustic frequencies in the water, and the non-acoustic operator (SS3) ensures that the radar is operable.

During the transit to the operational area, the 'Tube' crew has a quiet time and often naps. Before the P-3 reaches the operating area and calls 'on station', the nav/comm calls the submarine by secure radio to notify them that the aircrew is ready to begin training, and notifies base that they are going 'operational'. This means the P-3 is no longer under ATC control. The flight station calls any other aircraft or ships that might be in the area, to co-ordinate separation.

The crew comes alive as the P-3 descends to a low altitude for tracking. The IFT loads sonobuoys into the launchers and the Tacco directs the aircraft to specific points to drop them. As more and more are dropped to lay a blanket around the submarine, the acoustic operators tune the buoys and start analysing their returns. The Tacco receives the information from the SS1 and SS2 and decides where to lay the next pattern of buoys. The sub turns, speeds up, slows down and does everything possible to evade the sonobuoys.

Sometimes all the acoustic information may be misleading, or it may vanish as if the sub itself vanished. Quick action – or, sometimes, patience – is necessary to determine if the submarine has eluded the net of buoys. The Tacco directs the aircraft and the pilots pull on the stick as the P-3 banks and turns to a new point for a new pattern. As the cat-and-mouse game continues, the pilots practise their low-level flying and offer tactical advice to the Tacco, and the SSs train to distinguish the sounds of a submarine from those of a whale.

The training exercise will conclude with an exchange of information between the submarine and the P-3, and communication exercises. The pilots put the aircraft into a climb to return home. An intense debriefing follows landing, when experts analyse all parts of the mission and the tactics employed by the crew.

These P-3s, from VP-5 'Mad Foxes' and VP-23 'Sea Hawks', are seen on the Keflavik ramp in February 1980 during the heyday of the Orion's ASW career in Iceland.

Icelandic operators

Icelanders play a significant role in the day-to-day operations of the naval station. All air traffic control crews are Icelandic, which is important because the station is also Keflavik International Airport and local traffic is considerable. Much of the radio transmissions are in Icelandic, particularly ground radio. Most of the airport maintenance personnel are Icelandic.

The naval station fire department is totally manned by Icelanders, a unique situation on US military bases. The unit is very professional and has often received awards for being the best fire department at any naval station operated by the USN. Ice and snow removal is an additional responsibility, and the fire department has an excellent record for keeping the runways open when weather conditions are bad.

The ground radar system

The USAF originally built four radar sites in Iceland, one on each corner of the island. The complete system was operational by 1958. In 1960 and 1961 the two stations on the northern part of the island were deactivated, having proved too difficult to maintain on their mountain-tops.

The station close to Keflavik, named Rockville, and the one on the southeast corner at Stokksnes were maintained with their AN/FPS-93A search radars and AN/FPS-6 height finders until 1992, when they were replaced by modern facilities in hardened structures operating FPS117V5 phased-array radars. At the same time, the stations on the northern corners of the island were resurrected at different sites with the same modern equipment. The station at Stokksnes always suffered from being stationed close to a steep mountain range that effectively blanked the view to the north.

Right: ***Away from the multitude of airspace restrictions that hamper operations at home, the F-15s on Keflavik deployment get the opportunity to exercise to the full while still providing a notional air defence force.***

Left: ***This P-3C from VP-26 is seen as it patrols the approaches to Iceland's western fjords. It is at this point that the GIUK gap is at its narrowest and it would have been an obvious choke-point in time of war.***

Its contributions were particularly poor after the radar on Langanes in the northeast ceased operations.

These four new radar sites are maintained and kept operational by an Icelandic government agency, the Radar Agency, and are manned by Icelandic personnel. The new sites on the northwest and northeast corners are built on mountain tops and have an unobstructed view in all directions. The information they gather is used by two control organisations, the USAF and Icelandic ATC. It is ironic that by the time the new and advanced radar sites became operational, the traffic they were mainly designed to detect and track had disappeared.

All control of aircraft over and in the vicinity of Iceland is overseen by the Icelandic ATC. The 932nd Air Control Squadron, USAF, stationed at Rockville near NAS Keflavik, keeps vigil over unidentified aircraft and in case of any being encountered will scramble fighters from Keflavik to identify them. The control of military traffic, fighter, tanker and airborne radar outside designated training areas is undertaken by Icelandic ATC, but certain blocks of air are occasionally set aside for use by the fighters and their support aircraft. At those times, all other traffic is diverted by ATC.

The region in the desolate centre of the island, the Low-Level Manoeuvring Area, is very valuable to the fighters (and bombers when exercises are held). This area is only open during the summer months, however, and there are only narrow corridors for transition to and from it. Additionally, its use is time-restricted so that inland travellers are not too disturbed by the low-flying aircraft.

Iceland's continued importance

Positioned as it is in the middle of the Atlantic Ocean, Iceland has been a favourite refuelling spot for aircraft crossing the ocean since World War II. Most civilian aircraft of the smaller variety prefer to stop at Reykjavïk Airport. Larger aircraft and almost all military traffic go through Keflavik. In 1987 the new Leifur Eiriksson civilian terminal was opened at the northern perimeter of the airfield, thereby separating civil passenger traffic from the military base. The old terminal on the base is used as the military terminal for NAS Keflavik. Most of the traffic is transports – C-130, C-141 and C-5 – but occasionally mass flights of Dutch and Belgian F-16s, German and Italian Tornados, and German F-4s go through the naval station. When these aircraft remain overnight they are often parked on the remote 'hot cargo' parking area on the southwest side of the airfield.

Clearly, Iceland's position in the middle of the GIUK gap is not as important in world affairs as it was before the demise of the Soviet Union. NAS Keflavik still remains strategically significant as the transatlantic link between the United States and Europe, and as a staging and support facility for forward deployment of forces in the North Atlantic region. Anti-submarine warfare (ASW) remains a meaningful mission as long as Russia retains its effective (and slowly expanding) attack and ballistic missile submarine forces on the Kola Peninsula. Therefore, both US and Icelandic authorities agree on the need to maintain credible defence forces in Iceland for the foreseeable future in support of the bilateral defence agreement between those countries, and to preserve stability in the region.

Baldur Sveinsson

These Leuchars-based No. 43 Sqn Tornado F.Mk 3s are seen on the old 57th FIS flight line in April 1996, where once could be found F-89s, F-102s and F-4Es. The aircraft furthest from the camera has had its cockpit sealed after becoming unservicable and was awaiting repair.

In Sierra Leone EO personnel found themselves fighting alongside Belorussian pilots, who were also working on government contracts. The Belorussian-flown Mi-24V is here about to depart Freetown on an armed reconnaissance sortie.

Executive Outcomes

Dramatic changes in the political *status quo* of Africa have freed a small South African firm to make an unprecedented contribution to military operations in the region. Here, for the first time, *World Air Power Journal* talks to the people who were actually involved and tells the full story of Executive Outcomes' highly successful combat campaigns in Angola and Sierra Leone.

The rise of international terrorism in the last two decades, and its threat to multinational corporations, has made 'security' a world-wide growth industry. Established firms in London and Washington staffed by retired senior military officers discuss clients' needs in plush offices and despatch former special forces soldiers to sites around the globe. The services these firms have traditionally provided tend to be preventative in nature: establishing the physical security of oil fields, for example, or teaching executives how to avoid being kidnapped or assassinated. Proactive operations in the sense of actively seeking out those who might attack an oil field or murder an executive have never been part of a firm's prospectus. Never, that is, until the emergence in 1993 of a South African company which has captured the attention not only of the media, but of Third World governments faced with intractable and economically devastating bush wars they are incapable of winning themselves.

Angola I

Few people outside southern Africa had heard of Executive Outcomes (EO) until March 1993, when UNITA rebels captured Soyo, a petroleum maintenance and equipment storage site on the coast of Angola. The Forças Armadas Angolanos (FAA – Angolan Armed Forces), fighting the latest UNITA uprising in other parts of the country, had neither the training nor experience to oust the well dug-in guerrillas. Faced with the loss of millions of dollars' worth of drilling and ancillary stores, Heritage Oil and Sonangol, the state-owned oil company under the aegis of the MPLA government, approached EO, at the time a one-man operation based in Pretoria. Executive Outcomes was headed by Eeben Barlow, a veteran of military intelligence and the old South African Defence Force's (SADF) elite 32 Battalion. The company already had a reputation for providing intelligence and covert operations training to South African special forces, as well as security training for a major South African mining house.

Barlow accepted the contract and drew on his contacts among former black and white special forces soldiers to forge a 50-man strike force. Fifty men against several hundred guerrillas in well-prepared defensive positions was not a ratio with which they were totally unfamiliar, having fought similar engagements against moribund FAA units during the 1980s. However, against the more seasoned UNITA guerrillas the odds were less than reassuring. There were some positive aspects, though. Aside from the South Africans being arguably the most combat-experienced soldiers in the world, they were also well acquainted with UNITA, having trained and fought on the side of the guerrillas against FAA and their East Bloc advisers during South Africa's 1976-1988 war in Angola. Cobbling together the best intelligence available to them, including air reconnaissance photos provided by Angolan air force MiG-21s, EO's new unit designed an operational plan that appeared to offer the best chances of succeeding, took a deep breath and nodded.

EXECUTIVE OUTCOMES

A surprise ground attack was launched, supported by two Angolan air force Mi-17 gunships and a Mi-24, which, according to members of the EO team, "stayed so high you could barely see them and were as much danger to us as UNITA." Two FAA brigades, totalling 600 men, attempted an amphibious landing, but in a series of blunders lost all of their equipment and were effectively neutralised. A week of vicious fighting, during which three South Africans were wounded, ended with Soyo's capture and return to FAA control. Although Soyo was retaken by UNITA within weeks of Executive Outcomes' withdrawal, the company left an indelible memory in the minds of the Angolan general staff.

Angola II

The memory stuck, metamorphosing at the highest levels of the government into a scheme worthy of a Frederick Forsyth novel. In June 1993, Barlow was contacted by a senior Angolan general with an astonishing request. Would the South Africans of Executive Outcomes, men who had once been their nemeses, now be willing to train the Angolan army? The FAA was in desperate straits. No longer bolstered by thousands of Cuban and East Bloc infantry, armour and air force advisers and combatants, it was gradually losing ground

Executive Outcomes returned to Angola, after initial successes in early 1993, to assist in a fully-fledged military campaign against the once South African-backed UNITA rebels. EO pilots regularly flew FAPA MiG-23s on CAS missions.

to the battle-hardened UNITA guerrillas. A secret meeting was arranged at a game reserve in northern Namibia, where Barlow and Lafras Luittingh, who had emerged as the chosen leader at Soyo, discussed the proposed contract with the FAA general. Less than 24 hours later, a contract perhaps unique in the field of military training and advisory groups was agreed and sealed with the handshake of two men who had once been mortal enemies. EO had five months to turn FAA's 16th Brigade into a combat-ready unit capable of defeating UNITA. The irony was not lost on either the Angolan general nor Barlow, for the original unit had been virtually wiped out by the SADF at the Lomba River in 1988. Barlow remembers the general telling him, albeit good-naturedly, "You destroyed the 16th Brigade, now build the 16th Brigade."

The Soyo operation

"When we stood back and looked at the job, it was quite daunting," Barlow admitted to *World Air Power Journal*. "Fortunately, we could draw on the experience of former members of special forces, the parachute battalion, 32 Bn, engineers, armour, artillery and air force. We decided that the best way to approach it was as if we were training a South African unit. We took what we thought was the best of each discipline and put it together as our curriculum." Forced to think at both the tactical and strategic level, Barlow and Luittingh immediately understood that both logistical and operational air support would be crucial to the success of the fledgling company.

Executive Outcome's retaking and occupation of Soyo had been sustained by a Cessna 412 and a Cessna 310 chartered from Propilot in Windhoek, the capital of Namibia. "That entire operation was supported logistically, medically for casevacs, and in terms of transporting our people by those two aircraft flying between South Africa, Namibia and Angola," Barlow explained, "but this was something on an entirely different scale." The problems of supporting the Soyo strike force had been minuscule compared with the requirements the company faced in establishing a long-term presence that would eventually include up to 500 black and white South African personnel, and with retraining elements of the Angolan army in every aspect of conventional and COIN warfare. Although the client agreed to supply all weapons and ammunition (EO maintains only its own specialised equipement such as NVGs or secure comm systems), South Africa was the only guaranteed source of food, clothing, medical supplies and tents, which presupposed a major logistics effort. To the surprise of some observers, the most effective South African special forces/COIN units – Reconnaissance Commandos, 32 Bn and Koevoet – during the wars in Namibia and Angola were predominantly black. In keeping with this successful combination, 80-85 per cent of EO's personnel are black, all with an extensive covert operations or COIN background. The initial deployment of men and materiel was undertaken by two Beechcraft King Airs flying from Lanseria airport near Johannesburg to Cabo Ledo, a former Cuban air force base near the Angolan capital of Luanda. Loaded with 12 to 14 men for the six-hour flight, these aircraft were soon seen as inadequate to the task and eventually replaced by chartered Boeing 727s.

To appreciate the scale of EO's logistics requirements during their 28 months in Angola, which averaged almost 56 tonnes per month, one need only look at the aircraft and flight hours involved in transporting men and non-lethal materiel: Boeing 727 – 2,100 hours; King Airs – 2,600 hours; An-32 – 100 hours; An-12 – 70 hours; Il-76 – 46 hours; L-100-30 hours. The Antonovs and Ilyushins were dry-leased from Russian entrepreneurs operating in southern Africa and flown by EO pilots.

Above: The Mil Mi-17 became EO's preferred 'battlebus' for all its African operations. The Russian helicopters were cheap to acquire and could survive hits from ground fire that many of their South African pilots believed could not have been sustained by the Western helicopters they had previously flown.

Right: An Mi-17 arrives in a jungle LZ to pick up an EO mortar team after a fire support mission in Sierra Leone.

The Angolan air force had both Su-25s (as seen here) and Su-22s at its disposal, two types that were eminantly more suited to the attack missions for which EO was forced to use MiG-23MLs. The Su-25s were based at Saurimo and Luanda.

Above and left: Armed with 40-kg napalm tanks, this MiG-23ML is being readied for an operational mission. The 'Flogger' is precluded from carrying a much-needed ventral fuel tank because the two under fuselage stores stations are in use. UNITA's shoulder-launched SAMs were a major worry for the EO pilots – their effectiveness against FAPA combat aircraft had been clearly demonstrated during the fighting of the 1980s.

Looking to the future, EO has since become a major shareholder in South African-based Boeing 727-operator Ibis Air.

A major weakness of EO's client, and one the old SADF had used to great advantage during its involvement there, was FAA's adherence to the rigid military doctrine learned from its former Cuban and Soviet advisers. Nowhere was this weakness more glaring than in air operations involving combat aviation support, as the Angolan helicopter pilots' efforts at Soyo had so frighteningly demonstrated. Teaching the Angolan ground forces to co-ordinate tactical air support was only half of the solution. In order to maximise the effectiveness of the Angolan air force, it was decided that former South African air force (SAAF) pilots would have to be employed as instructors and to provide professional backup in the event that EO's infantry and armour advisors were attacked. Although Executive Outcome's primary role was that of training, it was clearly understood that UNITA would see the company as an asset of the Angolan military and therefore a legitimate target.

Under the terms of the new contract, the MPLA government agreed to provide EO with both rotary- and fixed-wing air assets, but it was four months after their arrival before an instructor from the Angolan air force arrived at Cabo Ledo to begin the former SAAF pilots' conversion to the Mil Mi-17. To the consternation of South Africans accustomed to state-of-the-art training aids, he began his lecture by drawing on a chalkboard a 'picture perfect' image of the cockpit panel, complete with Russian instrument labels and their English translations. The primitive nature of his presentation notwithstanding, he eventually impressed his students with his technical knowledge of controls, engines and sub-systems. Ground training encompassed three weeks, after which EO's pilots were finally allowed to fly the helicopter. Somewhat intimidated by the South Africans' reputation and experience, dual instruction lasted a mere 45 minutes and included neither practical emergencies nor night flying. According to Charlie Tait, EO's chief pilot, whereas the Angolan instructors were well versed in technical aspects, their knowledge of tactical utilisation was extremely limited.

The South Africans soon began to appreciate the Russian helicopter's considerable strengths in comparison with the Super Frelon, Puma/Oryx and Alouettes they had flown in the SAAF. "The Mi-17 is in the Super Frelon weight class," said Tait. "Its performance could be enhanced somewhat by removing extra weight intended for cold weather operations, and it could do with Western avionics and a more ergonomically-designed cockpit lay-out, but it is far superior to the Super Frelon in a hot-and-high environment, and is capable of carrying heavier loads. In some respects the Oryx compares favourably to the 17. It is approximately 10,000 lb lighter at MAUW and can carry comparable loads at reasonable distances. Its shortcomings versus the 17 are its limited cargo space and the need for many more skilled technicians to keep it maintained properly. Whereas the 17 is very rugged and robust with good serviceability in the field and capable of taking a real hammering – qualities that probably saved our lives on occasion – the Oryx needs far more pampering and TLC. As far as the Alouette is concerned, we used it to great effect in the old days as a close-in weapon platform with a door-mounted 20-mm. As a gun platform, we could not use the Mi-17 in the same way due to its target size and inability to maintain a tight orbit around a target because of its higher speed.

Maximum effort with the Mi-17

"The reliability of these Russian helicopters was fortunate, as the maintenance facilities in Angola were of a very poor standard, or non-existent," Tait added. "We had to rely on our host not only for the aircraft, but for spares and fuel as well, which often caused problems. The Cuban and East Bloc withdrawal had clearly left a hard-to-fill void. Engines being time-expired seemed to account for the majority of the unserviceabilities for all the (military) aircraft in Angola. Whether this was due to money or supplier, we never discovered."

As soon as the South Africans received their three Mi-17s (Mi-8MTV-1s), they replaced the rear clam-shell doors with cargo gates, and installed trooping steps and external GPS antennas. Two helicopters were fitted with 7.62-mm PKM GPMGs in the door and starboard hatch, and the third with a 12.7-mm DshK HMG as defensive weapons. In a commentary on the poverty of the country, they were forced to install lockable fuel caps to prevent the Angolan army sentries from siphoning the tanks.

As the helicopter crews were being shown the ropes, four former South African air force jet pilots were getting their own introduction to Russian equipment at Saurimo, a satellite field of Cabo Ledo. Lieutenant Colonel 'P' had seen his chances of promotion and getting his own squadron plummet with the rationalisation of the SAAF in the early 1990s, and left when he heard that EO had openings. A Mirage and Cheetah instructor, his logbook recorded over 3,300 hours, with 2,000 hours of operational time in Impalas, much of it over Angola in the 1980s, as well as 630 hours in Mirage IIIs and Cheetahs. As one of EO's pilots in Angola, he would eventually record almost 100 hours of PC-7 time, and add 23.2 hours of MiG-23 time on three familiarisation and 25 operational sorties against UNITA.

MiG-23 transition

"When we got to Saurimo," related Lieutenant Colonel 'P', "the Angolans didn't want to know about us flying their jets, and gave us PC-7s, which we flew for months. All the while, however, we were pestering them to fly their Su-22M4s, which is really a fantastic ground-attack aircraft. You could call it the Russian Buccaneer, and the only operational mud-mover they had. From a distance they appeared to be quite new, or at least extremely well maintained, and were the pride and joy of the Angolan air force. Our requests went right to the top and eventually came back approved, but in the end the chief of staff air ops, who was a Su-22 pilot himself, said no. So we started off on the PC-7s, flying top cover for the Mi-17s and doing reconnaissance and FAC work."

As the pilots familiarised themselves with their equipment, they compared notes on the tactical weaknesses of the Angolan pilots. Most of these were a result of Soviet air doctrine taught by instructors who, though often veterans of Afghanistan, had little concept of COIN warfare in southern Africa. As a result, the Angolan pilots were using tactics unsuited to the war that had already been going on for 20 years in their own country. Taught to react only to orders from a radar controller, their individual initiative was rare, resulting in pilots having difficulty in keeping abreast of fast-moving, constantly changing ground situations where new plans and improvisation had to be made on the spot. Not surprisingly, they had problems monitoring or operating more than one radio channel at a time. Because they generally flew at altitudes sufficient to remain tied to radar control, nap-of-earth flying was not something with which they were comfortable, while night flying – especially night formation flying – was almost unheard of. Where they did break with Soviet doctrine was their willingness to operate singly, or with only two to three other aircraft, which may have been out of necessity, given the poor aircraft serviceability. This all translated into the Angolan pilots having little competence for special tasks and flying techniques necessary in a COIN environment.

Executive Outcomes' extensive operations demanded an ever-increasing logistics chain to support them. From operating small Cessnas, the company rapidly graduated to its own dedicated fleet of two Angolan-registered Boeing 727-100s, operated by EO associate, Ibis Air.

Meanwhile, 16 Bde was being trained in a variety of disciplines, with an emphasis on offensive rather than defensive deployment due to the limited time EO had been given to prepare them for combat. "These included operating as motorised, mechanised or long-range foot infantry, the correct use of light and heavy armour, and how to co-ordinate artillery and tactical air support.," Barlow explained. "At the same time, our pilots were retraining the Angolan pilots in how to use their aircraft properly: the correct attack envelopes for the MiG-23 and Su-22 and co-ordinating it with ground forces; how to fly at tree-top level; and day and night navigation." Helicopter crews were likewise given instruction on NOE and navigation, as well as heliborne infantry assaults and casualty evacuation.

The results of previous training at the hands of East Bloc instructors, as well as a degree of war weariness among the Angolan pilots, were significant obstacles to their quickly learning and employing the more aggressive techniques demonstrated by the South Africans. Unwilling to force the Angolans into real-time combat situations that would be beyond their capabilities or, at worst, risk blue-on-blue incidents, EO's pilots found themselves supporting 16 Bde. Depending on tasking and aircraft availability, the South African helicopter pilots were logging 30 to 50 hours per month. The jet pilots, who until early May 1994 were still flying PC-7s, had finally proven themselves and were turned over to a MiG-23 instructor.

Flying the 'Flogger-G'

"Our instructor was a Portuguese-Angolan who spoke Russian, but no English," Lieutenant Colonel 'P' said. "He would laboriously translate the Russian flight manual into Portuguese, then the interpreter, who was not a pilot, would translate into English. We did pick up enough technical knowledge during the two-week conversion course to get us through and give us background that helped later, though we pretty much taught ourselves. Once the time arrived for our check ride, they kept delaying it because they wanted to do it in a dual MiG-23, but they were all unserviceable. We eventually cooked up a bit of a white lie and told them that in the SAAF we went straight into the Mirage because there were no duals. What we didn't mention, of course, was all the hours of simulator time before getting into the cockpit."

"Although the aircraft is optimised for ACM," Lieutenant Colonel 'P' said, "we decided that in the air-to-air role the MiG-23 is not as good as some people say. It's got a

While EO flew fast jets in Angola, it also used the Angolan air force's fleet of armed PC-7s to good effect. In many ways the PC-7s were best suited to fluid COIN operations in the dense jungle, but they were also very vulnerable to ground fire.

***Left:** Ibis Air is the notional owner and operator of Executive Outcomes' two Beech Super King Airs. Based at Luanda and Johannesburg, Ibis Air has a B200 and a B200T, alongside two Mil Mi-17s and a pair of Boeing 727s – all registered in Angola. The B200T can be fitted with 106-US gal (401-litre, 88.25-Imp gal) tip tanks and this example also has a ventral cargo pannier.*

***Below:** A Força Aérea Populaire de Angola (FAPA) PC-7 and an Executive Outcomes crew at Cabo Ledo. EO dubbed the PC-7 the 'United Nations lorry' – it was a Swiss aircraft with a Canadian engine, Brazilian rocket pods, American underwing pylons, Korean rockets and South African pilots.*

tremendous roll rate, but even when you bring it over it still wants to go straight. You really have to wolf it around the corner. The ergonomics of it are a total nightmare. Visibility is atrocious, with zero rearward vision. The side of the cockpit is at mouth level, so high it's like sitting in a bathtub. To look at your 3 o'clock, for example, you have to roll it. If I was engaging a Mirage in a MiG-23 and it tried to run away, I'd catch it up. But I'd prefer to be in the Mirage. If you break a lot of angle, the 23 can't turn with you. You can break him down and kill him, easy.

Limited systems

"The take-off run for the MiG-23 was about 4,000 ft. The manual said 280-290 km/h for take-off and 250-260 km/h for landing, but we always added a few knots for the wife and kids. It just felt better. The serviceability of the aircraft we flew was excellent. Extremely reliable and incredibly tough. I flew most of my sorties in the same one, C461, and it just never broke, in spite of minimal maintenance. But here I'm talking really about the engine and airframe, which were great. The systems themselves hardly ever worked. Radar? It was there in the nose, but I think the Angolans thought it was used for ballast. It never worked. There was no active EWC. The MiG-23 had an SPO-10 RWR, which is very crude; a Mk I eyeball is better. Neither did we have flares or chaff.

"For nav instruments there was an ARK, which is a military VOR or TACAN, but it was useless because no ground stations were working. There was an IRST with LAZUR system used in conjunction with a ground controller to provide discreet intercept courses, but again, it didn't work because there was not a single ground radar system in all of Angola that worked. After the Russians left, every radar system had turned into junk and was rusting away. There was an RSBN nav system that also didn't work. No ILS, no nav aids of any kind to get us back on the ground. As a result we only flew VFR. We used hand-held GPS for all our navigation, which worked brilliantly. Best thing the Yanks ever came up with. The Angolan pilots didn't fly if there were clouds, and never, never flew at night. Later on, when we flew night operations, they thought we were completely crazy.

"Of my 25 operational sorties in the MiG, four were at night using NVGs. The reason we didn't fly a greater proportion of night missions was due to the infrastructure problem at Saurimo. The runway had no lighting and we had to resort to filling tins of various sizes with sand and paraffin/jet fuel, which would be lit approximately 15 minutes before our return to the airfield. This worked well enough, but the locals stole the tins at such a rate that we eventually had to give up! Just before I left EO, we were seriously considering a mobile runway lighting system which could be laid out before landing and recovered again once we had finished flying for the night."

"The Saurimo airfield was terrible because of the pot holes and amount of debris. There had been a lot of Il-76 traffic and that aircraft's LCN (Load Classification Number) was way too high. The sheer weight of them was breaking up the runway. When the debris became too bad, we just refused to fly. One time I taxied out and came right back, thinking if I tried it I'd find myself farming with this thing. We'd make the Angolans get a truck and we'd go along the runway clearing it by hand. Fortunately, although we had lots of cut tyres, we never had a blow-out."

Into action at N'Dalatondo

The first major action by 16 Bde took place in November 1993, when one of its three combat teams, operating without EO advisors, successfully attacked and occupied a major UNITA base at N'Dalatondo. Hitherto, demoralised FAA troops had consistently been out-gunned and out-manoeuvred by the better (SADF-) trained and more determined UNITA guerrillas. N'Dalatondo was a significant victory that convinced General João Baptiste de Matos, Chief of the Angolan Armed Forces, of EO's worth. It also put the stamp of approval on EO's recommendation that 16 Bde attack the diamond fields at Cafunfo, a strategic asset held by UNITA and used to fund its military and political operations. Because of UNITA's strength and in-depth defensive positions, EO proposed that they 'monitor' the attack from both ground and air. Although the South African's had a professional interest in their students' success, there were also personal reasons: UNITA forces had infiltrated an FAA camp and killed one of EO's employees in his bed. There was a score to be settled. Lieutenant Colonel 'P', with three solo familiarisation flights recorded in his logbook, was soon in the air with his bomb-laden MiG-23 and hoping that all the brainstorming on anti-missile tactics was going to work.

Anti-SAM tactics

"We'd finally decided that the best way to get around the Stinger, SAM-7 and SAM-14 threat was by transiting high and at maybe 30 km from the target backing right off on the throttle, which reduced our noise to almost nothing on the ground. We'd roll in at idle power from about 6000 m and let the aircraft accelerate to about 1000 km/h in a 30° dive. We'd release our bombs at about 2000 m, pull out at 1500 m and hit max afterburner, betting on the slow reaction time of any SAM operator. Because the aircraft was so quiet at idle power, even if the operator already had the SAM on his shoulder he wouldn't know we were there until we'd already pulled out of the dive and gone to afterburner. With an advertised climb rate of 45,000 ft per minute, our defence was to simply out-climb a missile if it was fired. In no time at all we'd be between 6000 and 10000 m again, well out of range. If they ever did launch a missile at us, we never knew about it. The MiG-23's acceleration is just amazing. It really goes like the clappers. At 28,000 lb of thrust the engine is very powerful, but it's unbelievably

Above: At any one time the FAPA had three/four serviceable MiG-23s which operated from Lubongo and Saurimo. EO pilots never flew with Angolans, who did undertake 'their own' missions in the MiGs and Sukhois. EO rated the FAPA personnel as 'good pilots but bad operators' and it was not unheard-of for the Angolans to dump their bombs in the jungle and RTB without ever reaching a target.

Lt Col 'P' is seen here (right) in front of C454, an early mount, just before his second MiG-23 flight. Operations from Saurimo (below right) were hampered by the appalling condition of the runway, only one side of which was usable.

thirsty, which gives it a very short endurance. We never had the fuel to check the burn rate, but I would guess at low level in max afterburner it drinks around 1000 litres per minute. The other threat, of course, was ground fire, and when we were down and dirty we regularly had 23-mm coming at us, but none of us was ever hit.

A less-than-impressive performer

"As a mud-mover, on a scale of one to 10 the MiG-23 is about a two. It has four weapons stations, two on the belly and two on the wings inboard of the sweep. There is a centre-line station for a fuel tank only. You can't load the aircraft asymmetrically and you have to release both bombs from the belly stations at the same time. The same goes for the missiles. If you want to fire a missile, you have to fire two. If you're carrying a fuel tank, the two belly hardpoints are useless, and if you're carrying anything on the belly at all you can't use the cannon because of the shell casings hitting it. The sight seldom worked and even when it did a piece of chewing gum stuck on the windscreen would be about as good. Fortunately, just ahead of the cockpit are three 'Odd Rod' IFF antennas in line with each other. When the sight wasn't working, we'd line them up and with any decent aiming picture it worked like a charm. The chap I usually flew with took out a bridge on his first try with dumb bombs. You only have to ask people in the same business to realise it was a bloody impressive effort.

"A real problem was getting the Angolans to understand that different targets required different weapons loads. When we'd come back from a mission, the aircraft would be armed almost before we walked away from it. The problem was, they'd load it with whatever armaments were handy or they felt like at the time. I was once tasked to hit a bridge, but when I got to the aircraft, it was loaded with napalm. On another mission to hit a bridge, I found it had been loaded with rockets. The people who gave us our missions – I suppose if you really stretch it you could call them a 'tasking agency' – were often neither pilots nor even trained in target assessment, but very full of their own importance. They'd give us targets without understanding anything about them, and then got very touchy – even angry – when we said we wouldn't fly unless we had the correct weapons loads.

Praise for the weapons

"As far as armament, the MiG's twin-barrelled 23-mm cannon is an excellent piece of kit. Very accurate, very effective against ground targets. Our most common weapons loads were 250-kg or 500-kg bombs, but we occasionally carried napalm and rockets. Interestingly enough, we also had some Mk 82 bombs kindly provided by the Israelis, who had modified the American kit to fit the hardpoints on Soviet aircraft. The most effective bomb we used was the Russian RBK SWAB, a 500-kg cluster bomb. Once we'd pulled off and looked back at the target you could see hundreds of explosions going off over at least a 300-m radius. It was beautiful weapon for trenches."

All of EO's air assets were by then fully engaged, and their determination to give 16 Bde their best effort in the face of serious opposition from UNITA was reflected by the losses they incurred. Two EO-flown Mi-17s were downed, one by small arms fire in which, according to chief pilot Charlie Tait, the crew were "shaken but okay," and another by a SAM-7 in which the crew were "stirred but okay."

Mi-17 shootdown

The first incident is worth telling in Tait's own words. "In April 1994 we took off with two Mi-17s for a normal resupply mission for an element of 16 Brigade, which was on the move 220 km from our home base. When we arrived overhead it was obvious the LZ was too small to accommodate both helos simultaneously, so I waited until No. 1 had landed, unloaded and got airborne. As soon as he was clear I brought us around on a nice, easy approach and settled in. The guys in the back were already getting off, when, not five seconds after touchdown, we heard and felt small arms rounds slamming into the helo. The guys who had got off were already scurrying back to the relative 'safety' of the helicopter as the onboard port and starboard defensive PKMs opened up to try to keep the UNITAs' heads down, anything to give us time. Not knowing how many of our people were still on the ground, I was trying to decide whether to flee or to stay put. In the middle of the tremendous roar of both in-coming and out-going fire and the sound of the blades and engine, the flight engineer's voice came over the ICS.

"'The guys are taking hits inside the helo!'

"'Natasha', the Russian audio warning for emergencies, was screeching and the No. 2 engine oil pressure warning light was illuminated. I pulled collective and we got airborne, firing still going on full blast from us and the UNITAs on the ground . Our transition wasn't

While EO pilots did not rate the MiG-23 as a combat aircraft, they did have absolute faith in its mechanical integrity. For example, no pilot ever suffered a failure of the essential drag chute.

Left: Executive Outcomes operated two Mi-17 'Hip-H's in support of its mission in Sierra Leone. The helicopters were each christened **Bokkie** *and* **Daisy** *–* **Bokkie** *handled like a springbok,* **Daisy** *flew like a cow. Here* **Bokkie** *is seen in flight from the open tailgate of* **Daisy**, *inbound, from the east to Koidu base.*

Below: Former 22 SAS veteran Fred Marafano sits easily in an EO Mi-17 before lift-off from Lungi Airport, Freetown. He and his team of RSLMF troops are equipped with a mix of Russian- and Romanian-built AK-47s (the latter described as the worst ever made). Like many operators before them, EO immediately removed the rear clamshell doors of its 'Hips' to allow rapid deplaning/enplaning.

very lady-like, but we were out of that hellhole and I was just trying to fly the beast. Keep her airborne! Remember ANC! Aviate, Navigate, Communicate! I was definitely not relishing the idea of a 220-km walk. The co-pilot and flight engineer were assessing the damage and we were all wondering if we were going to make it home. We had badly wounded chaps in the back, some dying, others who were going to die if they didn't get treatment soon. Fuel was everywhere, a haze of Avtur inside the helo as a result of it being blown through the back without its clamshell doors. Visibility inside the cockpit and through the windscreen was not good. Fuel was also streaming down onto us from above.

"Me: 'Wipers, please!'

"Flight engineer: 'Fuel is on the inside of the windscreen!'

"Oh shit, I thought."

"By now we were 2 km from the LZ. It still wasn't a safe distance but we had to land in order to transfer the wounded to the No. 1 helo. The only choice I saw was an LZ littered with short tree stumps. Keeping our fingers crossed that we weren't going to land in another nest of UNITAs, we set down. The wounded were transferred as quickly as possible, while those people not employed threw out a defensive perimeter. We got airborne again and my satisfaction at not landing on a tree stump was cut short by the co-pilot's voice.

"'Main gearbox pressure zero! Main gearbox temp is against the stop! Fuel 800 litres. We've lost 1000 litres in five minutes. We've got a serious fire hazard!'

"I didn't know how close the UNITAs were, but if we stopped then we did not have the firepower to defend ourselves. I decided to push on past the next big river that I saw coming up, just to give the bad guys a bit of an obstacle. As soon as we were past it I picked an LZ big enough that the No. 1 helo could also get in to pick us up. We landed and lost little time shutting down and unbuckling. I grabbed my survival gear and headed towards the door, wondering where the other helo was, when someone shouted, 'Rotor brake!'

"'Fuck the rotor brake! Let's get out of here!'

"We scrambled out of the helo and there was No. 1 coming in, the defensive guns ready to give us covering fire if the bad guys suddenly pitched up. We sprinted for it, leaping on board in a tangle of weapons and kit. There was a quick, final check to make sure we were all there and the helo lifted off. As it made the transition and picked up speed for home, there was an audible sigh of relief in the back. We were the lucky ones. Five friends were dead."

At the end of July that year the fighting peaked between FAA and UNITA in north-western Angola, with FAA taking one rebel-held town after another as UNITA tried desperately to hold on to its areas of control. EO's training was paying off, not only on the ground but with the air force as well, which was keeping the advancing FAA units supplied by helicopter. Uys Roos (not his real name) had been tasked with resupplying a recently captured town in Lunda Province that was strategically crucial to both sides. UNITA, determined to halt the airlifts, soon blocked all the low-level routes out to 30 km with a heavy concentration of AAA weapons up to 23-mm. During his briefing Roos was assured by FAA that not only had they had cleared the area of UNITA for a 10-km radius around the town, but that there was no missile threat.

A second shootdown

Roos and his No. 1, both loaded with 2.5 tonnes of supplies, took off and climbed above 23-mm range. Flying with an Angolan co-pilot, Roos took the Vic Two position. Visibility and the handling of the heavily loaded helicopter deteriorated steadily as they climbed, until he was instrument-formation flying to maintain position. Two kilometres out they made a steep,

Here **Daisy** *deposits an EO mortar team at a hill-top LZ approximately 2 km east of the rebel-held town of* **Gandorhun**. *The intensive use of helicopters allowed EO to bring devastating mobile fire power to bear on the RUF.*

Above: The Sierra Leone government originally tried to buy its own Mi-24s, reportedly purchasing two aircraft for $9 million, only one of which was ever obtained. This led to the contract hire of two Belorussian 'Hind' crews to fly the Mi-24V 'Hind-E'. Note the green, white and blue flag of Sierra Leone on the tail fin.

Right: The Belorussian crews were veterans of the war in Afghanistan and made good use of their aircraft in Africa. Here the Mi-24V is seen attacking a target with flechette rockets.

spiralling descent to the runway west of the town, unloaded their cargo and took on troops. Because of the threat of long-range mortar, artillery and rocket fire, they did not wait to get airborne again. Roos gave his No. 1 approximately seven seconds before lifting off behind him.

"There was a ravine about 300 m ahead with high ground to the north and I turned left to be closer to the town," Roos said. "As I climbed through 200 m and 180°, I increased the bank to 45° to stay with the lead Mi-17, which was at my 12 o'clock. The next moment there was a tremendous flash and smoke of an explosion above my head as a SAM hit us. I shot a look out the window and saw the missile carry on a bit unstable towards the lead helicopter and pass just underneath them. My helicopter started to gallop viciously. I dumped collective, both to see if we were still flying and to get down as quickly as possible to avoid a second missile. The lead helicopter transmitted that a missile had just been launched and we'd better get out of Dodge. I told him I'd already been hit and was going down.

"As soon as I realised the aircraft was controllable I increased speed to lose height faster, heading for another runway about 1 km south of the town. It was then that the Angolan co-pilot finally realised we'd been hit and decided he had to take control. I was a bit busy, but my flight engineer helped him right. Then I had to listen to him screaming that the other helicopter must come and pick us up. Being otherwise engaged, I didn't bother answering. I landed safely, shut down and climbed out to assess the damage. The tail pipe was gone on the number two engine and a third of the pockets on one main rotor blade were gone. The blast had ripped open the engine cowling and then hit the main rotor blade, missing the main spar by 1 mm. One millimetre closer and we'd have died.

"Our people on the ground told me that the missile had been launched from the high ground on the far side of the ravine. The distinctive white trail they described confirmed to me that it was a SAM-7. The Angolans later said that I'd been very lucky. Fifteen of their helicopters were shot down before me, and three after me, all with no survivors."

Both incidents cemented the South Africans' affection for the Russian helicopter. "If they had been Pumas instead of Mi-17s," one of the pilots said, "I don't think they could have got down in one piece. Everyone would definitely have bought the farm." Two other Mi-17s were destroyed on the ground during a base attack by UNITA, and a PC-7 was lost to 23-mm ground fire. The Pilatus pilot made a successful landing and "the SAR operation worked beautifully," one of his colleagues recalled. Tragically, the downed pilot and his backseater were killed just as an Mi-17 was landing to pick them up. With his pursuers 100 ft away, the helicopter was forced to lift off under heavy ground fire.

Flame-out

The MiG-23s were also busy, and an action near Saurimo remains the most memorable mission in the flying career of Lieutenant Colonel 'P'. "It was one of my last sorties in the MiG-23," he recalled. "We knew where a large number of UNITAs were concentrating in two areas about 40 km apart, both roughly the same distance from Saurimo. It was about a 15-min flight and I was leading. My No. 2 was very experienced on Impalas but didn't have much time on the MiG-23. We found the target and I rolled in, dropped my bombs and pulled off to wait for him. At that point I started getting a spurious fuel warning light that's designed to come on when you're down to 600 litres. The fuel gauge said there was still plenty. I checked the fuel tally with my No. 2 and everything seemed okay. About two seconds later it came on again and stayed on, but I decided it was malfunctioning. We climbed to 20,000 AGL and were heading for the second target, when the engine flamed out.

"I tried to relight the fire, but nothing happened. I was out of fuel. I jettisoned the two remaining bombs and turned for home, which was 40 km away. I can tell you I was scared. I thought about ejecting, but immediately discarded the idea. Because of the poor maintenance I didn't trust the seat to work properly or the parachute to open. Even if it did work, we were over Indian country and I definitely didn't fancy my chances with UNITA. I had never read anything about the gliding characteristics of the MiG-23, but I decided it was my only option. My No. 2 stayed right with me the whole time, talking me through it, which was a big help. As I approached the Saurimo airfield I can tell you my heart was pounding. I got the wheels down, but they wouldn't lock. Just as I touched down the wheels collapsed and I made

The joint EO/RSLMF headquarters was located at Freetown, where Daisy *is seen on the ramp with the Mi-24V in the background. The well-worn Mi-17 bears signs of a hastily-applied Sierra Leonean (9L-) civil registration on the boom.*

a belly landing and went sliding down the runway. It was definitely the most frightening experience of my life.

"It's a real tribute to the strength of the aircraft that it suffered only superficial skin damage. Unfortunately, the Angolans had nothing to lift the aircraft with – no crane, no jacks, nothing – so it was just written off. A T-54 tank hooked a cable to it and dragged the MiG-23 off the runway. It's still sitting there today. It turned out that the fuel tanks had never been topped off. The fuel gauge itself is designed to be set by hand to what's been put in the tanks. Someone had set it to Full."

To the dismay of UNITA's military commanders, who had promised the political leadership that Cafunfo's defences were impregnable, the fierce ground and air battle ended with the mines securely in the hands of 16 Bde. It was a humiliating defeat for UNITA and one that placed its entire war effort in jeopardy. Correspondents who had covered the Angolan war in the 1980s were contacted and assured that UNITA's waning fortunes were the result of "over 5,000 South African mercenaries" operating on behalf of the MPLA government. In reality, less than 200 EO ground and air advisers had been involved in directly supporting the attack.

From Angola to Sierra Leone

By the time Executive Outcomes struck its tents and withdrew from Angola in January 1995, UNITA had long since sued for peace and sulkily joined the government. "When we arrived in Angola," Eeben Barlow said, "the army was in trouble. As part of the process leading up to the UN-supervised elections in 1992, FAA had pretty much been disbanded in accordance with the pre-election agreements. UNITA, which had not disbanded, refused to accept the election results and went back to war. Not only did we help our client turn the tide of that war, but, possibly more importantly, we earned the trust of the Angolan government and military. When you stop to consider that we had fought them as members of the SADF until 1988, this was a major achievement."

***Left:** The Mi-24 regularly operated from makeshift helipads around Koidu. Here the pride of the Sierra Leonean air force, AF-0010, is armed with two UV-32-57 rocket pods and two 30-mm grenade launchers.*

***Below:** For armed reconnaissance patrols it was routine to rely on rocket pods and the Mi-24V's own 9-A-624 four-barrelled 12.7-mm gun with up to 1,470 rounds in the USPU-24 turret.*

Executive Outcomes' reputation rippled across Africa. Geology and the arbitrary borders drawn during the colonial era mean that Sierra Leone's 27,000 sq miles (70000 km^2) contain 25 per cent of the world's known titanium ore, what may be the richest alluvial diamond mines in Africa, and major bauxite deposits. Gold, platinum and oil are also present, and it once exported rice and 20 per cent of the world's ginger. Today, Sierra Leone is the sixth most impoverished country on Earth. It was also the scene of a four-year war that had brought the tiny West African country to its economic knees. The undisciplined and ill-trained Republic of Sierra Leone Military Force (RSLMF) had been incapable of halting, much less reversing, gains made by the Revolutionary United Front (RUF). Nor had the Economic Community of West African States Military Operations Group (ECOMOG) contingents from Nigeria, Ghana and Guinea had any effect.

RUF opposition

The RUF is led by Corporal Alfred Foday Sankoh, 62, who was trained as a wireless operator by the British while serving in the Royal West African Forces in the 1950s and 1960s. Cashiered and imprisoned for his part in a coup attempt, he was pardoned in 1980 and fled to Libya. In 1991, armed by warlord Charles Taylor of neighbouring Liberia, Sankoh began a campaign of terror against the rural population of Sierra Leone. Other than demanding power and the removal of Western embassies, aid agencies and investors, Sankoh has no known political agenda, but maintains links with Libya.

The few convoys the RSLMF or ECOMOG commanders sent inland were regularly ambushed, providing the rebels with their major source of ammunition resupply. Mining sites which provided the bulk of the country's foreign currency earnings had been overrun and a number of Western hostages taken. The interior of the country had been cut off and the largely illiterate population terrorised by RUF thugs with a well deserved reputation for recreational murder and rape, and a penchant for ritual cannibalism.

The ruling military junta, the National Provisional Ruling Council (NPRC), had already agreed to democratic elections, but neither they nor the UN saw a way forward so long as the RUF, determined to seize power, refused to lay down their arms. Desperate to halt the rebels, who, by early 1995, were beginning to threaten the capital of Freetown itself, the NPRC contacted Executive Outcomes, which immediately despatched a small team to make an assessment of the situation. By April, EO had begun deploying a 100-man administrative and advisory group to Sierra Leone in Ibis Air Boeing 727s.

EO's pre-contractual analysis of the war stipulated the need for helicopters to move their own men and equipment in a country with limited infrastructure and vast areas of impenetrable, triple-canopy jungle. Additionally, resupplying remote Sierra Leonean bases by air, rather than convoy, would prevent a ready

source of ammunition from falling into RUF hands. Although the RSLMF was able to supply EO with individual and crew-served weapons, to include two BMP-2 IFVs, the Sierra Leone air force consisted only of one Mi-17 gunship, and an Mi-24V 'Hind-E', both flown by Belorussian contract pilots. Utilised for armed reconnaissance, the aircraft greatly intimidated the RUF but were largely ineffective in finding and attacking the rebels in the dense undergrowth. Potentially valuable, and one the South Africans had already factored into their plans as a transport helicopter, the 'Hind' was clearly inadequate to their needs.

Above: Viewed over a 7.62-mm PKM GPMG mounted in the door of an Mi-17, AF-0010 joins up after departure from Koidu en route to Kailahun. The Mi-24V has all its cabin windows open, to keep the occupants cool, but also allowing them to return fire with their own weapons if needed at the LZ. The 'Hind-E' itself is carrying a full load of four gun pods.

Right: Circling over a village destroyed by RUF rebels, the Mi-24V shows off a UV-32-57 pod – missions were often flown with half-full pods. The rockets are actually 55-mm projectiles, though they are fired from 57-mm tubes.

A renewed Mil fleet

Based on their pilots' familiarity with, and respect for, the Mi-17, EO initially leased and then purchased two examples at a cost of approximately $500,000 each. ("We soon dubbed them *Daisy* and *Bokkie*," chief pilot Tait said, "the former because it behaved a bit like a cow, and the latter due to its being as fleet-footed as a young springbok.") EO's ground crew quickly carried out the same modifications they had done in Angola, the only difference being the installation of a safety gate across the tailgate that doubled as a trooping step. A requirement for emergency casualty evacuation was satisfied by the acquisition of two Hawker Siddeley Andovers, one of which was placed on permanent standby at Lungi Airport near Freetown. Potential air assets included two Nigerian air force Alpha Jets, also based at Lungi, which would eventually prove their worth in joint operations with the South Africans.

While awaiting delivery of their own helicopters, the South African pilots were grudgingly taken in hand by the Belorussian contract crews to familiarise them with their gunships. Former Soviet front-line combat pilots, their technical knowledge was less extensive than the Angolans' had been, though the South Africans found the flight instruction of a much higher standard. The Belorussians were also less intimidated than the Angolans by the South Africans' considerable experience, and refused to turn them loose with the gunships until they had completed approximately six hours of dual instruction. Although the Mi-17 gunship was somewhat heavier and more sluggish than the Mi-17s they had flown in Angola, it was essentially the same aircraft. The Mi-24, however, exceeded all their expectations. "It's like flying a fighter!" Tait enthused over its handling characteristics after his first time at the controls.

Even though all of EO's pilots received conversion training in the Mi-24, the Belorussians refused to allow them to fly it on actual operations, clearly viewing the South Africans as a threat to their own contracts with the NPRC. This resentment may also have been coloured by EO's supremely confident (read: cocky) pilots, who immediately set about telling them how to fly in an African COIN environment. When the Mi-17 gunship, flown by an EO crew, was downed after ingesting a flock of birds while flying NOE, the relationship became distinctly prickly.

Foreign relations

By the time their own Mi-17s arrived the relationship between the Belorussian and South African camps was distant at best. Having studied the RUF and the terrain it operated in, EO's pilots recognised the synergistic potential of joint operations. In an attempt to heal the breach between themselves and the Belorussians, they took the initiative by volunteering to provide top cover for the immediate extraction of the Mi-24 crew in the event they were downed on their reconnaissance flights. The greatest problem with joint operations, however, was that neither group spoke the other's language. Until the gunship could be flown on operations by the EO flight crew, the interim solution was to place a Sierra Leonean officer who had attended university in Moscow on board the Mi-24 as a tactical translator between the Belorussians and the South African pilots and ground units. This was less than ideal, and limited the use of the gunship in a ground support role where the risk of a blue-on-blue incident is always high.

As the training of select units of the RSLMF went forward, Brigadier Bert Sachs, former CO of the SADF's 5 Reconnaissance Regiment and EO's commander in Sierra Leone, presented a formal operational plan to the NPRC. In it he recommended concentrating on three main objectives: first, evict the RUF from areas around Freetown; second, recapture and stabilise the diamond area around Koidu, 100 miles (160 km) to the east; and third, locate and destroy the RUF's headquarters.

Advancing from Freetown

The first attack was implemented with the same surprise and precision that had seen the old SADF win every engagement it had fought in Angola. RSLMF blocker groups supported by Executive Outcomes' personnel with BMP-2s were deployed southeast of Freetown, before EO's newly-arrived Mi-17s began inserting search and destroy teams. An intense, three-day campaign cost the RUF over 150 dead and threw the survivors into a panicked retreat. Before the RUF could assess and recover from its first defeat of the four-year war, EO and their freshly-trained RSLMF soldiers struck eastwards towards the second objective. Supported by BMP-2s, heavily armed Land Rovers and the Mi-24 flying top cover (which did no more than provide a degree of intimidation), a motorised force fought its way through successive rebel ambushes to capture the alluvial diamond fields around Koidu within two days. Additional equipment was immediately ferried in by the Mi-17s and a secure base, complete with *ad hoc* helipads, was established atop a volcanic outcropping overlooking the town. Within days, the first of over 30,000 inhabitants, forced to flee the year previously when the RUF had attacked, began to return.

The reaction of the NPRC in Freetown was jubilation. Discounting training, planning and preparation time, Executive Outcomes had accomplished more in a week than the RSLMF

Above: In Angola, three FAPA Mi-17s were seconded to EO. When they were handed over, the helicopters were still in Aeroflot's blue and white colour scheme, but all were quickly camouflaged.

Left: While the fixed-wing pilots were in Luanda for their MiG conversion, UNITA attacked EO's operations base. The Angolan guards fled, an EO employee was killed and two Mi-17s were destroyed in a night which could have ended far more badly.

Left: In Sierra Leone, EO's air wing worked with a pair of RSLMF BMP-2s. With large ID numbers painted on for recognition from the air, the BMPs were crewed by EO personnel – in this case all former members of the South West Africa Police counter-insurgency unit.

had in four years of bush warfare that had cost them over 500 dead and wounded. Losses under EO management had been two RSLMF soldiers killed, five wounded and three EO employees wounded, none seriously enough to be evacuated back to South Africa. Subsequent operations planned and executed by Executive Outcomes with client Sierra Leonean troops continued to whittle away at the RUF and drive the survivors deeper into the jungle or into neighbouring Liberia, where President Charles Taylor, himself a proponent of terror tactics, gave the rebels tacit support.

By now EO's air wing had convinced the Sierra Leonean government that the Mi-24's potential was not being realised due to the language problem and the subsequent risk of blue-on-blue incidents. As a result, two South Africans were soon at the controls of the Russian gunship when operations requiring close ground support were launched. "Before we climb into it, the Belorussian ground crew has serviced the aircraft and signed out the books, giving the Mi-24 a clean bill of health," Tait explained, "so all we need to do is a quick walk-around to confirm that all is in order. It's a formidable machine and we've grown quite fond of 'Renoster', so nicknamed because it is rather ugly and the 12.7-mm gun does give it a certain resemblance to a rhinoceros.

Flying the Mi-17

"In the 'front office', the co-pilot goes through the normal cockpit checks and gets the GPS on-line, while the aircraft commander silently runs through the pre-start in the slightly elevated rear cockpit. As is immediately apparent to anyone who has flown both types, a lot more thought went into the design of the Mi-24's cockpit than the Mi-17's. In terms of ergonomics, all the switches – electrical, start, fuel, radio, navigation, and armament panels – are effectively grouped together. The flight instrumentation is superior to the 17's, with the HSI, for example, situated at a higher and more comfortable level, while another nice feature is the electrically-operated seat in the rear cockpit. A great addition is the extremely efficient air-conditioner. Designed for an NBC environment, it also just happens to make operations in the tropics quite enjoyable.

"Once the start sequence has been initiated and all systems are on-line, one can, if necessary, get airborne within 2½ minutes. At sea level there is oodles of power, and even at MAUW we flash through transition with only a slight shake of the tail feathers. Gear up at 100 km/h and check NR at 95 per cent. Straight and level with full pods at 300 km/h, she is extremely stable. Visibility is good to the left and front, but restricted to the right for the pilot due to an air-conditioning duct and for the co-pilot as the result of missile/bomb-aiming equipment.

"The helicopter is extremely responsive in roll and one should have a steady hand. The auto-pilot is a great improvement over its sister ship and affords very good stability throughout the flight spectrum. In a turn one can observe a decrease in torque due to an increase in lift created by the wing stubs, which in turn reduces the load on the main rotor, allowing the application of more power to sustain speed in the turn. Below transition the opposite is true as a result of negative lift caused by the down-wash, which requires slightly more power. For an aircraft of 13 tons it is exceptionally agile and manoeuvrable. For instance, pulling up after a pass, one can zoom up at about 100 km/h and hoof in rudder to affect a quick turn-around. Where there's a threat of ground fire, you can create a side-slipping motion by flying cross-controls at a remarkably high air speed to present aiming difficulties for the bad guys.

'Hind' weapons

"With both cockpits and other vital components adequately protected, one feels quite secure under these conditions. The sense of security is bolstered by the weapons systems, which include 57-mm rockets, 30-mm AGS-17 grenade launchers, 7.62-mm Minigun packs and the 12.7-mm Gatling gun in the nose. Of these, the 12.7-mm is deadly accurate, and the rockets and grenades very effective as area weapons. Due to the density of the jungle, however, a large proportion of our targets would be better serviced with bombs.

"One of the main shortcomings of the Mi-24 is its relatively short range, which presents a problem even in a country as small as Sierra Leone. After one hour and 45 minutes, you had better start looking for a filling station. One can add an hour's flight duration with two 500-litre drop tanks, but the trade-off is losing two weapons packages. Because fuel is only available at Lungi airport, the trusty 17s are often used to cart around 200-litre drums. On these occasions we haven't had too much difficulty in landing and taking off in relatively confined spaces, where power in OGE was satisfactory."

RUF resurgence

Following UN-supervised elections and the beginning of the rainy season, a ceasefire was agreed by the RUF in April 1996. However, stories of RUF activities soon reached the ears of Executive Outcomes' combat intelligence unit via traditional native hunters, the Kamajos. Intimately familiar with the jungle, and sworn enemies of the rebels, they began reporting that the RUF was consolidating positions in remote areas still under its control. Weapons and ammunition, purchased with diamonds mined during its occupation of the Kono district, were arriving from Liberia and impoverished Guinean border troops. Villages were being looted for food and new recruits to fill its sorely depleted numbers; the illiterate farmers were offered the RUF's standard recruitment option of dying under torture or joining the movement.

Based on the Kamajos' reports, RUF infiltration routes, bases and possible avenues of attack were identified. The intelligence picture that was developing gave every indication that the rebels' ceasefire was little more than an attempt to recover from an uninterrupted succession of defeats at the hands of Executive Outcomes.

EO personnel and Sierra Leonean troops hustle to unload mortar ammunition after insertion to a firebase 25 km (15.5 miles) south of Koidu base. Mortar attacks would follow CAS sorties, if available, and preceded the insertion of troops against an RUF target.

EO's early prediction that the RUF would return to offensive operations was soon proved correct as the rains eased and the first RSLMF bases were attacked. The new government was given a detailed briefing and quickly gave EO the green light. The company's latest acquisition, a Cessna 337 Super Skymaster, was pressed into service to locate the rebels.

Working with local assets

"The Kamajos know the bush, but they don't understand radios or how a GPS works," one of EO's pilots said, "so it was up to us to confirm their information with aerial reconnaissance. It's a tricky task, since the RUF camps are well camouflaged under the dense jungle canopy. In order to positively identify the presence of rebels in the camps, orbit heights as low as 100 ft above the trees are necessary, which brings us well within the range of small arms fire." Although poorly maintained, the RUF's motley collection of AK-47s and H&K G3s were certainly capable of bringing down the Cessna. The one weapon that concerned the pilots far more, however, was at least one 12.7-mm weapon the rebels were known to have received from Liberia.

"When the camps are positively identified as being active," he continued, "an accurate plot is made and detailed planning takes places with the involvement of all the various players. The Alpha Jet pilots of the Nigerian air force give their input on dropping 250-kg bombs, while the Mi-24 crew decide which CAS packages they'll carry. Nearby LZs are selected for the insertion of mortar teams, and the Mi-17 pilots plan their approach and escape routes. Alternate LZs are determined, as well as SAR procedures for downed aircrew and missing ground troops. In the event of a casevac, the recovery procedure is discussed, and where the wounded will be flown before evacuation to a better equipped hospital than the one in Freetown. If additional fuel is anticipated, 200-litre drums will be flown to own forces security areas closest to the target.

Air support for combat troops

"On the day of the attack, the Mi-17s are loaded with 120-mm and 82-mm mortar teams and protection elements, ground troops are briefed and SOPs discussed. Radios are checked and frequencies allocated. The aircraft take off at planned times, so the mortar teams are set up as the attack is initiated by the Alpha Jets to shock the rebels into inaction. As soon as the Alpha Jets pull off, the mortar barrage begins, with the ground forces commander in the 337 providing fire control corrections, while the troop-carrying Mi-17s orbit a short distance away. Once the target has been saturated the Mi-17s head in, escorted by the Mi-24, which hoses down the area with its 12.7 to discourage anyone waiting to engage the 17s during the landing phase. Sometimes the LZs are so tight the jungle is only a few metres from the helicopters, making them sitting ducks for a rebel with an RPG. At moments like these, I have to admit we get slightly edgy.

After two days of supporting an attack on RUF positions at Gandorhun a mortar team is extracted by an EO Mi-17. Note the second 'Hip' circling prior to extracting the LZ protection team.

"The Cessna remains overhead to control the sweep lines, which can be difficult since the tree canopy is often too thick to maintain visual contact with troops on the ground. If they encounter rebel fire that prevents forward movement, the Mi-24 is called in to neutralise the pocket of resistance with, depending on the terrain, the 12.7, Miniguns, rockets or grenades. Once all resistance has ended, the troops gather prisoners, documents, weapons and equipment and move to a designated LZ. Prisoners are immediately uplifted and taken to the nearest RSLMF base for tactical interrogation, while the rest of the attack force is flown back to base before nightfall."

As this was written, the same ceasefire is in progress and negotiations are under way between Foday Sankoh, the RUF leader, and the new, democratically elected government of Sierra Leone. Not surprisingly, high on the RUF's list of demands is that Executive Outcomes be ordered to leave the country along with other foreign troops assisting the government, in particular the Nigerians. But Sankoh's lack of good faith, demonstrated by repeated attacks in which both civilians and RSLMF soldiers continue to die, has resulted in the South Africans being seen as liberators and protectors by the vast majority of Sierra Leone's population. The attitude in the rural areas was summed up by a teacher in Koidu in the diamond-rich Kono district. "We know the RUF," he said. "If the South Africans leave, we will suffer again. All the people of Kono will pack up and flee." The government, well aware that the RUF is continuing to re-arm and infiltrate, has asked the South Africans to remain until peace is assured.

EO – A legitimate success

The popular press has labelled EO as 'mercenaries' and the 'diamond dogs of war'. More sober commentators, including the BBC, have noted that the South African company has done something no one else was capable of doing: bringing peace to Sierra Leone. Whatever sobriquet is applied, however, Executive Outcomes remains a phenomenon, a proactive security company prepared to deploy a well co-ordinated team of professional soldiers and combat pilots in support of legitimate governments which have a limited ability to define their own countries.

Jim Hooper

High-altitude capability, long endurance and a worthwhile sensor payload are the chief attributes of the U-2R/S. The U-2R usually operates at over 70,000 ft (21335 m), from where its sensors can peer much further into denied territory than aircraft at lower altitudes. The aircraft's ability to remain on station for many hours makes it a highly useful surveillance tool to cover ongoing operations, as opposed to a one-shot reconnaissance platform. This is especially useful during Comint (communications intelligence) missions.

U-2 The Second Generation

Although public interest in the notorious U-2 waned soon after the Powers shootdown in 1960, the career of the aircraft was far from over. With one SAM attack the Soviets had made it obvious that the slender 'Angel' could no longer operate directly over well-defended territory, a fact reinforced by another shootdown over Cuba in 1962, but its sophisticated and far-reaching sensors could still provide excellent intelligence from safer airspace. With the U-2's capabilities much in demand, Lockheed undertook a complete redesign of the type in the mid-1960s to create a much bigger, better and further-ranging version: the U-2R. That aircraft was put back into production in the 1980s, and today forms the backbone of the USAF's high-altitude reconnaissance effort, having proved its worth in numerous conflicts, large and small, since its baptism of fire over Vietnam and China.

U-2 pilots are an elite crew, drawn from a variety of USAF backgrounds but with one factor in common: above-average ability. The wearing of the David Clark pressure suits is necessary on all but low-level training missions to protect the pilot in the event of a cockpit depressurisation. The main pressure suit is covered by an orange coverall containing lifevest, emergency oxygen and other paraphernalia.

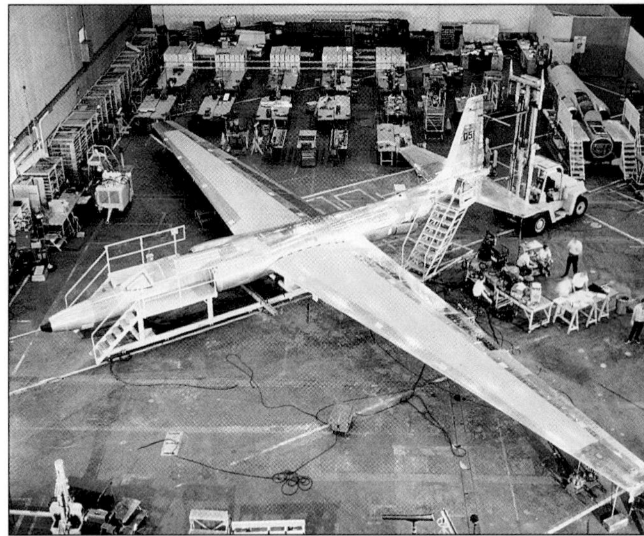

Right: Article 051 takes shape in the Burbank shop, while a second U-2R forward fuselage can be seen in the background. The use of the word 'article' dated back to the earliest days of the U-2 programme, when it was employed to shield the true nature of the project. The prototype U-2R flew with the civilian registration N803X.

Conceived by a visionary group of scientists and academics, sponsored by a civilian agency with virtually no record of aerospace endeavour, and born in the now-famous Skunk Works of Lockheed's sprawling Burbank plant, the U-2 was to become one of the world's best-known aircraft. Virtually everything about the aircraft was unconventional from the very start, including its expected life span – even designer Kelly Johnson gave it no more than two years. But as the CIA's audacious and ambitious programme to photograph the Soviet Union from great altitude stretched into a third, fourth and fifth year, more roles and missions kept emerging for the jet-powered glider. The USAF bought into the programme, eventually acquiring 35 of the total 55 aircraft built from 1955 through 1958. By the time Gary Powers was shot down over Sverdlovsk in May 1960, thus putting an end to the Soviet overflights, the aircraft's versatility could not be denied.

While the world's media and some in the US government wrote off the U-2, operations were quietly resumed by both the CIA and the USAF. The aircraft's possibly finest hour came two years later, when U-2 photography confirmed US intelligence about a Soviet military build-up on Cuba, and later revealed offensive ballistic missiles pointing at the US.

By 1963, CIA U-2s had been flying over mainland China for a year in a joint project with the Nationalist government on Taiwan. Using aircraft modified with an inflight-refuelling capability, Strategic Air Command was flying Elint missions along the eastern and northern borders of the USSR, probing the defences that its bomber fleet might meet. As both superpowers continued nuclear tests in the atmosphere, SAC was also running sampling flights for weapons diagnostics. Other U-2s were proving valuable as high-altitude testbeds for a variety of sensors destined for satellites.

In March 1963, Kelly Johnson noted in his diary that the U-2 was "in great use all around the world. We haven't got nearly enough of them." Twenty-one out of the original 55 had been lost by then, mostly to accidents, and he suggested building a new batch of 25 aircraft that would cost around $1 million each. However, the USAF was by then sponsoring the RB-57F, a bizarrely-modified B-57 which could theoretically haul a much greater payload to altitude than the U-2. It first flew in May 1963. Meanwhile, in great secrecy, the CIA was funding development of a Mach 3 successor to Kelly's 'Angel', known as the Oxcart programme. After three years of studies this had been given the go-ahead in February 1960 but the huge technical hurdles had been mounted only slowly. A first flight was made in April 1962, and the aircraft was slowly proving itself in flight tests from Groom Lake.

A larger 'Angel'

Kelly Johnson persisted. He well understood the continuing requirement for 'a good 75,000-ft airplane', despite the ongoing A-12 development. The original U-2 models were no longer capable of such altitude, having been weighed down by heavier payloads, ECM and more sophisticated navigation systems. Johnson did not think the RB-57F was a viable solution. He began drawing enlarged versions of the U-2, initially with two 30-in (76-cm) fuselage plugs. The project was given a boost by a new requirement from the intelligence community to evaluate Soviet satellites in orbit. Johnson proposed installing a 240-in (610-cm) focal length, upward-looking sensor in the space created by the fuselage extension. In September 1963, he formally proposed building 25 U-2L models for $1.1 million each.

In order to launch photo-reconnaissance missions against far-flung targets of interest without using foreign bases, with all the attendant political problems, the CIA had contracted Lockheed to modify some early-model U-2Cs to land and take off from aircraft-carriers. So, Johnson's new proposal was evaluated by the CIA, the USAF and the US Navy, which had by now become involved in the CIA's U-2 operations.

Rejected proposal

The days when a Skunk Works proposal would be approved and funded by a small circle of CIA and White House initiates were over. The Air Force was committed to the RB-57F; it was yet to learn that the General Dynamics project would be delayed by two years, cost much more than originally anticipated, become a maintenance nightmare, and – worst of all – never make it above 65,000 ft (19810 m). The U-2L idea was evaluated over a protracted period by the burgeoning defence intelligence bureaucracy, and eventually suffocated.

Throughout 1964 and into 1965, U-2s continued flying over China, Cuba and elsewhere. The USAF wing deployed aircraft to Vietnam for photo missions 'up north'. By May 1965, another nine U-2s had been lost, six in accidents and three to SA-2 missiles over China. Despite the ever-more sophisticated ECM packages, the U-2 was still vulnerable to these SAMs, which had just been identified around Hanoi and Haiphong as well.

Unfortunately for the USAF, a variety of technical and political problems still prevented the A-12 from being deployed, and suddenly its interest in an improved U-2 increased. Altitude was a key concern, so Kelly Johnson gathered a design team under Merv Heal to work on a new wing. The team studied swept wings, supercritical wings and higher aspect ratios, all of which proved unpromising. They investigated recent NASA studies into high-lift wings, including a new flap designed to increase the critical Mach number. After wind tunnel tests at Burbank, Johnson rejected the NASA wing, which added extra weight and did nothing for drag.

Advanced engine

At that point, Pratt & Whitney provided new direction to the project. The engine-maker had produced a new version of the J75-P-13 turbojet which increased sea-level thrust from 15,800 to 18,500 lb (70.29 to 82.30 kN). The J75-P-13A had replaced the original J57 in the CIA's U-2 fleet in 1959, in an attempt to obtain higher altitude. This "turned the aircraft from a Cadillac into a Porsche," according to one pilot, and the resulting U-2C model was never short of power.

Top: The prototype U-2R flies with gear down during an early test flight. Compared to the earlier U-2 design, the R model offered much greater range and load-carrying capability, even though it retained the same powerplant. The prototype was fitted with an air data probe with sensitive directional vanes.

Above: Bill Park (left) flew the U-2R on its first flight, and is seen here with the programme manager Ed Baldwin (centre) and Dick Boehme, who was Kelly Johnson's assistant.

Left: Another view shows N803X during flight tests. Fluttering of the tailplanes later required the addition of external stiffeners.

Five early U-2Rs, including the unpainted prototype, are seen at Edwards North Base. This facility was the main base for the CIA U-2R operations.

Providing a good illustration of the considerable differences between the two generations of U-2, this CIA U-2R shares the North Base ramp with a U-2C. The canopy sunshade was painted white to avoid heat build-up in the cockpit but was later changed to black.

The USAF, which was still flying J57-powered U-2As, immediately ordered some higher-thrust -13Bs to re-engine its dwindling fleet. Johnson realised that this latest power increase could be the key to a better U-2, and in October 1965 he instructed Skunk Works engineer Merv Heal to start a new study on the U-2, retaining the basic principles of the original design but scaling up to take advantage of the increased power. Bob Weile led the wing redesign. Retaining the same cross-section and taper, wingspan was increased by 23 ft (7.01 m) to 103 ft (31.40 m), and overall wing area by 400 sq ft (37.16 m^2) to 1,000 sq ft (92.9 m^2). As a result, the wing loading was reduced to original U-2A

values, and the lift/drag ratio returned to 25:1. Lift coefficient was 0.6 to 0.7, and the aspect ratio 10.667.

After various studies, the empennage-design group led by Herb Nystrom opted for the all-moving tailplane which had first been employed on the Lockheed Jetstar. The so-called Kelly Johnson tail effectively distributed the pitch forces to the entire horizontal tail, and the whole slab trimmed. The design helped widen the aircraft's centre of gravity limits and eliminated the need for ballast. Ed Baldwin led a complete redesign of the fuselage, which was wider and 25 per cent longer than the earlier aircraft. Systems which once had been 'bolted-on' to the exterior U-2C as an afterthought – such as engine oil cooler, HF radio and ECM System 9 – were now accommodated within its confines. Other systems variously added to specific U-2Cs – such as ILS, TACAN and Doppler – were now included as a standard fit. There were new avionics for flight reference and flight direction. Another bonus was the longer tailpipe, which helped mask the engine's infra-red signature.

The 45 per cent increase in cockpit area allowed pilots to wear the bulkier (but much more comfortable) full pressure suit, and it was now possible to install a 'proper' zero-zero ejection seat. The characteristic driftsight was retained, but not the sextant which had provided an alternative means of navigation in the early days.

The resulting U-2R (R for Revised or Reconnaissance) was a sensor platform of superb utility. The U-2R was about one-third bigger than the original model, but some of the performance numbers increased dramatically. Ferry range was more than 7,000 nm (8,050 miles; 12950 km), 2,500 nm (2,875 miles; 4625 km) better than the U-2C and fully twice that of the RB-57F. The total fuel capacity was 2,915 US gal (11035 litres), or nearly 19,000 lb (8620 kg) – enough to keep airborne for 15 hours, which was probably beyond the pilot's endurance. Maximum altitude, achieved at the end of the cruise climb, returned to 75,000 ft (22860 m). Payload was effectively quadrupled.

Sensor carriage

In the original U-2 models, cameras, Sigint and sampling packages could be interchangeably uploaded to the Q-bay behind the cockpit, an area spanning the entire width and height of the fuselage. That modular concept was retained, and also applied to the nose of the redesigned aircraft. Payload specialist Bob Anderson kept the aircraft's equipment segregated from its payload, in the area immediately forward of the front pressure bulkhead, and in a large E-bay aft of the Q-bay. A higher-capacity AC/DC electrical system was specified to accommodate increasing sensor power requirements. At the design stage, provision had been made for more payload to be carried in pods attached

The first batch of U-2Rs (FY68) numbered 12 aircraft. Six of these went to the Agency, the remainder going to the Air Force, primarily for operations in Southeast Asia. CIA aircraft like this one often flew with USAF markings.

Far left: Like its predecessor, the U-2R could be rapidly dismantled for carriage in transport aircraft. Here a shrouded U-2R is loaded on to a C-141 StarLifter.

Left: Construction is modular, the main sub-assembly being the central fuselage. The tail section, wings and nosecone are all built separately.

Above: The US Navy was interested in the U-2R from an early stage, its long endurance being of interest for patrol work.

Right: Following the success of operating the first generation of U-2s from carrier decks, it was decided that the U-2R should also be tested onboard ship. This CIA aircraft, serialled N810X, flew the proving flights from USS America *in 1969.*

to the wings. Although these were not initially used, the provision later proved invaluable.

In January 1966, Johnson presented the U-2R study to Dr Bud Wheelon, the CIA's Deputy Director for Science and Technology. To get the programme started, Johnson offered to build the first two examples for $12.5 million. Within days, the government responded with a request for costs and schedules on 25 aircraft. It was another three months before Washington started funding the project, and then only for continuing studies. However, Johnson brought in more engineers, and put Ed Baldwin in charge of the overall project.

Production authorisation

A go-ahead to produce eight U-2Rs finally came in September, and Johnson and his assistant Dick Boehme authorised tooling, expecting a substantial follow-on order. They were to be disappointed. Another four were ordered four months later, but the Pentagon had other priorities and did not pursue its original plan to order 25 aircraft. The 12 U-2Rs that were built were shared equally between the CIA and the USAF. The Skunk Works had two customers from the outset, unlike first time round, which created a number of management problems.

Sensing the lack of customer urgency, Johnson gave his team a full year to get the new aircraft airborne. "I expected nine months at maximum," said Baldwin. Johnson wanted higher-quality tooling than on the earlier models. There was also a static test article. The mock-up review was held in late November 1966. The Air Force wanted maximum cockpit commonality with its U-2Cs, so the old-fashioned round dials were retained. Bill Park, the Skunk Works test pilot who would make the first flight, preferred the contemporary strip instruments which were going into the 'Blackbird'. Park got his way for the prototype – only.

Above: Deck crew check over the U-2R by America's *island prior to take-off. Lift-off presented no problems.*

Right: Bill Park takes the wire in N810X. A simple arrester hook with an aerodynamic fairing was scabbed on to the U-2R forward of the tailwheel. Other carrier modifications included sprung-steel wingtip skids and a framework guard on the port tailwheel door to stop the wheel snagging the wire.

This is one of two aircraft used for the Navy's U-2 EPX (Extended Patrol Experimental) project. This aircraft featured a shortened nose housing search radar, and sensor-equipped wing pods. Ice regularly forms under the wings during the descent to warmer lower altitudes from a long mission.

A few problems emerged during development, including a slow rate of roll. That was solved by adding a second pair of hydraulically-actuated spoilers outboard on the wing. An inboard pair dumped lift during descent and landing, and the larger control surfaces and higher critical Mach number made the U-2R somewhat easier to control and land than the earlier models. Final assembly of the U-2R was accomplished in Building 309/310 at Burbank, with the aircraft trucked to the remote North Base at Edwards for its first flight. Bill Park took up Article 051 for the first time on 28 August 1967, in front of a crowd from CIA headquarters and the Pentagon.

Flight test

Flight testing proceeded smoothly. The bigger wing flexed as much as 4 ft (1.2 m) up or down at the tip and, for novice pilots, the aircraft was a handful to fly. The unboosted controls, worked by cables, push rods and bell cranks from a huge yoke in the cockpit, were unchanged. So was the U-2's most distinctive external feature: the bicycle landing gear and drop-out pogos. Above 60,000 ft (18290 m), the aircraft demonstrated weak static stability in all axes, requiring stability augmentation from a reliable autopilot. There was no doubt that pilots for the new U-2 would still have to be selected and trained with care.

By February 1968, the second U-2R was at North Base, which was also the location of the CIA U-2 unit. It was called Detachment G by the Agency, although for cover purposes the operation was designated the 1130th ATTG by the Air Force. Here, training of both CIA and USAF pilots soon commenced.

By December 1968 all 12 aircraft had been delivered, split equally between CIA and USAF. The military codenamed its new aircraft Senior Year, and this nomenclature survives as the overall U-2 programme name. Pilots and ground crew preferred to call it the 'Deuce' or the 'Dragon Lady'.

Carrier trials

One remaining flight test task which was not tackled until 1969 was the U-2R's carrier qualification. The new aircraft had been designed with a hinge so that the outer 6 ft (1.8 m) of wing folded back, enabling it to be moved to and from the hanger deck on the Navy's carriers. An unobtrusive arrester hook could be added forward of the tail gear, with cable deflectors attached to the tailgear doors and wingtip skids. Bill Park practised carrier landings on the lakebed at North Base before taking the navy's carrier qualification course at Pensacola. In November 1969 Park and four CIA pilots deployed to the NASA base at Wallops Island. USS *America* was waiting off the coast, but Park's first flight had to be aborted when he discovered that no-one had removed the locking pin for the tail hook.

***Far left:* CIA U-2Rs were flown from Taoyuan AB in Taiwan, in Taiwanese markings and with RoCAF pilots.**

***Left:* Among the many proposals for the U-2R was this aircraft, known as the Lockheed 351B. It was a two-seat derivative carrying missiles (presumably for anti-ship work) under the wings.**

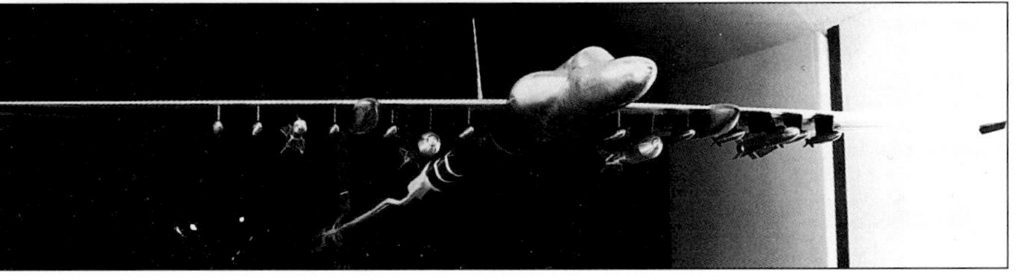

***Below:* A model of an armed U-2R is tested in a wind tunnel. The model has 14 hardpoints carrying a variety of bombs and missiles. None of the armed proposals was taken up, but decoys were launched from one aircraft during tests.**

***Right:** The* ***U-2R** served well in Southeast Asia, flying mainly from U-Tapao in Thailand. The operating unit was initially* ***OL-RU**, redesignated as the 99th SRS. The U-2s remained in-theatre until returning to the 100th* ***SRW**'s* ***HQ** base at Davis-Monthan in March 1976.*

***Below:** In addition to its* ***U-2R** squadron, the 100th* ***SRW** was also responsible for the reconnaissance drone operation (350th* ***SRS**). Occasionally, the two systems worked together. Here a* ***U-2R** formates on a* ***DC-130E** which is carrying an* ***AQM-34M(L)** drone.*

That mishap solved, everything else went according to Park's plan, which was to approach the deck at 72 kt (83 mph; 133 km/h) using a 45° flap setting. With a wind over the deck of 20 kt (23 mph; 37 km/h), and the spoilers deployed, the aircraft trapped easily. Take-offs were no problem either. With the help of a naval LSO assigned to the unit, CIA pilots remained carrier-qualified for the next few years. The U-2R carrier capability was never used operationally, although it was seriously considered on one occasion. The main reason for its non-use was the disruption that U-2 operations would cause to the carrier air wing. Nevertheless, the Navy was still interested in the U-2, as an ocean surveillance aircraft operating from land bases to extend a battle group's radar horizon. The threat to the fleet from long-range cruise missiles had increased, and the new aircraft's long endurance offered the prospect of round-the-clock cover.

EPX programme

Flight tests were conducted from Edwards from February 1973, using two CIA aircraft modified for the Electronics Patrol Experimental (EPX) programme. A heavily-modified RCA X-band weather radar was mounted in a new nose section, with an RCA return beam vidicon camera and a UTL Elint receiver carried in left and right wing pods respectively. The 'take' from these sensors was downloaded via a datalink in the E-bay to the navy's surface vessels.

In the aftermath of the Yom Kippur War, USAF U-2Rs were deployed to RAF Akrotiri on Cyprus to maintain a watch on the Arab and Israeli forces along the Suez Canal. This aircraft is configured for a photo mission and is fitted with a thermal blanket, colloquially known as a 'diaper'. Reconnaissance cameras were extremely sensitive to temperature change, and the blanket kept the Q-bay as cool as possible in the Mediterranean sun.

For navigation accuracy across large stretches of water, the Northrop NAS-21 astro-inertial system – similar to that carried by the SR-71 – was used (the NAS-21 became standard on the U-2R until more accurate INS, and eventually GPS systems, were developed).

The trials continued in 1975 with the more powerful Texas Instruments APS-116 radar, a purpose-built sea surveillance sensor which was developed for the S-3A Viking ASW aircraft, now rolling off the Burbank production lines. To get 360° coverage, the Skunk Works developed an air-pressure stabilised radome made from three layers of Kevlar. The radar was mounted in the Q-bay, with its antenna protruding below into this 'inflatable' radome. For access, Skunk Works engineers used a zipper taken from a U-2 pilot's partial pressure suit.

However, the advent of satellite systems that promised to provide constant, wide-ocean surveillance to the Navy's satisfaction meant that the U-2 EPX lost its appeal. Lockheed tried to keep maintain the Navy's interest by proposing the integration of Rockwell Condor AShMs, carried on mid-wing launch rails, but to no avail. The inflatable radome found a further use when the U-2R was selected as trials aircraft for the new Senior Lance side-looking reconnaissance radars.

A number of other exotic developments were also explored in the early 1970s. Briefings on other 'attack' versions of the U-2R were given to US and British officials. A scheme to launch two Beechcraft liquid-fuelled drones from the wing stations, as SAM missile decoys, reached the flight test stage. They were carried flush to the wing, and were extended on a trapeze for firing.

Camera systems

The truth was, the U-2 was best employed as a surveillance platform. A variety of camera systems were available. The original and revolutionary B-camera which had been developed for the Soviet overflights had been improved with new optics and lighter construction by the Hycon company. Redesignated HR-73B, it was still in use on the early U-2 models. The panoramic camera systems developed for the Corona satellites by Itek had been adapted for airborne use as the Intelligence Reconnaissance Imaging System (IRIS). Used on the SR-71 and later on the U-2R, these 24- and 30-in (61- and 76-cm) focal length cameras employed a folded optical path mounted on an Optical Bar Assembly (OBC). They scanned through 140° and provided good resolution across a 32-nm (37-mile; 60-km) wide swath below the aircraft. The most useful potential imaging sensor for the U-2R was the Type H, a 66-in (168-cm) folding focal length device developed by Hycon from the Type IV high-resolution camera used on the A-12. This was a LOng-Range Oblique Photographic

(LOROP) sensor which could image terrain many miles to the side of the aircraft's flight path. It was gyro-stabilised during the exposure, and employed temperature, pressure and image motion compensation. It was first introduced on the U-2C in 1965-66.

Operational deployment

As soon as the R model was finished flight testing, the CIA deployed two aircraft to Det H, the joint operation with the Republic of China air force (RoCAF). By then, overflights of mainland China had terminated, after the loss of a fifth U-2C to SAM missiles in September 1967. Using the H-camera from U-2 cruising altitudes, the 'Black Cat' squadron could fly along the mainland coast in international airspace, producing images of Chinese ports and coastal airfields, from where any preparations for aggressive moves against Taiwan would be mounted. Pilots could select photo targets ahead of the aircraft by 'eyeballing' them through the driftsight and storing them in the camera's memory.

When all worked well, the H brought back stunning imagery, actually much better than its predecessor on the A-12, partly thanks to the slower film transport past the lens required by the much slower U-2. The H was a temperamental beast, though, and had to be maintained at a constant temperature; Lockheed had to develop new air conditioners to hook up to the Q-bay during pre-flight preparation.

***Above:** Relieved of its duties in Southeast Asia, and bolstered by the influx of ex-CIA aircraft, the USAF U-2R fleet turned its main attention to the Cold War. Det 4 at RAF Mildenhall in England became the centre for European operations from 1976.*

***Above left:** There have been many reports of U-2Rs changing tail numbers, mainly sparked by obvious differences in paint style between the last two digits of the serial and the first three. However, changes usually occur because the rear fuselages are interchangeable between airframes. There have been a few real incidences of spurious markings, the best-known being this aircraft which returned to Mildenhall from Akrotiri with the serial '10345'. The official serial block ran from 68-10329 to 68-10340.*

The U-2Rs operating in Europe in the late 1970s were usually configured for signals intelligence gathering. This antenna suite, with a row of blades along the spine and a single paddle blade antenna under each wing, was believed to be called Senior Book.

68-10339 was used for a variety of equipment trials during the 1970s, one of the most visually striking being those concerned with the Senior Lance radar. This synthetic aperture radar was housed in an inflatable Kevlar radome under the Q-bay.

Right: Air sampling missions had figured prominently in the operations of the first generation of U-2s, and the capability was retained for the U-2R. The particulate sampler was an open-ended tube with internal filters. It was mounted on the Q-bay hatch.

The first loss of a U-2R occurred at Det H in November. A Chinese pilot lost control after applying power during a crosswind landing at Taoyuan. The aircraft rose steeply, then rolled left and crashed at the side of the runway. The 'Black Cat' squadron continued flying missions along the Chinese coast until August 1974, when the unit was closed after Sino-US relations improved.

In the meantime, the main excitement for the CIA's American and British pilots had been the ongoing conflict between Israel and its neighbours in the Middle East. The USSR supplied a complete air defence system to Egypt in spring 1970, and Israel's dominance of the skies over the Suez Canal was challenged. Tensioned increased through the summer, culminating in a large dogfight on 30 July. The United Nations brokered a ceasefire, and Det G was tasked to fly monitoring flights along the Canal, photographing the 64-mile (103-km) strip of territory bordering both sides of the Canal, within which Egypt and Israel had promised not to make any further deployments.

The UK agreed to provide basing facilities at Akrotiri, and two aircraft arrived there in early August via RAF Upper Heyford. Flights were mounted every few days for the next three months, with the 'take' processed at Akrotiri and then scanned for datalinking to the US by satellite. Neither party to the conflict had formally agreed the flights, and the U-2's defensive systems were frequently activated as Egyptian SA-2 and SA-3 missiles, and even Israeli fighters, threatened to shoot down the aircraft.

Long-range flights

The flights were halted on 10 November, and the U-2s were flown home a month later, again via Upper Heyford. This deployment certainly demonstrated the very long range of the U-2R. The first Canal overflight was actually performed from Upper Heyford, routing all the way around France and through the Mediterranean, with a recovery into Akrotiri (both France and Italy refused to allow the U-2 through their airspace). On one of the westbound ferry flights from the UK back to Edwards, a British pilot tested pushed the endurance to its extreme by arriving over the base and orbiting until fuel finally ran low. His total flight time was 14.5 hours.

In October 1973 fighting flared up again between Israel and Egypt in what became known as the Yom Kippur War. Det G deployed a U-2R to Upper Heyford and prepared to fly a mission down the west coast of France

Even before the Powers shootdown the gathering of signals intelligence (Sigint) was becoming an important part of the U-2's repertoire, and with the U-2R this role grew in importance. This aircraft is carrying the Senior Spear communications intelligence (Comint) suite, characterised by large farms of aerials. Senior Spear has received several updates, resulting in changing antenna configurations.

In 1978 the USAF announced that the U-2R line would be restarted to produce a variant known as the TR-1A (left), the primary role being radar surveillance of the central European theatre. The first aircraft from the line went to NASA, first flying on 11 May 1981. Shortly afterwards, on 15 July, the first production TR-1A (80-1066, below left) was rolled out at Palmdale, undertaking its first flight on 1 August.

(which again had denied overflight rights) and into the Mediterranean, with a recovery at Akrotiri. At the same time, the USAF prepared to deploy an SR-71 to RAF Mildenhall, but the British government refused to allow the flights. The U-2R went home, and SR-71s flew round-robin missions out of Griffiss AFB, NY instead, with the aid of multiple inflight refuellings.

In April 1974 the United Nations arranged for permanent monitoring of the latest stand-off between Israel and Egypt, with the full agreement of both parties. Once again, Det H headed for the Middle East, this time with British permission to fly out of Akrotiri. Later, airborne reconnaissance of the Sinai and (from 1982) the Golan Heights was formalised in the Camp David peace agreements, with the 'take' from the U-2's cameras being shared between all parties. The Akrotiri detachment was codenamed Olive Harvest, and when the CIA U-2R unit was quietly closed down at the end of 1974, it was taken over by the USAF's 100th Strategic Reconnaissance Wing (SRW).

Cuban watch and Southeast Asia

When it first received the U-2R in late 1968, the 100th SRW was responsible for continuing photo-reconnaissance of Cuba, and a single U-2R was deployed to OL-19 at Barksdale AFB for the Cuba mission. In late August 1970, OL-19 provided imagery of new construction at the port of Cienfugos, which led to the political furore over whether the Soviet Union was about to deploy offensive missile-carrying submarines from a Cuban base. Washington ordered daily flights from mid-September, and, for the first time since 1962, the U-2s were challenged by Cuban MiGs. Despite Cuban belligerence, the USSR eventually backed down.

In 1969, the 100th SRW also deployed the U-2R to OL-20 at Bien Hoa AB, South Vietnam. Because of the SAM threat, much of the photo mission 'up north' had been assumed by the SR-71 and OL-20's own Ryan-built reconnaissance drones. The U-2 was still flying photo, Elint and communications relay sorties in more permissive environments; the SA-2 was only deemed lethal within a 30-mile (48-km) radius of its launch pad. Careful mission planning was obviously essential.

In July 1970, OL-20 moved to U-Tapao air base in Thailand, by which time a new mission beckoned for the U-2R. Lockheed was asked to integrate a Melpar Comint sensor and datalink carried by one of the latest drone variants onto the 'Dragon Lady' (the USAF's nickname for the U-2). Using typical Skunk Works ingenuity, the company improved upon the drone set-up with better antennas and a new datalink from the Sperry company. The Senior Book programme was born, and Sigint soon became

The new designation TR-1 was adopted for various reasons, but usefully distanced the aircraft from the notoriety of the U-2 for its deployment to England. In fact there were few differences between the two aircraft, and subsequently all were restyled U-2R. This is the second production TR-1A, fitted with an optical Q-bay hatch.

Three TR-1A/U-2Rs pose on the Beale ramp, with the SR-71 barns and a TR-1B in the background. The central aircraft is configured with the PLSS (Precision Location Strike System). Intended for service in Europe, PLSS employed three TR-1As flying along the battlefront, each linked to a central ground station. Hostile radars were detected by the system, and the central station could rapidly compute the precise location of the radar by using triangulation based on the data from the three aircraft. This in turn would allow the location to be transmitted to strike aircraft so that they could attack the radar. The system was very complex and expensive, and was terminated in favour of cheaper methods.

the main activity for OL-20. From racetrack orbits high above the Gulf of Tonkin (GOT), the U-2 eavesdropped on Vietnamese national and air defence communications, transmitting the data in real time to a ground station at Nakhon Phanom on the Thai border. At the same time, it provided communications relay for US aircraft, and was even tasked to 'eyeball' the SAMs fired at US bombers during the Linebacker offensive in 1972.

The GOT missions were flown mostly at night, and lasted from 10 to 12 hours. They were a test of endurance for the pilots, and also for ground crews during those periods when the operations tempo increased and round-the-clock coverage was required. In January 1973 the U-2 operation at U-Tapao (by now redesignated the 99th SRS) clocked 500 hours, a first for the 'Dragon Lady' programme, and this was topped in December 1994 with a 600-hour month.

Extended Sigint coverage

The U-2's Sigint systems were continuously improved over the next few years. Coverage was extended from HF and VHF to the UHF bands; pre-set receivers that could only monitor a few frequencies gave way to scanning receivers that could be controlled by uplink from specialists sitting in the ground station. Antennas and receivers multiplied; in the Senior Spear system, some of them migrated from the fuselage to specially-adapted pods faired into the U-2's wing. Timely analysis of the downlinked data was also addressed in the Senior Stretch programme, which relayed Sigint data collected by the U-2 from the ground station up to satellites, and thence to the National Security Agency (NSA) in Maryland.

As the US finally withdrew from Southeast Asia, the focus of U-2 operations shifted, although the 'Dragon Lady' was finally withdrawn from Thailand only in April 1976. Three months earlier, the 100th SRW deployed U-2s to Osan air base, South Korea, where it had previously been operating the Comint drones. Despite their great contributions to intelligence gathering during the Vietnam War, drones fell out of favour as the US defence budget contracted. A virtual death sentence was passed on them when the USAF transferred their control from Strategic Air Command (SAC) to Tactical Air Command (TAC). The 100th SRW was left with only half a mission, and SAC's U-2 operation was therefore consolidated with that of the SR-71 at Beale AFB in July 1976.

NATO deployments

One month later, SAC made its first U-2R deployment to NATO, when 68-10336 arrived at RAF Mildenhall and flew during alliance exercises for the next four weeks. A longer deployment was made the following summer, and in 1978 the first aircraft to be equipped with the new E-Systems Senior Ruby Elint collection system (68-10339) was flown from Mildenhall for two months. The Ruby spiral antennas were carried at the front of new 'superpods', attached to the wing station at the same station as the Spear pods developed earlier, but they were three times larger. (Although the new pods were test-flown from Palmdale in 1975-76, it was only in the mid-1980s that the USAF ordered a full exploration of how these 24-ft/7.3-m long pods changed the flutter characteristics of the aircraft).

Western political and military leaders were worried about a growing disparity between the size of Soviet and NATO conventional forces in Europe. The Warsaw Pact now had the capability to mount an armoured Blitzkrieg, and might be able to advance several hundred miles in a surprise attack. To counter such an offensive, NATO needed to concentrate its statistically inferior fire power where it most mattered, and destroy WarPac forces as they were massing for attack. That would require effective and timely surveillance far beyond the East-West border, with the results sent quickly to the Army divisions and Air Force wings which would make the pre-emptive strikes. Spy camera satellites they could not see through cloud and were controlled by the super-secret National Reconnaissance Office (NRO) in Washington. The Sigint satellites sent all their 'take' to the NSA, which was also equally compartmented in the black world and not responsive to the needs of tactical commanders. The SR-71, now flying with production ASARS-1 radars as well as photo sensors, was a scarce and high-cost asset which was also controlled from higher headquarters.

PLSS

In Southeast Asia, the drones and the U-2 had demonstrated what might be achieved by high-altitude, long-endurance platforms equipped with real-time datalinks. Senior Lance had generated new confidence in the utility of side-looking radar for reconnaissance purposes. A development programme to identify air defence radar and communications sites for attack, by homing in on their emissions, was also underway. This was called the Precision Location Strike System (PLSS), and would also require high-flying platforms.

Although the drones had proved invaluable recce platforms in high-threat environments, the USAF hierarchy had lost faith in them. In the final analysis, it was now said, RPVs had been plagued by reliability and recovery problems. In an attempt to overcome these, the Compass Cope development programme had been funded, in which Boeing and Ryan produced all-new vehicles using the latest

In the 1970s the U-2R programme attracted competition from high-altitude long-endurance drones, principally from the USAF's Compass Cope programme. Two vehicles were produced, the Boeing YQM-94A (above) and the Teledyne Ryan YQM-98A (right). Proposals for an unmanned U-2R were also put forward.

Below: A U-2 floats across the Beale threshold during a training mission. For these sorties the aircraft usually fly without superpods, but with the defensive sub-systems in place. Antennas for them are located in the wingtip pods, in the fairing on the starboard wing trailing edge, and in the fin-tip. The rear-facing antenna at the top of the fin altered the fin profile, and is surmounted by the fuselage sump tank vent pipe.

Above: The PLSS birds featured an extended nose with slab sides for the emitter locator. The superpods featured slab sides, also for Elint antennas, while large fairings underneath housed DME (Distance Measuring Equipment).

composite materials, digital flight controls and powerplants. These RPVs were capable of reaching 70,000 ft (21335 m) and orbiting for 24 hours at a stretch. They also took off and landed conventionally, under their own power.

At Burbank, Kelly Johnson had retired from the Skunk Works in 1975 and his deputy Ben Rich had taken over. Rich began lobbying in Washington for a U-2 re-order. With the loss of a second U-2R in 1975, the fleet was already down to 10 examples. Against this background, in September 1977 the Pentagon tasked a group of USAF and US Army staff officers to urgently re-examine the services' reconnaissance resources, present and future. Headed by General Alton Slay, deputy chief of staff for R&D, they concluded that the U-2 was the best platform for PLSS and another side-looking reconnaissance radar now being developed by Hughes. They strongly recommended that control and tasking of the aircraft be vested in theatre commanders. In the past, they noted, the U-2 had been controlled by the SAC Reconnaissance Center in Omaha.

The study group's report was quickly approved by the Army and Air Force chiefs of staff. Compass Cope was cancelled, and the FY 1979 Defense Budget was altered just before publication in early 1978, to provide funds for a restart of the U-2 production line. To emphasise a break with the past, General Slay recommended that the aircraft be renamed TR-1 – for Tactical Reconnaissance. The chairman of the JCS, General David Jones, concurred. "We've got to get this spyplane label off the aircraft", he declared. As Ben Rich later noted wryly, "the Press simply called it the TR-1 spyplane instead."

TR-1 production

The FY 1979 budget signalled the intention to purchase at least 25 TR-1s, at a cost of about $550 million, including sensors and ground support equipment. Hughes Radar Systems Group in El Segundo, next to Los Angeles airport, gained further funding for ASARS-2. This much was out in the open, although the actual capabilities of ASARS-2 would be highly classified for many years. The intention to order another 10 aircraft with 'black budget' money went unreported. They would retain the U-2R designation and be used to augment the 9th SRW's small fleet engaged in Sigint and photo-reconnaissance duties in Korea, Cyprus and elsewhere.

The Skunk Works dusted off the old U-2R tooling and set up the production line again, this time at Palmdale. Under the direction of programme manager Fred Cavanaugh, some U-2 veterans were brought out of retirement to help the effort. Their experience was sorely needed; southern California's aerospace industry was booming, and Lockheed had to hire a number of unskilled workers to augment the workforce.

Only minor changes were made to the airframe. The engine was the same P&W J75, salvaged from retired F-105 and F-106 fighters and returned to P&W for overhaul and conversion into the -P-13B high-altitude version. That saved money, but the USAF procurement bureaucracy threatened to add cost. The 'old' U-2 – even the U-2R – had been procured under fast-track procedures, which accorded with the Kelly Johnson way of doing things. A new generation of Pentagon officials wanted to know why this 'new' TR-1 aircraft was not being built to MILSPECS.

The first TR-1A, 80-1066, was rolled out at Site 7 of the sprawling Palmdale airfield on 15 July 1981. This was a public occasion, unlike 1967 and 1955. The onlookers, ranging from Pentagon brass to the local Press, saw a smart black aircraft complete with the superpods. The only visible differences from the earlier U-2R were the slightly altered wingtip profile (for a new radar warning sensor) and a 'clean' horizontal tail (following some sonic vibration

The PLSS programme was developed from the ALSS trials undertaken by U-2Cs in the mid-1970s operating from RAF Wethersfield. If it had entered full-scale service, PLSS would have been a mission for the 17th RW at RAF Alconbury. That unit originally was to have been assigned an 18-aircraft fleet to provide continuous PLSS coverage in addition to its other theatre reconnaissance tasks.

A rare sight: NASA's three ER-2s cruise over the Golden Gate Bridge from their home base at Moffett, the aircraft in the foreground resplendent in the Administration's new house colours. The loaned aircraft (80-1069/NASA 708) may shortly to be returned to the USAF.

Right: The ER-2 has most of the U-2R's military systems removed. Like the Air Force aircraft, the NASA ER-2s are being re-engined with the General Electric F118 engine.

problems which threatened to cause fatigue stress, the U-2R stabilisers had been modified with stiffeners which protruded on the external surface as small ribs).

First flight

This first TR-1 had actually been preceded down the line and into the air three months earlier by a version for NASA designated ER-2 (of which, more later). Lockheed test pilot Ken Weir made the first TR-1 flight on 1 August 1981. There was no significant flight-test programme to accomplish, of course, so 80-1066 was in the customer's hands at Beale AFB by the end of the following month. By that time, the ASARS-2 radar was flying, on U-2R development aircraft 68-10336. A new, extended nose had been designed to house the long antenna, transmitter and receiver/exciter. The remaining black boxes for the radar were housed in the Q-bay, while the datalink stayed in the same place as the Sigint-equipped aircraft: in a pressurised cavity aft of the tail gear. Fibre-optic cables linked the various components. Early flight tests results confirmed the radar's promise. "It provides pictures of near-photo quality at remarkable stand-off ranges," declared General Thomas McMullen. "The combined increase in range, resolution and area coverage represents a quantum jump over currently operational systems."

Problems with PLSS

Unfortunately, the same good progress was not being made with PLSS, the other sensor intended for the TR-1. The complicated and expensive effort to produce an alternative to the Wild Weasels for SAM suppression had begun in 1972 with the Advanced Location and Strike System (ALSS). By orbiting a trio (or 'triad') of aircraft at high altitude, equipped with Elint sensors which were datalinked to a ground station, the accurate positions of threat emitters could be quickly calculated by triangulation. This overcame the problem of 'traditional' airborne Elint, where the emitter was required to stay on air long enough for the aircraft to move along track, so that the direction-finding process could be completed. The North Vietnamese had failed to co-operate in this endeavour, by quickly shutting down their transmitters. This also foiled the missiles launched at them by Wild Weasel aircraft, which homed on their radiated signals.

The ALSS ground station could not only fix a SAM site's position as soon as it came on air, it could also relay the co-ordinates to attacking aircraft, via the orbiting triad. To flight-test the new system, all seven remaining USAF U-2C aircraft had been equipped with ALSS antennas and datalinks in 1972. Development problems ensued, and it was not until 1975 that an operational test was conducted in Europe, with five U-2Cs deployed to RAF Wethersfield, UK. The results were unsatisfactory; datalinks failed, receivers and transmitters went offline, connectors failed to connect.

Undaunted, the USAF redefined and expanded the effort to a greater range of frequencies and signal types. The new PLSS contract was awarded in 1977 to Lockheed Missiles and Space Company (LMSC) as the main contractor. By the time that the TR-1 was flying, PLSS was supposed to be ready for flight test, but the first PLSS-equipped aircraft (80-1074) actually got airborne in December 1983.

Yet another nose was designed to house the E-Systems Elint antennas and receivers, while the superpods housed DME equipment. Another 18 months passed before the 9th SRW was finally able to launch a PLSS triad for weekly test missions over the China Lake weapons range. By this time, however, the Air Force top brass had lost patience, and the Wild Weasel community was openly hostile. PLSS lingered on as the Signal Location and Targeting System (SLATS) and was still being tested in a two-aircraft (dual) configuration in late 1987. There were other ways to accomplish the mission, and SLATS never did make it to Europe in 1988 as planned.

NASA's special

As noted earlier, TR-1 production was preceded by a single ER-2 version for the High-Altitude Missions Branch at NASA Ames Research Center, Moffett Field, California. NASA had been flying two U-2C models since July 1971 as Earth Resources Survey Aircraft. During that time, they had ranged across the US, using a variety of imaging systems to aid studies of the earth's surface. Some flights were tests of the sensors scheduled to be orbited on NASA's new, dedicated remote-sensing satellites (which were later named Landsat). The aircraft had proved themselves to be more than mere satellite surrogates, carrying a variety of sensors to 60,000 ft (18290 m) or higher to measure gases and particles in the atmosphere. Having started with a range of declassified imaging sensors from the CIA and USAF U-2 programmes, they were now carrying sensors which were custom-built by research scientists. The ability to fly above 95 per cent of the earth's atmosphere was good enough for many of them.

NASA had a similar operation at Ellington Field, Houston which used three former USAF RB-57F models and, as in military service, the Ames U-2s outperformed the WB-57. When the USAF re-opened the U-2 production line with the TR-1 order, NASA opted to retire two of its WB-57s and acquire two of the new aircraft. The greater volume offered by the superpods, larger Q-bay and detachable nose was required for new experiments, while the ability to combine sensors and experiments meant that the flight costs could be shared among a number of researchers. Maximum payload would be 2,600 lb (1180 kg).

ER-2 takes to the air

Smartly painted in blue and white as N706NA, the ER-2 was first flown by Skunk Works test pilot Art Peterson on 11 May 1981. NASA project manager Marty Knutson – a veteran U-2 pilot from the earliest days of the programme – picked up the aircraft from Palmdale and flew it to Moffett on 10 June. For the next six years, it flew alongside the two U-2Cs, but when the USAF decided to retire the last of its early-model aircraft, NASA followed suit. A second purpose-built ER-2 (N709NA) was delivered in 1989, by which time NASA had also acquired the former USAF TR-1A 80-1069 on loan as N708NA. The aircraft carry their USAF serials for administrative reasons.

The earth survey flights continued with improved imaging sensors, including the same Itek IRIS II 24-in (61-cm) focal length panoramic camera as used by USAF U-2Rs. The IRIS series was derived from the CORONA reconnaissance satellites, and offered very high resolution across a wide swath. Unlike the USAF, which was slow to adopt multi-spectral imaging, the NASA installation usually used colour and 'false colour' film. Such film is sensitive to the green, red and near-IR portions of the spectrum, and can reveal features on the earth's surface which could not be detected by panchromatic film. In addition to the IRIS, NASA uses Hycon HR-732 framing cameras with 24-in focal length lenses, but the workhorse is the Wild Heerbrug RC-10 mapping camera with 6- or 12-in (15- or 30-cm) lenses. One or more of these are flown on nearly every flight, and they can be mounted in the nose or superpods as well as the Q-bay.

High-altitude mapping

NASA's high-altitude aircraft had imaged large portions of the US (including Alaska), and an archive facility in Sioux Falls, South Dakota has over 500,000 photo frames, plus digital imagery data available. It handles hundreds of requests for the data from the remote sensing community.

The Daedalus Thematic Mapper Simulator (TMS) was introduced with the ER-2, a multi-spectral scanning radiometer recording digital data which could subsequently be computer-manipulated in ground analysis. This proved invaluable for geologists, oceanographers and agronomists in such applications as land use patterns, forestry, and disaster assessments. TMS has since been modified for many other environmental studies.

NASA flew the first-generation U-2C (above, background) on many high-altitude experiments. The larger U-2R airframe offered far greater load-carrying capability and NASA was an eager customer for the type. Two aircraft were procured as ER-2s, bolstered by a third aircraft (foreground) which was built as a TR-1A for the Air Force but subsequently operated by NASA on long-term loan.

The NASA ER-2 fleet is flown from Moffett Field. The aircraft in the foreground is configured for high-altitude atmospheric sampling.

Right and below: *The U-2 is a tricky aircraft to land, although the second-generation aircraft are more forgiving than the early machines. No trainers were included in the first batch of aircraft: U-2R pilots relied on the old U-2CT for conversion. However, the third and fourth aircraft of the FY80 batch were completed with a raised second seat in the Q-bay for training duties. Given a white scheme (soon changed to black), the aircraft were designated TR-1B and went into service with the 4029th SRTS at Beale.*

The ER-2 was deployed abroad for the first time in spring 1985, to Mildenhall, in support of a DoD programme named HI CAMP which used a multi-wavelength infra-red sensor to obtain a database of background measurements of the earth's surface. The most significant overseas trip came two years later, when an ER-2 and NASA's DC-8 were deployed to Punta Arenas in southern Chile to investigate the hole in the ozone layer which had recently opened over the South Pole each winter. Fourteen separate sensors were carried on 12 ER-2 flights across Antarctica.

Measurements from the two-month deployment added weight to the theory that man-made chlorofluorocarbons (CFCs) were to blame. In winter 1988-89, a similar deployment was made to Stavanger, Norway to investigate ozone depletion over the North Pole. From 1991 to 1994, more flights were mounted out of Eielson AFB, Alaska, Bangor, Maine, and Christchurch, New Zealand. The NASA flights led directly to the international conventions which have mandated a phasing-out of CFCs around the world.

In a variation of this theme, the ER-2 began investigations in 1992 to determine whether a future fleet of commercial supersonic transports would also cause ozone loss. It took measurements of the known ozone depletion catalysts from 60,000 to 65,000 ft (18290 to 19810 m) in the 15-60° N latitudes where most SSTs would fly. In one 1993 sortie, the ER-2 took samples from the wake of a specially-flown Air France Concorde over New Zealand.

The ER-2 is now also participating in the SUCCESS project (SUbsonic aircraft: Contrail and Cloud Effects Special Study) to measure the effect on cirrus cloud formation of the growing world fleet of subsonic airliners. Unusually, this sometimes requires it to fly at lower levels – around 40,000 ft (12190 m).

ER-2 down under

In early 1993, an ER-2 was flown out of Townsville, Australia as part of the highly-co-ordinated TOGA COARE project to explore the formation of tropical storms over the unique 'warm pool' of water in the Pacific Ocean northeast of Papua New Guinea. This was done by measuring the heat radiating from the earth's surface, as well as with atmospheric measurement. No fewer than nine sensors were carried during the flights. The ultimate goal is to develop satellite sensors which could help predict storm formations and movement.

A laser-based system weighing 1,000 lb has recently helped improve data collection during the ER-2's atmospheric study flights. The Lidar Atmospheric Sensing Experiment (LASE) was built by NASA Langley at a cost of $20 million to operate autonomously, and flights were conducted from NASA's Wallops Island airfield in Virginia in co-ordination with other Lidars on the Space Shuttle and NASA's lower-flying Electra. The LASE will eventually go into orbit, but, like many satellite sensors before it, the high-flying capability of the U-2 has been invaluable for proving flights.

New and improved earth-imaging systems have also been introduced. The AVIRIS (Airborne Visible-InfraRed Imaging Spectrometer) is a 224-band hyper-spectral scanner developed by the Jet Propulsion Laboratory which has been flown frequently since 1991, when one of its first overseas deployments was to RAF Alconbury, UK. An Electro-Optic Camera (EOC) has been developed at Ames, to capture high-resolution (15.8 ft/4.8-m) digitised images from a solid-state video camera.

Dedicated trainer

The decision to produce dual-cockpit versions of the TR-1 from the outset was a wise one. The U-2 programme had somehow managed without conversion trainers for the first 17 years, but at the cost of numerous bangs, prangs and write-offs. In 1972 and 1975, two early-model U-2s were adapted as trainers by replacing the Q-bay with a second cockpit. In 1983, they were joined at Beale by the two TR-1Bs, all four being assigned to the 4029th Strategic Reconnaissance Training Squadron. The 4029th was later renumbered the 5th SRTS, and is now the 1st RS (T). The two U-2CTs were kept on strength until 1988, when a third new trainer arrived, bought with 'black' U-2R money (80-1091). There are now four, and they have recently been redesignated TU-2S (80-1091 is still a TU-2R at the time of writing). A cockpit procedures trainer has recently been added, but there is still no full-motion simulator for the U-2.

Pilots who wish to enter the U-2 programme must have a minimum 1,500 hours. They come to Beale for a week of interviews and tests, which include a suiting-up to ensure they are comfortable in the hermetically-sealed atmosphere of the pressure suit, and three brief flights in the trainer. After selection, they return for a six-month course which starts with a month of instrument training in the T-38 companion trainer. Pilot training is strictly one-on-one, with each course consisting of two instructors and two students. Next comes the Initial Qualification phase, consisting of one month's ground study and one month during which six sorties are flown in the trainer. The instructor usually occupies the rear cockpit, which has most of the same displays as the front cockpit, although there is no driftsight.

Solo flight

The prized solo patch is then awarded, and the student moves on to the Mission Qualification Phase. He flies 14 increasingly long and complicated sorties in the U-2R, and also learns to play the role of 'mobile'. Each U-2 flight is assigned a second pilot, who deals with many of the pre-flight preliminaries, especially those that the space-suited pilot cannot easily perform, such as the pre-flight walkaround. 'Mobile' accompanies the aircraft to the runway for take-off and remains in radio contact throughout the flight. He acts as a second brain to solve problems which might arise during the flight, and provides height-above-ground readouts during the critical landing phase.

The U-2R is somewhat easier to land than the early-model aircraft, which had to be stalled onto the runway, but the experience is still likened to riding a bicycle without any handlebars while balancing a long pole laterally. The U-2 pilot really earns his pay when he descends from a nine-hour operational sortie, and finds fog or a crosswind at his recovery field.

Once they are qualified, new U-2 pilots spend their next 100 hours flying from Beale in the 99th SRS before they are ready to go overseas. The 99th SRS flies some interesting missions within the US, checking out new sensors or procedures, and supporting disaster relief and other environmental efforts with photography. It also flies in Red and Green Flag exercises, and launches short-notice flights to support search and rescue efforts.

The T-38 fleet at Beale numbers 12 gloss-black aircraft, which are also used by experienced U-2 pilots for standard USAF instrument check flights. They retained their standard training white colour for many years, until the 9th joined Air Combat Command where the rules dictated that their colour be changed to that of the primary wing aircraft.

When the RB-57F was retired in 1973, the U-2

Above: Normally based at Beale, the TR-1Bs occasionally deployed to RAF Alconbury while the 17th Reconnaissance Wing was resident with TR-1As to cater for mandatory check rides. A winter's evening provides a dramatic backdrop as a two-seater completes a check sortie.

Above left: After initially operating as the 4029th SRTS, the TR-1B/U-2RT squadron at Beale became the 5th SRTS. On the retirement of the SR-71 the training squadron adopted the old 'Sled' squadron number, becoming the 1st RS(T).

Below: One of the existing U-2RTs was among the first batch of three aircraft to be redelivered to Beale after re-engining with the F118. The two-seaters were redesignated U-2ST after re-engining (subsequently becoming TU-2S).

Lockheed ER-2 details

Above: This view shows two vertical sensors mounted in the Q-bay of an ER-2. A variety of Q-bay hatches are available with various sensor windows, and are usually insulated with some quilting.

Left: The ER-2's cockpit differs in some important respects from that of the U-2R/S. The most obvious is the extended dashboard to the right of the driftsight and rearrangement of the instruments. The all-important small rectangular indicator at the top left of the dashboard announces 'Food Ready', a reference to the in-cockpit food warmer.

The superpods can be used for a wide variety of sensors. The fixed portion of the pod (left) is shown with digitising and recording equipment (including a tape recorder on a drop-down rack), while the removable front section of the pod (right) is shown mounting a vertical optical sensor.

Wing fold
With a 31.39-m (103-ft 0-in) span, the U-2/ER-2 presents considerable hangarage difficulties away from its normal bases. To offset this, the outer 1.78 m (5 ft 10 in) can be manually folded to reduce span.

Lockheed ER-2/TR-1A NASA Ames Moffett Field, California

For many years NASA operated a pair of U-2Cs on a variety of test programmes and earth resources monitoring work. With the reopening of the U-2R production line to produce the TR-1A, the chance came to provide the Administration with new-build aircraft that were far more capable than the first-generation U-2s then in use. The designation ER-2 was applied to reinforce the 'Earth Resources' role of the aircraft, and the first example from the reopened line was assigned to NASA. Another aircraft from further down the line was also earmarked for NASA. The first ER-2 went into service supporting the two remaining U-2Cs pending their retirement. To allow them to retire prior to the delivery of the second dedicated ER-2, the Air Force loaned this TR-1A (80-1069) to NASA, and it became an ER-2. After a period of operating three ER-2s, NASA was due to hand back this aircraft to the Air Force.

Sensor carriage
The primary sensor locations are in the Q-bay behind the cockpit, in the detachable nose and in the superpods. In certain configurations the ER-2 has carried sensors in the rear of the superpods as well as the detachable front section. NASA aircraft have also been noted with sensors on underwing pylons in place of the superpods and with a streamlined pod carried under the rear fuselage. One ER-2 has been configured to carry a Senior Span-style dorsal fairing known as Starlink.

ER-2s are regularly reconfigured for various duties. The aircraft above has seven optical sensor ports, while the aircraft at right uses the superpod attachments to mount sensors on pylons.

Above: The ER-2 can carry a sensor pod under the rear fuselage.

Right: This aircraft has an extended Q-bay hatch for an optical sensor.

Lockheed U-2R/TR-1A cutaway drawing key

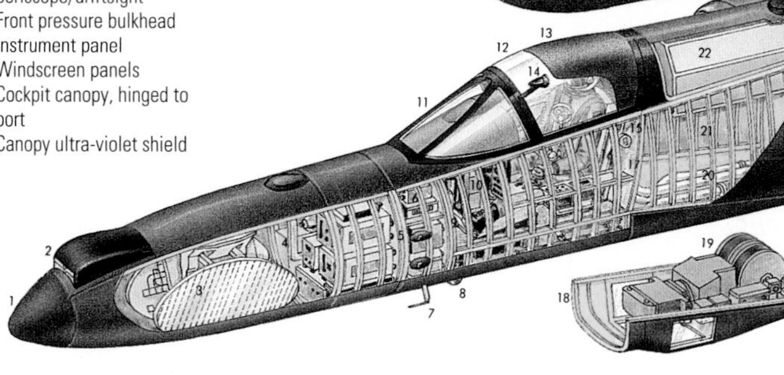

1 Nose radome
2 Radar cooling air intake
3 Hughes Advanced Synthetic Aperture Radar System (ASARS-2) antennas
4 Radar system equipment module
5 Interchangeable nose section mounting bulkhead
6 Avionics equipment bay
7 Pitot head
8 Downward vision periscope/driftsight
9 Front pressure bulkhead
10 Instrument panel
11 Windscreen panels
12 Cockpit canopy, hinged to port
13 Canopy ultra-violet shield
14 Rear view mirror
15 Canopy emergency release
16 Pilot's zero-zero ejection seat
17 Sloping rear pressure bulkhead
18 Photint system
19 Itec panoramic (horizon-to-horizon) optical bar camera
20 Equipment conditioning air ducts
21 Q-bay mission equipment compartment
22 Astro-inertial navigation system equipment package
23 Satellite antenna
24 E-bay avionics equipment compartment
25 Port engine air intake
26 Intake air spill duct
27 Mainwheel doors
28 Twin mainwheels, forward retracting
29 Landing/taxiing lamps
30 Main undercarriage wheel bay
31 Ventral antenna 'farm' – Senior Spear Comint package
32 Engine bay bulkhead
33 Engine compressor intake
34 Hydraulic pumps

Above: NASA pilot James Barrilleaux climbs aboard the first ER-2, which is configured for high-altitude optical surveillance. It has a twin vertical camera installation in the Q-bay, with another vertical sensor in the nose section. The camera ports are all fitted with optically-flat glass in a flat-bottomed fairing.

J75 engine
J75 engines were retrofitted to first-generation U-2s, and the powerplant was adopted as standard for the second-generation aircraft until the recent change to the F118. Designated J75-P-13B, the U-2's engine was a specially-built version of the standard J75 with a redesigned compressor stage for high-altitude operation and closer manufacturing tolerances to reduce weight. Nominal maximum thrust rating is 17,000 lb (75.65 kN) and standard cruise thrust is 15,100 lb (67.20 kN). The latter figure is rather academic as the thrust produced at operating altitudes is reduced to very low values. The engine itself is a two-spool design with coaxial shafts. The inner shaft mounts the second and third stages of the turbine, which drive the eight-stage low-pressure compressor. The hollow outer shaft connects the first stage of the turbine to the seven-stage high-pressure compressor. The compressor feeds air to the combustion chamber at a ratio of about 12:1 at take-off thrust. The eight cylindrical combustion chambers are each provided with six fuel flow nozzles, each suitably modified to handle the high-flashpoint JP-TS fuel. Ignition is initiated in chambers 4 and 5, with cross-over tubes subsequently igniting the other six burner cans.

Undercarriage
The U-2/ER-2 has a bicycle undercarriage by necessity of its slender configuration. Much of the weight is supported on the mainwheel, which is forward retracting and has two wheels with tubeless tyres. The forward-retracting tailwheel has a single solid rubber tyre. It can be steered up to 6° either side. The fully-castoring wing-mounted outriggers normally fall free on take-off, but can be fixed for initial flight training.

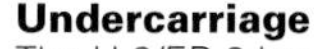

Cockpit

When compared with single-seat fighter cockpits, that of the U-2 appears roomy. However, the wearing on all but low-level training missions of a bulky pressure suit renders the cockpit quite cramped. During high-altitude cruise the pilot can collapse the rudder pedals for extra leg room. The aircraft is sluggish in roll control and a transport-style yoke is provided rather than a stick. The pilot sits on a Lockheed-designed zero-zero ejection seat. Ejection is initiated by pulling a D-ring on the front of the seat, and the sequence includes blowing off the canopy. Survival equipment is fitted in the seat bucket, and includes an emergency oxygen supply, which starts automatically on ejection. The cockpit is pressurised using an automatic schedule by bleed air from the engine compressor, which also supplies the air conditioning system. Ducted air also defogs the windscreen and canopy. The canopy itself (along with hatches for the Q-bay and E-bay, and the nose section break) is sealed using engine bleed air, with a nitrogen bottle backup system. The cockpit also has a food warmer, which heats up food contained in tubes. The tube has a pipe which can be inserted through a pressure seal into the helmet. Drinks are also consumed in this fashion.

Nav/comms equipment

Standard communications equipment for the U-2R includes an ARC-109 and -164 UHF radios, with built-in KY-58 secure voice equipment. VHF equipment is optional, but a 718U-7 HF set is provided for long-range communications. For navigation the primary aid is the LN-33 inertial navigation system, backed up by the ARN-52 TACAN system. Recently, the U-2R fleet has been fitted with GPS (Global Positioning System) receivers in a fairing on the port wing. An ADF (Automatic Direction Finder) system is fitted which provides long-range direction-finding of transmitted signals, and can be used for voice communications in emergency. An IFF (Identification, Friend or Foe) is fitted. The U-2R has an L-201 autopilot, but this has been replaced by a new digital system in the U-2S. An air computer takes pitot-static data to provide airspeed, climb speed, ambient temperature and altitude information. The air data system is located between the nose section break and the cockpit instrument panel.

Roll control and spoilers

The U-2 has narrow-chord ailerons on the outer portions of the wings, running between the fuel dump pipe and the wingtip. Each consists of two sections either side of the wing-fold joint. Both ailerons have inboard tabs, the left-hand tab being electrically adjustable in flight by means of a control on the left-hand console in the cockpit. Control of the ailerons is achieved mechanically by cable and push-rod linkage. The ailerons are hinged from the upper surface of the wing and can travel 16.25° either side of the normal neutral position. At low speeds, where roll control authority is considerably reduced due to the sheer size of the wing, the ailerons are augmented by hydraulically operated, electrically controlled roll-assist spoilers. These are located forward of the outboard flap sections, and are activated by a switch on the aileron actuation system. When the pilot applies bank, say to the right, the left-hand aileron deflects downwards and the right-hand aileron deflects upwards, the angle being governed by the deflection of the control yoke. When the right aileron deflection reaches 13° up the spoiler switch trips, activating the right-hand spoiler. The spoiler normally deploys to full deflection. When the control deflection is eased off, the right-hand aileron returns to its neutral position. As it passes through 13° the spoiler retracts.

As part of the gust alleviation system, the neutral point of the ailerons can be shifted to a 7.5° up position, in concert with a 6.5° upwards deflection of the flaps. This downloads the wing structure during turbulence or at high speeds. The gust alleviation system is controlled from the cockpit, and overrides the flap deployment switching. It increases speed pressure limitations from 180 to 250 kt. Situated inboard of the roll-assist spoilers, straddling the two outer flap sections, are lift-dump spoilers, controlled from the cockpit. These are normally held by springs in the faired position, but can be deployed hydraulically to a 60° deflection setting to dump lift during the landing roll. The springs provide an automatic retraction function of the spoilers in case of hydraulic failure.

Lockheed Martin U-2R
99th Reconnaissance Squadron
9th Reconnaissance Wing
Beale AFB, California

Known by a variety of nicknames, from the mysterious 'Dragon Lady' to the functional 'Deuce', the U-2 has been the USAF's premier high-altitude reconnaissance platform for over 30 years, proving of enormous value in both peacetime and war. Whereas the SR-71 was mainly used on occasional high-value 'snap-shot' forays against key targets, the U-2 (together with the lower-flying RC-135 Rivet Joint) provides the day-to-day continuous surveillance of regions of interest which keeps the US intelligence community in full-time work. Its ability to loiter at high altitude is the strength of the U-2, allowing it to listen in to hours of communications or watch a specific area over a long period with its Elint and radar sensors. In an era of increasing digitisation and electronics, its film-based cameras are still regularly called upon to gain high-resolution pictures in spot or swathe modes. The inherent flexibility of the airframe will allow it to carry many more types of new sensors as they are developed. A new lease of life has been given to the U-2 with the F118 re-engining programme and, despite the growing competition being offered by UAVs (unmanned air vehicles), funding for the U-2 programme remains a high budgetary priority for the DARO (Defense Aerial Reconnaissance Office) which controls it.

Production of the second-generation U-2 has amounted to 49 aircraft, in two batches. The first batch, funded in FY (Fiscal Year) 68, comprised six aircraft for the CIA and six for the US Air Force. In late 1974, the CIA aircraft were handed over to the USAF.

A requirement for surveillance in the Central European theatre was the spur to reopen the production line with FY 80 money to produce the TR-1A. The chance was taken to also procure three dedicated TR-1B/U-2RT trainers (to replace the first-generation U-2CTs), two special mission ER-2 high-altitude experimental aircraft for NASA, and to produce extra U-2Rs for the 9th SRW, partly to make good attrition and also to expand the fleet. Further production remains an option, and the aircraft has been offered for strictly-controlled export, notably to the RAF for the ASTOR (Airborne Stand-Off Radar) role.

Sensor carriage

Compared to the first generation of U-2s, the U-2R has a vastly increased sensor payload, although it utilises the same basic airframe locations. The principal locations are the Q-bay, E-bay, nose and superpods. The largest of these is the Q-bay, situated directly behind the cockpit. Fitted with an upper and lower hatch, the bay has a maximum load of 1,300 lb (590 kg) when the nose is empty or 750 lb (340 kg) with nose payloads, and a volume of 64.6 cu ft (1.83 m³). The upper hatch can be opened to provide access, and also for fitting a hoist which can lift heavy equipment into the bay from below. A variety of lower hatches are available, depending on the type of sensors carried. Some systems, notably ASARS-2, require the use of the Q-bay for the carriage of associated electronic equipment and recorders, precluding its use for the carriage of cameras. Behind the Q-bay in the lower fuselage, forward of the mainwheel, is the E-bay, usually used for aircraft electronic components. Some aircraft have been seen with a bulged radome on the E-bay hatch, for additional datalinks. A variety of nose sections are available, including 'slick', tracker camera, ASARS-2 and SYERS. The grossly elongated PLSS nose is no longer used. A special trolley is used to remove the nose easily, the break being located at FS (Fuselage Station) 169. The standard nose section offers 47 cu ft (1.33 m³) of capacity and is 7 ft 2 in (2.18 m) long and 3 ft 1 in (0.94 m) in diameter. The ASARS-2 nose requires additional air cooling, and a small scoop is provided on top. In some configurations the tip-mounted ADF sense antenna is displaced to a bulge on the top of the nose. The nosecone itself is removable at FS 99 to allow access to systems in the extrme tip of the nose. A further 800 lb (363 kg) of equipment can be accommodated in each of the wing superpods, which have now fully replaced the smaller 'slipper pods' used previously. These pods are attached to the underside of the wing with just four bolts, allowing their easy removal for reconfiguring the aircraft or for training sorties. Each pod offers an internal capacity of 83 cu ft (2.35 m³), and measures 23 ft 10 in (7.26 m) in length and 2 ft 8 in (0.81 m) in diameter. The pod itself has a break just forward of the wing leading-edge allowing the fitment of different nose sections (such as that containing the side-facing antennas for the Senior Ruby) system while several overall pod configurations are available, including the Senior Spear pod with a large 'canoe' on the underside of the centre section. Some equipment is held on drop-down racks for easy access. The rear of the pod is also detachable. In addition to these main locations for carrying mission equipment, the underside of the fuselage is used to mount large 'farms' of antennas for the Sigint system.

Fuel

The majority of the high-flashpoint JP-TS (thermally-stable) fuel is housed in integral wing tanks. Each wing has two tanks, the inboard tank housing 1,169 US gal (4425 litres) and the outboard tank accommodating 239 US gal (905 litres). In addition there is a fuselage sump tank (actually four tanks plumbed together) which wraps around the lower portion of the front of the engine. This houses a further 99 US gal (375 litres). The total internal capacity is 2,915 US gal (11034 litres), equating to 18,947 lb (8594 kg). Of this figure all but 35 US gal (132 litres) is usable. Fuel is fed from the wing tanks to the fuselage sump tank and then to the engine. In normal operations the outer wing tanks are drained last. Engine bleed air is used to create a positive pressure in the fuel system to aid feed to the sump tank, and there are two (primary and secondary) pumps to feed the engine. Each wing tank has a pump installed which can be used either for cross-transfer to maintain weight distribution, or to feed fuel into the sump tank as an emergency back-up to the primary feed system. A fuel dump system is installed in the wing tanks, fuel being dumped through pipes below the trailing edge of the wing between the flaps and ailerons. A small airscoop under each wing is used to provide ram air pressure to the tank in order to jettison the fuel through the dump pipe. The fuselage sump tank is vented to the outside via an outlet at the top of the vertical fin and prevents the fuel system overpressurising. For ground defuelling there are valves at the outboard end of the wing tanks so that sediment and water can be drawn off, and a similar valve is located in the bottom of the sump tank. Both the wing fuel feed lines and that from the sump to the engine have emergency shut-off valves.

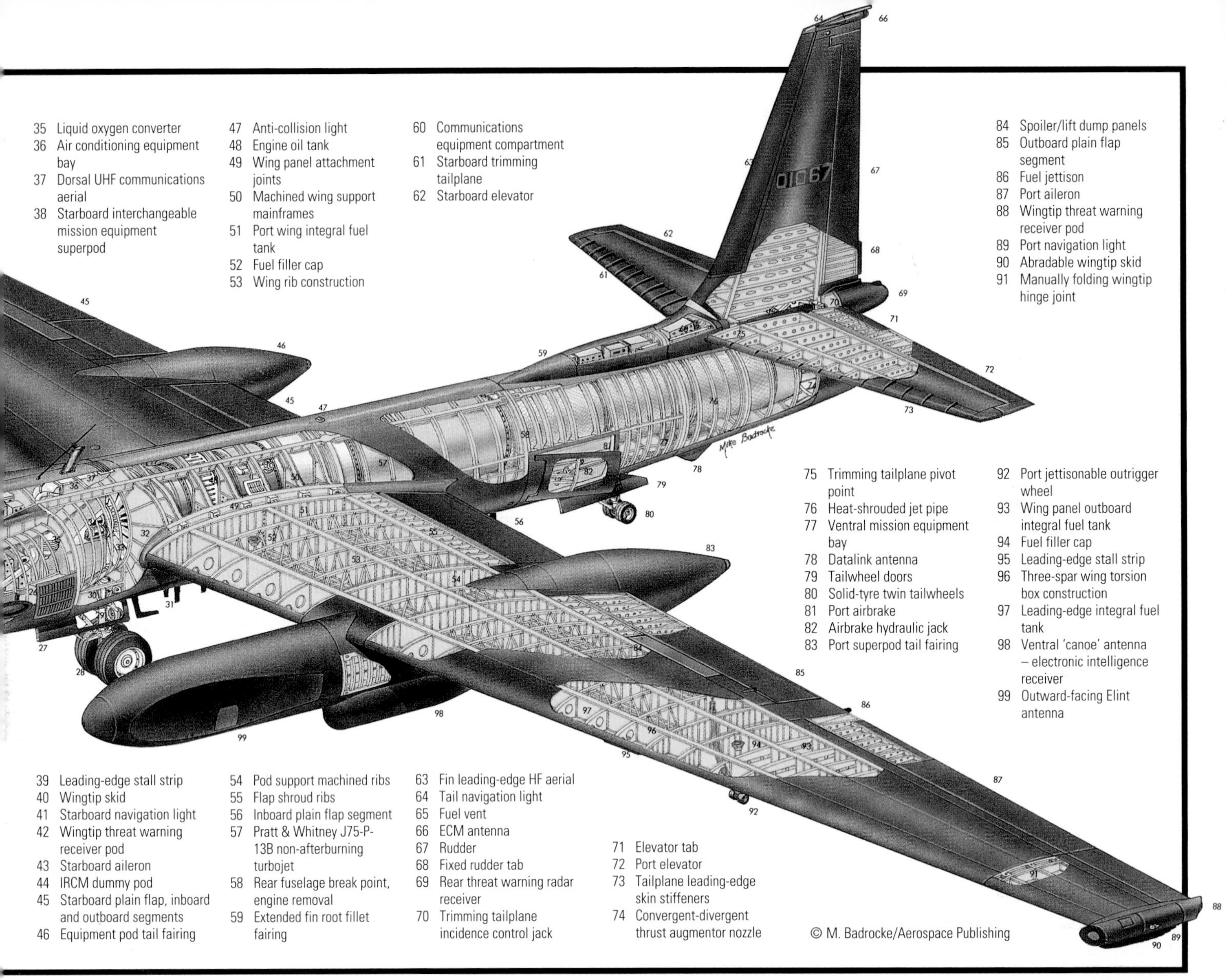

35 Liquid oxygen converter
36 Air conditioning equipment bay
37 Dorsal UHF communications aerial
38 Starboard interchangeable mission equipment superpod
47 Anti-collision light
48 Engine oil tank
49 Wing panel attachment joints
50 Machined wing support mainframes
51 Port wing integral fuel tank
52 Fuel filler cap
53 Wing rib construction
60 Communications equipment compartment
61 Starboard trimming tailplane
62 Starboard elevator
84 Spoiler/lift dump panels
85 Outboard plain flap segment
86 Fuel jettison
87 Port aileron
88 Wingtip threat warning receiver pod
89 Port navigation light
90 Abradable wingtip skid
91 Manually folding wingtip hinge joint

75 Trimming tailplane pivot point
76 Heat-shrouded jet pipe
77 Ventral mission equipment bay
78 Datalink antenna
79 Tailwheel doors
80 Solid-tyre twin tailwheels
81 Port airbrake
82 Airbrake hydraulic jack
83 Port superpod tail fairing
92 Port jettisonable outrigger wheel
93 Wing panel outboard integral fuel tank
94 Fuel filler cap
95 Leading-edge stall strip
96 Three-spar wing torsion box construction
97 Leading-edge integral fuel tank
98 Ventral 'canoe' antenna – electronic intelligence receiver
99 Outward-facing Elint antenna

39 Leading-edge stall strip
40 Wingtip skid
41 Starboard navigation light
42 Wingtip threat warning receiver pod
43 Starboard aileron
44 IRCM dummy pod
45 Starboard plain flap, inboard and outboard segments
46 Equipment pod tail fairing
54 Pod support machined ribs
55 Flap shroud ribs
56 Inboard plain flap segment
57 Pratt & Whitney J75-P-13B non-afterburning turbojet
58 Rear fuselage break point, engine removal
59 Extended fin root fillet fairing
63 Fin leading-edge HF aerial
64 Tail navigation light
65 Fuel vent
66 ECM antenna
67 Rudder
68 Fixed rudder tab
69 Rear threat warning radar receiver
70 Trimming tailplane incidence control jack
71 Elevator tab
72 Port elevator
73 Tailplane leading-edge skin stiffeners
74 Convergent-divergent thrust augmentor nozzle

U-2R/S cockpit

These two views show the cockpits of the U-2R (above) and U-2S (right), the cockpits of both being dominated by the circular driftsight. The U-2S cockpit differs mainly by having more digital instruments and a multi-function display in place of the autopilot controls to the left of the attitude indicator. The autopilot itself is new.

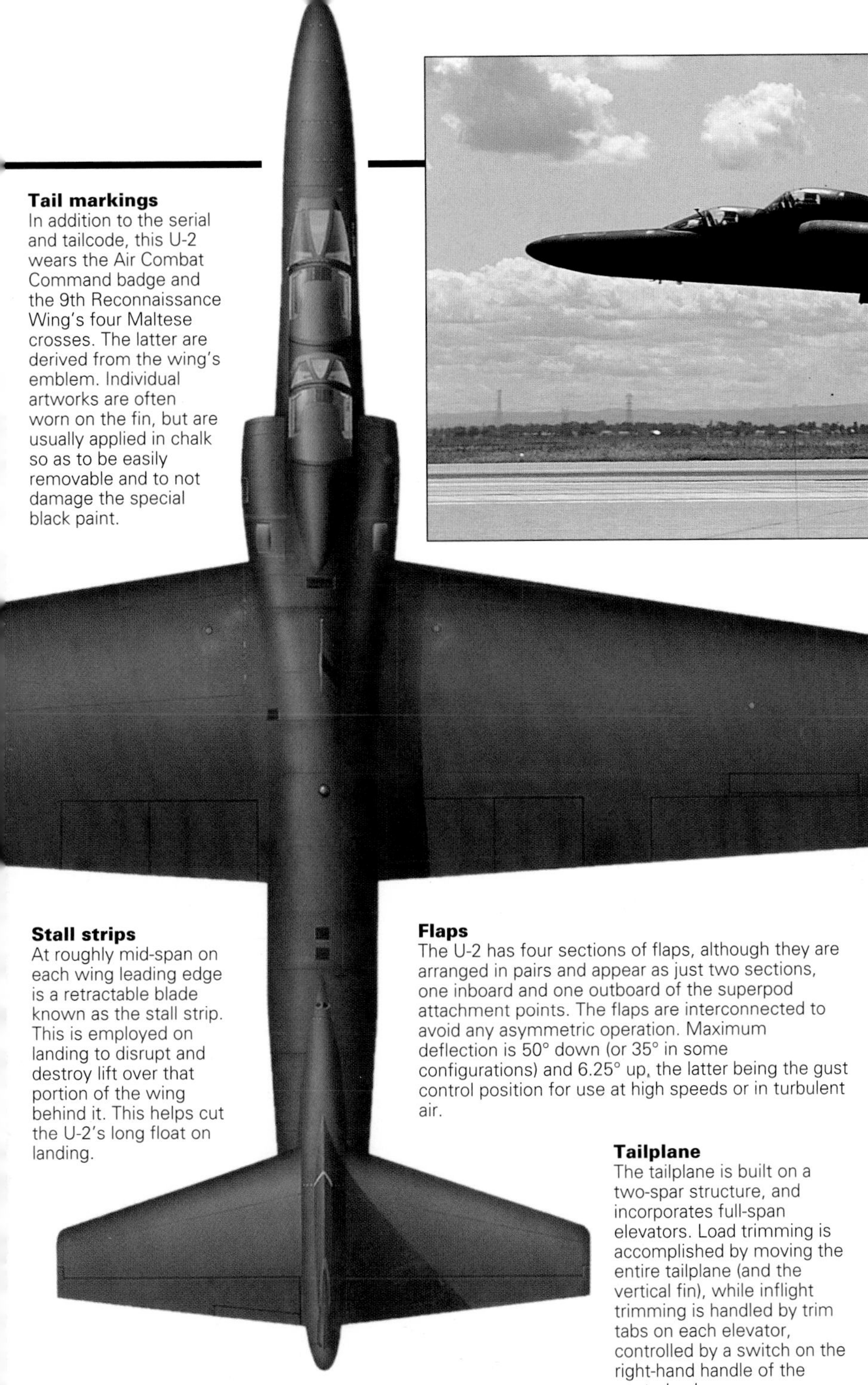

Tail markings
In addition to the serial and tailcode, this U-2 wears the Air Combat Command badge and the 9th Reconnaissance Wing's four Maltese crosses. The latter are derived from the wing's emblem. Individual artworks are often worn on the fin, but are usually applied in chalk so as to be easily removable and to not damage the special black paint.

80-0191 was the third of the two-seaters, and the first to receive the U-2RT designation. This new designation (instead of the previous TR-1B) reflected funding channels rather than any aircraft differences.

Stall strips
At roughly mid-span on each wing leading edge is a retractable blade known as the stall strip. This is employed on landing to disrupt and destroy lift over that portion of the wing behind it. This helps cut the U-2's long float on landing.

Flaps
The U-2 has four sections of flaps, although they are arranged in pairs and appear as just two sections, one inboard and one outboard of the superpod attachment points. The flaps are interconnected to avoid any asymmetric operation. Maximum deflection is 50° down (or 35° in some configurations) and 6.25° up, the latter being the gust control position for use at high speeds or in turbulent air.

Tailplane
The tailplane is built on a two-spar structure, and incorporates full-span elevators. Load trimming is accomplished by moving the entire tailplane (and the vertical fin), while inflight trimming is handled by trim tabs on each elevator, controlled by a switch on the right-hand handle of the control yoke.

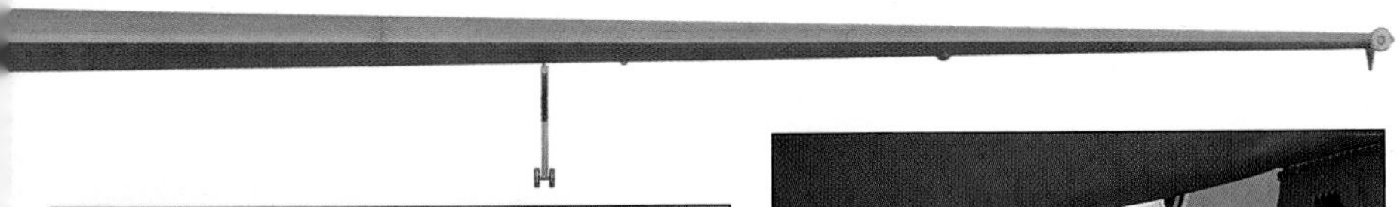

Above: A long jetpipe leads from the centrally-mounted engine to the tailpipe. This is the F118 installation in the U-2S.

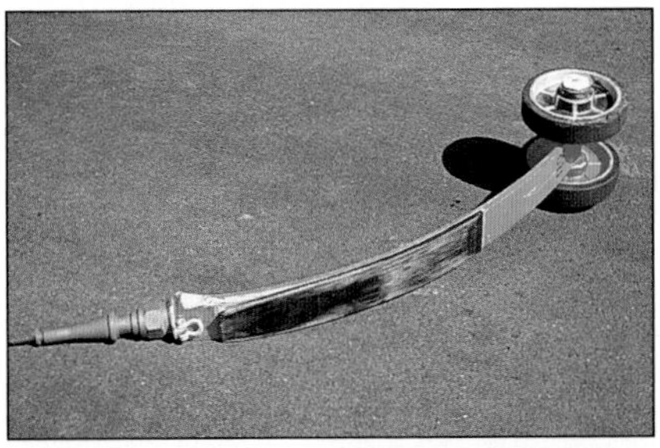

Fairings are mounted on the narrow fixed trailing-edge section between the flaps and the ailerons. On the starboard wing (above) is an IRCM fairing, while on the port (below) is the GPS receiver. The latter is fitted on operational aircraft only.

Below: The pogo is a simple sprung-steel unit with solid-tyre wheels. The simple fixture allows the strut to castor freely during taxiing.

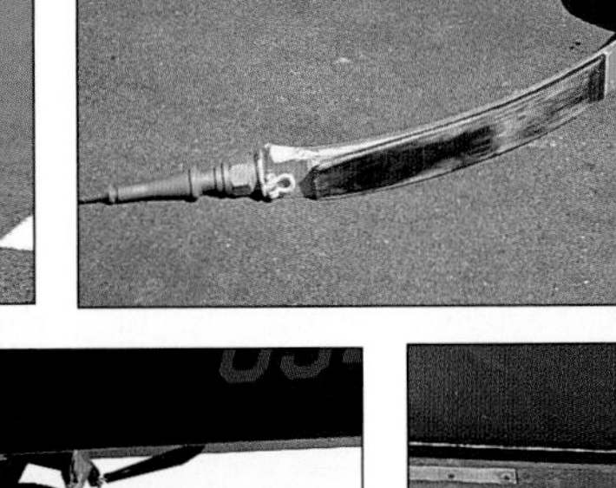

Below: This frame guard was added to the port tailwheel door of the U-2R used for carrier trials. It prevented the arrester wire snagging the wheel. The carrier aircraft also had sprung-steel wingtip skids.

Both undercarriage units have twin wheels. The tail unit (above) has solid tyres while the main unit (right) has tubeless 300-lb/sq in (2068-kPa) tyres.

Handling characteristics

With its wide-span wings and bicycle undercarriage the U-2 is notoriously tricky to land, although the larger aircraft is much improved compared to the first generation. Even with the overwing spoilers the aircraft lacks roll control authority at low speeds, but an experienced pilot can keep the wings level even when the aircraft is stationary, in a strong enough breeze. This makes the job of fixing the pogos back in much easier for the ground crew. Another peril on landing is weathercocking, caused by the central position of the mainwheel and the tall vertical fin. Crosswind limits are therefore very restricting. At high altitude great care is paid to airspeed, for the limiting Mach number and stall speed converge, giving a band of just a few knots for safe flight.

Senior Span

Several airframes in the U-2 fleet have been modified to carry the Senior Span pod on a hardpoint on the spine of the aircraft. The pod was first tested on TR-1A 80-1071, the rear half of the pod, together with the lower vertical tail, tailplanes and upper rear fuselage, being covered with wool tufts to visually monitor airflow. Other aircraft modified for Senior Span carriage to date include 68-10329, 68-10331, 68-10339, 80-1066, 80-1070 and 80-1095. The pod itself is a simple aerodynamic fairing mounted on top of a long-chord pylon. The pylon holds an upward-facing dish antenna for a satellite communications system. This allows the U-2 system to transmit its gathered data into a satcom link, in turn allowing the transmission of the data on a global scale in near real time. The normal downlink data transfer system has only line-of-sight range. The pod itself has a mid-section break with the front portion of the fairing sliding forward on rails to allow easy access to the satellite antenna for maintenance. The pod support pylon incorporates an airscoop to provide cooling air for the satcom equipment. The pod is almost 17 ft (5.2 m) long, and together with the pylon weighs 401 lb (182 kg). The Senior Span fit is for the transmission of data from the Sigint system only. A similar Senior Spur fit can transmit ASARS-2 radar imagery.

Sigint configuration

This aircraft is depicted in the full Sigint-gathering fit, consisting of the Senior Ruby Elint system and Senior Spear Comint system. The side-facing antennas for Senior Ruby are housed in the slab-sided front portion of the superpods. These detect and classify radars at long slant ranges. The Senior Spear system is housed in the rear portion of the superpods, with its characteristic lower bulge. The large 'farm' of hook and blade antennas also serves this system, which has been considerably updated and reconfigured since it first appeared in the early 1970s. Gathered data can be datalinked by either the Senior Span system, or by a direct datalink situated under the rear fuselage. This works on line-of-sight, restricting its range. The gathered data can be recorded on board, such equipment usually being located in the Q-bay, but is generally datalinked in near real time for analysis by ground stations.

Photographic and other configurations

For the photographic role the U-2 can carry four main sensors. The OBC and Iris III are panoramic cameras mounted in the Q-bay, peering through a bulged glazed hatch with three optically flat panes. For high-altitude framing purposes the ultra-high resolution H camera (HR-329) is used, this employing folding optics to create the equivalent of a 66-in (167.6-cm) focal length lens. This camera can be controlled by the pilot, who uses the driftsight to gauge the correct position to cover the objective. The Type H is used primarily in a LOROP (LOng-Range Oblique Photography) mode, and produces images of outstanding quality in the right atmospheric and meteorological conditions. A small T-35 tracker camera is usually carried in the tip of the nose for photographic missions to provide precise positional data. A new sensor being introduced to the fleet is the SYERS camera. This is mounted in a special rotating nose section with an optically flat window. The camera is a long focal-length unit, and lies lengthways in the nose section, using a 45° prism to peer out through the window. The rotating nose allows the camera to face to any angle, although in practice it is usually pre-positioned. A rarely seen configuration, but one which is still an option, is the air sampling kit, which is carried in the Q-bay. The special hatch mounts a sampling tube while the Q-bay houses the recovery and storage equipment.

Defensive systems
A variety of defensive systems has been fitted to the U-2R throughout its career. The most obvious is the System 20 aft-facing infra-red countermeasures sensor installed in a cylindrical fairing on the starboard wing trailing edge, first fitted to CIA aircraft operating out of Taiwan in the early 1970s. This equipment is no longer used, and the cylindrical housing is left empty with the tail end faired over. The early U-2Rs inherited the System 9 (air-to-air) and System 13 (surface-to-air) threat warning and jamming systems, together with the System 12 and OS (Oscar Sierra – colloquially known as 'Oh, Shit!) SAM warners. Today's more sophisticated System 27-1 radar warning installation has two receivers in each pod, facing forwards and backwards at 45° to provide complete coverage. A jammer known as System 29 is also carried, housed in the fairings on the engine intakes and in the E-bay, while System 28 was once carried, with antennas below the fuselage forward of the tail wheel.

Wing structure
The huge wings are manufactured separately and attached directly to the fuselage either side of the engine installation. Each wing is constructed on a three-spar structure, these being located at 15 per cent, 40 per cent and 65 per cent of the wing chord. Truss and web ribs complete the shape of the wing, apart from the outboard folding section, which has no internal ribbing. The leading edge is completed as a separate assembly and attached to the front spar. Virtually the entire internal volume of the wing inboard of the wing-fold is used for integral fuel carriage, the tanks filling the inter-spar area and forward to the leading edge.

Tailplane strengthening
When the U-2R was first built, the use of wing-mounted superpods had not been discussed. When these began to appear, they caused a buffet problem for the tailplanes. To counter this, a series of ribs was added to the external surface of the tailplane to strengthen the structure. These are only fitted to the FY68 aircraft, as here, and provide a unique identification feature. When production was reopened in 1980 the additional strengthening was accounted for within the internal structure, so FY80 aircraft do not have the external ribs.

U-2S programme
In the late 1980s the J75 engine of the U-2R was becoming increasingly difficult to support and, in the light of new powerplants entering service with other types, was seen as increasingly inefficient. In July 1989 Lockheed flew the first example of an aircraft fitted with General Electric's F101-GE-F29 turbofan, derived from the F101 used by the Rockwell B-1B (which has also spawned the F110 fighter engine and F118 for the Northrop Grumman B-2). After around 100 hours of testing the new engine was shown to provide a major improvement over the original powerplant, including around 15 per cent extra thrust, which restored some of the U-2's altitude capability which had been eroded by ever-heavier payloads. The new engine was also shown to be far more fuel-efficient, giving a healthy improvement in range/endurance, while the smaller number of components and modern manufacturing methods used in its construction made it more reliable and easier to maintain. As it is smaller than the J75 there was no problem fitting it into the existing engine bay, while the possible adverse effects on centre of gravity caused by its lighter weight were largely negated by the engine's central location within the airframe. A decision was taken to re-engine the entire fleet, the powerplant being redesignated F118-GE-101, to create the U-2S. At the same time, Lockheed Martin is installing some new systems, such as a new autopilot, some digital controls and a multi-function display. The work is undertaken at the Skunk Works plant at Palmdale, and should be complete by 1998.

U-2 details

Cockpit instrumentation
The front cockpit of the TU-2 is essentially similar to that of the single-seat aircraft, although key operational systems such as sensor controls and RWR are removed. The rear cockpit is more austere, lacking many of the secondary controls such as circuit breakers. The side consoles are rearranged compared to the front, and the rear seat lacks the large optical scope for the driftsight.

Second cockpit
The addition of the second cockpit required only minor airframe changes as it is situated in the Q-bay compartment. The floor is raised to provide adequate forward view for the instructor. The flight controls are interconnected with the front cockpit by means of push-rods and torque assemblies, mostly located in the lower fuselage beneath the raised cockpit.

Fuselage construction
The fuselage is built in three main sections. The central sub-assembly includes the cockpit, Q-bay (second cockpit in trainer version), engine intakes, wing attachment points and engine installation. The sensor-carrying nose section is attached just forward of the cockpit. There are several different nose configurations and these are routinely interchangable depending on mission requirements. The third sub-assembly attaches to the centre section aft of the wing trailing-edge, the break located at the start of the dorsal fin fairing. This section comprises the rear fuselage, tailwheel, empennage and airbrakes.

Lockheed TU-2R
1st Reconnaissance Squadron (Training)
9th Reconnaissance Wing
Beale AFB, California

Two trainer aircraft had been belatedly produced for the first-generation U-2 under the designation U-2CT, and these continued in use to serve as introductory aircraft for the first U-2R batch. When the line reopened for TR-1 production, the second and third aircraft (80-1064 and 80-1065) were completed as two-seater TR-1Bs to provide a fully capable trainer for the second-generation aircraft. These were later joined by a third aircraft (80-1091) which was initially designated U-2RT to signify its assignment as a strategic (U-2R) as opposed to tactical (TR-1) trainer. A subsequent rationalisation of the fleet dispensed with the TR-1 designation altogether, all two-seaters then being known as U-2RTs. Trainer aircraft which underwent the F118 re-engining programme became U-2STs. In the first batch of three F118-powered aircraft was a single-seater (80-1071), one existing two-seater (80-1064) and another two-seater (80-1078) which was produced by conversion of a single-seater which had been badly damaged. The four trainers have since been redesignated TU-2R and TU-2S to bring them in line with standard USAF nomenclature.

Markings
The first two TR-1Bs were completed in a white scheme to signify their training status but were soon painted in the matt black of the operational aircraft. The third and fourth trainers were black from the start. Originally the markings consisted solely of a red serial on the fin made up of the last five digits of the serial (80-1091 wore 01091). When Strategic Air Command was amalgamated into Air Combat Command, the U-2 fleet acquired Tactical Air Command-style serials consisting of the fiscal year (80) in small digits and the last-three (091) in large digits. At the same time the TAC-style two-letter tailcode was applied, the 9th RW adopting 'BB'.

Fin
The tall fin is a conventional two-spar and rib aluminium construction. Trimming adjustment is accomplished on the ground by means of a simple bend tab.

Speed brakes
An electronically-controlled and hydraulically-operated airbrake is situated on either side of the rear fuselage. Maximum deflection is 60°.

The wing fold incorporates three interleaving fixtures which maintain the dynamic loads on the spars. A pin is fixed through the leaves to lock them, and a small strip then fairs over the small gap left in the skin surface.

The turned-down wingtip has abradable strips on the bottom to protect the structure on landing. The cylindrical fairing added on the end accommodates radar warning receiver antennas facing outwards at 45° and the wingtip navigation light.

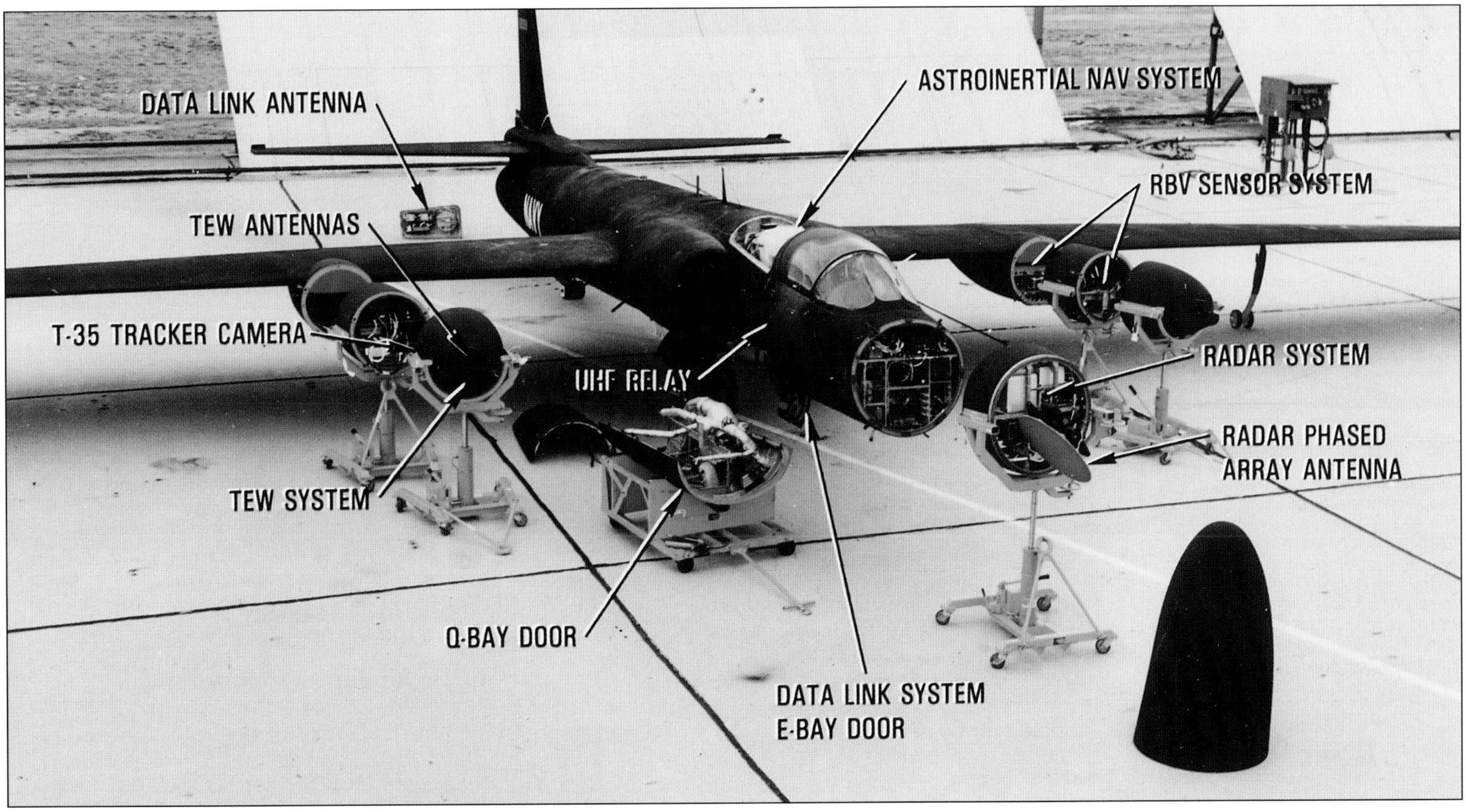

***Above:** This view of the **U-2EP-X** provides an example of how a reconnaissance system can be accommodated in the **U-2** airframe. Note that the **EP-X** had slipper-type wing pods rather than the full-size superpods used by later **U-2R** variants.*

The most distinctive of the U-2 nose sections is that housing the ASARS-2 radar (left). This has a cooling air scoop on the top (right). ASARS-2 has undergone an upgrade to provide full MTI capability.

***Left:** Aft of the tailwheel is this fairing for the datalink equipment.*

***Below:** The cockpit is provided with internal mirrors either side and an external mirror to port. The latter is primarily used to check for contrails. Note the cockpit ventilation fan.*

***Above:** Located under the cockpit are pitot/air data tubes and the glass bubble for the driftsight. The latter can be controlled from the cockpit to provide a near-hemispherical view under the aircraft.*

***Above:** The vertical and horizontal stablisers are bolted together, so that when the horizontal surfaces are moved for trimming, the vertical fin also pivots, accounting for the small silver strip at the leading edge. U-2s are always towed tail-first.*

***Left:** The outrigger pogo is shown in position.*

Seen from a T-38, a 99th RS U-2R flies over northern California. On the rare occasions that the U-2 is flown on a purely low-level training sortie, the pilot can enjoy the comfort of flying in a standard flight suit and standard helmet as opposed to the bulky pressure kit.

resumed the high-altitude air sampling role, a capability now also maintained by the 99th. After the Chernobyl disaster in 1986, a U-2 flew over Western Europe, configured with the specially adapted hatch and Q-bay assembly, which includes an airscoop, gas bottles and particle filters.

The standard USAF aircrew duty day is 12 hours, and a U-2 pilot scheduled for an operational mission will likely use every minute of it. The reporting, suit-up and pre-breathing phase takes about two hours, and post-flight reporting at least 30 minutes. That leaves time for a nine-hour 30-minute flight, although longer missions are technically possible with special waivers.

Climb profile

The U-2R climbs quickly to beyond 50,000 ft (15240 m), whereupon it enters a gradual cruise climb for the rest of the flight, ascending as fuel is burned off to 70,000 ft (21340 m) or above. The numbers vary depending on the mission weight, range required, outside air temperature and other factors. When it is time to return, speedbrakes and landing gear are deployed – otherwise, the U-2 will not leave altitude until the engine quits. Contrary to popular misconception, U-2 pilots never cut the engine and glide to increase the range.

Stories of high-altitude emergencies and deadstick landings are part of U-2 lore, and could fill a book. Suffice to say, the aircraft has a safety record better than average. The 1980s were virtually accident-free, apart from three write-offs in 1984 when – for the only recorded time – a design factor was to blame in two cases. (The engine adaptor/tailpipe link failed, and had to be redesigned. Luckily, all three pilots made successful ejections).

Beale also trains mission planners, who are the hidden heroes of the U-2 community. Focusing on the targets requested by intelligence, the planners devise the ground tracks which will enable a flight to cover them. When the limitations of particular sensors, national borders, and terrain-masking factors are taken into account, this becomes a complicated process. Extreme accuracy is required; for instance, the H-camera used on some flights covers only a 2-mile (3.2-km) swath of territory when operating at nadir (e.g., looking straight down). As pilots say, it's like viewing the ground through a soda straw, and an incorrectly plotted track will miss the target completely.

Permanent European detachment

Having deployed the U-2R and the SR-71 to Mildenhall with increasing frequency in the late 1970s, the US eventually gained British permission for sustained operations. Det 4 of the 9th SRW was established at the Suffolk base in April 1979 with a single U-2R (initially 68-10338). While the Blackbird's role was still photo, the European activities of the 'Dragon Lady' were dedicated to Sigint. In the dying days of 1979, the 9th SRW deployed its first Senior Glass aircraft to Europe (68-10339). In this configuration, the Senior Ruby Elint system was combined with the Senior Spear Comint system to produce a versatile collection capability. The classically clean profile of the 'jet-powered glider' was no more. Multiple radio monitoring and direction-finding (DF) antennas protruded from the lower fuselage and the superpods, which were now asymmetric since the left pod sported a 'canoe'-type fairing housing parts of the Spear system.

The detailed capabilities of these two collection systems remain classified; they have since been updated and are still primary U-2R sensor systems. The basic capability was revealed in 1985 by the main contractor, E-Systems Melpar Division, when it gained permission to market the Airborne Remotely Controlled Electronic Support Measures System for export. Its brochure described the advantages to be gained by orbiting a small aircraft at high altitude with its sensors datalinked to a Ground Control Facility (GCF). "The critical signal processing equipment, data bases, and skilled operator/analysts with their support electronics and displays are in a safe haven," it noted. Only the antennas and receivers would be "compromised" if anything went wrong.

Sigint system

The radio monitoring system used 24 receivers in the HF, VHF and UHF bands, to detect AM, FM, CW, SSB and WBFM transmissions. Direction finding was via multi-baseline phase interferometric techniques. The radar detection system also used 'highly accurate' phase interferometer DF, and had automatic scan and reporting capability. Operators in the ground control facility could specify the search strategies. The datalink was highly directional, and provided a full-duplex HF voice or RTTY capability. The GCF itself was housed in transportable shelters, with as many as 18 consoles displaying data in full-colour graphics.

The Sigint mission was codenamed Creek Spectre by US European Command (EUCOM), and was flown by Det 4 from Mildenhall until February 1982, when the newly

Right: The sole aircraft built as a U-2RT (80-1091) taxis in after a rainstorm, its crew wearing low-level flight gear.

Below: Taxiing from its barn at Beale, this U-2R displays the three-pane windows for the small T-35 tracker camera mounted in the tip of the nose. Also noteworthy is the discrepancies in paint between the first three and last two digits of the tail number. This arises from the regular switching of rear fuselage sections.

The first ASARS-2 radar was flight-tested in U-2R 68-10336, seen here over the Palmdale runway. The long antenna required an extended nose, while other black boxes were housed in the Q-bay. It was rapidly to become possibly the most important sensor to the U-2R. Note the externally stiffened tailplane, a characteristic feature of the FY68 aircraft.

activated 17th Reconnaissance Wing took it over from nearby Alconbury. The 17th was a former bomb wing which was revived to fly the TR-1s in Europe. The 95th Reconnaissance Squadron was the operating squadron, and the reporting line was ostensibly back to SAC Headquarters in Omaha. Following the principles established by the 1977 Joint Recce Study, the 17th's operational tasking came from EUCOM.

The first TR-1A for the 17th (80-1068) was flown from Beale via Patrick to an icy Alconbury on 12 February 1983. This was its second visit to the UK, having been displayed by Lockheed at the Farnborough air show in the previous September in an attempt to interest NATO nations in the aircraft's battlefield reconnaissance capability. The British government was the main potential customer, but the MoD was about to launch its own CASTOR programme and so it did not pursue the matter. (Thirteen years later, the MoD was still trying to launch the programme, by now renamed ASTOR, and the U-2 was back in contention.)

The 17th was expanded only slowly, since the ASARS-2 radar sensor was not yet ready for deployment. With its first two aircraft, the routine nine-hour Creek Spectre flights were continued. The wing's first serious mishap occurred in October 1982 when a bus containing security police was driven into its third aircraft (80-1069). The aircraft was returned to the US inside a C-141 for repair, and subsequently redelivered. The 17th pilots and ground crews insisted that it did not fly correctly after the accident, and the USAF eventually gave up on the aircraft and leased it to NASA. The maintenance at Moffett Field was contracted to Lockheed engineers, who promptly re-rigged 069's control surfaces, and NASA pilots have flown it ever since without complaint.

ASARS arrives in Europe

In March 1985, the 17th RW received three more TR-1s and the long-awaited ASARS-2. On 9 July 1985, 95th RS commander Lieutenant Colonel John Sander flew the first operational ASARS-2 sortie. The world of airborne reconnaissance would never be the same. For the first time, tactical commanders were provided with timely results from an imaging sensor which could operate round-the-clock, with no regard to cloud cover or whether it was day or night. The U-2/TR-1 was the ideal platform for ASARS-2. It provided the highest-possible operating altitude, thus enabling the radar to see over and around terrain which would be masked from view at lower levels. By flying far above the earth's weather patterns, the aircraft

Every U-2 landing is accompanied by the 'mobile', a fast car driven by another U-2 pilot in radio contact with the landing aircraft. As the U-2 crosses the threshold, the car accelerates behind it, allowing the driver to aid the pilot to land the aircraft, chiefly by calling off the height from the runway as the aircraft slowly sinks to earth.

The UK government announced its permission for the TR-1 fleet to be based at RAF Alconbury shortly before the aircraft's first flight in 1981. The first aircraft arrived with the 17th RW's 95th Reconnaissance Squadron in February 1983. This is the third production aircraft, seen configured for the photo mission with an optical Q-bay hatch.

Although the 95th RS fleet performed occasional photo missions, Sigint duties were far more important. This aircraft has a Senior Spear Comint fit. Initial plans called for the 17th RW to have 18 aircraft, 12 at the parent base at Alconbury and six detached to Wethersfield. In the event, the total was cut to 14, all at Alconbury. The force was run down with the end of the Cold War, the 17th RW being deactivated while the much-reduced 95th RS was reassigned to the 9th SRW.

provided the extreme stability which is demanded by the 'synthetic' array.

ASARS-2 operates in X-band to produce constant scale imagery in plan view, even when operating at long stand-off ranges. Ground resolution can be independent of range, by increasing the 'length' of the array in direct proportion to the area under investigation. Increased resolution can be commanded in the 'spot mode' by changing the look angle of the antenna as the aircraft moves along track, so that it repeatedly maps a smaller area of particular interest.

Like the Sigint sensors, ASARS is controlled from the ground via the wideband datalink in real time. For the European theatre, a new ground station was ordered from Ford Aerospace, which later became part of Loral (before it too was subsumed into Lockheed Martin). The TREDS (TR-1 Exploitation Demonstration System) was set up in trailers at a former missile maintenance facility near Hahn AB, Germany, codenamed Metro Tango. This interim system was scheduled to be replaced by two fully hardened underground stations named TRIGS (TR-1 Ground Stations), but the first TRIGS was never completed due to the end of the Cold War.

Operational evaluation

When ASARS flights began from Alconbury in 1985, the Cold War was still a reality. For the next three years, the system was 'wrung out' above NATO's Central European front. The process included the complicated task of integrating the operation of the Sigint systems with that of the radar. For instance, the radar's spot mode might be cued by an emission detected by the Ruby sensor. It would then image and allow identification, perhaps of vehicles belonging to a surface-to-surface missile battalion which had moved position recently.

In theory, the TR-1 could reconnoitre territory up to 350 miles (565 km) across the Warsaw Pact border. That is the horizon for the Sigint sensors, although the radar's useful range is about 100 miles (160 km) less. The range from aircraft to ground station can be more than 300 miles (480 km) in ideal conditions.

NATO ground force commanders were excited by the new capabilities, but demanded more flexible methods of distributing the data. The US Army ordered a mobile ground station from Westinghouse known as the TRAC (Tactical RAdar Correlator). This was housed in a 40-ft (12-m) container, and could deploy to the field and operate independently from the TREDS/TRIGS. The UK and US jointly funded a programme to process and disseminate ASARS data to NATO. The TADMS (TR-1 ASARS Data Manipulation System) was built by GE and Ferranti in 1989, and manned by RAF personnel.

The 17th RW received more TR-1As directly from the production line, and was eventually assigned 12 aircraft. Although the PLSS had been cancelled, the wing needed enough aircraft for its wartime task of providing two TR-1 orbits across Central Europe on a 24-hour basis, which would mean launching six aircraft each day. Expensive new facilities were built as Alconbury, including 13 unique wide-span hardened aircraft shelters and a hardened avionics and sensor maintenance facility known as Magic Mountain. The USAF's only hyperbaric chamber in Europe was built for the 17th's Physiological Support Division.

On a typical day, seven or eight training or operational flights would be launched. There were occasional long photo sorties under SAC control codenamed Senior Look, as well as the Creek Spectre missions for EUCOM. The 17th wing grew to more than 500 personnel, and the 95th RS had an authorised strength of 18 pilots. The wing helped develop a new flight planning system running on a minicomputer, which automated much of the drudgery involved in devising flight tracks. It was the most advanced in the USAF.

Final delivery

TR-1A 80-1099, the last of the new-build aircraft, was accepted by the USAF on 3 October 1989 and reassigned to Alconbury six months later. After various changes of plan stemming mainly from the protracted development and ultimate cancellation of PLSS, a total of 37 aircraft was built at Palmdale from 1981 to 1989. They comprised 25 TR-1As, two dual-control TR-1B trainers, two ER-2s for NASA, and the 'black budget' U-2Rs – seven U-2Rs and a single dual-control U-2R (T). Three of the first five TR-1As had already been 'converted' to U-2R configuration.

Operations at Alconbury usually involved at least one mission launch each day to patrol the West/East German border. Regular training missions were also mounted, the aircraft being flown without mission equipment fitted (illustrated).

The USAF professed itself well satisfied with the deal. General Mike Loh, commander of AFSC, declared that "this programme was built on partnership and trust. We kept the auditors and inspectors to the minimum. We knew that Lockheed would keep their side of the bargain, and adhere to the 14 operating rules of the Skunk Works – especially the one about not surprising the customer."

The concept of real-time reconnaissance had received a boost from the TR-1 programme, but the system which evolved in Europe had one important drawback: the aircraft remain 'tethered' to the ground station by the datalink. If a U-2 needed to roam further afield than the 220 miles (355 km) line-of-sight distance to the ground station, the sensor 'take' had to be recorded for relay when the ground station was once more within range. Moreover, political or military circumstances might not always be such that a ground station could actually be deployed.

Data uplink

Back in 1975, Skunk Works engineer Bob Anderson had devised a solution to the problem. Why not install a satellite antenna on the U-2, and uplink the data for transmission back to the US? The US military was then launching its second-generation Defense Systems Communications Satellites (DSCS) with multiple channels. Although satellites were already relaying U-2 data to the US from ground stations in the Senior Stretch programme, it was another 10 years before the USAF adopted Anderson's idea, when it approved the Senior Span development. (Anderson became U-2 programme manager when Fred Cavanaugh retired.)

Lockheed worked with E-Systems and Unisys Government Systems Group (previously named Sperry) to devise the U-2's satcom link. The three contractors had to overcome considerable technical challenges to turn the concept into reality. Unisys had provided the U-2 air-ground datalink, and now provided the buffer into which the aircraft's sensor data could flow and be configured for transmission by an airborne modem. A 30-in (76-cm) parabolic antenna was designed, steerable in both azimuth and elevation at 60° per second and capable of elevation angles up to 85°.

The challenges for the Skunk Works were to build a lightweight composite radome for the antenna and attach it so that U-2's delicate centre of gravity was not disturbed, nor its inflight vibration increased; to provide a high-voltage power supply; and to interface the aircraft's INS system.

Aerodynamic flight tests of the Span pod began on 80-1071 in 1985. The unpressurised radome was nearly 17 ft (5.2 m) long and the whole system weighed 400 lb (180 kg). It was mounted on the upper fuselage immediately aft of the ADF antenna. Someone outside the fence at Palmdale photographed the secret new configuration from a side-on position at some distance, and sent his snap to *Janes's All The World's Aircraft*, describing it as an AWACS development of the U-2.

The programme moved slowly forward as the considerable problems were overcome, such as the requirement to constantly track the DSCS satellite through the various aircraft manoeuvres. Pointing commands of the Span antenna depended on extremely accurate positioning data being provided by the aircraft's INS (and on the satellite being in the expected location at the expected time).

A U-2R equipped with ASARS, Spear and Ruby lands at NAS Jacksonville. Operational missions launched from the mainland United States have been aimed at Caribbean flashpoints and, especially in the 1980s, Central America.

Global deployments have been a regular feature of U-2 operations throughout the aircraft's career. In addition to England and Cyprus, the U-2 force has operated for many years from Osan AB in South Korea. From here the 'Black Cat' aircraft of the 5th Reconnaissance Squadron (previously Det 2) provide constant surveillance of developments north of the 38th Parallel.

Moreover, the whole installation had to transmit and receive through a single antenna, since the principle was preserved that the sensors could be reconfigured by ground-based operators who received and analysed the 'take'.

The first deployments with fully-configured Senior Span U-2R 68-10331 were made to Patrick AFB and Suwon AB, South Korea. In March 1989, the first deployment to Europe was made when 80-1070 arrived at Alconbury. Airborne reconnaissance had finally entered the space age.

New electro-optical sensor

When Iraq invaded Kuwait in August 1990, 80-1070 was one of the first two U-2s sent from Beale to Saudi Arabia in response. The second was also in a new configuration. It was equipped with SYERS – the Senior Year Electro-optical Relay System. SYERS had evolved from the new generation of photo reconnaissance satellites in the late 1970s, in which digitised imagery was relayed to ground stations for processing. This was made possible by replacing the traditional 'wet' film exposed by the camera lens with light-sensitive semi-conducting silicon. The silicon was arranged in arrays of charged-coupled devices (CCDs), which transformed the light energy into electrical charges, ready to be amplified and transmitted as a string of numbers.

The SYERS camera was developed for the U-2 in the mid-1980s by Itek, a division of Litton which had dominated large optics for satellite imaging. When the new concept was first presented to Lockheed, Itek assumed that the new camera would be fitted in the Q-bay, where the U-2's existing film cameras were housed. This would have entailed designing a new Q-bay optical hatch, but Lockheed had other ideas. The company dusted off the old drawings for a rotating nose section, which had been designed to house a sensor for the tracking of re-entry vehicles. This was been one of the earliest proposed applications for the U-2R, but had fallen by the wayside. The Senior Open nose was thus fabricated, with one optical glass aperture in the first 4 ft (1.2 m) of the nose, which was rotated by a servo to 'look' left, right or below the aircraft flight path. The camera's mirror system was housed here, while its body remained fixed within the rest of the nose section.

Specifications for the SYERS camera have not been released, but after it was developed Itek was cleared to market an Electro-Optical LOROP sensor which has a 110-in (280-cm) focal length and uses a 10,240-element CCD array as the detector. This camera is 43 in (110 cm) long and weighs 490 lb (220 kg), with another 90 lb (40 kg) for the control electronics and EO processor. It provides panoramic coverage with high resolution to the horizon.

After flight tests, the first SYERS system was deployed for operational testing at the 9th SRW's Det 2 in Korea, where a hardened ground station had already been established for ASARS operations. The ground portion of SYERS is codenamed Senior Blade, and performs similar functions to the ASARS ground station: control of the sensor, processing, display and reporting of the imagery. As with ASARS, the U-2 can record SYERS imagery onboard when it flies beyond line-of-sight to the ground station.

Lockheed Martin provides support for the U-2R/S fleet from the Skunk Works Plant 2 facility at Palmdale. Here three ASARS-equipped aircraft are seen after returning from the Gulf. A further three aircraft are in the U-2 maintenance hangar.

Desert Shield

The SYERS and Span aircraft touched down at King Fahad Royal Saudi Air Base, Taif on 17 August 1990, just 15 days after the Iraqi invasion. Two days later, both aircraft mounted their first patrols of the Kuwait border, thanks to a minor miracle of logistics. Within two weeks, 160 personnel and aircraft support equipment, including a three-week supply of the U-2's special JPTS fuel, had been airlifted to the Saudi base. The Senior Blade van had been positioned nearer to the Kuwait border at Riyadh, so that the SYERS aircraft would remain 'on-tether' for most of the time.

It was quickly decided to send TR-1s from Alconbury to the new location, which had been designated Operating Location CH (for 'Camel Hump'). Although they had only begun operational testing in March, the TRAC and TADMS mobile ground stations were airlifted from

U-2 sensors

From its lofty perch the U-2 can use a range of sensors depending on mission requirements. The SYERS, H-camera and Iris are all electro-optical sensors for long-range oblique, overhead or panoramic imagery, using either daylight or infra-red. The ASARS-2 radar produces radar images of photographic quality at long oblique ranges. A comprehensive signals intelligence gathering suite can be carried, knwon as Senior Glass. This comprises the Senior Ruby Elint system (distinguished by the flat-sided forward portion of the superpods, and the Senior Spear Comint system with large antenna farm). Data can be downlinked over short distances by the antenna under the rear fuselage, but for global transfer of intelligence the data is uplinked via the Senior Span system (for Senior Glass data) or Senior Spur (for ASARS data).

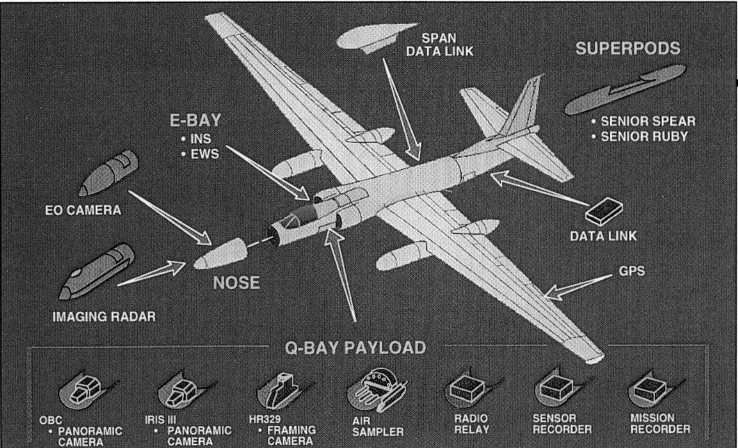

This diagram shows the main sensor-carrying areas of the U-2, with some of the different Q-bay hatches available. There are three different nose options: ASARS, SYERS (EO camera) and the standard 'slick' nose.

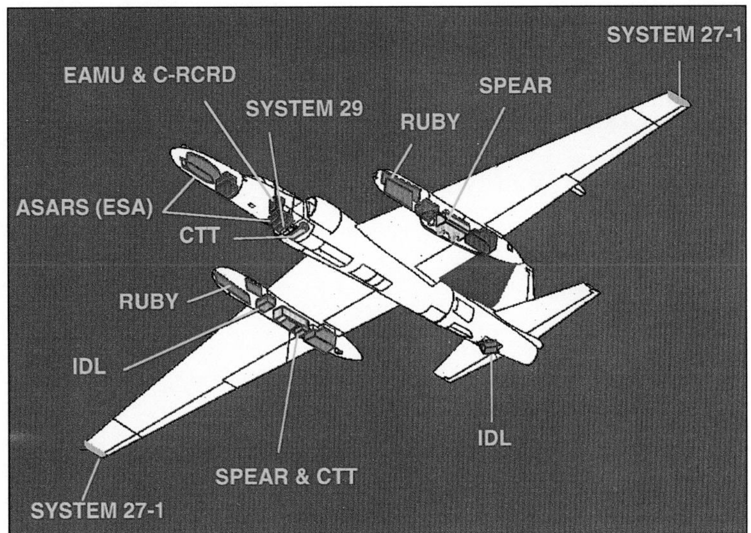

Shown above is a typical mission configuration for an ***ASARS/Sigint*** *aircraft, with radar recording equipment in the Q-bay. The self-protection electronic suite (Systems 27-1 and 29) is also shown.*

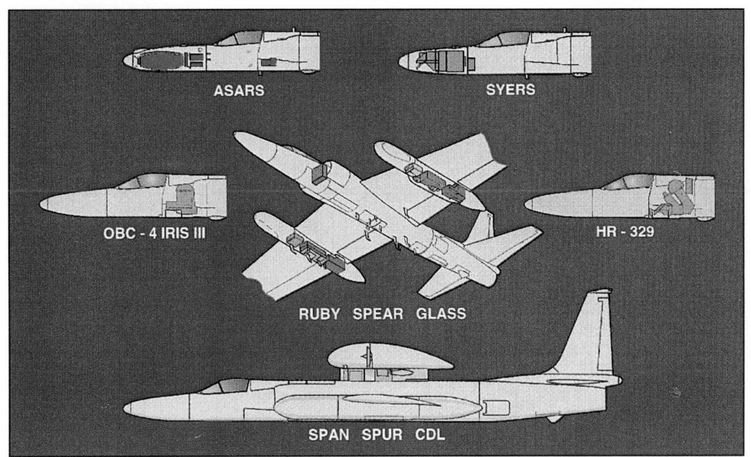

Above are the main payload options, comprising ***ASARS*** *and* ***SYERS***, *the* ***Iris*** *or* ***H-cameras***, ***Senior Ruby Elint*** *and* ***Senior Spear Comint*** *systems (together known as* ***Senior Glass***), *and the* ***Senior Span/Spur*** *datalink.*

One of the most important sensors carried by the ***U-2R/S*** *fleet is the* ***Hughes ASARS-2*** *synthetic aperture radar, which can produce high-resolution imagery at long slant ranges on either side of the flight path. Shown at right is the first production radar being loaded into the purpose-built nose – note the two canted antenna arrays. Shown left is an example of* ***ASARS*** *imagery, depicting the* ***Los Angeles International Airport*** *area. A spot mode is available to provide far greater detail of much smaller areas.* ***ASARS*** *has recently received a major modification to improve its* ***MTI*** *(moving target indicator) capability.*

Below is ***H-camera*** *imagery of another* ***U-2*** *of the* ***9th SRW's Det 5*** *at* ***McCoy AFB*** *in* ***Florida***. *Note the ground crew in appropriate formation.*

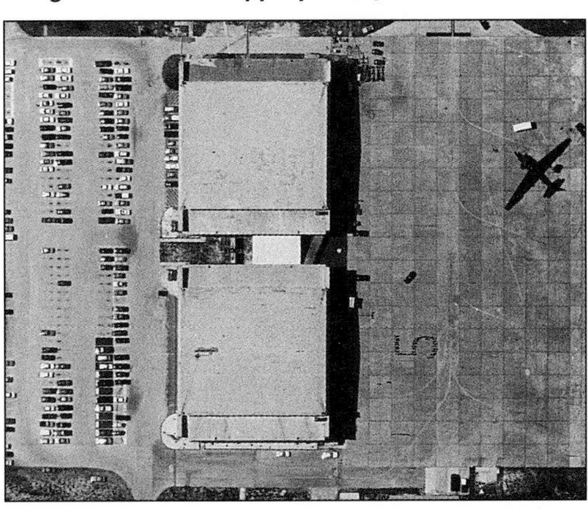

The ***Iris III*** *and* ***OBC*** *cameras provide panoramic coverage across a wide area. This oblique image shows damage after a* ***California*** *earthquake.*

From high altitude, images like this false-colour infra-red photograph show the curvature of the earth. Here the target is ***San Francisco Bay***.

When it was first seen by outsiders, the dorsal fairing later identified as Senior Span was thought to house a form of AEW radar. Its true purpose is to uplink data from the Sigint collection systems to satellites, which then relay the data across global distances. This allows commanders and analysts half a world away to receive data in near real-time.

Right: Groaning under the weight of the Senior Span pod and a comprehensive Senior Glass (combination of Spear and Ruby) fit, this U-2R taxis for a mission from Alconbury. Span-equipped aircraft appeared in Europe primarily in response to the crisis in former Yugoslavia.

Germany and set up next to the Blade van in the compound of the US Training Mission (USTM) at Riyadh. (They were joined there by more ground stations for the RC-135 Rivet Joint Elint aircraft and the J-STARS, which led to considerable overcrowding.)

A pair of 17th RW TR-1As arrived on 23 August, and the first ASARS mission was flown six days later. The 17th RW was tasked to support OL-CH by performing phase maintenance on the deployed aircraft, and so a steady shuttle of personnel and aircraft developed between Alconbury and Taif. OL-CH was redesignated the 1704th Reconnaissance Squadron (Provisional) when SAC established the 1700th Strategic Wing (Provisional) alongside CENTCOM's forward-deployed staff at Riyadh. Another SYERS-equipped U-2R was sent from Korea to the desert on 11 October.

By the end of November, the five aircraft at Taif had performed 204 missions, some of them lasting 11 hours. They were flown under normal peacetime rules which required that the flight tracks be no closer than 15 miles (24 km) to the Iraqi border. Even so, from 70,000 ft (21335 m) and above, the SYERS and ASARS sensors could image most of southern Iraq, while the Sigint sensors on the Span aircraft covered most of Iraq, including Baghdad. The usual routine was to fly a SYERS mission every day, an ASARS mission every night, and a Span mission every second day.

Iraq 'painted' the U-2 flights with its air defence radars, and in mid-September began launching MiG-25 fighters in response. They flew along the border, parallel to the U-2 and 5,000 ft (1525 m) below. In response, the System 20 IRCM pod which had not been regularly used on the U-2 for some years was reactivated. A direct voice link to the USAF E-3A AWACS was established for the first time – in Europe, all communications from the U-2 pilot to the outside world were channelled via Metro Tango. F-15 fighters were tasked to fly MiG-CAP in support of the U-2 flights.

Call for photos

CENTCOM commanders liked what they saw from the U-2, but those planning the air war in the 'Black Hole' at Riyadh wanted more, including hard-copy photos. (The ground stations could print ASARS and SYERS imagery, but it was a protracted process.) The call went back to Beale for camera-equipped aircraft and photo-processing vans. The 9th Reconnaissance Technical Squadron (RTS, or 'recce-tech') scrambled to bring the 15-van Mobile Intelligence Processing Element (MIPE) back into service. It had been mothballed when the SR-71 was deactivated. The MIPE deployed to Riyadh in mid-December, and the 9th deployed U-2Rs with IRIS III and H-cameras to Taif in late December and early January.

Taif was also the base for the F-111Fs of the 48th TFW

from RAF Lakenheath. Their pilots and mission planners approached the U-2 squadron directly for target information, trying to short-circuit the system. The solution was to send a 48th pilot to the ground station at Riyadh, where he could view the imagery on-screen and interpret it for his colleagues. In the last week of December, the 'Aardvark'/'Dragon Lady' alliance was cemented when an exercise confirmed the practicality of relaying target information derived from SYERS and ASARS to airborne F-111s, via the TRAC, TACC (Theatre Air Control Center), and ABCCC aircraft. Within 10 minutes of a target being imaged, its co-ordinates were in the TACC's hands.

As the United Nations' deadline for an Iraqi withdrawal approached, CENTCOM made plans to send the U-2 over Iraq if war broke out. A second Senior Blade van was requested, to be deployed closer to the border. The U-2's reconnaissance capabilities, and potential additional roles as an airborne data relay and a 'high-altitude FAC', were explored and explained to CENTCOM planners, most of whom had no knowledge of 'Dragon Lady' operations.

Desert Storm

As soon as there was enough light for SYERS on 17 January, Major Blaine Bachus flew the first U-2R mission across the border. His task was to image the fixed 'Scud' missile sites at H2 and H3 airfields, and to perform bomb damage assessment (BDA) from the initial F-117 attacks. The 'Scuds' were a high-priority target, given their potential for chemical warfare, and they soon became the major priority when Iraq began firing them at Israel.

Mission planners drew up flight tracks which ensured that Bachus and those who followed flew at least 10 miles (16 km) from known SAM sites. The exigencies of war quickly intervened, and many U-2 flights during Desert Storm were retasked when airborne, requiring pilots to replot their own tracks and make critical judgements about whether to fly near or over SAM sites. In fact, the U-2's supposed vulnerability to SAMs was did not prevent the aircraft from providing valuable intelligence about them. Some missions were specifically flown to pinpoint SAMs, such as one flown by Captain Bryan Anderson on 22 January which identified multiple SA-2, SA-3 and AAA sites in western Iraq. Lieutenant Colonel Steve Peterson (the 1704th RS commander) and Major James Milligan both flew missions which were deliberately routed within lethal range of known SAM sites. An estimated 15 fixed 'Scud' sites were identified from U-2/TR-1 imagery and eliminated during the first week of the war. Ten of them were assessed as destroyed by one strike package which launched on the second day of the war, less than one hour after they were identified by a TR-1 flown deep into northern Iraq flown by Lieutenant Colonel James Burger.

Mobile 'Scud' sites were a more difficult proposition. The U-2 had to go 'off-tether' in order to cover the more distant parts of Iraq, although commissioning of the second Senior Blade van helped increase real-time SYERS processing. There was a time delay while the U-2 returned within range of the ground station to download its imagery. The Iraqis learned to hide their 'Scud' Transporter/Erector/Launchers (TEL) by day, and quickly move into place, fire and withdraw by night. The 'Black Hole' responded by co-ordinating the night-time patrols of a U-2R and an F-15E. When the ASARS sensor located a suspected TEL, the Strike Eagle was primed to destroy it. Several mobile 'Scud' kills were claimed with this technique, but subsequent analysis showed that the 'kills' were of decoys, shorter-range FROG missiles, or ordinary trucks.

Some of this analysis is disputed, and U-2s were certainly responsible for some TEL kills. These include the one that misfired a 'Scud' on the night of 22 February, which detonated just 3 miles (4.8 km) from a TR-1 flown by Captain Mark McDonald. (In fact, U-2 pilots observed most of the 'Scud' launches from their lofty perch.) Undoubtedly, too, the Iraqi mobile 'Scud' crews knew they were being hunted. As a result, their launch rate and accuracy declined significantly.

When Desert Storm was initiated, the 1704th had nine aircraft at Taif, and another three were quickly added. At least five missions were flown each day during the air

***Top:* A logical outgrowth of the Senior Span programme was Senior Spur. Whereas Span could uplink the data from the Sigint system, Spur provides a similar function for the ASARS-2 radar imagery. Shown here is Lockheed's original test aircraft for the ASARS/Spur configuration.**

***Above:* Operational trials of the Senior Spur equipment were undertaken from Alconbury in 1992 using 68-10339, also equipped with Glass Sigint gear. The modified Skunk Works badge is noteworthy, as is the dielectric portion of the ASARS nose.**

U-2Rs have remained at Taif since the end of the Gulf War, monitoring the ceasefire terms and subsequent United Nations Security Council resolutions. The unit, manned from Beale, is known as the 4402nd Reconnaissance Squadron (Provisional), and the aircraft received 'UN' tailcodes.

campaign, rising to eight on some days during the land campaign. Most lasted more than eight hours, and some were voluntarily extended by their pilots to 11 hours when the need arose.

More outfits sent pilots or artillery officers to the U-2 ground stations, from where they could convey exactly what they saw on the screens to their flight crews or gunners. On one occasion, a B-52 bombardier in the TRAC van spotted a likely bomb dump and diverted a B-52 strike inbound from Diego Garcia to hit it, with spectacular results. Towards the end of the war, U-2 pilots became 'high-altitude FACs' by identifying tanks concentrations and relaying the co-ordinates for attack by allied artillery. On many occasions, U-2 pilots co-ordinated search and rescue attempts for downed pilots.

Assisting the ground war

When the ground forces attacked on 24 February, a TR-1 provided hour-by-hour imagery updates of precise Iraqi front-line armour and troop movements. Coalition troops advanced more quickly than expected, and another TR-1 mission the next day proved invaluable in keeping CENTCOM commanders abreast of the fluid situation, so they could cut off the Iraqi retreat.

The day after the war ended, a U-2 equipped with the IRIS camera flew back and forth across large parts of the battlefield to take a synoptic view of the carnage below. When this film was eventually analysed back in Washington, it indicated that CENTCOM had seriously overestimated the number of Iraqi weapons which had been destroyed in the air campaign. U-2 photography had been used for BDA during the war. With so many 'smart'

Below: A 9th RW U-2R cruises serenely over the California countryside near its base at Beale. On operational missions the engine is run at full power until the descent from altitude. Rated at 18,000 lb (80.10 kN) thrust at sea level, the thrust level falls off as the aircraft climbs into the thinner air at altitude.

Above: Towards the end of the 1980s the J75 engine of the U-2R was becoming increasingly difficult and costly to support, while newer engines were offering greater levels of thrust, performance and economy. Using 80-1090 as a testbed, Lockheed fitted the General Electric F101-GE-F29 engine, the aircraft flying first in 1989. This engine, a non-afterburning derivative of the Northrop B-2's powerplant, was soon redesignated F118-GE-101.

missiles and bombs flying through windows and air vents to destroy buildings, a high-resolution sensor was often needed to confirm a kill. The IRIS and especially the H-camera could do the job, but their 'wet film' take had to be flown from Taif to Riyadh on a C-21 courier aircraft for processing at the MIPE. There, it could take all day just to handle a single IRIS mission with its 10,000 ft (3050 m) of film. It all took too long.

The overall contribution made by the U-2 to Desert Storm was substantial. The 1704th RS flew 260 missions totalling over 2,000 hours, with 80 per cent of this time spent above Iraq or occupied Kuwait. The vast majority of missions took off when scheduled. The U-2 community calculated that they had supplied over 50 per cent of all imagery intelligence and 90 per cent of the Army's targeting intelligence. So much for reconnaissance satellites,

This aircraft is a U-2R in the classic clean-wing, slick-nose configuration. There are only a small number of detailed external differences between the models, including the repositioning of the external start and nitrogen panels to a position higher on the fuselage, and the deletion of the engine bleed air exhausts from the U-2S.

Pilots from the 1704th Reconnaissance Squadron (Provisional) pose in front of a U-2R at Taif. From this Saudi base the five U-2Rs maintained a vigil on Iraq throughout Desert Shield and Desert Storm, and long after. The U-2 was vital to the prosecution of the war, providing much data on Iraqi force dispositions while being used on the 'Great Scud Hunt'. The force remained alert for, but relatively untroubled by Iraqi defences, although aircraft were sometimes tracked by MiG-25s.

This U-2R of the 99th Reconnaissance Squadron (the operational unit) is seen at relatively low altitude over Lake Tahoe. A relatively recent addition to the antenna fit is the GPS pod on the port wing. This has replaced the Northrop star-tracker system as the primary navigation aid.

which were often defeated by haze, smoke or bad weather; when they did take useful images, the product was simply not available to the right people at the right time.

When it was all over, most of the plaudits went to J-STARS, the hugely expensive battlefield radar flown in two converted Boeing 707s, which was still under development. This had a Moving Target Indicator (MTI) as well as a Synthetic Aperture Radar (SAR) mode, with the data also downlinked to ground stations. Partly because the Span and SYERS sensors were still classified, the U-2 remained an unsung hero.

The end of the Cold War eliminated the TR-1's role in Central Europe, yet Desert Storm had proved that there was no substitute for the U-2. In June 1991 the 17th RW was deactivated, but the USAF kept the squadron structure and five TR-1s at Alconbury. For a while, it seemed that some of the other TR-1s would go into storage, but continuing instability in southern Europe, the Persian Gulf, the Korean Peninsula and elsewhere forced a re-evaluation. Soon, the 'Dragon Lady' was flying over war-torn former Yugoslavia.

Force reorganisation

In October, the TR-1 designation was dropped. In June 1992, the deactivation of Strategic Air Command swept away most of the centralised control and tasking of U-2

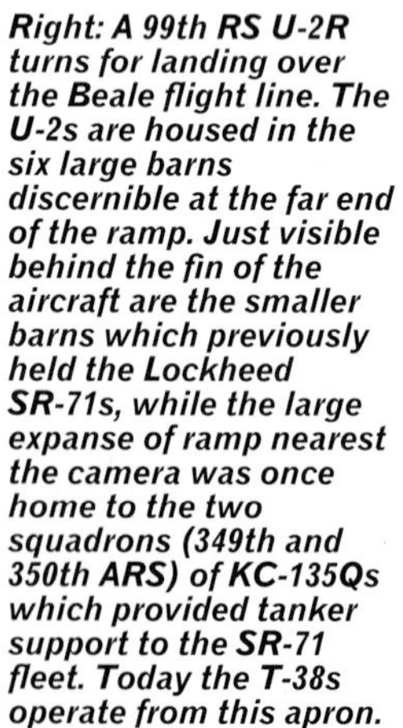

Right: A 99th RS U-2R turns for landing over the Beale flight line. The U-2s are housed in the six large barns discernible at the far end of the ramp. Just visible behind the fin of the aircraft are the smaller barns which previously held the Lockheed SR-71s, while the large expanse of ramp nearest the camera was once home to the two squadrons (349th and 350th ARS) of KC-135Qs which provided tanker support to the SR-71 fleet. Today the T-38s operate from this apron.

operations, and the 9th Wing became part of Air Combat Command (ACC). Theatre commanders no longer had to go through bureaucratic hoops in Washington and Omaha to get a mission flown. The 'lessons learned' from Desert Storm were slowly being applied, as the communications architecture was improved and the U-2 slowly but surely became a reconnaissance system.

More Senior Span uplinks were procured, and the principle of transmitting the 'take' via satellite was extended to ASARS imagery. This was not a simple task, since much larger bandwidths were required. The DSCS satellites were unsuitable, so the system was adapted to use NASA's Tracking and Data Relay Satellite (TDRS) which operates in Ku-band instead of SHF. A prototype of the new Senior Spur system was deployed to Alconbury and Sigonella, Italy for operational testing in 1992-93.

CARS and CDL

On the ground, Metro Tango in Germany had been inactivated, but the equipment which had already been ordered for the TRIGS, and subsequently stored, was reconfigured as a deployable system named Contingency Airborne Reconnaissance System (CARS). The first CARS, consisting of Sigint, SYERS and ASARS modules, was put together at ACC headquarters, Langley AFB in 1992. A new Common Data Link (CDL) replaced the long-serving L51/L52 (AN/UPQ-3A) on the U-2.

The sensors were also improving. Cameras were back in vogue to some extent after Desert Storm, and after receiving rave reviews ("better resolution than the satellites"), the venerable H-camera was given solid-state electronics. SYERS became a dual-band sensor with the addition of infra-red. Of most significance, perhaps, the USAF finally approved the addition of Moving Target Indicator (MTI) capability to ASARS.

In 1995, the 5.7-litre '95 Chevrolet Camaro began replacing 5.0-litre '87, '88 and '91 Ford Mustangs as the standard chase car. Shown below is the new car next to a line of the Mustangs. The Camaro has a top speed of more than 140 mph (225 km/h) and lightning acceleration, allowing it to catch up with the landing U-2 with ease. According to the pilots, the biggest danger is from spinning out on a wet runway.

This fine overhead view shows the enormous wing of the U-2R. A variant proposed for NASA has wingtip extensions to extract a few more thousand feet in operational altitude. The detachable superpods do little to impair performance, although they required a reconfiguration and reduction in overall area of the trailing-edge flaps. Note the open airbrakes, which can be augmented by overwing spoilers and leading-edge stall strips to help the aircraft descend.

Hughes had received a development contract to adapt the ASARS to show moving as well as fixed targets back in 1988. This entailed adding components to the receiver/exciter and processor control unit in the aircraft, and software changes in the ground station. The development was overshadowed by the J-STARS, which was first and foremost an MTI system, and one which needed large amounts of funding. It was also held up by the Gulf conflict, which interrupted operational tests of an ASARS-MTI prototype by the 17th RW in Europe.

In the ground station, the ASARS MTI shows the speed and location of moving targets in search or spot modes, against either a cartographic or synthetic aperture radar map background. While Grumman loudly proclaimed the virtues of J-STARS, Hughes quietly but firmly insisted that ASARS was "the most advanced reconnaissance radar in the world." The tests were completed in October 1991, and the ASARS MTI finally went operational in 1995 with the U-2R in Korea.

One of the keys to the success of ASARS on the U-2 has been the navigation data interface. For years, the Litton LN-33 P2/P3 INS was used, updated periodically by the Northrop NAS-21 astro-inertial star-tracker. The advent of the Global Positioning System and its lightweight receivers allowed Lockheed to dispense with the excellent but complicated NAS-21. The GPS receiver was faired into the U-2's left wing trailing edge.

Re-engining programme

Undoubtedly the most significant upgrade to the U-2 this decade has been the re-engining programme. When the last F-106 fighter was retired, the U-2R became the sole remaining user of the P&W J75. The support costs threatened to become unaffordable. Moreover, the weight

Several Northrop T-38As are assigned to the 9th Reconnaissance Wing to provide additional flight hours for the U-2 pilots. The aircraft were first used by the SR-71 fleet, as the landing characteristics of the Talon and 'Sled' were not dissimilar.

Above: *The first U-2S deliveries were made to the Air Force in 1994, with the first batch of three aircraft leaving Palmdale together. The batch comprised one single-seater, one two-seater and this aircraft (80-1078). It had entered the Lockheed Martin plant as a single-seater which had been damaged in an accident at Alconbury, and emerged as the fourth two-seater.*

Left: *The first three U-2S/ST aircraft taxi out to the Palmdale runway for their short redelivery flights back to Beale. All re-engining is expected to be complete by 1998.*

80-1071 was the first single-seater to get the F118 engine. The new engine offers far greater operating economy in both fuel and maintenance terms, and provides a boost to altitude or range.

of new sensor and datalink systems were restricting the aircraft's operating performance. (This was history repeating itself; the same problem in the late 1950s had prompted the re-engining of the early U-2s with the J75 in the first place.) Lockheed selected the General Electric F101-GE-F29 turbofan as a potential replacement for the J75. It was a low-bypass ratio (0.8:1) unit with a three-stage low-pressure compressor and a nine-stage high-pressure compressor. It was being developed for the then still-secret B-2 'Stealth Bomber'. Rated at 18,300 lb st (81.4 kN), the GE powerplant offered equivalent thrust for the U-2R, but a significant weight reduction and improved fuel consumption. And it was a good fit.

Once again, the USAF took a long time to approve the idea. A refurbished ground test engine from the B-2 programme was eventually released to the Skunk Works in

What had once been a wing of aircraft at Alconbury rapidly eroded to become a detachment of the 9th RW. In 1994 the OL-UK (Operating Location – United Kingdom) moved to RAF Fairford, from where its aircraft continued to monitor the war in former Yugoslavia. This aircraft is unusually configured with an ASARS-2 nose and an optical Q-bay hatch. As the ASARS radar requires some equipment to be installed in the Q-bay, this aircraft must be in a photo fit, with the non-operational ASARS nose left on from a previous mission.

1988. It was fitted to 80-1090, and made its first flight with Lockheed test pilot Ken Weir at the controls on 23 May 1989. This was four months before the B-2 first flew, incidentally. Over the next 15 months, 82 flight hours were logged. Initial flights were limited to engine-out gliding distance of Edwards AFB, because, unlike the J75 turbojet, the new turbofan could not be restarted inflight by windmilling. An emergency air-start system was then added, comprising compressed air and jet fuel which was ignited in a two-stage compressor. This was heavy, so when the re-engining programme did get the green light a hydrazine system capable of spooling up the engine to 45 per cent core rpm was developed.

Further engine trials

Before the pre-production flight tests started in late 1991, the GE powerplant was redesignated F118-GE-101, and the re-engined aircraft was designated U-2S. A host of evaluations was addressed in the next 38 flights, including some distinctly U-2-specific investigations, e.g., whether vibrations from this different engine would affect sensor or INS performance, and whether the ninth stage air bleed which provides the pilot's pressure suit cooling was satisfactory.

The flight test results showed a weight saving of 1,300 lb (590 kg) and a fuel saving of 16 per cent compared with the J75. These translate into a maximum altitude increase of 3,500 ft (1065 m), an increased payload, a 1,220-nm (1,400-mile; 2260-km) increase in range, or increased time on station. Other benefits include increased reliability and maintainability, an improved centre of gravity, and a digital engine control which provides linear thrust with stall-free operation throughout the flight envelope. Those famous U-2 flame-out incidents should now become rare events.

The first production U-2S conversion was 80-1071, flown again with the F118 on 12 August 1994. On 28 October a delivery ceremony was held at Palmdale, when the first three conversions were handed back to the USAF. (The others were two-seaters 80-1064 and 80-1078. The latter was built as a single-seater, but was damaged in a landing accident at Alconbury and rebuilt as a trainer.)

Fleet standardisation

The entire fleet is being converted as major overhaul becomes due – every 3,400 hours or five years. The last aircraft will be re-engined in 1998. At the same time, wiring and mounting provisions are being standardised, so that each aircraft can carry the entire inventory of sensors. Depot maintenance of the U-2R has always been performed by Lockheed at Palmdale Site 2, and the unique relationship between contractor and customer extends to the field, since the Skunk Works is responsible for line maintenance at some of the overseas detachments (and also at NASA Ames).

After a year or so of operations from Fairford, an otherwise successful deployment marred by a fatal crash, OL-UK became OL-FR when the U-2s moved to Istres in France. This significantly reduced the transit time to the operational area from where surveillance of Bosnia and surrounding nations was undertaken.

Four of the original 12 U-2R models produced in 1967-68 are still in service. Like the U-2A/H series before them, they have outlived their reputation as supposedly fragile, short-lived aircraft. In fact, the fatigue life of the U-2R was originally envisioned as 20,000 hours, but in August 1994 68-10338 became the first aircraft to pass that milestone with no problems. A new limit of 30,000 hours was set. Unfortunately, 68-10330 was destroyed in the tragic accident at RAF Fairford in August 1995, during an attempt to release a pogo which had 'hung up' on take-off.

Diverted funds

The accident was a blow to the programme, since the USAF lost the pilot, the aircraft and one of the Span systems. Such sophisticated equipment is expensive, of course, and the U-2's collection systems have been under-funded in recent years, according to some intelligence community insiders. U-2 money has been diverted to fund the accelerated development of new Unmanned Aerial Vehicles (UAVs), which it is claimed are capable of performing the U-2's mission, but a debate has raged over their utility, maturity and total cost. Observers with long memories can recall the same debate over the relative merits of Compass Cope and the U-2 in the mid-1970s.

"The performance parameters published for the UAVs and their sensors to date do not approach what the U-2 already has in many cases," notes Garfield Thomas, vice-president for reconnaissance systems at the Skunk Works. "Weather avoidance, flexibility, ground support systems and logistics support have not received a great deal of attention from the UAV proponents to date, and when they are honestly included in the trade studies, the result may shock some people."

Thomas says that the only thing the U-2 cannot do today is penetrate heavily-defended territory. "A very stealthy asset is needed to do that," he says. Lockheed is

***Above and left:** Much use has been made of the Senior Span equipment over Bosnia, allied to the Spear and Ruby Sigint collection system. In 1996, the Rapid Targeting System (RTS) was deployed to the theatre. Known as Gold Strike, this system relays ASARS imagery from the U-2 to a ground station at Rimini, where it is then processed and uplinked by the MOBSTR (Mobile Stretch) system back to a ground station at Beale. There the imagery is analysed and annotated before being transmitted back to the theatre, and then into the cockpits of fighter aircraft. This provides a recognition aid during the attack run for positive target identification.*

The U-2Rs of OL-FR operate from a giant hangar at Istres, which provides ample comfortable accommodation. The use of Istres is not without its problems for the strong mistral wind often poses crosswind problems for the delicate U-2s.

Thanks to the F118 re-engining programme, the immediate future of the U-2 is assured. Even with the return of the unmanned air vehicle as a major means of intelligence-gathering, there is a growing requirement for the type of reconnaissance that the 'Dragon Lady' can provide. More sophisticated sensors are being developed for the type, along with more capable means of transferring the gathered intelligence to the commanders and war fighters who require it.

Opposite page, bottom: With his U-2S in the background, a 9th RW pilot poses with the portable air conditioning and oxygen system which he carries until connected to the aircraft's own systems. The David Clark S-1031 suit is now being replaced by the S-1034, a revised suit with no inside liner, improved wrist locks and less weight.

developing the Tier 3-minus drone for this purpose, but the programme has been delayed by the crash of the prototype on its second flight.

Meanwhile, the U-2 is as busy as ever. The 9th RW is hard pushed to support the deployments, and its people undertake TDYs far beyond the call of duty. The aircraft has operated continuously out of Korea and Cyprus for more than 20 years. Unfortunately, five U-2s have been lost in accidents during the last five years, reducing the fleet to 30 operational U-2Rs, plus four trainers and the three NASA ER-2s.

Monitoring Iraq and Bosnia

U-2 flights over Iraq continue from Taif, under United Nations auspices. Using the IRIS and H-camera systems, over 300 flights since August 1991, codenamed Olive Branch, have been instrumental in identifying the weapons of mass destruction that Iraq has been hiding. The imagery is routinely used by UN officials to plan inspections, and has sometimes provided 'smoking-gun' evidence of Iraqi non-compliance with its obligations. The Iraqis do not like it, of course, and their foreign minister complained in March 1996 about the "material and psychological damage caused by the violations of its airspace by this aircraft."

At least two other U-2s have been kept in Saudi Arabia since the Gulf conflict, providing intelligence support to coalition forces. Part of the CARS-1 ground station is deployed there from Langley.

Most attention in recent years has been focused on Bosnia. On nine-hour round trips from Alconbury, the 95th RS and its successor, OL-UK, used aircraft configured for either ASARS, Span or camera missions. When Alconbury closed, the three aircraft were moved temporarily to Fairford. In December 1995 they were moved again to Istres, France which offers a shorter transit time to the area of interest. Most of the 'take' from the Bosnia flights is processed and first analysed in the US. A new trailer-based satcom system nicknamed Mobile Stretch and located at Rimini, Italy compresses ASARS radar and other data downlinked from the U-2. It is then transmitted to the lower-bandwidth DSCS satellites and transferred to Beale AFB. A second CARS ground station was set up there in 1994-95, and can operate exactly as it would do if deployed in the field. The two-way link is maintained so that, for instance, if the Sigint sensors pick up a radar, the same U-2 could be tasked to image the location and determine if missiles are present.

The advantage is that all the ground personnel can stay at home, and the logistics burden for a U-2 deployment is much reduced. The complete CARS configuration would need seven C-5 transports to deploy, although the ground station modules are getting smaller all the time. An enhanced version of the TRAC now being manufactured for the US Army by Westinghouse can be carried in two C-130s and set up to receive the ASARS downlink in 90 minutes.

New system for NASA

The NASA operation also now benefits from 'electronic co-location'. The prototype Senior Spur system was transferred to NASA last year and has been adapted for use on one of the ER-2s as STARLink. Data from various

experiments can be transmitted in near-real time via TDRS and domestic satellites to NASA's Payload Operations Control Center, and can even be further distributed via the Internet. Scientists can control their experiments inflight, and no longer need to accompany the ER-2 to remote airfields in Chile, Norway or the Australian outback.

Looking to the future

What does the future hold for the U-2? The new engine has given the programme a considerable boost, and there has been talk of re-opening the production line. Most of the fleet has a structural life beyond 2025, and the airframe has consistently proved to be the most suitable platform for modern reconnaissance sensors. Having been disappointed with the performance of new high-altitude research vehicles such as Perseus and Strato-2C, NASA has even explored the possibility of increasing the ER-2 wingspan. By adding at each wingtip removable 10-ft (3-m) extensions made of composites, the aircraft could operate in the 75,000 to 80,000 ft altitudes.

New Sigint sensors are being developed for the U-2, and multi-spectral capability is being added to the camera systems. In May 1996, Hughes received a contract to provide more enhancements to ASARS, including onboard processing. This has favourable implications for U-2 payload flexibility and data relay. For instance, it will be possible to fly cameras and ASARS on the same flight.

While its sensors are collecting, an orbiting U-2 can perform an important secondary role as a data relay platform. The E-Systems Commander's Tactical Terminal (CTT) has been integrated with the aircraft, and can rebroadcast data from the U-2 ground stations (or other parties). A higher-capacity X-band relay system could be carried as an alternative.

The drive is ongoing to get U-2 sensor information quickly to the people who really matter. In a test exercise last year, ASARS imagery was transmitted from a U-2 via the ground station and a GBU-15 datalink to the rear cockpit of an F-15E. The Strike Eagle's weapons system operator then used it to cue his own APG-70 radar and lock on to the target; this was a simulated 'Scud' missile, and it was destroyed.

Although it remains a relatively simple airframe, the U-2 has been kept at the forefront of reconnaissance collection and dissemination science. It is still the world's foremost air-breathing intelligence aircraft. **Chris Pocock**

Above: Once one of the many rare jewels in the crown of Strategic Air Command, the U-2 is now firmly integrated into wider USAF operations. The 'Deuce' still retains much of the mystique which has surrounded the U-2 since the earliest days of the programme.

Individual aircraft details

The following table lists all U-2R, TR-1 and ER-2 production. The first number is the Lockheed 'Article Number' (e.g. construction number) followed by the USAF serial. The first batch manufactured in 1967-68 comprised Articles 051 to 062, which were all U-2R models. The second batch from 1981 to 1989 comprised Articles 063 to 099, which were a mix of U-2R, TR-1 and ER-2 models. USAF serial numbers were allocated to coincide with the Article Numbers in the second batch only.

The prototype U-2R and some subsequent aircraft sometimes carried 'civilian' registrations when serving with the CIA units (such as N803X, N810X, N812X, and N8032X). The CIA units used the 'correct' USAF serial numbers on other occasions, and RoCAF numbers (such as 3925) when deployed to Det H. In the mid-1970s, some USAF aircraft were repainted with false serials such as 10342 and 10345. These came from a batch of serials (68-10341 through 10353) which had been allocated for additional U-2R production, but not taken up.

The remaining TR-1s were redesignated U-2R in October 1991. All remaining U-2R aircraft are being converted to U-2S standard with the new engine. For ease of reference, neither redesignation is noted in the tables below (except for the first U-2S conversions).

051/68-10329: First flight 28 August 1967 as N803X, unpainted. Subsequently reworked to production standard and repainted as 10329 for use by Det G/H. Reallocated to flight test in 1975 and was first aircraft to carry superpods. To 9th SRW by 1981.
052/68-10330: Delivered to 100th SRW by late 1968. Returned to flight test around 1970 for US Navy EPX trials. 100th SRW again by early 1972. To 9th SRW in 1976. Written off by OL-OH at Akrotiri on 7 December 1977 (Capt Robert Henderson killed).
053/68-10331: Delivered to Det G. To 100th SRW in early 1975. To 9th SRW in 1976.
054/68-10332: Delivered to Det G. To 100th SRW in early 1975. To 9th SRW in 1976. Written off by Det 2 off Korean coast on 15 January 1992 (Capt Marty McGregor killed).
055/68-10333: Delivered to Det G. To 100th SRW in early 1975. To 9th SRW in 1976. Damaged by OL-OH at Akrotiri on 24 April 1980. Written off by Det 2 at Osan on 22 May 1984 (Capt David Bonsi survived).
056/68-10334: Delivered to 100th SRW. Written off by 99th SRS in Gulf of Thailand on 15 August 1975 (Capt Jon Little killed).
057/68-10335: Delivered to Det G. Written off by Det H/35th Sqn at Taoyuan on 24 November 1970 (Maj Denny Huang killed).
058/68-10336: Delivered to 100th SRW. To 9th SRW in 1976. Returned to flight test: first ASARS aircraft (1981), first Senior Spur aircraft? Still with flight test.
059/68-10337: Delivered to 100th SRW. Damaged by 99th SRS at U-Tapao on 16 May 1975. To 9th SRW in 1976. Damaged by Det 5 at Patrick on 24 May 1988.
060/68-10338: Delivered to 100th SRW. To 9th SRW in 1976. First aircraft to reach 20,000 hours, on 11 August 1994. Written off by OL-UK at Fairford on 29 August 1995.
061/68-10339: Retained for US Navy EPX trials. Delivered to 100th SRW by early 1972. To 9th SRW in 1976. Written off at Beale on 13 December 1993 (Capt Rich Snyder killed).
062/68-10340: Delivered to 100th SRW. To 9th SRW 1976. Written off by Det 2 in Korea on 5 October 1980 (Capt Cleve Wallace survived).
063/80-1063/N706NA: First new-batch aircraft to fly, on 1 May 1981. Delivered as ER-2 to NASA in June 1981.
064/80-1064: Delivered as TR-1B to 9th SRW in March 1983. Converted to TU-2S and redelivered in ceremony on 28 October 1994.
065/80-1065: Delivered as TR-1B to 9th SRW on May 1983.
066/80-1066: Second new-batch aircraft to fly, on 1 August 1981. Delivered as TR-1A to 9th SRW in September 1981.
067/80-1067: Delivered as TR-1A to 9th SRW in July 1982. Returned to flight test in 1989.
068/80-1068: Delivered as TR-1A to 9th SRW in July 1982. First aircraft to enter service with 17th RW in February 1983. To 9th SRW in April 1987.
069/80-1069/N708NA: Delivered as TR-1A to 9th SRW in July 1982. To 17th RW in July 1983. Damaged by vehicle collision at Alconbury in October 1983. To Lockheed in March 1987, converted to ER-2 and loaned to NASA.
070/80-1070: Delivered as TR-1A to 9th SRW in October 1982. To 17th RW in February 1983. To 9th SRW in May 1988.
071/80-1071: Delivered as U-2R to 9th SRW in November 1993. Returned to flight test as first Senior Span aircraft in 1985. Returned to 9th SRW by late 1988. First U-2S production conversion, redelivered in ceremony on 28 October 1994. Damaged at Beale in February 1996.
072/80-1072: Delivered as TR-1A to 17th RW in November 1993. To 9th SRW in March 1984. Written off at Beale on 18 July 1984 (Capt Tom Hubbard survived).
073/80-1073: Delivered as TR-1A to 9th SRW in February 1984. To 17th RW in January 1991. To 9th Wg in September 1992.
074/80-1074: Delivered as TR-1A to 9th SRW in February 1984. PLSS configuration 1984-85. To 17th RW in December 1990. To 9th SRW in October 1992.
075/80-1075: Delivered as U-2R to 9th RW in 1984. Written off by Det 2 in Korea on 8 October 1984 (Capt Tom Dettmer survived).
076/80-1076: Delivered as U-2R to 9th SRW in 1984/85.
077/80-1077: Delivered as TR-1A to 17th RW in March 1985. To 9th SRW in November 1989.
078/80-1078: Delivered as TR-1A to 17th RW in March 1985. Damaged at Alconbury on 24 April 1990 and returned to Lockheed for storage. Converted to TU-2S and delivered in ceremony on 28 October 1994.
079/80-1079: Delivered as TR-1A to 17th RW on March 1985. To 9th SRW in January 1991.
080/80-1080: Delivered as TR-1A to 9th SRW in May 1985. Damaged at Beale on 25 May 1988.
081/80-1081: Delivered as TR-1A to 17th RW in October 1985. To 9th SRW in August 1991.
082/80-1082: Delivered as TR-1A to 9th SRW in November 1985.
083/80-1083: Delivered as TR-1A to 17th RW in March 1986. To 9th Wg in December 1991.
084/80-1084: Delivered as TR-1A to 17th RW in April 1986. Damaged by vehicle collision at Alconbury in December 1987. To 9th SRW in 1988/89.
085/80-1085: Delivered as TR-1A to 17th RW in August 1986. To 9th SRW in February 1991.
086/80-1086: Delivered as TR-1A to 9th SRW in 1986/87. To 17th RW in April 1987. To 9th SRW in August 1991.
087/80-1087: Delivered as TR-1A to 9th SRW by May 1987.
088/80-1088: Delivered as TR-1A to 17th RW in December 1987. To 9th SRW in August 1991. Written off near Beale on 7 August 1996 (Capt Randy Roby killed).
089/80-1089: Delivered as U-2R to 9th SRW in 1988.
090/80-1090: Built as TR-1A in 1988 and retained by flight test at Palmdale. Prototype U-2S re-engined aircraft, f/f on 23 May 1989.
091/80-1091: Delivered as U-2R(T) to 9th SRW in March 1988.
092/80-1092: Delivered as TR-1A to 17th RW in April 1988. To 9th Wg in December 1991.
093/80-1093: Delivered as TR-1A to 17th RW in June 1988. To 9th Wg in April 1992.
094/80-1094: Delivered as TR-1B to 17th RW in September 1988. To 9th Wg in December 1991.
095/80-1095: Delivered as U-2R to 9th SRW in 1988.
096/80-1096: Delivered as U-2R to 9th SRW by April 1989.
097/80-1097/N709NA: Delivered as ER-2 to NASA in 1989.
098/80-1098: Delivered as U-2R to 9th SRW in 1989. Written off by Det 2 at Osan in August 1994 (Capt Chuck Espinoza survived).
099/80-1099: Delivered as TR-1A to 9th SRW in final delivery ceremony on 3 October 1989. To 17th RW in March 1990. To 9th Wg in December 1991.

U-2 tail artwork

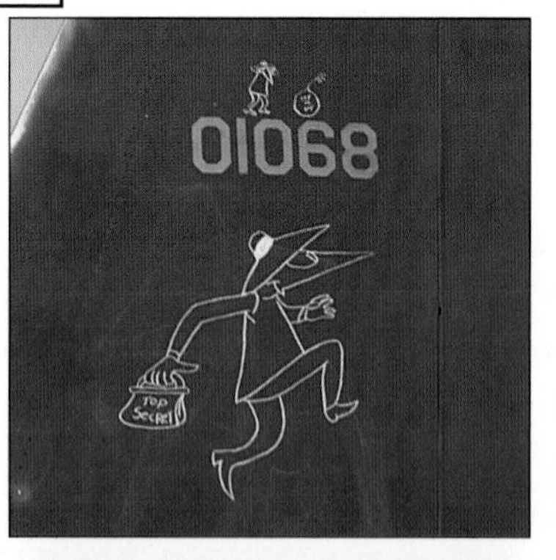

U-2R/TR-1 Operators

Central Intelligence Agency

Detachment G, Edwards North Base, California

This was the base for the CIA's U-2 operations, where training, development and maintenance activities took place. The unit was named the Fourth Weather Reconnaissance Squadron (Provisional) (WRSP-4) for cover purposes until mid-1969, when it was redesignated the 1130th Air Technical Training Group (ATTG). It was manned by a mix of CIA and USAF personnel, with maintenance provided by Lockheed. As part of the overall UK-USA intelligence co-operation agreement, two RAF pilots were always attached to the unit.

Det G received its first U-2R in February 1968, when Colonel 'Curly' Schambers was unit commander. Det G supported the Taiwanese U-2 operation (see below), and also conducted its own reconnaissance operations when directed by Project Headquarters in Washington, DC. These included annual deployments to the UK to demonstrate the aircraft's capabilities to senior British personnel. From August to December 1970, Det G deployed to RAF Akrotiri, Cyprus and flew reconnaissance missions along the Suez Canal ceasefire zone. Colonel Roger Cooper took command of the unit in 1971.

In April 1974 a permanent detachment was established at Akrotiri, to monitor the peace agreement between Israel and Egypt arranged by the United Nations. In December 1974, the CIA ended 14 years of U-2 operations. The USAF's 100th SRW took over the Akrotiri detachment as OL-OH, while North Base was closed.

Detachment H/35th Squadron, RoCAF, Taoyuan AB, Taiwan

The operation to conduct reconnaissance operations against mainland China was established at Taoyuan AB near Taipei in 1961. The CIA provided the aircraft and training, while the Republic of China air force provided the pilots. Lockheed maintained the aircraft, and other contractors provided sensor support. Both countries contributed intelligence and logistics support. As a cover story, the US announced the 'sale' of two U-2s to the Republic of China air force, but, in reality, the two aircraft remained the property of the US government, and were regularly rotated with others from the Edwards-based CIA fleet. At Taoyuan, the aircraft usually wore RoCAF insignia.

The unit was nicknamed 'The Black Cat Squadron' and was jointly commanded by a RoCAF and a USAF officer (the latter on a 360-day TDY). When the U-2R arrived in mid-1968, Colonel Yang Shi Chuen was the RoCAF commander, subsequently succeeded by Colonels Wang Shi Chuen, Tom Hwang and Wong Tao.

Following the improvement in Sino-US relations, the unit closed in August 1974.

The U-2Rs of Det H wore RoCAF serials and carried the Taiwanese star national insignia.

United States Air Force

100th Strategic Reconnaissance Wing

The 100th SRW had been created at Davis-Monthan AFB, Arizona in June 1966 by a renumbering of the previous USAF U-2 operating wing, the 4080th SRW. It reported to SAC headquarters through the 15th Air Force. In addition to the Davis-Monthan-based U-2 squadron (see below), the 100th controlled the 350th SRS which operated RPVs and the associated DC-130 launch and CH-3 recovery vehicles.

Although training was conducted at Davis-Monthan, most operational missions were conducted from deployments which were designated Operating Locations (OLs – see below).

When the U-2R arrived at Davis-Monthan in 1968, the wing was commanded by Colonel Marion 'Hack' Mixson. He was succeeded by Colonel Ray Haupt (August 1970), Colonel Don White (June 1972), and Colonel Chuck Stratton (May 1974).

On 1 July 1976, SAC decided to consolidate U-2 operations with that of the SR-71, under the 9th SRW at Beale. The 100th SRW designation was also transferred to Beale, becoming the 100th Air Refueling Wing in control of the KC-135Q tanker fleet which supported SR-71 operations.

349th Strategic Reconnaissance Squadron

Created by a renumbering of the 4028th SRS in June 1966, the 349th SRS conducted training in the U-2C, U-2F and (from September 1968) U-2R models. It also flew domestic reconnaissance missions in support of various US government agencies. From 1972, it was allocated responsibility for the operational trials of the Advanced Location and Strike Systems (ALSS), and deployed five U-2C models to the UK for this purpose in 1975. When U-2 operations were moved to Beale AFB in July 1976, the 349th squadron number transferred with the 100th wing designation to the KC-135Q operation already there.

Operating Location 19 (OL-19)

After the Cuban Missile Crisis in 1962, the 100th SRW was tasked with regular reconnaissance missions over Cuba to monitor compliance with the informal agreement between the US and the USSR, that no offensive strategic weapons would be deployed there. In 1969, a single U-2R was deployed to OL-19, recently moved back to McCoy AFB, Florida from Barksdale AFB, Louisiana.

Operating Location 20 (OL-20) and Operating Location RU (OL-RU)

OL-20 was created at Bien Hoa AB, South Vietnam in February 1964, when the U-2 was one of the first USAF aircraft types to be deployed in Southeast Asia. In October 1964, OL-20 expanded with the arrival of the wing's reconnaissance RPVs and DC-130 launch aircraft (CH-3 recovery helicopters were based at Da Nang).

The U-2R joined OL-20 in mid-1969. In July 1970, the unit moved to U-Tapao AB, Thailand and was redesignated OL-RU. In November 1972 it gained full squadron status as the 99th SRS (see below). During 1972, the unit was awarded the Paul T. Cullen Trophy in recognition of its work in support of the war, to be followed by a host of other awards.

9th Reconnaissance Wing

Designated the 9th Strategic Reconnaissance Wing until September 1991, and then simply the 9th Wing until October 1994, the 9th RW has been based at Beale AFB, California since June 1966, when it assumed control of the newly-established SR-71 operations there. U-2 operations were consolidated with the SR-71 at Beale in July 1976, when the 99th SRS became the U-2 squadron while the 1st SRS remained the SR-71 squadron.

At that time, the wing reported to SAC through the 14th Air Division of 15th Air Force. From September 1991 it reported through 2nd Air Force. After SAC was deactivated in June 1992, the wing joined Air Combat Command, and the 'BB' tailcode began to appear on all its aircraft. The reporting line changed from 2nd AF to 12th AF in July 1993.

The wing has since also controlled at various times the 5th RS and 97th RS (see below).

Control of U-2 (and, since its comeback in 1996, SR-71) flying operations is today vested in the 9th Operations Group, which was established in September 1991. But operational control of the overseas U-2 deployments is chopped to the relevant theatre commander (EUCOM, CENTCOM, PACOM etc.). The 9th OG also controls the 9th Intelligence Squadron, which produces and stores all domestic U-2 and SR-71 imagery.

Commanders of the 9th RW since its association with the U-2 first began in 1976 have been Colonel John Storrie (until September 1977), Colonel Lyman Kidder (until January 1979), Colonel Dale Shelton (until July 1980), Colonel Dave Young (until July 1982), Colonel Tom Pugh (until July 1983), Colonel Hector Freese (until January 1985), Colonel Dave Pinsky (until July 1987), Colonel Rich Graham (until November 1988), Colonel James Savarda (until June 1990), Colonel Thomas Keck (until November 1991), Colonel Richard Young (until June 1993), Colonel Larry Tieman (until June 1993), Brigadier General John Rutledge (until September 1995), Brigadier General Bob Behler (current).

1st Reconnaissance Squadron (Training)

Today, the 1st RS (T) recruits and trains all U-2 pilots. After initial interviews, orientation flights and selection, the new pilot undergoes six months of training, including 20 sorties in the U-2, mostly the squadron's four U-2RT/ST two-cockpit trainers. The 1st RS (T) also flies the wing's 13 T-38 companion trainers, and trains the U-2 mission planners. It graduates about 20 pilots and two mission planners each year.

Having been 'grounded' when SR-71 operation terminated in March 1990, the 1st designation was revived in July of that year when the U-2 training squadron was redesignated from the 5th SRS (T) (see below) to the 1st SRS (T).

5th Reconnaissance Squadron

The 5th RS is based at Osan AB, South Korea, from where U-2s have been monitoring the tense situation on the Korean peninsula continuously for 20 years. The unit usually operates two aircraft, and was the first overseas location to receive the U-2S model in October 1995. The aircraft are maintained under contract by Lockheed Martin.

Until October 1994, the unit was designated Det 2 of the 9th RW (Det 2 is now the revived SR-71 operation based at Edwards AFB). U-2 operations have been conducted continuously in Korea since February 1976, when OL-AO of the 100th SRW was established. These operations soon inherited the Black Cat emblem of the RoCAF's former 35th Squadron. OL-AO became Det 2 in July 1976.

In 1986 the USAF redesignated the 4029th SRTS training squadron at Beale as the 5th Strategic Reconnaissance Squadron (Training), thereby renewing the 5th squadron's previous association with the 9th wing. The 5th SRS (T) became the 1st SRS (T) in July 1990.

99th Reconnaissance Squadron

Today, the 99th RS is the Beale-based operational U-2R squadron which supports the overseas deployments and conducts domestic reconnaissance missions for various US government and non-government agencies. These have included earthquake and flood damage assessment, and environmental change detection flights. The 99th also conducts some operational testing of newly-fielded systems.

Having been the SR-71 training squadron at Beale until deactivation in April 1971, the 99th first became a U-2 squadron in November 1972 at U-Tapao AB, Thailand (see OL-RU, above). As the US military presence in Indo-China wound down, the 99th SRS left Thailand in April 1976, and was re-established at Beale in July of that year.

Other Current Detachments and Operating Locations

Det 1 is the continuing deployment at RAF Akrotiri, from where one or two U-2R

The Beale-based 9th RW supports all U-2 operations worldwide, including pilot training and intelligence data processing.

A U-2R wheels over the Beale tower, an SR-71 being displayed outside. In addition to its U-2 operation, the 9th RW operates the two SR-71s recently brought out of retirement. These fly with Det 2 at Edwards AFB.

models have continuously monitored compliance with United Nations resolutions since mid-1974. The detachment re-equipped with U-2S models in February 1996, and uses Lockheed Martin contract maintenance.

OL-FR is the detachment at Istres AB, France which continues to monitor the Bosnian conflict. The U-2 has flown over Bosnia for the last five years, originally from the UK as the 95th RS and OL-UK (which see). It usually operates three aircraft with differing sensor fits.

4402nd RS is based at Taif in Saudi Arabia, reporting for operations to the 4404th Composite Wing at Dhahran AB. It conducts the Olive Branch photo-reconnaissance monitoring flights over Iraq on behalf of the United Nations, and has operated two or more other aircraft for coalition force reconnaissance requirements. It re-equipped with U-2S models in August 1996.

Previous Detachments, Operating Locations and Squadrons

Det 2 was the designation of the U-2 operation at Osan AB, South Korea from 1976 until 1994 (see 5th RS above).

Det 3 was a redesignation of OL-OH at RAF Akrotiri in September 1980. The operation was again redesignated, to Det 1, in 1994.

Det 4 was created in April 1979 at RAF Mildenhall, UK to fly the U-2R (and the SR-71) in the European theatre on a routine basis (previously, missions had been flown on a temporary deployment basis). At most times a single U-2R aircraft was deployed. The U-2R element of Det 4 ceased operations in February 1983 when the first TR-1A reached the 17th RW at RAF Alconbury. The SR-71 operation continued until December 1988.

Det 4 was re-established at Howard AFB, Panama in 1991, but closed again in late 1993.

Det 5 was a redesignation of OL-OF at Patrick AFB in January 1983. It was closed in November 1990.

Det 8/FT was a flight test organisation created in late 1977 to work in conjunction with Lockheed's U-2 flight test and depot-level overhaul activities at Site 2, Palmdale, California. (Det 8 itself was the logistics support activity for the U-2, based at Robins AFB, Georgia.) Control of this activity was transferred to the 412th Test Wing at nearby Edwards AFB in April 1993 as **OL-HM**. Due to the ongoing nature of sensor and equipment development for the U-2, OL-HM usually has two aircraft and two pilots assigned. They share post-depot acceptance flights, and flight test sorties.

OL-OF (for Olympic Flare) was established at Patrick AFB, Florida in January 1982. Redesignated Det 5 in January 1983.

OL-OH (for Olive Harvest) was the operation at RAF Akrotiri in support of United Nations and other objectives, which was taken over from the CIA in mid-1974. It was redesignated Det 3 in September 1980.

OL-UK (for United Kingdom) was established in September 1993 to take over three U-2Rs from the 95th RS at RAF Alconbury. When Alconbury closed in March 1995, the unit relocated to RAF Fairford. In December 1995, it moved to Istres AB, France and was redesignated OL-FR.

OL-CH (for Camel Hump) was opened at King Fahd RSAB, Taif, Saudi Arabia in mid-August 1990, as coalition forces responded to the Iraqi invasion of Kuwait. Initially operating two U-2R aircraft, two TR-1A aircraft were added from the 17th RW after one week. As the Desert Shield deployments mounted, SAC chopped tactical (though not operational) control of OL-CH to CENTCOM, whereupon it was redesignated on 21 September as ....

1704th RS (Provisional) reporting to the 1700th Strategic Wing (Provisional). Another U-2R was added from Det 2 in October 1990, and when Desert Storm was mounted on 16 January the squadron had nine aircraft and had already accomplished 325 sorties. Eventually, squadron strength reached 12 aircraft (six U-2Rs and six TR-1As), allowing another 195 sorties to be performed during the war. After the war, the squadron remained at Taif in slimmed-down form, until it was redesignated 4402nd RS (P).

4029th Strategic Reconnaissance Training Squadron

The 4029th SRTS was activated at Beale in August 1981 to train all U-2 and TR-1 pilots. Until then, training had been conducted by the 99th SRS, but the arrival of the TR-1 and the consequent greater demand for new pilots mandated the creation of a separate training outfit. The 4029th SRTS received the first two-seat TR-1B trainer in March 1983. (In earlier times, this squadron number had been assigned to the 4080th SRW, the original USAF U-2 wing.) Redesignated 5th SRTS in 1986.

17th Reconnaissance Wing

The 17th RW was reactivated in October 1982 at RAF Alconbury, UK to operate the TR-1 in Europe. It reported to SAC through the 7th Air Division and 8th Air Force, but operational tasking came from USAFE and NATO (via US European Command). In 1990-91, the wing supported Desert Shield/Desert Storm by deploying aircraft and personnel to the 1704th RS (P) in Saudi Arabia. Following the end of Desert Storm and the Cold War, the wing was deactivated in June 1991.

Colonel George Freese was the first commander of the 17th RW at Alconbury (until July 1983), followed by Colonel Tom Lesan (until August 1985), Colonel James Wrenn, Colonel Art Saboski, Colonel John Sander, and Colonel Doug Cole.

A 95th RS TR-1A returns from a mission along the German border. The original plans for the 17th RW involved basing 12 aircraft at Alconbury and six at Wethersfield. In the event the 17th only had 11 aircraft at most.

95th Reconnaissance Squadron

The 95th RS was reactivated alongside the 17th RW in October 1982 at Alconbury, and received an initial two TR-1A models to continue the Det 4 Sigint mission. More aircraft were steadily added, particularly from 1985 when the ASARS sensor was deployed. By early 1989, the 95th RS operated 11 TR-1As. The 95th RS survived the deactivation of the 17th RW in June 1991, remaining at Alconbury under the control of the 9th Wing at Beale. However, it was reduced in size, and eventually deactivated in September 1993, when Alconbury became a TDY location as OL-UK.

The badge of the 95th RS was the famous 'Kicking Mule' insignia first used in World War I.

Variant Analysis
Sukhoi 'Flanker' family

Part One: Su-27 (T10) 'Flanker-A' to Su-27UBK (T10UK) 'Flanker-C'

***Above:** Early Su-27s remain in widespread use. Here an aircraft from the test centre at Akthubinsk rolls away, revealing a weapon load of only two R-73 and two R-27 missiles. The Su-27 can routinely carry 10 AAMs, or 12 in the case of the latest production aircraft.*

***Left:** The first Su-27 was the prototype T10, officially the T10-1 and simply coded 10 on its forward fuselage. Anti-flutter weights were added to the leading edges of the fin, tailplanes and wings during the flight test programme, and weapons pylons were also added. The outboard underwing R-60 (AA-8 'Aphid') pylon is very close to the undersurface of the wing, threatening difficult launch/separation conditions for the missile.*

The Sukhoi 'Flanker' is one of the most successful families of fighter aircraft ever to emerge from the former Soviet Union. Analysts have compared it favourably to the best Western fighter aircraft, and many have marked it as the 'threat to beat'. In fact, the Sukhoi OKB has been very good at showing off the aircraft's strengths, while simultaneously hiding some fundamental weaknesses. Here, *World Air Power Journal* presents the first in-depth and objective analysis of one of the world's most significant fighters.

One difficulty facing people trying to assess the capabilities of the aircraft against which they might have to fight lies in the large number of markedly different variants produced. There is the world of difference between a standard early production Su-27 and the latest Russian navy Su-27Ks (to say nothing of the Su-27M, if and when its development is successfully completed). Difficulty is posed by the need to distinguish actual capabilities and equipment fit from Sukhoi's statements of future intended capabilities, which are often presented as though they are currently, actually available. Yet another difficulty has been posed by some Western intelligence estimates of the Su-27's capabilities, which have sometimes been deliberately over-stated in order to help win funding for advanced Western fighters, weapons and avionics.

The Sukhoi Su-27 has come a very long way since its ill-starred beginning. The original design was seriously flawed and had to undergo a total redesign before it was suitable for operational use in even its original, rather narrow role. Since then, the Sukhoi Design Bureau has improved and refined the aircraft to fulfil a variety of roles, giving the resulting sub-variants a bewildering array of new designations. During the Cold War, new sub-variants of Sukhoi designs were simply given a new designation suffix, but, in the financially austere period following the disintegration of the former USSR, a minor change has often led to the allocation of an entirely new designation. Sukhoi has used such designation changes to try to attract scarce funding, reasoning that new aircraft (or aircraft which appeared to be new) may have had a better chance of attracting resources than simple modification or modernisation projects.

Airframe production at the Gagarin Aircraft Manufacturing Factory at Komsomolsk na Amur (Su-27, Su-27SK, Su-27K, Su-27M), the Joint Stock Company Irkutsk Aircraft Manufacturing Association (Su-27UB and Su-30) at Irkutsk and the Novosibirsk Aircraft Manufacturing Association plant at Novosibirsk (Su-27IB/34) has dwindled to little more than a trickle, but the allocation of new designations has continued at an astonishing rate. "They produced more new designations than airframes this year," observed one distinguished analyst

Right: The third prototype (T10-3) takes to the air with the aid of the ski-ramp at Saki. Development of a naval carrierborne Su-27 began at an early stage, though the programme took many years to bear fruit. The T10-3 made the first 'Flanker' ski-ramp take-off on 22 August 1982. The T10-3 was the first AL-31F-engined 'Flanker', and differed from most early aircraft in actually having a gun fitted in the starboard LERX.

Below: Despite undergoing a major redesign for production, the initial batch of T10 prototypes was able to play a useful part in Su-27 development. Some aircraft (like T10-11 seen here) were fitted with radar and IRST for early weapons system work, while the third and fourth aircraft provided a representative environment for testing of the definitive AL-31F engine, with an almost identical inlet to the eventual production aircraft.

during 1995. Some Su-27 sub-variants have worn as many as three successive designations without actually undergoing any change, making the identification of members of the 'Flanker' family fraught with pitfalls. Nor can one simply use NATO ASCC reporting names. New 'Flanker-' codename suffixes are only allocated to aircraft which are on the verge of entering service, so many of the versions still in development have not yet received official new reporting names. Furthermore, some Western analysts have jumped the gun by pre-empting officialdom and have 'assigned' new reporting name suffixes which may or may not be later applied by the Air Standards Co-ordinating Committee. We have chosen to use the official Russian air forces' designations for Su-27 variants, using OKB designations only in parentheses, or for dedicated export aircraft which have no air forces' designations. NATO ASCC reporting names are given only where they are confirmed.

The political ascendancy enjoyed by the Sukhoi Design Bureau since the collapse of the old regime seemed to have ensured that the re-equipment of the Russian air force would be based around variants of the Su-27, with many newer projects and modifications of other OKB's aircraft having been abandoned or sidelined. Thus, the Su-27 'Flanker' in all its various forms is becoming an aircraft of increasing importance and interest. Once used primarily as an IA-PVO long-range air defence interceptor (a role in which it remains without peer), the Su-27 and its close relatives will soon dominate Frontal Aviation and Naval Aviation as well. The two-seat Su-27IB (OKB Su-34) and Su-32FN may even supplant the heavier bombers of Long Range Aviation, albeit while serving with Frontal Aviation regiments.

The most remarkable thing about this success story is that it has reportedly been based as much on politics and personalities as it has on the attributes of the Su-27 itself. It is widely believed that some versions of the aircraft have succeeded in the face of competition from superior aircraft designed by other OKBs. As

The transformation of the T10 is nowhere more evident than in Sukhoi's Su-32FN/Su-34 long-range strike aircraft, which marries the Su-27's basic fuselage with a broad side-by-side-seating 'platypus' nose. These two closely related aircraft have their roots in the Su-27IB demonstrator and are seen as Su-24 replacements.

Above: The Su-27's massive internal fuel capacity allows it to fly over extended ranges without inflight refuelling or the carriage of external fuel tanks. These features have made it a natural choice for overseas demonstration and display flights. The Gromov Flight Research Centre's 'Test Pilots' team have used a number of demilitarised Su-27s (equipped for long-range navigation, inflight refuelling and extended endurance operations) for their displays. This single-seater is an Su-27P.

Left: Although modern Russian fighter airfields are generously provided with hardened aircraft shelters, peacetime practice is to use them as little more than hangars, and to conduct flying operations from a single flight line. These aircraft served with the 159th IAP in Poland.

Perestroika and *Glasnost* swept away the old Soviet Union, political and especially economic 'liberals' were able to gain power at the expense of anyone considered tainted by Stalinism or hard-line Communism. As part of this process, the Sukhoi OKB's head, Mikhail Simonov, was able to gain more and more influence; he eventually sat on the committee of the Supreme Soviet which oversaw the operation of the military-industrial complex. He was energetic in promoting and safeguarding the interests of his design bureau, apparently influencing procurement decisions in favour of his own 'company'. He was able to ensure that the first 'experimental' grouping of design and production facilities in Russia was one between Sukhoi and the factories with which it had traditionally been associated, especially the production plant at Komsomolsk na Amur.

As funding dwindled for defence projects, Simonov was able to minimise the effect on Sukhoi, so that while funding for the MiG-31M declined, work on the Su-27M (and even the Su-30 interceptor) continued. Similarly, work on the intended replacements for the MiG-29 and Su-27 was not cut back equally. While work on the MiG-29M (actually the better aircraft for the post-Cold War world, being cheaper and more flexible) ground to a halt, work on the Su-27M programme (which had reportedly reached a less advanced stage, and was more beset by troubles) progressed unabated. Similarly, the MiG-29K was abandoned in favour of the Su-33, originally envisaged as an air defence complement to the more modern, multi-role MiG for Russia's carrier air wings. Most analysts agree that had it been possible to acquire only one aircraft type, then it should have been the MiG-29K, which was analogous to the full-up night-attack F/A-18C, and not the Su-27K, which was more analogous to the basic F-14A Tomcat. The Su-27K had no appreciable air-to-ground capability, and no real improvement in air-to-air capability, except in terms of range, radius and endurance.

If the production MiG-29M and MiG-29K remain unbuilt, today's political realities will have succeeded in killing off the Su-27's lightweight competitor, which had been born as a result of operational and financial necessities. This will put the Su-27M and the other advanced 'Flanker' derivatives in the same status as had originally been intended for the basic Su-27. The 'Flanker' will finally represent the single future fighter for the Russian air forces. This will in one way mark a final realisation of the original plan which resulted in the Su-27, which had originally called for a single tactical Prospective Frontal Fighter.

Roots of the Su-27

In 1969, the same year that the McDonnell Douglas F-15 Eagle was chosen as the winner of the USAF's FX competition to find a new-generation fighter, the Soviet Union launched its own Perspektivnyi Frontovoi Istrebeitel (Prospective Frontal Fighter), or PFI, programme to design what would effectively be a counter to the new American super-fighter. The aircraft to be produced as a result of the competitive programme was quickly nicknamed the anti-F-15. The PFI requirement specifically mentioned the F-15, but emphasised that the new fighter would have to counter all potentially hostile advanced aircraft, including fighters and strike aircraft, operating from 30 m (100 ft) above the ground to altitudes of 17 to 18 km (55,000 to 60,000 ft). Performance figures of between 1350 and 1450 km/h (840 and 900 mph) at sea level and between 2300 and 2500 km/h (1,430 and 1,555 mph) at altitude were required, while climb and acceleration requirements dictated a thrust-to-weight ratio of 1.2:1.

The Su-27's distinctive profile has won it the nickname 'Zhuravlik' (Crane) in service. Here an Su-27 of the 159th IAP lands at Kluczewo, shortly before the withdrawal of Soviet units from Poland. Most Su-27s were delivered to the IA-PVO for defence of the Soviet motherland, and only a small number were assigned to Frontal Aviation units.

Above and right: The Russian air forces' 234th Guards Fighter Aviation Regiment at Kubinka serves as a demonstration unit, and includes three formation display teams, equipped with the Su-25, MiG-29 and Su-27. The Su-27 team is known as the 'Russian Knights'. The team flies a a six-ship mix of single- and two-seat aircraft – which remain combat-capable (as demonstrated by the photo opposite). Their last public appearance was at LIMA 95, Malaysia, when sadly the team lost three aircraft and four members in a crash en route to Cam Ranh Bay.

Sukhoi worked towards meeting a low-level radius of action requirement of 500 km (310 miles) (inferring a low-level range of at least 1200-1400 km/745-870 miles) and a high level radius of 1700 km (1,050 miles) (with a range of 4000 km/2,485 miles).

These range and performance characteristics dictated that the new aircraft would have to carry at least 9500 kg (20,950 lb) of fuel, which in turn inferred a take-off weight in the 25000 to 30000-kg (55,110 to 66,130-lb) class. This was not far short of the massive MiG-31 which would soon take shape as a MiG-25 replacement. To build such a fighter would clearly be a great undertaking, even without the extraordinary agility requirements also demanded of the successful PFI contender, which required very high sustained and instantaneous turn rates, small turn radii, and high acceleration. These ensured that the new fighter would require a very high thrust to weight ratio, together with a very high lift coefficient and very low drag characteristics. Lastly, the aircraft would be expected to operate from what the Russians classified as 'third-class airfields', with runway lengths of only 1200 m (3,940 ft). Yakovlev, Mikoyan and Sukhoi competed to produce a design, although Yakovlev dropped out at an early stage to concentrate on a new VTOL aircraft for the AV-MF, which became the Yakovlev Yak-141.

Sukhoi versus MiG

Sukhoi submitted the T10. Mikoyan responded with an aircraft designated MiG-29, which was very different to the 'Fulcrum' we know today and had MiG-25-type intakes flanking the fuselage. In many ways, the aircraft looked like a single-seat MiG-31, but with LERXes leading forward along the upper edges of the intakes, with more curved wingtips, and with tailfins and tailplanes carried on booms extending aft of the jet pipes.

Sukhoi did not have to contend with designing a weapons system for their new aircraft, since the design of this was tackled by other agencies. The OKB merely advised the weight and space constraints of the new fire control system, and the power and hardpoint requirements of the armament. The aircraft was apparently originally intended to be armed with new K-25 missiles (Soviet copies of the Sparrow, compromised in Vietnam). The identity of the organisation responsible for this missile remains unknown, as is the missile's eventual fate. In the event, the Su-27 was equipped with the heavier, long-range version of the R-27 (AA-10 'Alamo') SARH missile. It was one of two missiles (the other being the short-range IR-homing R-73) developed by Vympel from the mid-1970s specifically to equip the new fourth-generation fighters as part of a unified armament system. The R-27 was developed in semi-active radar homing and IR-homing versions, each produced in long- and short-range forms. The lighter, shorter-ranged missile was specifically intended for the lightweight PFI (which became the MiG-29) but was eventually to be carried by the Su-27 as a back-up to its long range R-27s (which weighed almost half as much again).

Before Artem Mikoyan died, he proposed following the American example even more closely – perhaps mindful that his MiG-29 was arguably not as radical as Sukhoi's original T10, and perhaps worried that he might not get the order. It is more likely that Mikoyan had realised that no single aircraft could meet the PFI requirement's contradictory demands for very long range and very high agility, and realised that a smaller, simpler fighter optimised for agility would be required in addition to the longer-range machine. The USAF had just announced that it would fund a lightweight (lower-cost) fighter to complement the capable but colossally expensive F-15, and Mikoyan proposed that Russia should do the same, producing a pair of aircraft (one large and expensive, one small and cheap) which could replace the MiG-21, Su-15 and MiG-23 in service with the IA-PVO and with Frontal Aviation. A few months later, Gleb Lozino-Lozinsky submitted the specification of a smaller MiG-29 (the 'Fulcrum' we know today, which was initially known as the MiG-29D – D for Dubler, or double). After a brief examination of a lightweight version of the T10, Mikoyan was instructed to proceed with their aircraft under the new LPFI (the new L prefix stood for Logiky, or lightweight) programme. In 1971 Sukhoi was instructed to continue with the T10 under what became the TPFI programme (the T suffix stood for Tyazholyi, or heavy).

The complex behind-the-scenes evaluations had led to a situation resembling that in the 1950s, when Mikoyan had tended to produce

The Soviet 4th Air Army in Poland included two Su-27-equipped fighter regiments at Chojna and Kluczewo-Stargard. They were tasked with long-range escort and air defence duties. Here an Su-27 from the Kluczewo-based 159th IAP taxis past the unit's standard during the 1992 return to Russia.

light multi-role fighters for Frontal Aviation and Sukhoi had tended to produce heavier aircraft for intercept duties with the IA-PVO. Mikoyan lost nothing from the result of the competition, since development of the MiG-31 (the ultimate heavy interceptor) continued apace, while Sukhoi had effectively lost the opportunity to design the affordable lightweight multi-role aircraft which would inevitably serve in larger numbers, and which would probably be produced in even larger numbers for export, too.

Happy to conveniently forget that the original requirement had become two quite different requirements, Mikhail Simonov remembers the order for the MiG-29 in his own way. "We won, but as so often happens it was decided to adopt the losing aircraft as well," he said at the Farnborough air show, in 1992. Despite any disappointment they might have felt, the Sukhoi OKB set about transforming its basic configuration into an operational fighter. After an expensive false start with the original T10 prototypes, they mounted a major redesign that resulted in the T10S, the Su-27 'Flanker' which we know today.

Aerodynamic concepts

When they were first seen in the West, the Su-27 and MiG-29 were frequently described as being mere copies of the latest Western fighters, clever Soviet amalgams of some of the features of the F-14, F-15, F-16 and F/A-18. In fact, the similarities to the latest generation of US warplanes were limited in most areas, and the Su-27 was no more a copy of the F-14/F-15 than those aircraft were copies of the MiG-25. Common problems often demanded common solutions, the most obvious being the use of twin fins to ensure adequate longitudinal control at high angles of attack.

An even more important similarity (at least to the F-14 and F-16) lay in the use of what the Russians called an 'integrated aerodynamic concept', in which a highly blended wing/fuselage combined with a high-lift fuselage to produce a 'unified lifting body'. This was designed to generate high lift during manoeuvres, while reducing wave drag at transonic speed and above. The use of a blended wing and fuselage also conferred enormous internal volume for fuel and avionics, while giving a relatively low wetted area and allowing a smooth distribution of cross-sectional area, in accordance with Whitcomb's area rule.

The engine nacelles were added below the lifting body, and were widely separated to prevent airflow disturbance in the event of a compressor stall, and to reduce the possibility of collateral damage if one engine broke up after sustaining battle damage. The underwing/fuselage position helped keep the intakes supplied with a relatively clean airflow even at high angles of attack. Differences from the US aircraft emerged because of the emphasis placed

An unarmed Su-27 of the 159th IAP sits in front of its hardened shelter. The aircraft's dimensions meant that it could not use facilities designed for the previous generation of Frontal Aviation fighters such as the MiG-21 and MiG-23, or even for the contemporary, but significantly smaller, MiG-29.

***Right:* Two demilitarised Su-27PUs of the 'Test Pilots' team refuel from an Il-78 'Midas' tanker, with the Su-27IB prototype taking fuel from the centre hose. The Su-27PU formed the basis of a family of extended-endurance interceptors and fighter-bombers known to the Sukhoi OKB as the Su-30 family.**

***Above:* Two early production Su-27s of the Ukrainian air force attended the Bratislava air show in 1995. Ukraine is the largest operator of the Su-27 outside Russia itself, having inherited two Su-27 regiments when the USSR split apart. Other former republics of the USSR operating Su-27s include Belarus, Kazakhstan and, perhaps, Georgia, Armenia and Azerbaijan.**

on keeping the engines running at high AoA, which necessitated a straight-through intake design. The Soviet emphasis on rough field operations also necessitated the provision of retractable anti-FOD intake screens for use on take-off and landing. On the Su-27 these were simply meshed, whereas the MiG-29 (which was expected to use even more primitive strips) used a system with solid doors and auxiliary intakes above the wings.

The engine air intakes were of similar design to those of the F-14 or the Panavia Tornado: steeply raked and rectangular, with an integral splitter (and a series of perforations) to remove sluggish boundary layer air, and with additional louvres which could act either as spills or auxiliary intake doors in the lower surface of the intake. The intake incorporated three variable ramps to optimise airflow to the compressor.

Su-27 wing layout

The wings of the Su-27 are often overlooked, since they are of conventional construction and their planform is so ordinary, modestly swept and with only small taper. In fact, the wing section has a deformed mid-section to give greater aerodynamic efficiency at high angles of attack, when maximum lift is being generated. The new section tends to give a less disturbed airflow at higher angles of attack, and also redistributes air density spanwise and chordwise, giving more even lift and coming closer to the optimum parallel airflow pattern by reducing induced drag. The efficiency of the deformed wing is further improved through the provision of automatically scheduled leading-edge flaps and trailing-edge inboard flaperons.

In order to obtain the necessary degree of agility, the stability of the Su-27 was reduced to a point at which a sophisticated fly-by-wire control system was required to provide artificial stability. The aircraft was not unstable in the same way as the BAe EAP, or as modern fighters like the Rafale, and used a quadruplex analogue FBW control system rather than a digital system as favoured in more modern, truly unstable aircraft. Sukhoi had gained experience with fly-by-wire control systems in its abortive T-4, the fuselage of which flexed so much that it had to be artificially stabilised in pitch. This control system formed the basis of the SDU-10-27 system used by the Su-27. The yaw and roll controls remain electro-mechanically controlled, although there is a sophisticated aileron/rudder interconnect which is used at high angles of attack. This means that the tailerons are actuated by the FBW computer when they move symmetrically for pitch control, but that differential movement, for roll control, is not handled by the FBW FCS computer. The fly-by-wire system includes a sophisticated angle of attack, pitch rate and *g* limiter, although this can be manually overridden by the pilot.

LERX enabled

One of the features which helped to reduce the longitudinal stability of the Su-27 was the provision of ogival-shaped wingroot leading-edge extensions (also known as leading-edge root extensions, or LERXes). They produced more lift at high angles of attack, and provided a powerful nose-up pitching moment. At angles of attack of more than 10° they also generated powerful vortices which flowed back over the wings (keeping airflow attached and reducing the tendency to stall) and tailfins (improving controllability in yaw at high angles of attack).

The Su-27's empennage virtually designed itself. Twin fins imposed a higher structural weight for the fin area, but brought about improvements in directional stability and controllability at high angles of attack. The interac-

The Su-27s of the 582nd IAP at Chojna wore dark blue codes, distinguishing them from the other Poland-based Su-27 regiment, which used red codes. Rivalry between the two units was intense, and both maintained a high level of morale right up until their withdrawal from Poland.

Above: Carrying Sorbtsiya ECM pods on its wingtips, an Su-27 of the 61st IAP, Belarus air force, taxis in at Baranovichi. Belarus inherited the 61st IAP, then converting from the MiG-25 to the Su-27, upon the break-up of the former USSR. The unit remains equipped with a mix of aircraft types, though the Su-27s are now augmented by MiG-29s withdrawn from units previously based in the former East Germany.

Right: This Su-27 is one of those used by the 760th ISIAP (part of the air force training centre at Lipetsk). Several of the unit's Su-27s wear sharkmouths on their intakes, but only one has the full silhouette. The 760th ISIAP uses a mix of Su-27s, Su-25s, Su-24s, MiG-29s and MiG-23s for tactical training and operational evaluation and development.

tion of the vortices generated by the LERXes and the tailfins was complex, varying according to Alpha, and the fins were carefully positioned for optimum effectiveness. The tailplane of the Su-27 was mounted low on booms adjacent to the outer edges of the engine nacelles, considerably below the trailing edge of the wing.

This locates the tailplane well below the mean chord line of the wing and below the decaying and disturbed airflow behind the trailing edge, instead laying in the wake of the more evenly distributed airflow below the wing. The tailplane is located far aft, to give the most powerful moment arm possible. This was especially important in the longitudinally unstable Su-27, which needed powerful pitch controls.

The same broad configuration was retained even after the T10 was redesigned to become the definitive T10S, which was the internal designation given to the Su-27 which we know today. The original T10 configuration (and the reasons for the redesign) are explained in detail in the T10 and T10S entries, while the definitive Su-27 fighter is described in detail here.

Structure

The Su-27 is of predominantly metal construction, mostly of conventional aluminium alloys but with some titanium and steel in areas around the engine nozzles and perhaps around the cannon port, and with a relatively small proportion of composites. The fuselage and wing centre-section were constructed as a single integrated unit, to which were joined the empennage, nose and outer wing panels. The fuselage was an all-metal semi-monocoque, spilt into three sections, comprising the nose, centre-section and rear. The centre fuselage section was built around three mainspars and a number of ribs, and also contained the two main fuel cells, various racks of avionics equipment and the 150-round ammunition box for the internal cannon. The upper part of the centroplane (as Sukhoi called the assembly) was of riveted aluminium alloys, and the lower part was primarily of welded construction with a high proportion of titanium alloys. Above the upper part of the centre fuselage was the 2.6-m² (28-sq ft) hydraulically actuated airbrake. It extended up to 54°, and could be used at speeds of up to 1000 km/h (620 mph).

Below the centre section were the mainwheel wells, and the attachment points, for the forward-retracting main undercarriage units. Each main undercarriage unit carried a single KT-156D (1030 x 350 mm/40 x 14 in) braked mainwheel. The lower part also included the mounting points for the engine intakes, and for the tandem weapons racks between the engines. The fuselage spine was built in three sections, one central and two outer, consisting of longerons, arched formers and inspection hatches. They contained the control linkages and other services.

Nose and cockpit section

The nose section was of stressed skin construction, with stringers and longerons reinforcing the bulkhead frames. Capped by a separate glass-fibre radome, the nose accommodated the radar, the electro-optical system and other avionics forward, and the pilot's cockpit, an under-cockpit equipment bay area, the nosewheel well and the forward parts of the LERXes. The nosewheel well contained a single forward-retracting, steerable, semi-levered oleo, to which was attached a single braked (680 x 260 mm/27 x 10 in) KN-27 wheel. The pilot's cockpit was fully pressurised and was covered by a two-piece canopy. The windscreen was fixed and the rear section hinged upwards. This had an internal frame well aft which gave it the appearance of being built in two sections. The pilot sat on a Zvezda K-36DM Series 2 ejection seat. It contained a NAZ-8 survival pack, with a Komar 2M survival radio/SAR beacon and a PSN-1 dinghy in addition to rations, flares and emergency medical equipment, and was integrated with the KKO-5 oxygen system. The pilot wears a PSU-36 28-segment 60-m² (645-sq ft) parachute, and can wear a high-altitude pressure suit or an immersion suit. The starboard LERX contained the internal Gryazev/Shipunov 9A-4071K GSh-30-1 single-barrelled 30-mm cannon. This was the same weapon as was fitted to the rival Mikoyan MiG-29.

Rear fuselage and powerplants

The rear fuselage section contains the engine nacelles, which are covered with access panels. The aft-most pair of bulkheads are removable downwards and backwards to give access to the engines for removal and replacement. Between the nacelles was the central tailboom, which was a continuation of the centre fuselage spine and housed a fuel tank, avionics equipment and the brake chute compartment. Outboard of the nacelles were two more tailbooms which supported the empennage and housed the RPD-1 electro-hydraulic power control boosters for the tailerons; the latter could move differentially through ±10°, or symmetrically from 15° leading edge up, to 20° leading edge down. The twin fins carried tall rudders which could deflect through ±25°.

The wing centre-section was joined to the outer wing panels immediately outboard of the LERXes. The outer wings were built around a three-spar wing box and incorporated integral fuel tanks. Strengthened ribs carried underwing hardpoints and the wingtip missile launch rails. The latter doubled as anti-flutter masses and could be replaced by Sorbtsiya ECM pods. The 42° swept leading edge incorporated full-span leading-edge flaps (4.6 m²/50 sq ft) which could deploy down to 30°, while single-slotted flaperons occupied the inboard 60 per cent of the trailing edge (4.9 m²/52 sq ft). They could deploy up to 35° and down to 20° and were actuated differentially for roll control, or symmetrically to alter the wing profile. The slats and flaps were actuated manually for take-off

Above: Sukhoi is now throwing the full weight of its marketing expertise behind the advanced Su-35. The Su-35 has been, at least nominally, entered in every international fighter competition of recent years, though Sukhoi has had more success in selling the proven, baseline Su-27.

Right: Development of the Su-27M has been long and protracted, and it remains unclear which radar will actually be fitted to any production version of the aircraft. This Tupolev Tu-134UBL, based at Zhukhovskii with the LII Gromov Flight Research Institute, has an extended nose with an Su-27M radome attached. Latest reports suggest that the Su-35 will have an electronically scanned, phased array antenna, which is believed to have been tested in this aircraft.

and landing, but are otherwise scheduled by the flight control system controller.

The Su-27 is powered by a pair of NPO Saturn/Lyul'ka AL-31F afterburning turbofans. The engine is of similar configuration to the Klimov/Isotov RD-33 turbofan used by the MiG-29, but is considerably larger, with increased mass flow and commensurately higher thrust ratings. Some sources have suggested that the two engines were designed by the same state institute (presumably TsIAM) and represent small and large versions of a common design (refined, improved and put into production by their respective OKBs), in the same way that the Su-27 and MiG-29 have sometimes been seen as large and small versions of a common TsAGI aerodynamic configuration.

The AL-31F is described as being of modular design, and as having a four-stage low-pressure compressor, a nine-stage high-pressure compressor, an annular combustor and single-stage high- and low-pressure turbines. It also has a fully variable convergent/divergent nozzle. The same description could apply equally well to the MiG-29's engine. The AL-31F has a claimed pressure ratio of 23:1 (compared to 20:1 for the RD-33) and a maximum TET of 1,427°C (2,600°F) (compared to 1,397°C/2,550°F TET). Specific fuel consumption figures are given as 0.67 lb/lb/hr dry and 1.86 lb/lb/hr with afterburning (compared to 0.77 lb/lb/hr and 2.1 lb/lb/hr for the RD-33).

The mature production engine is reportedly less powerful than had once been hoped, but its thrust rating of 74.53 kN (16,755 lb st), or 122.59 kN (27,588 lb st) with afterburning, is

Left: The second prototype Su-27UB, sometimes referred to as 02-10, was used to test some of the features of the Su-27PU, but also carried out trials on the ski jump and dummy carrier deck at Saki. The aircraft had a new retractable inflight-refuelling probe, necessitating the relocation of the IRST to the starboard side of the nose. Its constant-section cylindrical tail sting was replaced by a more streamlined fairing, fatter further forward and curving in to more of a point. This pointed upwards, reducing the risk of tail scrapes during high-Alpha landings.

nonetheless more than sufficient to endow even a heavily laden Su-27 with breathtaking performance figures. The availability of better materials, and the ability to manufacture to closer tolerances, has led to the development of at least one (and perhaps two) higher thrust versions of the AL-31F, known as the AL-31FM and AL-35F (it is not certain whether these designations apply to a single engine, or to two slightly separate engines). Such highly evolved versions of the AL-31F are expected to power advanced versions of the Su-27, including the Su-27M and Su-27IB, although prototypes of these subtypes are understood to retain their existing AL-31F engines rather than any of the more advanced powerplants.

The Su-27's fuel system was arranged in three main fuselage tanks, with additional tanks in the outer wing panels. The basic Su-27 has no provision for inflight refuelling or for the carriage of external fuel tanks (but see under individual variant entries for exceptions). The maximum capacity of the tanks was 12000 litres (9400 kg at the accepted standard specific gravity of 0.785) but 3400 kg (7,496 lb) of this was regarded as internal auxiliary tankage, used for long-range missions but imposing lower *g* and a limits. All of the tanks are lined with reticulated polyurethane foam to reduce the danger of explosions, and the tanks are believed to be pressurised with inert halon gas.

Powered systems

The MiG-29 is believed to have made extensive use of pneumatic systems (which were considered to be less vulnerable to battle damage, since they did not rely on inflammable hydraulic fluid) for braking, undercarriage extension, etc., but the Su-27 used pneumatics only for pressurisation and for the back-up of certain hydraulic systems. The Su-27 had two separate 280 kg/cm^2 closed-circuit hydraulic systems, which powered undercarriage and air-brake retraction and extension, control surface actuation, wheel brakes and the retractable intake screens. Each system is driven by a separate engine-mounted pump and the systems provide full redundancy. The Su-27's electrical systems operate on either 27 volt DC or 115 volt/400 Hz AC current. The aircraft has two engine-driven AC generators and two 20NKBN-25 NiCad batteries.

The Su-27 made its public debut at the 1989 Paris Air Salon at Le Bourget, less than one year after the MiG-29's ground-breaking appearance

The first photo of what later became known as the Su-27IB, 'blue 42', showed it approaching the deck of what was then the Tbilisi. With no arrester hook the aircraft could not actually make a carrier landing, and with no wing folding and no double-slotted flaps it was not really suitable for carrier operation, but the fiction was maintained that it was actually the prototype for a dedicated carrier-based trainer with the designation Su-27KU. It is unknown whether there was a kernel of truth in the story, or whether the picture was part of a pure disinformation exercise.

Above: The 1st Squadron of the Severomorsk Regiment made its first operational cruise aboard the carrier **Kuznetsov** *in 1996, sailing from its Northern Fleet base to the Mediterranean. Here one of the regiment's aircraft, decorated with a diving eagle fin badge, takes a wire, its tyres streaming smoke. Although the aircraft were loaded with weapons for port visits, they usually flew in clean configuration.*

Right: Burners blazing, one of the **Kuznetsov's** *Su-27Ks blasts off from the carrier's ski jump. The aircraft are reportedly designated Su-27K by the AV-MF, although the Sukhoi Design Bureau uses the designation Su-33. This photo shows to advantage the Su-27K's generous double-slotted trailing edge flaps and short tailcone.*

at Farnborough. The MiG-29 had astonished Western observers with its unprecedented tailslide, and the Su-27 made a similarly dramatic debut by demonstrating the dynamic deceleration which became known as Pugachev's Cobra. The aircraft had been specially stripped and was flying with very little fuel, but the manoeuvre demonstrated an astonishing level of benign handling, and a hitherto-unimagined ability to point the nose away from the direction of flight.

The aircraft pitched 120° nose up from level flight until the nose was pointing up, back past the vertical, while the aircraft flew on belly and tail first, before the nose pitched back forward to level flight. This was achieved at air show altitude, with no appreciable loss or gain in altitude, demonstrating that the manoeuvre was reliably and safely repeatable. The manoeuvre was entered from level flight at speeds of less than 400 km/h (250 mph), decelerating to about 115 km/h (70 mph) within about three seconds. The pilot overrode the pitch limiter by pulling the stick back hard, holding it there before firmly pushing forward, using sufficient pressure to pull and push through the 'soft' limits.

The manoeuvre was apparently developed as a flight test AoA limit check point by Valery Menitsky, Mikoyan chief test pilot, using the MiG-29, but was cheekily borrowed by Pugachev, Sukhoi's chief test pilot, who wanted a unique air show manoeuvre for the Su-27's Western debut. He succeeded beyond his wildest dreams, and in the process won countless column inches of free publicity.

The Su-27 in combat?

Assessing and analysing the combat potential of the Su-27 remains difficult. Whereas many front-line pilots have flown against MiG-29s in simulated combat (especially since NATO-member West Germany integrated a full squadron of former East German MiG-29s into its force structure), the Su-27 remains much more of an unknown quantity, familiar only from intelligence reports and air show appearances. At one time it seemed likely that this might change, when the US company Greystone Technologies Inc. announced that it would be using Su-27s and MiG-29s to act as hostile 'aggressor' aircraft during NATO exercises, initially at a NATO Tactical Fighter Weapons Instructor Course at Leeuwarden. Unfortunately, the plan was defeated by the difficulty (which should surely have been foreseen) of a civilian company operating uncertificated military Su-27s in normal airspace.

Some have assumed that the Su-27 is closely comparable to the MiG-29, and at very low weights, at the end of a mission (or for an air show appearance), the comparison is probably valid. Although a MiG-29 at air show weight and a MiG-29 at combat weight are relatively similar, the difference between two Su-27s in these configurations is enormous. Somewhat larger than a MiG-29, with bigger wings and more powerful engines, the fully laden Su-27 nonetheless has a higher wing loading and a lower thrust-to-weight ratio than the MiG-29. It can thus be expected to be less agile at normal mission weights. This vital factor has not always been fully appreciated, and a nightmare scenario for Western air defence fighter pilots for many years was the prospect of Su-27s escorting long-range bombers almost to their targets, where they would be able to outfight (and outmanoeuvre) locally based air defence fighters. With sufficient fuel to return to base, the Su-27 would have represented a formidable BVR threat at the very edge of its mission radius, but would not have been so dangerous in a close-in turning fight.

This difference is relatively unimportant, however, since the intelligent fighter pilot will always avoid the close-in turning fight if possible. Close-in dogfighting is simply too unpredictable, and a superior pilot in a superior aircraft can be defeated almost by chance factors in

Left: The Su-27M is even more agile than the basic Su-27, thanks to its new digital FBW control system and canard foreplanes. This aircraft is actually the T10M-11, the prototype for what Sukhoi call the Su-37, which also features vectoring engine nozzles. The vectored-thrust 'Flanker' made its Western debut at Farnborough in 1996, astonishing onlookers by replicating some of the manoeuvres demonstrated by the Rockwell X-31 at the previous year's Paris Air Salon.

Below: The Sukhoi Su-37 introduced a combination of breathtaking supermaneouvrability and real combat potential at the 1996 Farnborough air show. Opinions were immediately split between those who saw no advantage for a thrust-vectoring aircraft in the BVR era and those who pointed to its unique combination of agile weapons and agile airframe. To answer this question chief designer Simonov challenged any Western manufacturer, there and then, to an aerial duel either at the show or an ACMI range.

the confusion of the fur-ball. The Su-27 pilot will always aim to sneak up on his opponent undetected, like an assassin in the night, and then shoot him in the chest from the maximum possible range. Some aircraft do not have a sufficient BVR missile warload to rely on being able to make a long-range kill every time. The basic MiG-29, for example, has only two BVR missiles (representing only one-third of its missile load) and thus relies on being able to cope in a close-in fight. The basic Su-27, on the other hand, can carry six (or even eight) BVR missiles with only four IR-homing 'dogfight' missiles, which thus represent only a last-ditch contingency option.

Su-27 weights and performance

The Sukhoi OKB recognised the impossibility of making the Su-27 as agile as the MiG-29 at maximum weight by quite deliberately setting two separate groups of limits, for a low-weight aircraft (at what might be called dogfighting weight) and for the fully-fuelled, fully-equipped interceptor. This philosophy of having two different weight-class fighters within the same airframe is a novel one, and allows the Su-27 to be used as a low-weight, agile, short-range fighter if required. It is achieved by having two basic fuel configurations, with three of the internal tanks being regarded as a 3400-kg (7,496-lb) auxiliary tank, used for most missions, but left empty for dogfight-type missions. Although providing space for this dictated a larger airframe, it was considered to be a more efficient and lower-drag solution than providing for the carriage of external or even conformal auxiliary tanks, especially because the auxiliary tankage would inevitably be required for the Su-27's primary role.

At low weight, the Su-27 is unquestionably a very fine close-in fighter, with a low wing loading and a very high thrust-to-weight ratio. Its turn radius is small, and the aircraft handles well at high angles of attack, allowing the pilot to manoeuvre with confidence even at low airspeeds. The air show manoeuvres described by some as 'circus stunts' represent a stunning demonstration of the aircraft's ability to point its nose, and have proved effective in some combat scenarios when used by the MiG-29. The Su-27 pilot can enhance his dogfighting advantages through use of the helmet-mounted target designator. This allows him to cue the seeker heads of his IR-homing missile armament onto a target by looking at it through the fixed monocular eyepiece mounted on the helmet, which also incorporates head position sensors. The computer can work out where he is looking, and 'tells' the missile seeker heads to point in exactly the same direction. Use of this system allows the Su-27 pilot to fire his R-73 (AA-11 'Archer') missiles at targets well offset from his nose (off-axis). Use of the same system by MiG-29 pilots has proved a decisive advantage in engagements between Luftwaffe MiG-29s and USAF and Dutch F-16s, or USMC F/A-18s.

Engagements between NATO-operated MiG-29s and aircraft like the F-15, F-16 and F/A-18 have tended to demonstrate that the MiG-29's BVR capability is relatively unimpressive, despite the long range of its radar. This is partly a function of the complicated switchology necessary for missile arming and selection, and for manipulating the radar's modes, which reduces the pilot's situational awareness, and is partly due to the inadequate onboard computer processing which makes autonomous targeting difficult and effectively precludes multiple simultaneous target engagement. Moreover, the R-27 (AA-10 'Alamo') missile is generally ranked slightly below the current models of the AIM-7, with considerably lower pK than the AIM-120, SkyFlash or even the latest AIM-7M.

BVR capabilities

Since the Su-27 uses basically the same missile armament as the MiG-29, and has generally been assumed to have what is essentially the same radar, it has often been thought that the Su-27's BVR capabilities are similar to those of the smaller aircraft, albeit with slightly greater radar range (made possible by the larger antenna diameter and more powerful transmitter), and with greater combat persistence (due to the larger number of missiles carried). The more astute observers have also concluded that the Su-27 would enjoy some advantages due to its better supersonic acceleration, which could impart higher acceleration (and thus range) to its missiles, and that its pilots (primarily PVO specialist interceptor pilots) would be more experienced and better trained in BVR tactics.

Superior Sukhoi?

In fact, the Su-27 enjoys some other advantages, too. The big Sukhoi can carry some long-range versions of the R-27 which have not been seen carried by MiG-29s, including the extended-range R-27ER and R-27ET. The basic Su-27 is fitted with an active ECM jammer (only fitted to the 'Fulcrum-C' and advanced MiG-29 variants) and probably has better RHAWS coverage, while the electro-optical system's IRSTS and laser rangefinder are understood to have a slightly longer range (IRST range is more than 40 km/25 miles for a rear-hemisphere, non-reheat target).

Although both the Su-27's N-001 radar and the MiG-29's N-019 bear the same NATO 'Slot Back' reporting name, they are believed to be entirely separate radars rather than large and small, long- and short-range members of the same family. Whereas the MiG-29's 'Slot Back' is the Phazatron-built N-019, the Su-27 'Slot Back' is NIIP's N-001. These differences may help to explain why Sukhoi claimed a simultaneous dual-target engagement capability long before it was claimed for the MiG-29 (in its N-019M-equipped MiG-29S form). It may also help to explain why the Su-27 is sometimes described as being compatible with the 'Foxhound's' R-33 missile, a weapon known to be incompatible with the 'Fulcrum's' 'Slot Back'. NATO fighter pilots are now familiar with the MiG-29's radar, but they have not had the same access or exposure to the Su-27's radar, and so some elements of the Su-27's BVR capability must remain a matter for educated and informed supposition. Despite Sukhoi's claims, this author would tend towards the belief that the baseline Su-27 in service with the Russian air force in 1996 probably does not enjoy a simultaneous dual-target engagement capability – a conclusion supported by a non-NATO air force which nevertheless expected to meet the Su-27 in combat. Sukhoi figures suggest that the N-001 (at least in the form fitted to the export Su-27SK) has a look-up or level range (for a MiG-21-type target) of more than 100 km (62 miles), with a look-down range of more than 97 km (60 miles) for the same type of target.

The Su-30MK is a genuine multi-role, two-seat, high-endurance strike fighter. Here, one of the demonstrators takes off in full burner, toting an impressive array of air-to-air and air-to-surface ordnance. The first customer for the Su-30MK is to be India, which may receive aircraft with canard foreplanes and thrust vectoring.

Of course, only the basic Su-27 is equipped with the fundamental, standard N-001 radar, and subsequent variants and derivatives have modernised or modified versions of the radar, or, in the case of the Su-27M, an entirely new radar. This demonstrates how different 'Flanker' variants can have such different capabilities. Details of all of the major Su-27 sub-variants are given in the following pages. **Jon Lake**

The first prototype Su-27IB was converted from the airframe of a redundant Su-27UB, and was little more than an aerodynamic prototype for the full-standard side-by-side strike/attack aircraft which followed, and which the OKB refers to as the Su-34 and Su-32FN (in naval anti-ship configuration).

Sukhoi Su-27 'Flanker' variants

The earliest days of the Su-27 project remain shrouded in mystery. The overall concept of using a blended wing and forebody, with widely spaced underslung engines and twin fins, was decided early on, but details took longer to finalise. An early model of the Su-27 in the bureau's archives (seen right) had canted fins and dramatically canted intakes, with four hardpoints under each wing (the two outboard pylons carrying 'Aphids', and those inboard carrying what were recognisable as early 'Alamos') and with no pylons under the intakes. This aircraft had an entirely frameless canopy, like that of the F-16. Another model of what is claimed to have been an early Su-27 configuration was recently discovered in the Ilyushin OKB museum, reportedly placed there as part of a disinformation exercise. This model shares some common features with the Su-27 configuration described above, but was unarmed and had a conventional two-part windscreen. The aircraft had intakes much closer to those fitted to the flying T10, but had cropped wingtips like those of the F-15, rather than the smooth curved wingtips of the Sukhoi model and the original T10 itself.

Right: This early Su-27 configuration differed from the definitive T10 in a number of areas, but had the same Gothic wing planform and placed a similar emphasis on combat persistence. It carried four BVR missiles and four WVR missiles underwing, and perhaps more between the engines.

Below and bottom right: The model in the Ilyushin OKB museum bore some resemblance to the F-14, with its intake configuration, square-cut beaver tail and tapering ventral strakes, while its wing planform was similar to that of the F-15.

Su-27 (T10) 'Flanker-A'

Aircraft designed by the Sukhoi OKB have inevitably received an internal sequential numerical designation based on wing planform, using the prefixes S, for *Strelovidnyil* (arrow-shaped, or swept), or T for *Treugoinyi* (triangular, or delta). The original Su-27 was known internally as the T10, indicating that it was the 10th delta-winged design drawn up by the bureau. The T10 was created around a cleverly designed blended forward fuselage and a Gothic wing (with graceful curved tips), optimised for low drag and high lift, with prominent chines (or LERXes) running forward from the wingroot. To this basic core unit were added widely separated twin engine nacelles, twin tail fins and twin engines. An early configuration had wingtips much like those of the F-15, and the engines were separated by a broad flat beaver tail, much like that fitted to the F-14. This configuration also had shallow ventral strakes below the engine nacelles, and these, too, were similar to those fitted to the F-14. From the start, Sukhoi intended that its fighter would have an unusual degree of combat persistence, and added hardpoints below each wing (totalling four) and below each nacelle (two more), with two more in tandem on the centreline, between the engine nacelles. This was two more usable hardpoints than the MiG-29, whose centreline pylon was used only for a ferry tank, and whose carriage prevented use of the internal cannon. The main undercarriage doors doubled as airbrakes, opening forward and downward.

Sources differ as to exactly who designed the basic configuration of the Su-27 (and the MiG-29, since the smaller aircraft uses virtually the same configuration). Certain sources within the Sukhoi OKB suggest that the design was 'theirs', while others infer that the configuration was brought to Sukhoi by two designers who joined the bureau from Mikoyan. According to the accepted 'legend' within the Sukhoi OKB, the original configuration layout was produced by only three men, who worked over a single weekend in order to avoid interruptions. These men were said to have been Oleg Sergeyevich Samolovich, chief designer on Su-24 and Su-25 (working under P. O. Sukhoi himself), and deputy designer general Yevgeny Ivanov, together with a graduate student (sometimes named as Vladimir Antonov). Mikhail P. Simonov later took over from Ivanov while Samolovich later became a professor at the Moscow Aviation Institute. Antonov later rose to become a senior figure within the OKB.

Regardless of who designed the original Su-27 wing/forebody, it is known that a variety of shapes was studied (at angles of attack of up to 180°) in SibNIA's T-203 subsonic wind tunnel, and by TsAGI, the state's own aerodynamic research centre, and the LII. In the Soviet Union of the late 1960s and early 1970s (then still a highly centralised and directed society), it is likely that the two competing design bureaus actually performed only definition and detailed design work on a configuration given to them by TsAGI (or CAHI, as it should be more correctly transliterated). This helps explain the inconvenient fact that Mikoyan ('copiers' of the configuration in

The first T10 prototype takes shape in the OKB's own experimental workshop. The square-cut beaver tail and close, uncanted tailfins are apparent in this very early view of what would become the Su-27.

Right: The first T10 is pictured shortly before its maiden flight, in one of the open-ended sheds south of Zhukhovskii's runways. The rear of the hangarette has had a canvas awning rigged to hide the still-secret prototype, which was soon 'captured' on film by a prowling US satellite and allocated the provisional US DoD reporting name of 'Ram-K'.

The first T10 was soon retrofitted with distinctive leading-edge fairings which contained anti-flutter weights. The jetpipes also seem to have been extended or replaced, or perhaps to have suffered heat damage at the fuselage/jet pipe intersection.

The T10-1 was flown with dummy R-60 (AA-8 'Aphid') missiles underwing, and with dummy R-27 (AA-10 'Alamo') missiles between the engine nacelles. Inboard underwing pylons were not fitted but their locating lugs can just be seen. The value of the main gear doors as airbrakes is also clear.

most scenarios) actually got it right the first time, while Sukhoi's first configuration was badly wrong.

Indeed, the first Su-27 configuration, used by the initial batch of T10 prototypes, was very badly wrong. So wrong, in fact, that the aircraft had to be entirely redesigned before it could enter production, with a new wing, new tailplanes, more outboard tailfins and a redesigned nose.

Nine of the original T10s were built and flown, however, and they played a part in the Su-27 flight test programme even after it had been decided to redesign the aircraft. The first of the prototype batch made its maiden flight on 20 May 1977, in the hands of Vladimir Ilyushin. It was not until many years later that the Western public got its first look at this early 'Flanker' when a brief clip of the first prototype was shown on Soviet television, and stills from the sequence appeared in Western aviation magazines. Western intelligence agencies had already seen the aircraft, via satellite imagery and photos gathered by other means. This data resulted in the allocation of the provisional reporting name 'Ram-K', indicating that it was the 10th (I was not used) new prototype seen at what the West still referred to as Ramenskoye, but which by then had been renamed as the Zhukhovskii Flight Research Institute. One overhead satellite photo found its way into print before even the TV segment, but it had been so dramatically degraded that it gave little indication as to what the aircraft really looked like, and even led some analysts to conclude that the aircraft had a variable-geometry wing. Observers in the West were not aware of the difficulties experienced by the T10, and, assuming that the aircraft was on the verge of entering service, the reporting name 'Flanker' was allocated, with the original configuration being known as 'Flanker-A'.

Photos of the first T10 before and during its initial flight reveal many differences between its configuration then and its appearance at the end of its useful life. The aircraft was retired to the air forces' museum at Monino, where it can presently be inspected. For its first flight, the aircraft was remarkably clean (perhaps with a pair of overwing fences well inboard). The aircraft was soon to be seen with four large fences above the wing, quite close to the root. The outboard pair was later removed, but large anti-flutter weights were added in fairings which projected forward from the leading edges of the tailfins, tailplanes and wingtips. These modifications represented futile palliatives intended to cure the many aerodynamic problems suffered by the T10.

Subsequent T10 prototypes differed in detail from the first prototype, with a

Sukhoi T10-1 first flight configuration

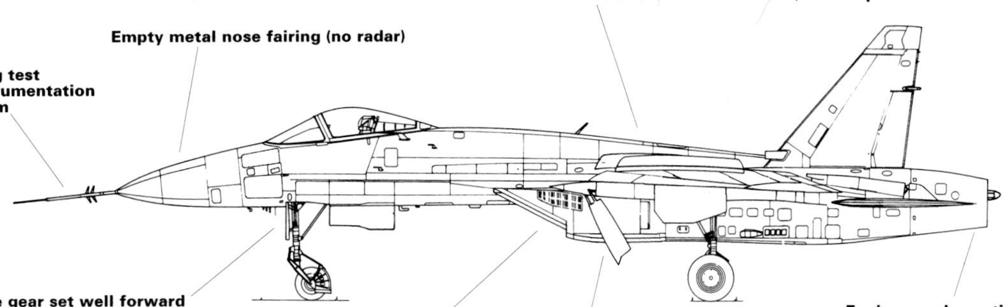

Two and then four fences (inboard pair later removed)
Empty metal nose fairing (no radar)
Long test instrumentation boom
Nose gear set well forward
'Crease' in intake lip
Main gear door functions as airbrake
Engine nozzles entirely contained within rear fuselage

Sukhoi T10-1 late configuration

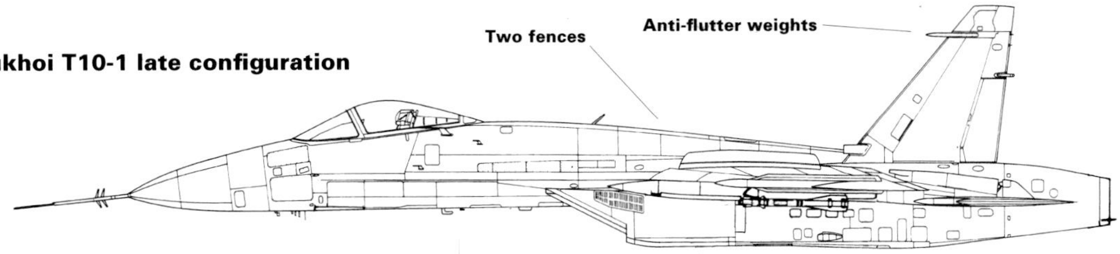

Two fences
Anti-flutter weights
Anti-flutter weights on wing leading edge
R-60 AAM on very shallow pylon
Anti-flutter weights on tailplane leading edge

Sukhoi T10-11

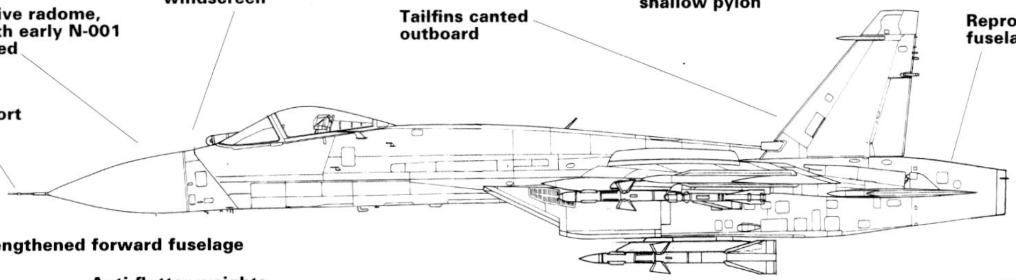

Representative radome, probably with early N-001 radar installed
IRST sensor in front of windscreen
Tailfins canted outboard
Reprofiled rear fuselage
Standard short pitot probe
New lengthened forward fuselage

Sukhoi T10-1

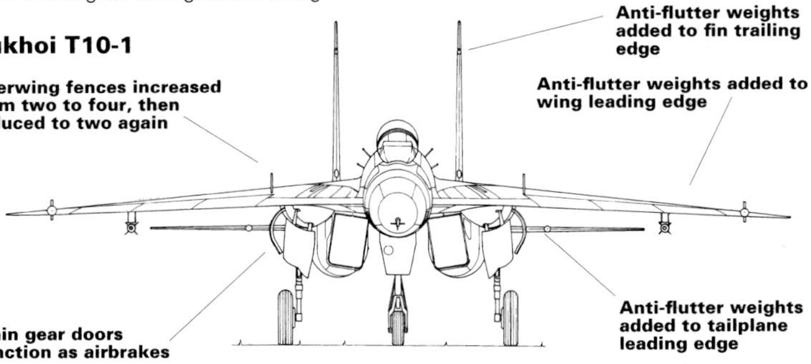

Overwing fences increased from two to four, then reduced to two again
Anti-flutter weights added to fin trailing edge
Anti-flutter weights added to wing leading edge
Main gear doors function as airbrakes
Anti-flutter weights added to tailplane leading edge

Sukhoi T10-11

Two overwing fences
Tailfins canted outboard
IRST sensor in front of windscreen
Gun fitted to T10-3 and perhaps some other prototypes, but not T10-1, T10-5 or T10-11
Production-type radome

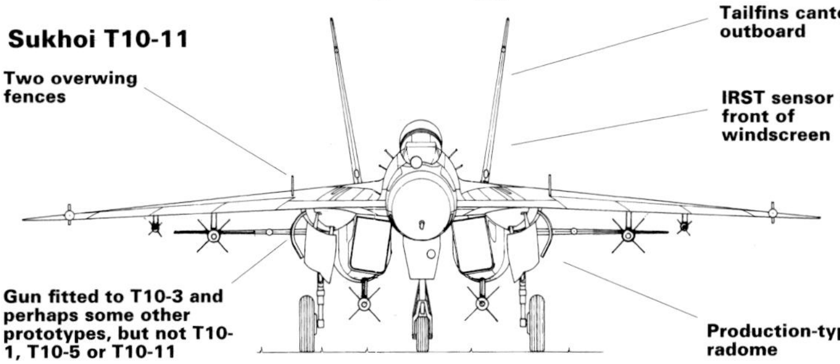

Sukhoi 'Flanker' variants

The canted fins fitted to later T10 prototypes are just visible in this view of the fifth aircraft, seen here with a full missile load of six R-27 and two R-73 (AA-11) AAMs.

Above: This early view of the fifth aircraft shows it fitted with an IRST above the nose, but with no radome. The T10 prototype batch aircraft differed from each other in detail, and fulfilled different tasks within the overall development programme. The OKB-built third and fourth aircraft had definitive AL-31 engines, and may have had an internal gun.

sharper, flatter LERX and (from T10-3) with slightly canted tailfins that also appear to have been slightly enlarged and more widely spaced. The later aircraft also had an extra 2,205 lb (1000 kg) of fuel, bringing tankage to 10000 kg (22,045 lb). Some of the aircraft (perhaps from T10-2, and almost certainly from T10-5) had leading-edge flaps, while some of the aircraft (probably from T10-4) were fitted with radar. The later aircraft were probably fitted with the fin-, tail- and wing-mounted anti-flutter weights from the start, and appear to have had the inboard overwing fences, too. A landing light was set into the port side of the main nosewheel door (the modified door later being retrofitted to the first prototype). It is uncertain as to whether the GSh-30-1 cannon was ever fitted to any of the T10 prototypes, or even whether the aircraft was originally intended to have an internal cannon at all, although photos of the third T10 appear to show a cannon port and adjacent airframe strengthening in the upper surface of the starboard LERX.

The second prototype (which was the first T10 to introduce the FBW control system, according to some sources) had a brief life, crashing on 7 May 1978, killing its pilot. Soloviev ejected outside seat parameters after flight control system problems resulted in severe airframe resonance, which led to a structural break-up. The third and fourth prototypes (coded '310' and '410') were built in the bureau's own Moscow workshops (using wings, tails and other sub-assemblies from the production plant at Komsomolsk na Amur) like the first two aircraft, but unlike the other T10 prototypes were powered by a pair of Saturn/Lyul'ka AL-31F engines and fitted with new convergent/divergent fully-variable nozzles. Five additional T10 prototypes were assembled at Komsomolsk between 1980 and 1982 (T10-5, T10-6, T10-9, T10-10 and T10-11), but these retained the AL-21F-3 engines used by the original prototypes. The 109.84-kN (24,692-lb st) AL-21F-3, a tried and trusted engine which already powered versions of the Su-17, MiG-23 and Su-24, actually offered greater dry thrust (76.49 kN/17,195 lb compared to only 74.53 kN/16,754 lb) than the new 122.59-kN (27,588-lb st) AL-31, but had a considerably higher specific fuel consumption and could not match the AL-31F's promised reliability. It was also longer and fatter than the new engine.

It was once thought that the original T10s were powered by Tumanskii R-29 engines, rated at 125 kN (28,100 lb st). This was not the case, although the engine may once have been considered as an alternative to the AL-21F-3.

Despite the repairs and modifications, computer simulations based on T10 flight test data revealed that instead of enjoying a 1.35:1 advantage over the F-15, the aircraft was inferior to the American fighter by about the same degree. Flight tests confirmed that the T10 was failing to meet its specification in many areas, and would be completely unable to meet the F-15 on anything approaching even terms. Aerodynamic difficulties imposed higher-than-predicted drag and handling problems, while performance was lower than expected. The conventional outboard ailerons were prone to reversal, forcing the wing to twist rather than encouraging the aircraft to turn, while the combined gear door/airbrakes caused severe tailplane flutter when actuated. As if this was not bad enough, much of the Su-27's equipment was overweight and under-spec, while the engines had a much higher specific fuel consumption than had been predicted, radically reducing the aircraft's range and endurance characteristics. Salt was rubbed in Sukhoi's wounds by the continuing success of its smaller rival, the MiG-29, which proved to be better than had ever been predicted.

A major redesign was inevitable, and two T10 prototypes taking shape in the bureau's workshops (reportedly T10-7 and T10-12, and not T10-8 which was a static test airframe) were completed as the T10S-1 and T10S-2. (The revised T10S is described in greater detail below.) There were reports that production of the original T10 continued even after the T10S-1 and T10S-2 were being converted, with the aim of providing a large fleet of development hacks for radar and weapons trials. Some sources suggest that 20 T10s were eventually completed, but this cannot be confirmed, and much evidence supports the supposition that only nine of the original aircraft ever flew. These were, however, used in support of the T10S programme.

Su-27 (T10S) pre-series 'Flanker-B'

Sukhoi T10S (Pre-series Su-27)

Following the dramatic failure of the original T10 to live up to expectations, the aircraft was entirely redesigned, and two partially complete airframes (which would have been T10-7 and T10-12) being constructed at the OKB's workshops in Moscow were finished to the revised design, under the new designation T10S. The S suffix was optimistically added to signify 'series', and not Simonov, as has often been suggested (not least by senior figures within the Sukhoi OKB). The scope of the redesign was such that Sukhoi insiders joke that only the K-36 ejection seat and mainwheels were retained from the original T10. This is a slight exaggeration, since the entire centre-section, including the engine intakes and nacelles, remained virtually unchanged, and the position of the shoulder-mounted wing and mid-set tailplane remained constant. The overall configuration was retained, too, and the aircraft stayed as a twin-finned, high-winged fighter with twin, widely-separated engines and with prominent wing leading-edge root extensions. The fact that the same basic description could be applied equally to the T10 and the T10S hides the fact that there were major changes and that few areas of the airframe were not refined in some way or other.

The wings were entirely redesigned, with reduced leading-edge sweep, and lost their fences. They were increased in area (to 62 m² from 59.4 m² – 667 sq ft from 639 sq ft) and were given square-cut tips mounting missile launch rails which also acted as anti-flutter weights. This effectively raised the number of weapons pylons from eight to 10, and allowed the aircraft to carry four short-range IR-homing 'dogfight' missiles in addition to its six longer-range semi-active radar homing BVR weapons. The trailing-edge flaps and separate outboard ailerons were replaced by single-section flaperons extending out from the root to about 60 per cent span. The leading edge gained computer-controlled flaps.

The tailfins were increased in size and moved outboard to slender booms beside the engine nacelles, but were returned to the vertical, having been canted outboard on most of the T10s. The vertical fins were augmented by new ventral strakes carried below the same tailbooms. They were intended to enhance directional stability and increase spin resistance, but positioning them proved troublesome, and required a long series of flight tests. (These may have involved one of the original T10s, as well as the T10S.) The tailplanes were increased in size (span, chord and area) and gained distinctive cropped tips, like the wingtips of the F-15 Eagle. The flat, shallow, spade-like beaver tail between the engine nozzles was replaced by a lengthened cylindrical tail sting, tipped by a conical fairing, which reduced drag, provided a housing for enlarged twin braking parachutes and provided space for chaff/flare dispensers. The fuselage cross sections were reduced and the wing fillets were of reduced radius.

The nose was lengthened and refined in shape, with a more bulbous radome and with considerably more droop. The nosewheel was moved aft to reduce the aircraft's turning circle and to reduce the likelihood of debris being thrown up into the intakes. The oleos of the main undercarriage units were altered to slope forward, allowing them to retract better into the wing/fuselage centre-section. The undercarriage doors were also redesigned, with a large dorsal airbrake replacing the forward doors, which had functioned as speed brakes. Even the cockpit canopy was redesigned, being given a longer, flatter, more streamlined profile. The definitive AL-31F engines (with top-mounted accessories gearboxes) were housed in redesigned nacelles. They remained less powerful and more fuel heavy than the OKB had hoped. Gridded intake screens were added in the main intakes, to reduce the danger of FOD ingestion during take-off and landing. The aircraft initially lacked the extended tailcone of the production Su-27.

The first T10S (the former T10-7) made its maiden flight on 20 April 1981, with Vladimir Ilyushin at the controls. The aircraft was lost on 3 September 1981, due to fuel system problems, although pilot Ilyushin ejected safely.

The second T10S (the former T10-12) was lost shortly afterwards, on 23 December 1981, killing its pilot, Alexander Komarov. The cause of this accident was a mystery, until Nikolai Sadovnikov attempted to duplicate the fatal flight in T10-17. He escaped with his life, force-landing the aircraft after losing almost his entire port wing. Both accidents were caused by uncommanded pitch-ups after separation of the new automatic leading-edge flaps, which damaged the tailfins and tore off the outer wing panels. The forces acting on the flaps in a turn had been miscalculated. The solution was to redesign the leading-edge flaps, reduce their extension angle and strengthen the structure. This problem aside, the Su-27 had clearly been transformed, and its pilots raved about its handling and performance characteristics. The Su-27 was by then running late, and the decision was taken to put the T10S into production; this began in 1982, with the first production aircraft rolled out in November 1982. All T10S aircraft were powered by AL-31F engines with the top-mounted accessories gearboxes.

Despite the redesign, the Su-27's problems were far from over. Deliveries of production-standard radars were slow, and the aircraft also suffered from fuel system and engine problems. Stability problems necessitated severe flight restrictions until the flight control system could be redesigned (or perhaps only until the software was rewritten). If it had only one of these problems, the aircraft could probably have entered limited service in an interim state, but with so many difficulties it was not worth completing many of the airframes. Apart from a handful of aircraft used for ongoing development work, most rolled off the line as part-fitted hulks and went straight into storage outside the factory. Production was actually halted during mid-1986. This at least prevented the stockpile of incomplete Su-27s from growing larger, while the aircraft flying at Zhukhovskii and Akhtubinsk were used to solve the various problems.

Fortunately, the T10S flight test programme did at least progress smoothly in one area – that of engine development. Many of the AL-31F's teething problems had already been solved using the two AL-31F-engined basic T10s, and the only serious problem (excessive fuel consumption and low thrust) was not bad enough to justify expensive rectification and remedial action. Even as it was, the engine was considerably better than any alternative, and could be regarded as a success.

The earliest T10Ss differed in small details from the definitive production Su-27. The early aircraft had slightly different fin-caps, without the top of the trailing edge cropped, which gave them a fin-tip profile similar to that of the tails of the last T10s and the latest Su-35s. The number of aircraft completed with this early fin-cap profile is uncertain, but there may have been enough to equip the first evaluation squadron (although all of the earliest aircraft encountered by the Norwegian air force had the full production standard tailfins fitted). The early pre-series aircraft were also fitted with long nose probes, probably housing extra Alpha and sideslip probes to feed data to the comprehensive test instrumentation carried.

Many test aircraft were known by a T10-series numerical designator, but it is unknown whether this reflected their sequential position in the overall tally of T10s produced, or whether the sequence was restarted with the first T10S. For example, it is unclear whether the aircraft designated T10-17 was the 17th Su-27 completed (and thus the seventh or eighth T10S, there having been nine or 10 T10s, excluding the two aircraft converted to T10S standards) or whether it was the 17th T10S. This aircraft had vestigial ventral fins below the booms which carried the tailfins and tailplanes, but it is unclear if the earlier T10S prototypes were fitted with these fins. The aircraft tended to carry a two-digit 'regimental'-type code which corresponded to their sequential identity. By T10-22 (and perhaps as early as the T10-20), the aircraft had acquired a short, production-standard nose-mounted pitot probe, and the canopy had been redesigned to incorporate an extra frame just behind the pilot's ejection seat headrest. The early style uncropped fin-caps were fitted to the T10-25, but photos of the T10-24 show the aircraft with production-type tailfins, perhaps installed by retrofit. The T10-20, T10-24 and T10-25 are described separately, as is the record-breaking P-42, which was modified from an early aircraft from the pre-series batch. Western intelligence agencies allocated the new reporting name 'Flanker-B' to differentiate the new configuration from the original prototypes.

Right: The T10-26 was one of the first Su-27s to fly without fin leading-edge anti-flutter weight fairings. It is seen here with production-type cropped fin caps (probably retrofitted), but lacks the standard IRST sensor ball ahead of the windscreen.

Below: Some sources suggest that this aircraft (T10-17) was actually the T10S prototype (converted from the T10-7). It is typical of the earliest T10Ss, with square cut fin caps and an unframed rear canopy. The colour scheme is unusual, apeing one of the early F-16 paint finishes.

P-42 (possibly T10S-3)

Little is known about the motivation behind the modification of the third T10S (which was actually the first aircraft built as a T10S from the ground up, and not converted from a T10) to become the P-42. The source of funding for the project is unclear, but the aim was to establish the outstanding performance characteristics of the Su-27 by shattering the time-to-climb records previously set by the McDonnell Douglas F-15 Streak Eagle.

The T10S-3 (T10-13?) was stripped of all radar, armament and operational equipment and lightened for its record attempts, under the direction of Rollan G. Martirosov. In the interests of saving weight, the leading-edge flaps were disabled and locked shut, and their actuators were removed, while the tail sting, wingtips and fin-caps were also removed. The rear fuselage was left with a spade-like straight trailing edge inset from the engine nozzles. The normal radome was replaced by a lightweight aluminium fairing, and the aircraft was stripped of paint and highly polished. Ventral fins were not fitted.

Take-off weight was reduced to 14100 kg (31,085 lb), and thrust was increased by over 9.8 kN (2,204 lb) per engine. In the documentation given to the FAI, the engines of the P-42 were described as being TR-32U afterburning turbofans, rated at 133.25 kN (29,955 lb st) with afterburning. The Su-27's standard brakes could not hold the P-42 at anything approaching full power and, instead, the aircraft was anchored to a heavy AFV by twin cables and an electronic lock. The standard brakes may even have been removed to save weight.

Among the 27 world records (for time-to-climb and level speed) set by the P-42 between 1986 and 1988 were five absolute time-to-height records previously held by the F-15 Streak Eagle. On 27 October 1986 Victor Pugachev reached 3000 m (9,625 ft) in 25.373

The P-42 climbs steeply during one of its record-breaking flights. The combination of a stripped, lightened airframe and specially tuned engines brought the thrust to weight ratio to something approaching 2:1.

seconds, and reached 6000 m (19,250 ft) in 37.050 seconds on 15 November. On 10 March 1987 Nikolai Sadovnikov went through 9000 m (28,875 ft) in 44.176 seconds to reach 12000 m (39,370 ft) in 55.542 seconds in the same climb – breaking two records at once. The same aircraft subsequently reached 15000 m (49,210 ft) in 70.33 seconds, almost seven seconds faster than the F-15 Streak Eagle. The aircraft also set a class C sub-class (aircraft with a take-off weight between 16 and 20 tonnes, normally dominated by executive jets) height record of 19335 m (63,435 ft) and class C (take-off weight 12 to 16 tonnes) time-to-height records with and without payload. On 11 March 1987 the aircraft set a number of records for class N aircraft (STOL aircraft with a take-off run below 500 m/1,540 ft, with and without a 1-tonne payload), including times to 3000, 12000 and 15000 m of 25.4, 57.4 and 75.7 seconds, respectively. On 10 June 1987 the aircraft was used to set a sustained altitude record for a STOL aircraft of 19335 m. The last record set by the P-42 was a climb to 15000 m (with a 1-tonne payload) in 81.7 seconds. This was flown by Victor Pugachev.

The P-42 remains in open storage at the OKB's facility at the LII's Zhukhovskii airfield, where it could be returned to flight status if another record attempt becomes necessary – however unlikely that may be.

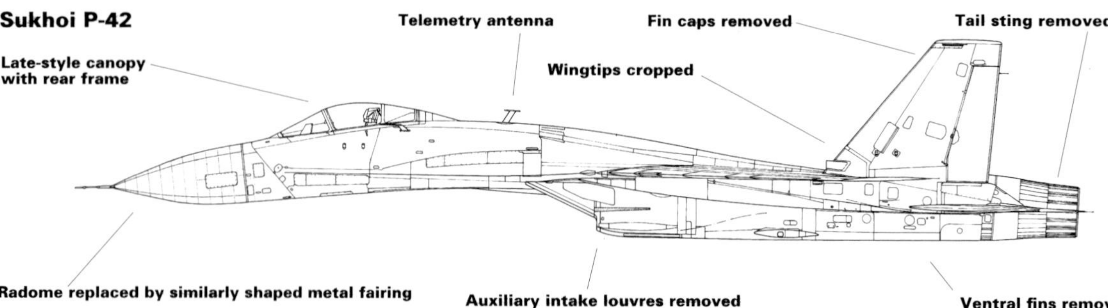

Many of the records set by the P-42 still stand, and the aircraft today languishes in open storage on one of Zhukhovskii's crowded ramps. If funding permits, there have been suggestions that the aircraft may one day form the centrepiece of an enlarged OKB museum but, in today's harsh economic climate, this seems unlikely.

T10-20R

The T10-20 was converted to make an attempt on the speed record over a closed circuit distance of 500 km, and was intended for prolonged supersonic flight. Its take-off weight of 26600 kg (58,643 lb) included an astonishing 12900 kg (28,440 lb) of fuel.

The T10-20R was based on an early T10S airframe, and so lacked the box-like chaff/flare dispenser fairings on each side of the tailcone, and featured the early canopy without the rear frame. Further modifications for the record attempt included installation of a lengthened tailcone, which improved the overall fineness ratio and accommodated an extra fuel tank. The nose radome was replaced by a simple conical fairing (which contained another auxiliary tank) and lacked the compound curvature of the normal nose shape. The fin-tips were cropped, losing their dielectric tips, and the wingtips were rounded off, forfeiting their wingtip launch rail/anti-flutter masses. Ventral fins were also removed. The aircraft was bereft of RWR antennas and pylons, and all non-essential items were deleted. Even the pneumatic reservoir for the braking system disappeared from the nosewheel door, and the landing lights were similarly omitted. Had the aircraft been used for a record attempt, it may be assumed that it would have been completely stripped of paint. Its patchwork finish was remedied by a hasty respray before it was retired to the Central Armed Forces Museum at Khodinka.

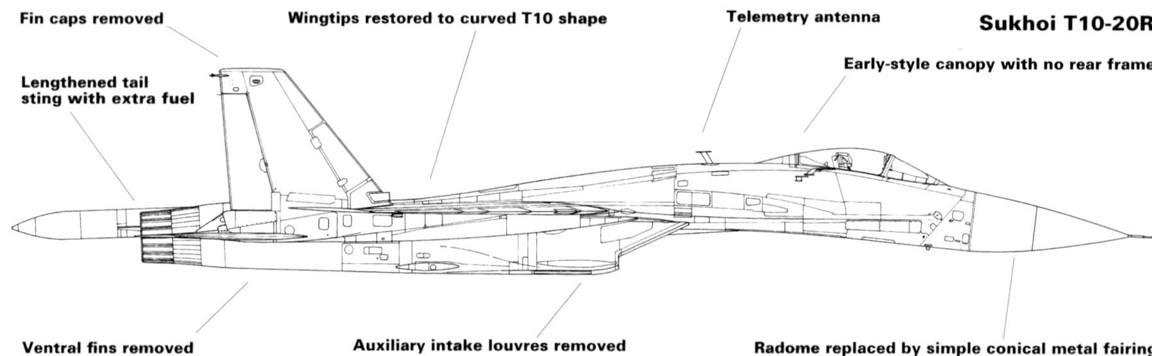

***Right:** The T10-20R was stripped of radar and armament, and its tailcone was replaced by a long tubular fairing containing a small fuel tank. The tailfins themselves were cropped, since the aircraft was not expected to need enhanced stability at higher angles of attack.*

***Below right:** The Su-27's gracefully curved radome was removed and replaced by a simple conical metal fairing. This is believed to have covered another extra fuel tank.*

***Below:** The T10-20R was not used for its intended record-breaking flight, but was instead retired to the Central Museum of the Armed Forces, where it replaced another early Su-27. It is unclear as to whether it was intended to carry external fuel tanks for its record attempt.*

T10-24

The Sukhoi OKB reportedly began working on the installation of canards on the T10 in 1977, even before the first prototype had made its maiden flight. Unfortunately (according to the semi-official Russian Aircraft, published by Moscow Mashinostroenie), "flights of the Su-27 experimental aircraft fitted with the front horizontal empennage (aircraft 10-24) failed to bring positive results expected from installation of the empennage until 1985." Quite what this statement meant is uncertain, since the T10-24 did not actually fly with its canard foreplane fitted until May 1985, with Victor Pugachev at the controls. Perhaps tunnel tests, static tests and taxi trials significantly delayed the first flight of the new configuration, which had reportedly been finalised in the spring of 1982. By this time the aircraft had been fitted with production-style fins, with cropped tips, and wore prominent camera calibration markings on its radome.

The T10-24 (sometimes known as the T10-24-PGO) was used to prove the canards used by the Su-27K (and later by the digital FBW Su-27M and Su-27IB), and as such was a testbed for overall Su-27 development, and was not exclusively dedicated to the Su-27K programme, although it did make many take-offs from the ski-jump at Saki. It was not equipped with an arrester hook, nor did it have the shortened tail sting of the Su-27K; the first canard-equipped 'Flanker' with these features was the first Su-27K prototype (T10-37). The T10-24 may have initially flown with its canards locked in position, perhaps for an extended period.

The T10-24 gets airborne from the ski-jump at Saki, an airfield in the Crimea which incorporated a full-size dummy carrier deck and various ski ramps. The aircraft's primary purpose was to serve as a testbed for the canard foreplanes designed for the naval Su-27K and the advanced Su-27M, but it was also used for ski jump take-off tests. The aircraft made its maiden flight with canards fitted during May 1985.

T10-25

The Sukhoi T10-25 was used extensively as a trials and support aircraft for the Su-27K carrierborne naval fighter programme, and was similar in configuration to the T10-17, with the early square fin-tips. The (sole) aircraft was so associated with the Su-27K programme that it wore the AV-MF flag below its cockpi from its earliest dayt. The T10-25 was fitted with a crude square-section arrester hook below the modified and raised tail sting. This itself was modified, like that fitted to the T10U-2 (Su-27PU demonstrator), being raised and given a higher, more upward-pointing centreline and a slightly sharper point. The alteration reduced the danger of tail scrapes during high-Alpha landings. The T10-25 made the Su-27's first arrested landing on the dummy deck at Saki on 1 September 1984, in the hands of Victor Pugachev. The same aircraft was used for ski jump take-off trials, making the first ski jump take-off on 25 September 1984. (This milestone was achieved two years after the MiG-29KVP made its first ski jump take-off on 21 August 1982.) Pugachev and Nikolai Sadovnikov were the pilots for the first ski ramp take-offs. Later, the aircraft flew approach and landing trials using the Rezyestor radio landing system, and night landings using the Luna-3 laser optical landing system. The airframe was later reportedly used for captive carry trials of the Kh-41 anti-ship missile.

The T10-25 naval trials development aircraft was an early-model T10S fitted with an arrester hook for deck landing trials at Saki, in the Crimea. The aircraft also undertook ski ramp take-off trials, making the Su-27's first take-off from the fully-inclined ramp, after the T10-3 took off from the less radically inclined original inclined deck.

Su-27 (T10S) early series 'Flanker-B'

Small numbers of Su-27s began entering service in late 1986, flying from bases in the Kola Peninsula. (The US DoD estimated that five were in service with the PVO, and 10 more with Frontal Aviation, during October 1986.) They were almost certainly flying with an evaluation/development unit, and not with a front-line regiment. The aircraft operated with similarly new Ilyushin/Beriev A-50 'Mainstay' AWACS aircraft, and ran mock intercepts against NATO aircraft flying over the Barents Sea. These engagements were usually broken off while still outside visual

Sukhoi Su-27 (early production series)

range, but it was inevitable that the aircraft would soon be seen 'close-up' by Western fighter pilots. Norwegian F-16 pilots began photographing Su-27s during early 1987, and in September the crew of a Norwegian P-3 got an even closer look at the 'Flanker' when one of the latter clipped the Orion's propeller with its tailfin during a close intercept. Fortunately, both aircraft landed safely.

The first Su-27s encountered by NATO pilots were usually seen carrying only their R-27 (AA-10 'Alamo') BVR missile armament, with two underwing, two under the engine nacelles, and two in tandem on the centreline. The wingtip and outboard underwing pylons were almost inevitably empty. This may have been because initial production of the new short-range missile was given primarily to the MiG-29s of Frontal Aviation, although when the latter were encountered in an armed configuration they were usually carrying a pair of R-27s and a pair of older R-60 (AA-8 'Aphids') IR-homing AAMs outboard. Perhaps this indicated that development problems delayed the service introduction of the definitive R-73 (AA-11 'Archer') AAM. The wingtip missile launch rails of the Su-27 may not have been compatible with the R-60, which has never been seen carried by the Su-27.

Soviet combat aircraft reached their units known only by a simple designation, and were never officially named. Inevitably, such aircraft received nicknames, and often more than one. The Su-27 soon became known as the 'Azure Lightning' (the publicist's choice) or as the 'Crane' (Zhuravlik), reflecting its rather individualistic and broken-backed appearance in flight, while some pilots preferred to use the NATO 'Flanker' reporting name. As in every air force, people from outside the Su-27 community tended to apply less flattering epithets, often based on the long-delayed entry into service.

Many early production Su-27s remain in service today, in virtually their original configuration. The distinctive anti-flutter weights on the leading edges of the tailfins have been removed in recent years, without apparent ill effect, and the mounting holes are often visible. The number of chaff/flare dispensers have been increased, by the simple modification of adding the distinctive

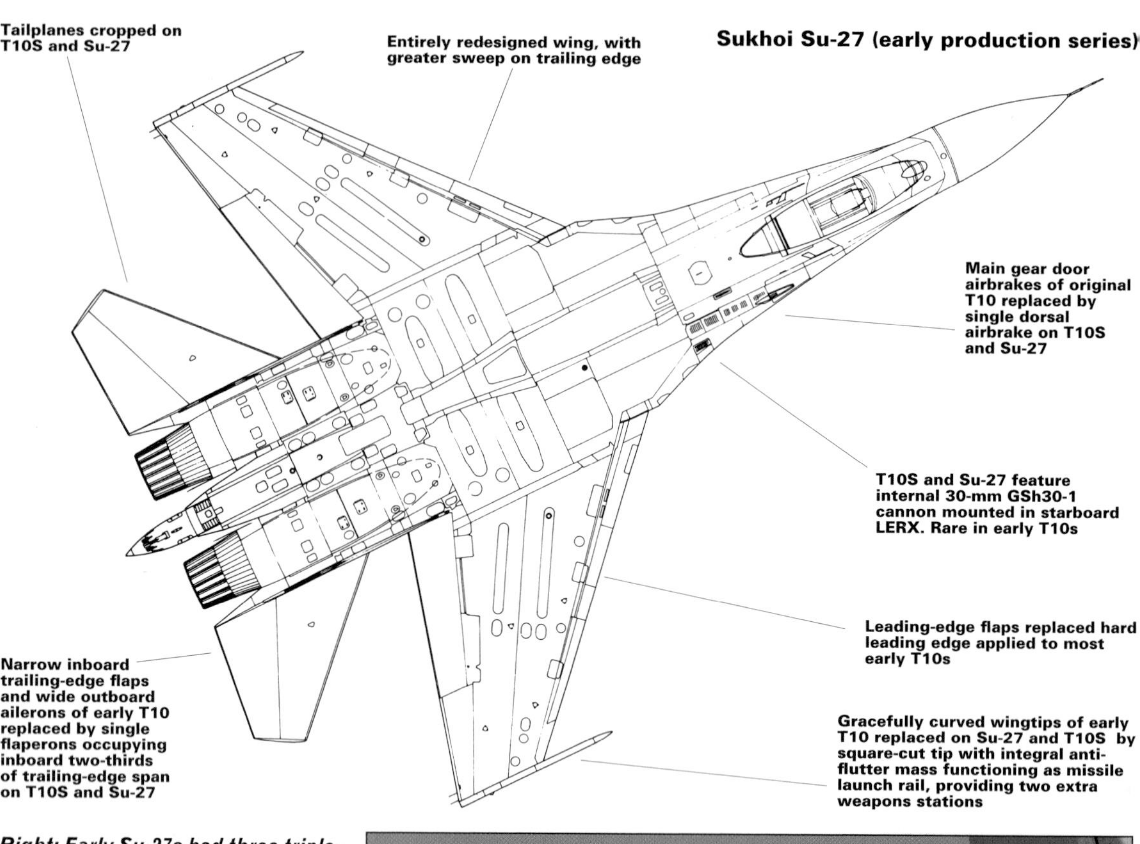

***Right:** Early Su-27s had three triple-shot chaff/flare launchers above each side of the tailcone, with another underneath on each side. This gave a maximum of only 24 chaff or flare cartridges. Newer aircraft carry 96.*

***Below:** It is rare to be able to spot an early production Su-27 today, since most have been modified so that they externally resemble the later production aircraft. Few still fly with the prominent leading-edge fairings on their fins, and many have even had their tailcones modified to accept the increased number of chaff/flare dispensers. This Ukrainian Su-27 is an exception, showing clearly the strakes alongside its tailcone, rather than the newer boxes.*

box-like fairings which accommodate extra chaff/flare cartridges on later production Su-27s, and which may allow installation of the Pallad jammer. Early and late production Su-27s often serve side-by-side in the same regiments, and both types were used by the two regiments based in Poland until the Soviet withdrawal.

The early series Su-27s may not originally have been compatible with the use of air-to-ground weapons at all. If this is the case, then the aircraft were almost certainly fitted with new or reprogrammed stores management systems, new weapons aiming software and new HUD symbology generators, when they were upgraded. This would have allowed them to carry the most basic air-to-surface weapons, including unguided rockets and 'dumb' iron bombs.

Fin leading-edge flutter weights have been removed from most surviving early-series Su-27s, such as this Ukrainian aircraft. Some aircraft have also had the tailcone box-fairings added, making them externally indistinguishable from the later production aircraft.

Specification
Su-27 'Flanker-B'

Dimensions: fuselage length including probe 21.935 m (72 ft 0 in); span over wingtip missile launch rails 14.7 m (48 ft 3 in); area 62.037 m² (667.8 sq ft); tailplane span 9.88 m (32 ft 5 in); tailplane area 12.24 m² (131.75 sq ft); fin area 15.4 m² (165.76 sq ft); overall height 5.932 m (19 ft 6 in); wheel track 4.34 m (14 ft 3 in); wheelbase 5.88 m (19 ft 4 in)

Powerplant: two Saturn Lyul'ka AL-31F afterburning turbofans each rated at 74.53 kN (16,755 lb st) dry and 122.59 kN (27,558 lb st) with afterburning

Weights: empty operating 16380 kg (36,112 lb); normal take-off 23000 kg (50,705 lb); maximum take-off weight 28300 kg (62,391 lb)

Fuel and load: internal fuel (normal) 5270 kg (11,620 lb), (maximum) 9400 kg (20,723 lb) or 12000 litres (2,640 Imp gal); maximum theoretical weapon load 8000 kg (17,636 lb); normal weapon load 4000 kg (8,818 lb)

***g* limits:** 8-9 at basic design gross weight

Performance: (estimated) maximum level speed at sea level 743 kt (1370 km/h; 850 mph); maximum level speed 'clean' at altitude 1,236 kt (2280 km/h; 770 mph); limiting Mach No. 2.35; (estimated) practical service ceiling 17700 m (58,070 ft); absolute ceiling 18500 m (60,700 ft); range 1,987 nm (3680 km; 2,285 miles) at altitude; 740 nm (1370 km; 851 miles) at low level; high-altitude radius of action 590 nm (1090 km; 677 miles); low-altitude radius of action 227 nm (420 km; 261 miles); take-off run 500 m (1,640 ft) or 450 m (1,476 ft); landing roll 600 m (1,968 ft) or 700 m (2,297 ft); take-off speed not given; landing speed 121-124 kt (225-230 km/h; 140-143 mph)

Note: All of the specifications given here should be treated with some caution. Sukhoi has released widely differing performance figures on different occasions (and even releases different dimensions for the same aircraft), while rarely specifying the loads carried for particular range or performance figures. Whereas accurate performance figures for other Soviet fighters (e.g., the MiG-29) have been revealed by export customers, but the only overseas customers for the Su-27 (China and Vietnam) are even more secretive than the Russians themselves.

Su-27 (T10S) late series 'Flanker-B'

The first major improvement to the Su-27 came with the addition of box-like fairings on each side of the cylindrical tail sting. They accommodated 28 upward-firing triple-shot APP-50 (L-029) chaff/flare dispensers, housing 84 chaff/flare cartridges, on the upper surface. A total of 32 dispensers (96 cartridges) augmented the four set into the top of the tail sting. They extended back as far as the hinged brake chute compartment cover and were each tipped by a dielectric antenna fairing. These were described as Sigint antennas on an official Sukhoi diagram, but this is taken to refer to the SPO-15 Beryoza (L-006) RHAWS system.

The new tail sting configuration was standard by the time the Su-27 made its Western debut at the 1989 Paris Air Salon at Le Bourget. Its radomes and dielectric panels were white, while the early Su-27s had dark green dielectric panels and antenna fairings. Dark green nose radomes were replaced by white radomes on the production line, and later aircraft had all dielectric panels and fairings in white. The radome was actually also increased in diameter and length. As far as can be ascertained, the aircraft with white radomes never had the fin leading-edge fairings fitted to the first Su-27s.

In the very latest production series, maximum take-off weight was increased by 4700 kg (10,360 lb) to 33000 kg (72,750 lb). There may have been a minor increase in fuel capacity in these aircraft, since published range figures were increased to 2,160 nm (4000 km; 2,485 miles). Somewhat inexplicably, figures for the take-off run and landing roll were reduced to 400 m (1,312 ft) and 500 m (1,640 ft) respectively, although there were no changes to flaps or engine ratings.

Another important change to some late production 'Flankers' was the addition of an extra pair of underwing pylons, bringing the total number of hardpoints to 12. They were believed to have been provided so that aircraft fitted with the optional (and removable) L-005

Sukhoi Su-27 (late production series)

No anti-flutter weights on fin leading edges

Revised tailcone with box-like fairings on the sides housing extra chaff/flare dispensers

Some aircraft may have upgraded radar capable of simultaneous two-target engagement

Minor variations in antenna configuration between production blocks

Revised tailcone with square-section boxes scabbed onto the sides replacing the original strakes

The late series Su-27 is intended to be compatible with a wide range of weapons, both air-to-air and air-to-ground. The 10-station aircraft can carry up to 16 FAB-500 bombs, six B-13M rocket pods or 38 FAB-100 bombs. The Russian air force is not believed to utilise the Su-27's ground attack capability operationally, even in its Frontal Aviation regiments, although trials may have been undertaken and training units may have explored air-to-ground operations. Aircraft from the very latest production batches have a total of 12 external weapons stations.

Maximum AUW raised to 3300 kg (72,750 lb)

Minor changes to fuel tanks give slight increase in range

Sorbtsiya ECM pods can replace the wingtip missile launch rails on late production Su-27s

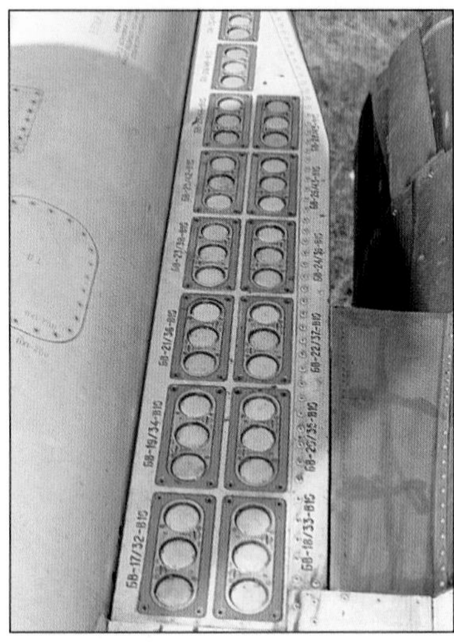

Above: The box-like fairings added to the sides of the late Su-27's tailcone each contained 14 triple-shot chaff/flare dispensers, and another four were mounted in the top of the tailcone itself.

Below: This Ukrainian late-series Su-27 is unusual in displaying a squadron badge on its tailfin. The aircraft was assigned to the 62nd IAP at Belbek alongside a number of early production Su-27s.

Sorbtsiya-S wingtip ECM pods in place of the wingtip missile launch rails would still have 10 weapons stations available. Late production Su-27s can carry unguided air-to-ground weapons, although, as far as can be ascertained, only a handful of Russian specialist and trials units have actually practised this capability. Strangely, the extra new pylons have seldom been seen in photos of late production Su-27s (even those showing aircraft fitted with wingtip ECM pods), suggesting that only a handful of aircraft were fitted in this manner. The new three pylon wing configuration was adopted by subsequent 'Flanker' variants, however, including the Su-27K, Su-27PU, Su-27IB and Su-27M.

Apart from the increased number of chaff/flare dispensers and new rear hemisphere RHAWS antennas, the late series Su-27 is believed to have the same avionics and equipment fit as its predecessor. The aircraft is designed around the RLPK-27 (RadioLokaatsionni Pritselnaya Komplex-27) radar complex, which integrates an NIIP S-27 Myetch (N-001) coherent pulse-Doppler radar with a TsVM-80 digital computer. This is the weak link in the Su-27's weapons system, offering insufficient processing capacity for onboard target allocation and prioritisation of the multiple threats which could be detected and tracked by the extremely powerful radar. This effectively condemned the Su-27 to an undue reliance on ground-based controllers in many circumstances, using a Spectre datalink, or on an AWACS-type aircraft, using the TKS-2 secure air-to-air datalink. The Su-27 was more capable of autonomous operation than previous aircraft, like the Su-15 or MiG-23P, but was far from being able to operate in the way that the F-15 or F-16 could.

The radar had a search range of about 130 nm (240 km; 150 miles), and could track targets out to 92 nm (170 km; 105 miles). The radar could simultaneously track up to 10 targets, and is now understood to be capable of engaging two targets simultaneously, although this is thought to be the result of a recent modification that has not yet been incorporated fleet-wide. The radar used a primitive-looking and bulky inverse cassegrain antenna, which imposed the provision of a radome that was bulbous quite far forward.

During the late 1970s, as the Su-27 and MiG-29 were taking shape, Russian tacticians realised that the use of radar to detect, track and engage a target could betray the position and intentions of the attacking aircraft, if the target was equipped with a radar warning receiver, and might actually place the attacker at a disadvantage. They perceived that the provision of an emission-free subsidiary target acquisition and tracking system would allow the attacking aircraft to approach its target undetected. The Su-27's radar is thus augmented by the OEPS-27 (Optiko-Electronikaya

Above: This aircraft (possibly T10-85) was probably the first Su-27 fitted with the distinctive 'boxes' on each side of the tailcone. Interestingly, it retains the original dark green radome and dielectric panels, and is fitted with the distinctive fin leading-edge anti-flutter weight fairings usually associated with early Su-27s.

Pritselnaya Sistyema) electro-optical system, which integrates an OLS-27 IRST with a laser rangefinder.

Although it lacks the absolute detection range offered by radar, the OLS-27 could track a rear-hemisphere target out to 27 nm (50 km; 31 miles) with greater angular accuracy than radar, while the laser offered more accurate ranging information over shorter distances. For close combat, the Su-27 pilot could use a Shchel-3U helmet-mounted monocular target designator (with its associated Ts-100 computer), which could cue the missile seekers (or the radar) wherever the pilot pointed his head. This allowed him to designate a target for his IR-homing missile armament simply by looking at it, and gives the Su-27 pilot the ability to engage targets well off-axis.

The Su-27 is fitted with a Parol IFF set, and an SO-69 transponder, with R-800 and R-864 radios, an ARK-22 radio compass, A-317 SHORAN, and a marker beacon receiver. Defensive avionics include an L-006 SPO-15 Beryoza RHAWS, with antennas on the intake sides and the tailboom. This is augmented by a Pallad ECM jammer in the tail sting itself, which may not have been fitted to early series Su-27s, and which is probably not fitted to export Su-27SKs.

Some reports suggest that Su-27s assigned to Frontal Aviation units are actually designated Su-27S, and that IA-PVO aircraft are designated Su-27P. *Jane's All the World's Aircraft* suggests that the Su-27S is distinguished by the carriage of wingtip Sorbtsiya ECM pods, but these are interchangeable with wingtip missile launch rails and are not restricted to Frontal Aviation aircraft. Additionally, the Su-27P designation has already been assigned to a stillborn extended endurance interceptor, which will be described in the next volume of *World Air Power Journal*.

Gun
The Su-27 carries a single 30-mm GSh-30-1 single-barrelled cannon in the starboard LERX, fed by a 150-round ammunition tank. The gunsight system uses the laser for ranging, and is reputedly extremely accurate.

Secondary sensors
The radar of the Su-27 is backed up by an OEPS-27 IRST, coupled to a laser rangefinder, while the Su-27 pilot may also use a helmet-mounted target designator to point the radar or missile seeker heads at off-boresight targets. This close-in, no-emission part of the Su-27's weapons system is second to none.

Radar
The basic Su-27 is fitted with a pulse-Doppler NIIP N-001 radar, codenamed 'Slot Back 2' by NATO's ASCC. Although built by NIIP, the radar is a development of the rival NIIR/Phazatron's N-019 'Slot Back 1' fitted to the MiG-29, using a larger version of the same twist-cassegrain antenna and a higher-power transmitter to obtain better range performance. The N-001 radar forms the main element of the RLPK-27 weapons system, but inadequate onboard processing effectively ties the 'Flanker-B' to ground stations .

Air defence armament
The baseline 'Flanker-B' is fitted with three hardpoints on each wing, one under each engine nacelle, and two in tandem on the centreline. Some versions have an extra underwing pylon, too. The wingtip hardpoint can mount a Sorbtsiya ECM pod or a wingtip missile launch rail for a short-range IR-homing missile (usually an R-73). The outermost underwing hardpoints also carry R-73s, while the other pylons carry different versions of the BVR R-27 missile.

Structure
The basic Su-27 makes little use of composites or advanced alloys, with some stainless steel and titanium in areas subjected to high temperatures.

Sukhoi Su-27 'Flanker-B'

The Air Forces Training Centre at Lipetsk controls a number of units, including the Russian aviation medicine establishment (an Su-27 operator) and the 760th ISIAP. The 760th ISIAP operates Su-27s, MiG-29s, MiG-23s, MiG-27s, Su-25s and Su-24s and is primarily concerned with the development of tactics and the training of qualified weapons instructors (QWIs) and tactics instructors. Sharkmouthed intakes are by no means rare on Lipetsk-based Su-27s, but only one has the full shark silhouette painted along its flanks. This aircraft participated in the massive 80-aircraft 1995 VE-day flypast over Moscow, which involved 23 Su-27s, most of them drawn from the 760th ISIAP at Lipetsk, but including five Su-27Ks from the AV-MF. Several of the Lipetsk aircraft wore patriotic white, blue and red Russian tricolours around the fins and even around the forward fuselage. For the flypast all but four of the Su-27s actually flew from Kubinka, the others operating from Khotilovo (PVO).

Defensive systems
The Su-27 uses an L-006 (SPO-15) Beryoza RHAWS to detect threats, and also has a Pallad ECM system, provision for wingtip L-005 (Sorbtsiya-S) ECM pods and an APP-50 chaff/flare dispenser system. The Pallad jammer can be used in the rear hemisphere only when the Su-27's own onboard radar is in use.

IRST
The Su-27 has an OEPS-27 electro-optical complex which includes an OLS-27 Infra-Red Search and Track system. This has a range of 50 km against a rear-hemisphere target.

Flight control system
The SDU-10-27 has a quadruplex analog flight control system. This controls the automatic *g*/Alpha limiter (which can be turned off by the pilot), the pitch control channel, and the actuation of flaperons and slats, except for take-off and landing.

Su-27SK (T10SK) 'Flanker-B'

Using the designation suffix letters S (for Series) and K (for *Kommercial*) to differentiate it from the carrierborne Su-27K, the Su-27SK is externally indistinguishable from the standard late series production Su-27, although it almost certainly has downgraded equipment and weapons systems, like export versions of the MiG-29. The aircraft has only 10 external hardpoints, and the undercarriage is strengthened (by comparison with the basic Su-27) to permit a maximum take-off weight of 33 tonnes. Unfortunately, there have been no published photos of Su-27SK cockpits, or of fully armed Su-27SKs, so one can only speculate as to the exact equipment fit and capability of the aircraft. It is known that the aircraft had an LTTS defensive complex which included the Gardeniya internal active jammer, which is claimed to be broadly comparable to the American AN/ALQ-135, and which marks an improvement over the basic Su-27's internal Pallad jammer.

It seems likely that the aircraft has a slightly different version of the radar (probably lacking current Russian IFF) and reduced anti-ECM capability. The electro-optical complex may also be of reduced capability, and the aircraft lacks the full-standard PVO/Frontal Aviation EW capabilities.

The largest and highest-profile customer for the Su-27K so far has been the People's Republic of China. The addition of the Su-27 to the Chinese inventory has been of enormous significance, despite the relatively small number of aircraft delivered. The aircraft gives China its first truly modern fighter, with a modern pulse-Doppler radar and modern BVR missiles. It also allows China to provide its forces with much longer range air defence and air superiority, of great importance for power projection in areas like the much-disputed Spratly Islands.

China signed an initial contract for 24 Su-27SKs in 1991, paying approximately $1 billion (mainly in goods) for the aircraft, with an additional pair of two-seat Su-27UBKs. The first aircraft were reported to have been delivered by June 1992. They equipped a single regiment of the 3rd Air Division at Wuhu, although the unit has since been moved around in response to various crises, and was briefly stationed on Hainan Island. These aircraft were painted in a different camouflage scheme to Russian Su-27s, with a dark grey-overall top surface and darker grey radomes which incorporated a 'cut-out' in the lighter grey lower surface colour. The aircraft wore two-digit codes on their noses and at the top of each rudder, with a five-digit serial on the fin and an abbreviated construction number on the engine intake. An example is 13148 (code '18') which has the c/n 38919 on the intake. Aircraft coded '22' and '24' were serialled 13242 and 13244, respectively. Post-delivery photos of the Chinese aircraft (notably the aircraft coded '12') have shown them carrying single B8M 80-mm rocket pods under each inboard underwing pylon, perhaps indicating that the secondary ground attack capability is actually practised. The Su-27SK can carry up to six B8M or B13M rocket pods, or 10 bombs of up to 500 kg weight, or 16 bombs of up to 250 kg weight, or up to 38 100-kg bombs.

An additional Chinese contract for Su-27SKs was signed in 1995, covering the supply of 24 more aircraft, including another pair of two-seat trainers (11 of the batch were complete by April 1996) and another contract was signed in 1996. This will cover the licence-production of the Su-27 in China (using Russian sub-assemblies) at a factory to be built by the Russians. Production is anticipated to average between 10 and 20 aircraft per year and China has reportedly paid $2.5 billion for production rights. China is expected to build between 72 and 78 Su-27s, sufficient to equip three PLA(AF) regiments.

The chief difference between export-standard Su-27s, the Su-27SKs, and their predecessors lies in the Su-27SK's ground-attack capability. While not able to carry as heavy a load as the attack optimised Su-27SMK, the SK can be fitted out with a range of weapons. Arrayed here are R-27 and R-73 AAMs, various FAB bombs plus S-13 122-mm and S-8 80-mm rocket pods. KMG-U cluster munition dispensers are another standard option.

The Chinese licence-production agreement will provide Sukhoi and its associated factories and suppliers with useful foreign currency at a time when Russian air force funding is becoming ever more scarce. Unfortunately, the deal may still be cancelled, having attracted strong criticism from some powerful voices within the Russian government, including President Yeltsin's former security chief, General Lebed. The criticism centres on the potential danger of transferring advanced technologies to a potential enemy, but also on the possibility that cheap Chinese-built 'Flankers' could one day represent competitors for Sukhoi's own Su-27s in certain markets. Critics are realistic enough to accept that the Chinese may not always abide by the terms of agreements limiting where they could sell their own Su-27s.

The second customer for the Su-27SK was China's neighbour, Vietnam, which purchased six Su-27SKs for $195 million ($32.5 million each). This was a remarkably low price, since Sukhoi has quoted a price of $85 million for a single aircraft with spares and ground support equipment (plus $4 million for each spare engine). The 'Flanker' represents a quantum leap in capability for Vietnam, although the small quantity of aircraft purchased will allow only very limited operations, with insufficient numbers to maintain even a two-aircraft CAP for more than a day or so. Unless and until more aircraft are delivered, Vietnam may choose to use its Su-27s as mini-AWACS platforms to direct and control the more numerous MiG-21s.

The Su-27 remains an attractive aircraft to export customers, although it is considerably more expensive to buy, operate and maintain than the MiG-29, which is arguably more capable in the tactical role. Potential customers for the basic Su-27, who need the extended range and endurance of that aircraft, and its high combat persistence, include Syria, Libya, Iran and perhaps Algeria. The aircraft was also offered to India (two aircraft visited New Delhi on their way home from the 1990 Asian Aerospace Show), Finland and Iraq. In 1989 it was reported that an agreement to sell the aircraft to Iraq had been signed, and that a limited number of aircraft had been delivered to Afghanistan, but these reports later proved to be unfounded. Perhaps the most likely next customer for the aircraft is Syria, which has a requirement for about 14 very long-range interceptors, and which reportedly already operates a similar number of Su-15 'Flagons' to train suitable pilots. Some sources suggest that Syria has already taken delivery of 17 Su-27SKs.

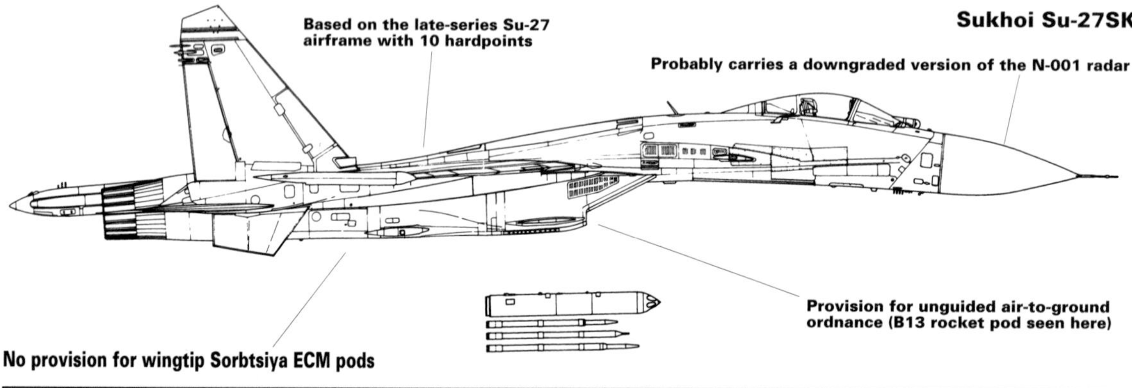

The PLA(AF) has leap-frogged several generations with its acquisition of the Su-27. China's proposed licence-production deal with Sukhoi will alter the entire balance of power in the region.

Su-27SM

There have been reports that a mid-life upgrade has been proposed for the Su-27. It would offer improved air-to-air and air-to-ground capability with RVV-AE 'AMRAAMski' active radar homing AAMs and compatibility with a wider range of air-to-surface weapons. The level of capability required could be attained by simply upgrading and modernising the existing 'Slot Back' radar, but, instead, Sukhoi has offered the Russian air force the possibility of fitting one of the derivatives of the significantly more effective Zhuk radar. The aircraft could even be re-engined with more powerful AL-31FM or AL-35Fs. These two measures would transform an existing Su-27S into a 'poor man's Su-35', albeit one lacking the lighter, stronger airframe, canards and digital FBW control system. These omissions would have relatively little impact on operational capability, however, and the Su-27SM would represent a cost-effective aircraft for the Russian air forces. In the end, the mid-life upgrade will depend on funding, and Sukhoi will aggressively market the new-build Su-27M rather than settle for less work in upgrading existing aircraft.

Su-27SMK

Contrary to the impression given by the designation, the Su-27SMK is not simply an export version of the Su-27SM. It has a different proposed radar fit, based on a development of the original 'Slot Back' radar and not on the advanced Zhuk family. The Su-27SMK remains a 'paper' project, but could be delivered from 1998 if orders are placed during 1996. The aircraft has been offered as a multi-role version of the standard Su-27, and is firmly aimed at the export market, and especially at those nations for whom the Su-35 is either too expensive or for whom its likely delivery schedule lies too far in the future. The Su-27SMK has an extra pair of external hardpoints underwing, which allow the same missile armament to be carried even when wingtip Sorbtsiya ESM pods are fitted. These pods are not usually offered as an option on export 'Flankers'. The aircraft has increased internal fuel capacity, enough to allow an unrefuelled endurance of five hours, or a radius of 675 nm (1250 km; 777 miles). The Su-27SMK will feature a retractable inflight-refuelling probe and a state-of-the-art long-range GPS-based navigation system, similar to the equipment developed for the Su-27PD and Su-30.

The basic N-001 (RLPK-27) radar will reportedly be modified for compatibility with the RVV-AE (AA-12 'Adder') or 'AMRAAMski' missile, and a second stage modification will allow carriage of the Kh-29 and Kh-31 ASM, or the KAB-500 laser-guided bomb.

Sukhoi announced that the Phase One Su-27SMK would be available for delivery from late 1997/early 1998, with the ground-attack capable Phase Two Su-27SMK available one year later. It was further announced that the Su-27SMK would be offered with provision for auxiliary underwing fuel tanks, and that the Su-27K-type IFR probe might also be offered.

These alterations will transform the basic Su-27 into something which more closely resembles the Su-35, and could presumably be offered as retrofit options. There is no reason that the Su-27SMK could not be delivered with Zhuk radar rather than a modified N-001; this might be a likely scenario for China, in the light of Zhuk orders for the upgraded Shenyang J-8IIM and the new J-10 lightweight fighter currently under development.

This late-series Su-27 was painted to serve as an Su-27SMK demonstrator. The aircraft has 12 hardpoints, but the inboard pylons are not fitted here. The aircraft wears an overall dark grey colour scheme similar to that applied to Chinese Su-27SKs.

Su-27UB (T10U) 'Flanker-C'

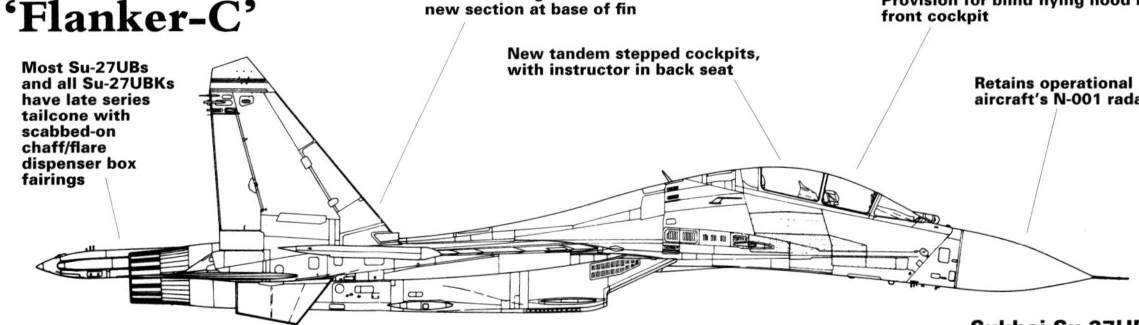

Sukhoi Su-27UB

Plans for a two-seat conversion and continuation trainer version of the Su-27 were drawn up at an early stage of the programme, but were put on hold while problems with the single-seater were sorted. It is understood that a two-seat basic T10 was due to be the next aircraft to be produced in the OKB experimental workshops when the original T10 design was abandoned.

When the single-seat fighter had to be redesigned, it was decided that every effort should be put into getting the operational aircraft right, and work on the Su-27UB went ahead only very slowly. While this undoubtedly caused its own problems (introducing a radically new fighter without a two-seat trainer version was never going to be easy), it was a courageous decision and one which history proved to be correct. When single-seat Su-27s began to enter service, the first operational regiments were allocated MiG-23UB and MiG-29UB two-seat trainers, which proved to be a suitable alternative in the interim.

After all of the difficulties and problems with the single-seater, it was

Although PVO and Frontal Aviation Su-27 regiments originally used two-seat MiG-23s and MiG-29s for training, two-seat Su-27UBs were eventually available in sufficient numbers to supplant them. By 1990, when the two Poland-based regiments returned to Russia, each included six Su-27UBs and neither had any 'Flogger-C' or 'Fulcrum-B' two-seat trainers on charge.

Above: The first prototype Su-27UB was broadly equivalent to early-production series single-seaters, with the original 'unboxed' tailcone and with anti-flutter masses on the leading edges of the tailfins. It made its maiden flight on 7 March 1985, but remained unknown in the West until shortly before the 1989 Paris Air Salon, when the first photographs were released.

decided that the two-seat trainer version would differ as little as possible, and would retain the same overall dimensions and centre of gravity, as far as was possible. Sukhoi's own figures would suggest that the provision of the second cockpit has been achieved with no sacrifice in internal fuel capacity. Aerodynamic, structural, equipment and systems changes were also kept to an absolute minimum. Wind tunnel testing confirmed that the Su-27UB had the same characteristics as the single-seat fighter, and this was later to be confirmed in flight testing.

The two-seat trainer version of the Su-27 is thus fully combat capable, unlike the two-seat MiG-29UB. The aircraft retains its 'Slot Back' radar and differs from the single-seater only in having a second cockpit behind the first. The cockpits are highly stepped, and are covered by a single upward-hinging canopy, which probably produces slightly more drag than the cockpit canopy of the single-seater. The backseater benefits by enjoying the best view forward over the nose of all Russian tandem-seat trainer versions of front-line fighters. The increased keel area forward produced by the new cockpit canopy was compensated by a slight increase in tailfin area. This was achieved by adding a full-chord section below the rudder, retaining the same planform from the bottom of the rudder up to the fin-tip. The Su-27UB is also slightly heavier than the single-seater (1120 kg/2,470 lb heavier empty, 1140 kg/2,515 lb heavier at normal take-off weight, and with a 2150-kg/4,749-lb increase in MTOW). This resulted in the least possible impact on performance, with a 70-km/h (44-mph) reduction in low-level speed, a 155-km/h (96-mph) reduction at altitude, a 30-m (100-ft) increase in landing distance and a 100-m (328-ft) increase in take-off run. Fuel load is slightly reduced, with a marginal impact on range and endurance figures, but this is not operationally significant. Some sources suggest that fuel load was actually increased, by refining the shape of the spine, but this seems unlikely.

Left: The rear cockpit of the Su-27UB lacks some of the instruments and equipment in the front cockpit, and has only a primitive HUD repeater. The two cockpits are well stepped, however, and the backseater enjoys an excellent view forward, over the nose and over his pupil. Unlike the instructor in a two-seat MiG-29, the 'Flanker' instructor has no need of a retractable periscope. Whereas the Su-27M/Su-35 has a cockpit dominated by modern multi-function display screens, the Su-27 used a conventional arrangement of analog dials with a small radar display screen. It was broadly equivalent to the cockpits of aircraft like the Phantom and was thus about a generation behind contemporary Western fighters.

The dorsal airbrake has been lengthened by one fuselage frame, changing its shape and area. It is believed that its maximum extension angle is rather smaller than that of the single-seater's airbrake.

The first Su-27UB prototype flew on 7 March 1985 piloted by Nikolai Sadovnikov. The Su-27UB prototype and the first few production two-seaters were built to broadly the same standard as early series production single-seaters, but without production-style cropped fin-caps and without the distinctive chaff/flare dispenser box fairings flanking the tail sting. The most familiar photos of the aircraft show it with cropped fin caps and white dielectric panels, but these features were added after the first flight, together with the code 01. Most production two-seaters, however, have been delivered in the later configuration, with the increased number of chaff/flare dispensers. Maximum take-off weight was increased by 3050 kg (6,724 lb) to 33500 kg (73,854 lb) in the last production series. Production of the Su-27UB has been undertaken by the Joint Stock Company Irkutsk Aircraft Manufacturing Association since 1986, and it is not known how many Su-27UBs were produced in Moscow and at Komsomolsk before 1986. The first picture of the Su-27UB was not published until early 1989, shortly before the variant made its debut at the 1989 Paris Air Salon at Le Bourget.

The primary role of the Su-27UB has always been one of providing conversion and continuation training (including training in instrument flying, for which a track-mounted blind-flying curtain is

provided). Su-27UBs have also been used for a number of other roles, offering a unique high-Alpha, high-*g*, long-range and very high-speed capability in a multi-seat aircraft. One of the best-known test Su-27UBs is used for aeromedical experiments and for the training of aviation medicine specialists. This aircraft (red 16) is based at Lipetsk, alongside other Su-27s used by the Russian aviation medicine establishment. The aeromedical Su-27s are used for a wide variety of human factors work, including the development of cockpit displays, and frequently operate from Zhukhovskii. Other Su-27UBs have been used as chase aircraft and for test-pilot training. The Su-27UB also formed the basis of the Su-27PU, designed as a dedicated long range, high endurance interceptor and mini-AWACS platform, able to carry two pilots or a pilot and a dedicated fighter controller.

Above: The aviation medicine institute's Su-27UBs wear a distinctive circular badge on their port air intake, consisting of the red cross superimposed on the blue and yellow sunburst flag of the Russian air forces. Red 16 is the best known of the unit's aircraft, and is used for the development of cockpit displays and controllers.

Specification
Sukhoi Su-27UB
Dimensions: fuselage length including probe 21.935 m (72 ft 0 in); span over wingtip missile launch rails 14.7 m (48 ft 3 in); area 62.037 m² (667.8 sq ft); tailplane span 9.88 m (32 ft 5 in); tailplane area 12.24 m² (131.75 sq ft);overall height 6.357 m (21 ft 5 in); wheel track 4.34 m (14 ft 3 in); wheelbase 5.88 m (19 ft 4 in)
Powerplant: two Saturn Lyul'ka AL-31F afterburning turbofans each rated at 74.53 kN (16,755 lb st) dry and 122.59 kN (27,558 lb st) with afterburning
Weights: empty operating 17500 kg (38,580 lb); normal take-off 24140 kg (53,220 lb); maximum take-off weight 30450 kg (67,130 lb)
Fuel and load: maximum 9400 kg (21,725 lb); maximum theoretical weapon load 8000 kg (17,636 lb); normal weapon load 4000 kg (8,818 lb)
***g* limits:** 8-9 at basic design gross weight; (estimated) maximum design gross weight 7 *g*
Performance: (estimated) maximum level speed 'clean' at sea level 705 kt (1300 km/h; 810 mph); maximum level speed 'clean' at altitude 1,150 kt (2125 km/h; 1,325 mph); limiting Mach No. 2.0; (estimated) practical service ceiling 16700 m (54,790 ft); absolute ceiling 17500 m (57,400 ft); range clean 5,530 nm (3000 km; 6,360 miles) at altitude, 2,340 nm (1270 km; 2,690 miles) at low level; take-off run 750-800 m (2,460-2,625 ft); landing roll 650-700 m (2,130-2,300 ft)

The front cockpit of the Su-27UB is broadly representative of the single-seat cockpit. It is astonishingly old-fashioned by contemporary Western standards, though it is well laid out.

Su-27UBK (T10UK) 'Flanker-C'

The Su-27UBK designation is applied to two-seat Su-27UBs built for export customers. The aircraft is broadly equivalent to a Russian late-production Su-27UB, with extended chaff/flare dispenser fairings on each side of the tail sting. The Su-27UBK is a very rare beast, since only two (one of them coded '04') were delivered with China's first batch of 'Flankers' and, as far as is known, the Vietnamese order did not include any two-seaters. Subsequent Chinese batches may include further pairs of Su-27UBKs (the second batch including aircraft coded 28 and 29, for instance), but the total number of aircraft involved will doubtless be small. Future Su-27 customers are probably more likely to opt for Su-30 two-seaters, which retain full dual controls, but which have much improved combat capability, with inflight-refuelling probes and the ability to mount extended-range or extended-endurance missions.

China is the only operator of the Su-27UBK, having taken four aircraft alongside its 46 single-seat Su-27SKs. The UBKs (will) wear the same colours as Chinese SKs.

Western Vortex
The RAF at Goose Bay

With adequate low-level training areas at a premium in Europe, the RAF has for many years rotated its operational squadrons to Labrador. A huge tract of virtually uninhabited land allows a degree of tactical freedom not found at any other available training area, making any squadron's two-week stay at Goose Bay a highly valuable one.

Every year the RAF sends its Tornado squadrons to the remote wilds of Labrador for some of the finest training the world has to offer. In RAF parlance the deployment is known as Western Vortex, and it usually occupies the months from June to September (the official flying season according to the Canadian government agreement is 1 March to 30 November).

On 10 February 1996 the Canadian government signed a new 10-year memorandum of understanding covering the continued use of the Goose Bay training area by UK, Dutch and German forces. This followed some considerable uncertainty over the future of the training area, and was delayed until an enivronmental impact study had been completed. The principal concerns had arisen from the local population, although this amounts to just 0.1 person per square kilometer, and from the environmental effects on the osprey and caribou populations, both of which are of great significance in this wilderness area.

Until the new agreement, the training area had featured 90000 km² of low-flying region. Like the current area, it was arranged in two sections, north and south of the environmentally-sensitive Churchill River area. However, under the old scheme there were two narrow link routes between the two areas, whereas now there is a long corridor along the river which can be crossed at any point at a minimum of 250 ft (76 m). Apart from the caveat that the crossing must be made quickly (i.e. to be in the corridor for as short a time as possible), the new arrangement provides for far greater tactical freedom in transiting between the two areas. The new area has also been shifted as a whole southwards, thereby avoiding the traditional grounds of the George River caribou herd. This denies the use of some mountains that previously fell into the northern area, including the infamous Harp Lake valley – one of the deepest and most spectacular to be encountered by low-level fliers anywhere.

The RAF unit at Goose Bay has a long history of supporting the North American operations of the air force. For many years the base supported Vulcan operations before the Tornado became the prime type. 'Goose' is also the main stop-over point in North America for the transport fleet.

Altogether the new area provides 130000 km² (50,197 sq miles) of contiguous training area, of which the Canadian government guarantees the

Left: In terms of colour scheme the RAF Tornado is in a period of transition. All-grey examples like this No. 12 Sqn GR.Mk 1B fly side-by-side with aircraft in the original grey/green camouflage.

Right: Screaming through a valley on its way to the target, this Tornado clutches a dummy 1,000-lb (454-kg) laser-guided bomb to its belly. The crew is from the LGB-specialist No. 17 Sqn, and the Goose Bay detachment provides them with a rare opportunity to drop the real thing. All warheads dropped at Goose Bay are inert, and the guidance systems are usually time-expired.

availability at any time of 100000 km². There are small areas within the main region where flying is discouraged (for instance in the vicinity of fishing camps) and these small areas are subtracted from the 130000 km². The range area is then automatically cut further to 100000 km² by taking out an area in the northwest near the Smallwood Reservoir. This giant lake is a prime habitat for birds, and is usually avoided as a matter of course for the good of the health of both the birds themselves and the jets.

Further stipulations of the new agreement include a maximum of 18,000 sorties per year for all users of the training area, of which a maximum of 15,000 can be at low level. At present the NATO forces are nowhere near this level of utilisation. Under the old agreement the three nations which use Goose Bay paid on an equal-share basis, but a user-pay scheme is now in place, whereby the individual countries pay according to the amount of use they make of the area. In the RAF's case, 85 per cent of the funding comes from support channels.

Right: The North American Tornado fleet normally numbers nine or ten aircraft, drawn from UK squadrons. The result is a mix of markings (Nos 14, 31 and 617 Sqns being seen here). In addition to regular GR.Mk 1s, the GR.Mk 1B is also used, although only as a standard bomber rather than its specialised anti-ship role. The Tornado GR.Mk 1A is rarely used due to the current operational commitments of the reconnaissance force.

Training range

Goose Bay's vast range offers an unrivalled low-level training environment. Despite having lost the mountains in the north after the restructuring, the new area now incorporates some mountains in the south. The southern area is also far more heavily forested than the north. Across the whole area is uncluttered airspace where aircraft are cleared down to 100 ft (30 m) altitude. The airspace restrictions previously mentioned are few and far between, allowing a large degree of tactical freedom in planning training missions and exercises.

Out in the range the Canadians maintain several targets. There are around 90 tank targets around the region: some inflatable and some made of wood. These provide excellent targets for reconnaissance as well as for attack. However, the main focus is the PTA – practice target area – a circular area some 20 nm (37 km; 23 miles) in diameter. This area contains several targets, the most important being a mock airfield hacked out of the scrub and forest. This has vehicle targets, wooden aircraft and mock helicopters for attack with a variety of inert weapons. A simple dummy aircraft shelter has been constructed by bulldozing dirt into a suitable shape and adding a wooden 'door'.

There are no live weapons used anywhere on the range due to the very real danger of starting forest fires (the Province of Newfoundland maintains a summertime detachment of water-bombers at Goose Bay). Similarly, the use of chaff and flares is not allowed. Another drawback is the lack of any scoring facilities. The range can theoretically be used for gunnery with inert rounds, although this is not practised at the moment. It is a facet which is expected to be added soon.

Situated in a wide depression, the mock airfield in the PTA is overlooked by Lima Hill, which is occasionally used as a base by forward

444 Squadron

Previously the Base Air Rescue Flight, 444 Squadron is the only permanently assigned CF unit at Goose Bay. It has recently upgraded from the CH-135 (Bell 212) to the CH-146 (Bell 412, below). In addition to a rescue role for the range and surrounding area, 'Treble Four' also provides helicopter transport for FAC teams (right) and range support personnel.

Canadian Forces

Once the location of a permanent Canadian air defence alert detachment, Goose Bay now hosts only periodical detachments of Bagotville-based CF-188s (a CF-188B of 425 'Alouette' Squadron illustrated). These aircraft operate from the alert barn area at the end of the main runway. CT-133s are also regular visitors, principally operating in an ECM training function or occasionally as air combat adversaries.

air control teams. Ground laser designation of targets on the airfield is possible from Lima Hill, allowing Tornados to practise LGB delivery.

RAF Unit Goose Bay is the official title of the resident UK organisation, which handles all RAF operations at the base. This consists of a 108-person permanent unit which is at Goose Bay all year. The posting is for one year (extendible to two) for unaccompanied personnel and two years (extendible to three) for married/accompanied personnel. Apart from base administration and operation, the permanent unit provides maintenance on the transport aircraft which transit through Goose Bay all through the year.

During the flying season two Permanent Support Parties, each of 30-40 personnel, are assigned to Goose Bay to aid Tornado servicing. When a Tornado squadron deploys for a Western Vortex exercise, it brings about 130 personnel, preceded by an advance maintenance party of about eight. If an aircraft requires specialist maintenance during the flying season, specialist teams are flown out from the UK to perform the work. Goose Bay also supports the North American exercise detachments such as Red Flag and Purple Star. A proportion of the personnel accompany these detachments.

Giant hangars

Apart from its people, the biggest asset of the RAF at Goose Bay is the excellent hangarage. The unit uses two giant hangars, each with three internal towers which house administration, operations and briefing facilities. The hangars themselves are big enough to accommodate a TriStar, six Hercules and a whole squadron of Tornados at a squeeze. The largest aircraft admitted to date is a KLu KDC-10. In winter the hangars provide the only workspace on the base for large aircraft, although with the temperature

Left and below: During the daytime operations the Tornado fleet operates from the line, aircraft then being towed into the hangar for security overnight (Goose Bay is an open base). Normally two pushes are launched each day, with an occasional third night wave added.

The PTA

Above: Tornados often work with army FAC teams at the PTA. The teams deploy by helicopter to Lima Hill for days at a time to provide ground designation for LGBs.

Left: A dummy 1,000-lb LGB is guided to its target by the FAC team on Lima Hill.

Right: A mock airfield has been carved out of the bundu. It has a simulated shelter half way down the runway. Visible on the near end of the runway is a dummy helicopter target.

Below: Aircraft dummies are positioned for take-off on the 'runway'. The PTA also has vehicle targets available for attack.

outside often at around -35°C (-31°F) plus wind chill factor, each opening of the doors can cost $1,000 in heating bills.

Goose Bay was originally a large Strategic Air Command base, and accommodation was built on a grand scale, providing plenty for the air arms which currently use the base. Although the local township of Happy Valley offers only limited recreation, the surrounding countryside offers a slice of the 'great outdoors' for visiting squadrons. Log cabin stays out in the *bundu* (a southern African slang term for the wilderness, which survives today in the British forces), fishing trips and the boat club are all available. Every two years RAF aircrew are expected to undertake a wet-winching exercise to keep their survival ratings current, and Goose Bay provides a good opportunity thanks to 444 Squadron, the locally-based Canadian Forces helicopter squadron. Germany-based squadrons are especially grateful of this opportunity as there is little chance of gaining the rating in the course of everyday squadron operations.

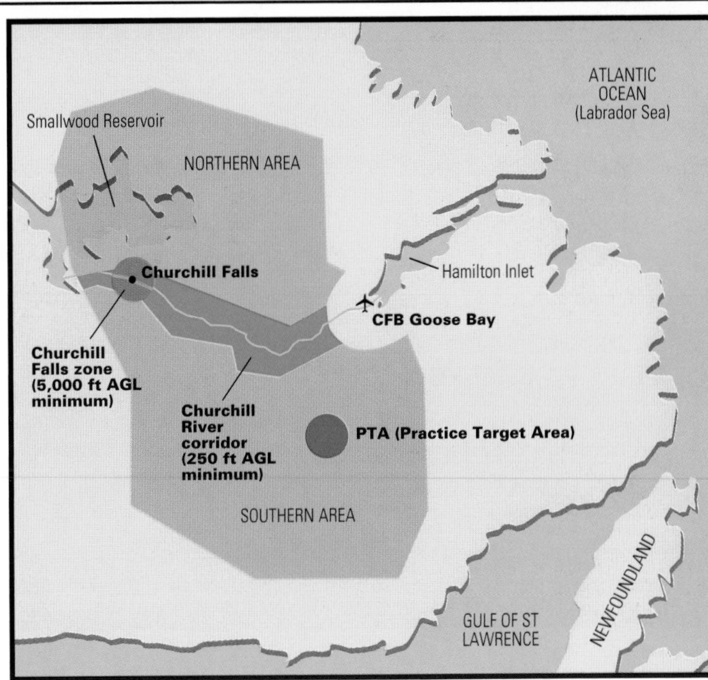

This map shows the full extent of the Goose Bay Military Training Area following the 1996 agreement. The 130000-km² (50,197-sq mile) area is roughly 310 miles (500 km) long and 180 miles (300 km) wide, and is arranged into two main regions (northern and southern) bisected by the Churchill River corridor. The corridor is provided primarily to protect the wildlife habitat along the river, and to avoid undue disruption to any traffic along the Trans-Labrador highway. Apart from a small service road running north from the Churchill Falls area to dams on the Smallwood Reservoir, the Labrador highway (from Quebec, via Churchill Falls, to Goose Bay) is the only road in the region. The reservoir is usually avoided due to the high density of birds in the area.

Helicopter operations

'Treble Four' operates the Bell CH-146, and is tasked with both SAR duties and utility transport duties. The former cover both the range area and a national responsibility along the coast of Labrador. Most transport tasks are concerned within the range itself, flying maintenance teams in to tend to targets or FAC teams into the PTA. Wet-winching exercises provide the helicopter squadron with useful experience.

As described earlier, a Western Vortex Tornado detachment lasts for two weeks, and is preceded by a small engineering group which prepares for the arrival of the squadron's main engineering party. Deployment from the UK or Germany is made en masse, utilising either a single TriStar or VC10, or two Hercules. Western Vortex is not a set exercise scenario, allowing the squadron to tailor its flying programme to its individual needs. In this way aircrew can concentrate on achieving their next goal. During the two-week deployment each squadron will expect to achieve many qualifica-

A Tornado approaches its target at very low level. The bundu is heavily forested and riddled with lakes. The latter provide a great many radar offset points to update en route navigation and to provide fixes for IP to target runs. The area contains many valleys down which the art of OLF (operational low flying) can be fully exercised.

Above and left: Tornado GR.Mk 1s with No. 31 Sqn markings (and No. 17 Sqn crews) set out on a training mission from Goose Bay. One of the great benefits of Goose training is that there is no set syllabus: squadrons can tailor their activities to meet their own requirements. On missions where fighter opposition (provided by German F-4Fs, Canadian CF-188s or Dutch F-16s) is not available, the squadron assigns an experienced crew to 'bounce' duties.

tions for its aircrew (OLF-qualified, pairs leader, four-ship leader, etc.).

Uncluttered airspace and lack of restrictions make Goose Bay the main area where aircrew achieve their OLF ratings. OLF stands for operational low flying, and requires crews to be able to fly at 100 ft (30 m) AGL. To get comfortable at this height requires several missions in a stepped approach down from the normal 250-ft (76-m) minimum flown in the low-level flying areas of the UK.

Missions are planned in the same fashion as they would be elsewhere. A typical route would seek to include several targets. Care is naturally taken to avoid the few restricted regions within the area. The flight-plan is entered by the navigator into a computer maintained at Goose Bay for monitoring low-level routes. The computer dispatches the route to a central location in Ottawa by modem. The route and timing information is stored so that any reported infringements of restricted airspace can be investigated.

Training missions from Goose Bay can take a variety of forms depending on the requirements of the participants and the assets available. At the lowest end of the scale are unopposed pairs or four-ship attack sorties. To add further realism to the scenario one extra Tornado is often dispatched as a 'bounce' to attack the other aircraft as they fly round their route. This requires some planning as the 'bounce' has to be able to cut corners off the strike formation's routing to be able to attack them several times during the mission.

Multi-force exercises

Goose Bay is well-placed to provide ComAO (combined air operations) exercises by integrating the aircraft of the four nations which fly from the base. These can be simple affairs whereby, say, Dutch F-16s provide fighter opposition for RAF Tornados, or can get quite sophisticated with large packages. A strike package could typically include eight RAF Tornados, eight German Tornados and eight Dutch F-16s acting as bombers, being opposed by a fighter force of eight Dutch F-16 fighters and four Canadian

The KLu at Goose Bay

During the flying season the KLu maintains up to 20 F-16A/Bs at Goose Bay. These operate from a ramp next to the civil terminal, in front of the maintenance hangar (illustrated). The operations room, however, is across the base in the old SAC operations building, known locally as the 'Mole-hole'.

CF-188s. Such packages can be the equivalent of those found at TLP (Tactical Leadership Programme) and provide a challenge for the senior members of the squadron in terms of planning.

Large ComAO operations are usually planned and briefed in the Dutch operations centre, which is the best-equipped on the base. Locally known as the 'mole-hole' thanks to the several tunnel-type entrances, the building was formerly the SAC operations centre. ComAO operations also benefit from periodic detachments of NATO E-3 Sentries to Goose Bay. Quite apart from the exercise advantages these aircraft provide during the flying portion of the mission, they provide a good means of debriefing afterwards. There is no ACMI range at Goose Bay, although the idea of a GPS-based low-cost system has been raised as a possible addition for the future. Air defenders do provide an added element to the realism of the attack training, but the training area is not ideally suited to their own requirements, and the fighter assets available are therefore naturally limited.

Canadian participation

Canadian CF-188s are regular participants in ComAO operations, terming their involvement Free Alliance. The opportunity for ComAO at Goose Bay is especially important for the Canadians: since their complete withdrawal from Europe, Free Alliance offers the only chance to train with other NATO nations outside of the rigid schedules of Flag-type exercises. The CF-188s usually deploy from Bagotville every other week, and while at Goose Bay maintain a QRA detachment (albeit only with guns). This does have a considerable training value, and the aircraft are regularly scrambled to practise their quick alert capabilities.

For the future the RAF is hoping to expand the range facilities to make Goose Bay even better training value for the squadrons. In 1997 the addition of RAF Regiment Rapier teams will not only give those teams valuable experience, but also provide a ground EW threat. Apart from occasional visits from Canadian Forces CT-133 jammers, there is at present no electronic warfare simulation available. Rapier sites have been surveyed close to the Trans-Labrador highway (the only road in the entire region) so that they can be easily supported by ground vehicles.

In the winter the Goose Bay area is available for Special Forces Hercules training. Close to the main airfield is the Webber Drop Zone, available for paradropping small loads. Luftwaffe Transalls also use Goose Bay for tactical airlift training during the summer months, employing the small airstrip at Churchill Falls for practising austere base operations.

Once considered in doubt, the future of Goose Bay as NATO's low-level training ground is brighter than ever. A consensus of opinion between the user nations will see the facilities increase to provide ever more realistic training. The RAF and its Tornado squadrons are seen as the prime movers behind the move towards greater assets.

For those squadrons, Goose Bay offers the best possible environment for their own training needs, and the deployment is often used as a means of working up towards a Red Flag exercise or a real-life operational deployment.

David Donald

German operations

Germany maintains a sizeable detachment of Tornados (about 15), drawn from both Luftwaffe and Marineflieger (MFG 2 illustrated). In addition the Luftwaffe bases a similar number of F-4Fs during the summer months, and three Transall C-160Ds. The latter regularly use the Churchill Falls airstrip.

A No. 14 Sqn Tornado taxis from the line at Goose Bay. Even in 1996 the last vestiges of Gulf War camouflage could still be found in the Tornado fleet, mainly on fuel tanks and Sky Shadow ECM pods.

US Army Aviation: *Part Two*

In this, the second part of our landmark Air Power Analysis, we detail the organisation, unit structure and order of battle of the US Army's major front-line combat units. This includes the ConUS-based Armies plus their Europe- and Pacific-based equivalents; also Forces Command, the unifying command for all the Army's war-fighting units and its constituent Corps.

Third US Army (3rd ARMY)

The 3rd Army is the US Army theatre command assigned to US Central Command. USCENTCOM is the joint war-fighting command that is responsible for maintaining American military interests in the Southwest Asia theatre, covering 20 countries in the region from eastern Africa to western Asia.

The command headquarters, located at Ft McPherson, Atlanta, Georgia, spends most of its time preparing for theoretical, future conflict scenarios. These range from large operations with armoured formations such as were executed during Operation Desert Storm, to limited warfare options of a special operations nature, to peace-keeping and humanitarian missions, and everything in between. In order to determine personnel and materiel requirements for possible land warfare operations, the command staff routinely conducts studies, analyses and command post exercises (CPXs) that essentially provide commanders with multiple 'what if' simulations to assess and overcome potential problems and opportunities that would be encountered in any future operations, anywhere in the theatre.

The command was reactivated in 1982 as the Army component headquarters for CENTCOM, composed of Army elements of what had previously been known as the Rapid Deployment Force (RDF). The Third Army is supplied primarily from Forces Command (FORSCOM) units for potential contingency operations, with the forces of XVIII Airborne Corps (XVIIIABNCORPS) and US Army Special Operations Command (USASOC) constantly preparing for rapid deployment to the theatre to deter, reinforce and fight, if so directed by the National Command Authority (NCA). Additional war-fighting assets are also tasked to reinforce the command from reserve components assigned to FORSCOM. The pace of training deployments, exercises and combat operations since Desert Storm has forced the Army to prepare additional units for possible deployment, including forces assigned to US Army Europe/7th Army (USAREUR/7A) and III Corps. For most of the command's history, it was a 'paper' force with a full battle staff of experienced, professional soldiers, in constant readiness in case the need arose for the command to activate its resources and deploy for combat.

Few outside the US military establishment paid any attention to Third Army until it was tasked to command American and coalition forces deployed for what became known as Operation Desert Shield/Storm. At its peak strength during that conflict, 3rd Army commanded over 350,000 soldiers, including US Marines from the 1st and 2nd Marine Divisions, reinforced with an Army armoured brigade from the 2nd Armored Division. Additional coalition forces from nearly a dozen other countries were under the operational control of the command. No coalition soldiers or materiel were in place when Iraq invaded Kuwait, and Third Army logisticians played a critical role in managing the arrival and dispersal of vast quantities of ammunition, food, fuel and manpower that arrived via aircraft and ships. From their ports of arrival, many units drove their vehicles and armour right to their defensive positions, forward deployed in the desert.

Desert Storm debut

The air war was initiated when eight AH-64As from the 1-101 Aviation Regiment conducted a mission to destroy an Iraqi radar site in order to clear a corridor for strike aircraft heading to Baghdad. They were led by a pair of AFSOC Enhanced MH-53Js because of that type's sophisticated navigation systems.

Between 17 January and 3 February, two corps were relocated from defensive to attack positions. VII Corps moved 140,000 soldiers, 32,000 wheeled vehicles, 6,600 tracked vehicles and their aviation assets an average distance of 140 miles (225 km). XVIII Airborne Corps managed the movement of more than 115,000 soldiers, 21,000 wheeled vehicles, 4,300 tracked vehicles and their aviation assets an average of 360 miles (580 km), as they executed the 'Hail Mary', left-hook movement deep into the desert. Vehicles crossed paths at critical intersections and aviation units played 'leap frog' as they set up refuelling points on the way to new forward bases. Along with the combat units and their equipment, immense quantities of ammunition, food, fuel and water had to be repositioned and stockpiled to allow for a 60-day supply, at peak war-fighting levels. This massive repositioning allowed these formations ample room to manoeuvre outside the ring of fixed Iraqi defensive positions.

At the start of the ground war on 24 February 1991, 3rd Army directly controlled over 2,080 US Army combat and support aircraft, along with several hundred Marine Corps helicopters plus aviation assets belonging to the coalition countries. 3rd Army had about 100 aircraft directly assigned at the EAC level, including the aviation brigade detached from the 2nd Armored Division, SOA aviation units from the 160th Special Operations Aviation Regiment (Airborne), and the famous 'Camel Express' with five brand new C-23B Sherpas providing logistics support to aviation units scattered over thousands of square miles of Saudi Arabian desert. VII Corps was supplied with six aviation brigades and the 2nd Regimental Aviation Squadron (4-2 ACR), plus military intelligence and corps support aviation assets, totalling 957 aircraft. XVIII Airborne Corps had five aviation brigades, three assigned to divisions and two corps-level brigades, plus 4-3 ACR and aviation units assigned to their intelligence brigade and corps support assets; over 1,025 aircraft.

When the ground war began, the two US Army corps were in attack formations west of the Marine and coalition forces, across a featureless desert front of 144 miles (232 km). VII Corps was composed of four heavy armoured divisions – three US and one British – plus the 2nd ACR, and was tasked to flank the western Iraqi units and penetrate into northern Kuwait to destroy Republican Guard units based there. XVIII Airborne Corps – with one US armoured division, one French light armoured division, 2nd ACR, 82nd Airborne Division and the 101st Airborne Division (Air Assault) – was assigned to move due north and control the Euphrates River Valley, to support VIICORPS and to prevent any reinforcement or supplies coming from the west, and also block any escape routes of retreating Iraqi units. XVIIIABNCORPS conducted the largest air assault operation in history when the three infantry brigades of the division were moved over 100 miles (160 km) during one night.

Fifteen battalions of AH-64As, many having received their aircraft just in the year before the war, employed almost 300 Apaches to provide firepower that proved highly lethal to Iraqi armour, vehicles and fortifications. The presence of 141 AH-1Fs assigned to nine cavalry units has been largely ignored, but these aircraft were also in the thick of the fighting, conducting anti-tank and armed reconnaissance missions. The Army used the 15 armed OH-58Ds, but they were embarked onboard US Navy vessels, conducting operations in the Persian Gulf. Special operations aircraft assigned to the 160 SOAR flew many missions, operating with a estimated 50 aircraft. Armed AH-6Gs and MH-60A/Ls performed gunship and CSAR roles, and MH-6Hs, CH/MH-47Ds and MH-60A/Ls executed the covert insertion and extraction of special forces soldiers, often behind Iraqi lines.

The remaining helicopter fleet was equipped primarily with machine-guns for defensive purposes as they performed a variety of missions including air assault, air ambulance, combat support, command and control, general support, intelligence gathering, medium lift, reconnaissance, and target acquisition. The Blackhawk community represented the numerically largest fleet of any type of Army aircraft, with at least 529 UH/EH-60s operating in the theatre. Four hundred and ninety OH-58A/C/Ds performed

Above: The 3rd Army's aviation elements distinguished themselves during Operation Desert Storm and still remain on alert in Saudia Arabia.

Below: Fuel tanks carried on the Blackhawk's ESSS pylons extend the UH-60's range considerably.

Above: The arrival of the Longbow Apache will advance Army Aviation's warfighting capability to a devastating level.

Below: Existing UH-60A Medevac Blackhawks will eventually be augmented by dedicated UH-60Qs.

as scouts and to acquire targets for field artillery. The Air-To-Air Stinger had just been tested with the OH-58C/D, and was deployed to provide a rudimentary air defence capability to attack battalions and cavalry squadrons. At least 301 venerable UH-1H/Vs provided support and air ambulance capability. The heavy-lift CH-47D moved all types of materiel and weapons, with at least 156 aircraft in-theatre at the peak. Three military intelligence battalions operated 45 OV/RV-1 and 26 RU-21/RC-12s, giving commanders vital intelligence on Iraqi movements and positions. At least 25 fixed-wing types, including U-21A/Gs, C-12C/D/Fs and C-23Bs, were deployed.

The contribution of Army aviation in this campaign has been largely overshadowed by the dramatic results of the air war and by the imagery of sleek strike fighters that caught the media's attention. In the years prior to the war, the service came under intense scrutiny for the alleged failings of the Apache, questioning whether the force was ready for conflict. From the beginning of the ground war, the aircraft were employed offensively to destroy Iraqi armour formations, prior to the arrival of US armour columns, and they advanced so rapidly that refuelling and re-arming sites had to move at unexpected speeds just to keep up with them. US Army aviation came of age for a second time during this conflict; post-war reviews by senior Army leadership led to significant doctrinal changes that will affect the force well into the 21st century.

The conflict did not come without cost. Nearly 65 Army helicopters were involved in crashes in FY91, many of them in-theatre. Army safety officers were at a loss to explain the increase over previous years, except to state that many aviators might have become a little careless while preoccupied with the threat of upcoming combat. The harsh conditions of high heat, high humidity, blowing sand and smoke from burning oil wells contributed to much higher than normal wear on the fleet. The Army initiated Project STIR in November 1991 to return the aircraft to an operational status. All told, 911 aircraft, nearly half of all the Army helicopters involved in the conflict, passed through nine different locations, the last being completed by late 1994. Returning the aircraft to pristine condition cost over $500 million and involved a labour force of 2,300.

The 244th Aviation Brigade was previously based in Georgia and did not deploy with the 3rd Army to Saudi Arabia. The headquarters unit relocated to Illinois in the early 1990s. By the end of 1996, it was the only remaining aviation brigade assigned to the Army Reserve Command (USARC). The units attached to the command will all be drawn from the USARC or ArNG components. The brigade has been in transition since late 1994 and it is expected that additional changes to the structure will be made before the end of 1996. The lean force structure of the theatre aviation brigade can be strengthened with additional units as needed and in time of conflict.

3rd US Army, HQ Ft McPherson, GA; THREEUSA/3rd Army

(3rd US Army, Forward, Riyadh, Saudi Arabia)

167th Support Command, Montgomery, AL; 167 SUPCOM
AL ArNG-assigned unit

C/7-159 AVN, Scott AFB, IL

UH-60A	2	AVIM

USAR-assigned unit

244th Aviation Brigade, Aurora, IL; 244 AVNBDE
USARC-assigned unit. Brigade relocated from Ft Sheridan, IL in 1994

1-147 AVN (CMD), Truax Field, Madison, WI

UH-60A(C)	8	C&C
UH-60A	8	CS
UH-60A	8	GS

WI ArNG-assigned battalion. Converted from ATK to CMD role in 1995, replacing 3-158 AVN (USARC). Units in IA and IL

5-159 AVN (MHB), Felker AAF, Ft Eustis, VA

CH-47D	48	MH

USARC-assigned battalion relocated from Tipton AAF, Ft Meade, MD in 1995 with units assigned in KS and WA

2-228 AVN (TA), NAS Willow Grove, PA

C-12C/F		TA/GS
C-12R	16	TA/GS
C-23B+		TA/GS
U-21A		TA/GS

USARC-assigned battalion with units in WI. 16 C-12Rs replaced U-21/C-12C in 1994-96. C-12R in 1994-96. 'C' and 'D' companies to activate and gain 16 C-23B+s from 1997

US Army Europe/7th Army (USAREUR/7A)

US Army Europe/7th Army is the war-fighting component of the US European Command (USEUCOM or EUCOM), the joint unified war-fighting command assigned to command US forces in the European theatre. Both commands are headed by four-star generals. EUCOM is headquartered in Stuttgart, Germany and composed of US Air Force and Army units based on the continent plus seaborne Navy and Marine Corps forces deployed to the eastern Atlantic Ocean and Mediterranean Sea. Both of these commands represent only a fraction of the land warfare capability available to the Supreme Allied Commander, Europe (SACEUR) and its HQ element, the Supreme Headquarters Allied Powers, Europe (SHAPE). SHAPE is the military command of NATO that is tasked with the defence of Europe from Norway to the Mediterranean Sea, and from the Atlantic to eastern Turkey.

The four-star leader of USAREUR/7A is in charge of the two commands in the designation. US Army Europe represents the peacetime structure and denotes the military and political nature of the command's relationships with its international allies, as well as potential adversaries. Seventh Army is the war-fighting side of the command, and in the event of conflict it becomes a theatre army, conducting operations in the field, and structured to fight alongside other numbered allied armies. The command has been headquartered in Heidelberg, Germany, the country where most of its forces have been deployed since the end of World War II.

European exercises

USAREUR/7A forces regularly exercise with allied military forces from throughout NATO and recently they have begun conducting training with eastern European and Russian forces, building greater co-operation and understanding. Eastern European forces have even rotated through US combat training centres as they begin to operate alongside US Army forces in peacekeeping operations such as Operation Joint Endeavor in Bosnia. The 7th Army Training Command (7 ATC) operates the Combat Maneuver Training Center (CMTC) at Hohenfels, an instrumented training and evaluation facility that allows manoeuvre training over 40,000 acres (16190 ha) of Bavarian terrain. Units are rotated through the CMTC with an average of 2,000 soldiers undergoing training at any one time. The Opposing Force (OPFOR) is composed of a battalion-sized task force built around the 1st Battalion/4th Infantry Regiment (1-4 INF) and reinforced with aviation elements that provide threat emulation and air assault for the OPFOR.

USAREUR/7A underwent a tremendous expansion beginning in the mid-1980s, coinciding with the deployment of the upgraded CH-47D and OH-58D variants plus the procurement of the UH-60 and AH-64s. The composition of the Army's heavy divisions' (those composed chiefly of armour and mechanised infantry forces) aviation brigades was structured so that they were supplied with two attack battalions at full strength, and only the four divisions assigned to Europe during that period were so equipped. Additional forces were rotated to Europe for short training periods under a programme known as Return of Forces to Germany (REFORGER). Entire battalions of Apaches were deployed in these exercises, and some remained to be reassigned to the theatre to provide a deep strike capability with the constantly growing 11th and 12th Aviation Brigades. These corps-level aviation brigades were also assigned many Army National Guard and Army Reserve aviation units, with hundreds of additional helicopters to supplement these brigades if they were actually required to go to war. The battalions with regimental affiliations of the 158th and 159th Aviation Regiments were built around these requirements, at least on paper.

At its peak, the command directly operated over 325 front-line attack helicopters along with hundreds of scout, combat and general support, medical evacuation and medium helicopters. USAREUR/7A modernised its airborne intelligence assets by transitioning from RU-21H to RC-12D and eventually to RC-12K aircraft. The latter is equipped with improved generations of Guardrail systems optimised to collect intelligence of command and control, and communications signals (Comint), with increasingly sophisticated location and direction-finding sensors. OV-1Ds provided infra-red and optical reconnaissance capability and RV-1Ds were fielded to conduct Elint on high-value, electronic emitters, such as radars. The command also operated large quantities of U-21s and C-12s for general support between the far flung units of the command.

The Army was denied an opportunity to test whether its forces could master the battlefields of Europe, but when Iraq invaded Kuwait in August 1990, the massed armoured forces of 7th Army were more than prepared. Units assigned to both V and VII Corps were deployed to Saudi Arabia under the command of US Central Command (USCENTCOM). 12th Aviation Brigade was one of the first Europe-based units to deploy, being assigned to augment XVIII Airborne Corps. VII Corps headquarters, and its assigned 11th Aviation Brigade, was also deployed; it commanded the bulk of the armoured and mechanised infantry units assigned to the theatre, comprising nearly half of all the Army combat units .... Army aviation units that deployed from the European theatre included those assigned to 2nd Corps Support Command, 1st Armored Division, 3rd Armored Division, 2nd Armored Cavalry Regiment, 7th Medical Command, and the 205th Military Intelligence Brigade. These units contributed almost 700 aircraft, nearly one-third of total Army aviation assets and 25 per cent of the forces deployed in-theatre.

Post-Gulf changes

More than any other command, US Army Europe has undergone far-reaching upheaval in its organisation, force structure and inventory. Since late 1991 the command has been involved in the Retrograde Europe (RETROEUR) programme, which moved large quantities of materiel, weapons and aircraft back to ConUS for redistribution to active-duty and reserve component forces. The command had 213,000 soldiers and civilians on strength at the beginning of Fiscal Year 1990; by the end of FY95, it was down to 65,000. The withdrawing soldiers took with them almost every aircraft, piece of equipment and weapon that still had value, plus tens of thousands of dependants, privately owned vehicles, and thousands of tons of personal effects. Many facilities that had been occupied by the US military since World War II have been returned to the host nations, most in Germany. The direct-reporting unit responsible for managing most of this massive movement is the 21st Theater Army Area Command (21 TAACOM), which had traditionally been tasked to manage the flow of materiel to the theatre from reinforcing and sustaining units. The command's small aviation element supports the movement and co-ordination of these war stocks throughout the theatre. In the RETROEUR programme, the 200th Theater Army Material Management Center (200 TAAMMC) and B Company/70th Transportation Bn (AVIM) handled the movement of hundreds of aircraft exiting the theatre.

End of VII Corps, beginning of EC3

Since the beginning of the decade, USAREUR has lost more than half its combat and support forces, with many units forced to stand down completely while others were reassigned, principally to the continental US. VII Corps, which had been responsible for the southern portion of 7th Army's area of responsibility was inactivated in March 1992. This manoeuvre headquarters had been deployed to Germany since the 1950s and, once it was inactivated, V Corps remained to assume command for all remaining manoeuvre forces in the European theatre. Many remaining units changed their designations prior to inactivating, a confusing situation to both casual observers and military personnel. The flags of the 3rd Armored and 8th Mechanized Infantry Divisions were inactivated, along with materiel and personnel equivalent to the unit's assigned strength. The 3rd Infantry Division (Mech.) designation remained assigned to Europe, but its aviation brigade headquarters was redeployed to Ft Bragg, North Carolina to become the 159th Aviation Group (or Regiment) in January 1992. Two European Apache battalions were also redeployed to Ft Bragg to form the nucleus of the newly activated 229th Aviation Group, all executed under the Enhanced ConUS Contingency Capability (EC3) programme. The two armoured cavalry regiments, 2nd and 11th ACR, were inactivated along with their regimental aviation squadrons (RAS). Many combat support and combat service support units were also packed off, including two CH-47D medium-lift companies.

By 1994, the equivalent of five full aviation brigades had been retrograded. This massive movement coincided with the ARI restructuring which led to the almost complete withdrawal of the Vietnam-era UH-1H, AH-1F and OH-58C fleets, which were considered unable to survive on the modern battlefield and incapable of self-deployment to contingencies as were the majority of Europe-based helicopters, the UH-60 and AH-64. By the end of 1996 the last of the HueyCobras had been reassigned to ArNG units in the states, and the only OH-58Cs were those

Above: These were the spartan conditions that greeted the men and machines of the 7th Army during their Provide Comfort deployments.

Right: These IFOR-dedicated AH-64As of 2-227 AVN are seen here preparing to depart for Bosnia in early 1996. Note the non-standard codes on the exhaust shrouds.

Above: Intra- and extra-theatre deployments by USAREUR units are supported by the 7th Army's fleet of C-12s, such as this 6th Avn Det C-12F seen at Budapest.

assigned to target acquisition/reconnaissance platoons, performing spotting duties for the field artillery units assigned to the divisions. The last Hueys remaining in Europe are employed for general support, administrative tasks and as threat surrogates for the CMTC.

Manoeuvre forces currently assigned to the command are aligned with V Corps, based in Frankfurt, Germany. The corps commands two armoured divisions, 1st Armored Division and 1st Infantry Division (Mechanized), which was redesignated from the 3rd Infantry Division in early 1996. Many specialised brigades are assigned to the corps, including the 3rd Corps Support Command, 30th Medical Brigade, 12th Aviation Brigade, and 205th Military Intelligence Brigade, all of which operate aviation components. Additional combat forces are assigned to the Southern European Task Force (SETAF), a unit composed of allied military forces and headquartered at Vicenza, Italy. SETAF is subordinate to the Allied Land Forces, Southern Europe and the US Army has built its forces up to a brigade-sized, composite force that has recently served to initially secure key staging areas and to remain on call as a back-up force for NATO deployments to Bosnia. A few aviation units of fixed- and rotary-wing aircraft provide support to the force.

The history of military and political changes in Europe from the late 1980s has caused planners to reassess the roles and missions of their assigned forces. The force structure of US Army Europe/7th Army remains one of a mobile, armoured strike force that is available for deployment within the theatre or for assignment to other commands to reinforce contingency operations. Since Operation Desert Shield/Storm, USAREUR/7A has been tasked to support assorted, non-traditional, short- and long-term missions throughout its area of operations, while continuing to maintain peak proficiency supporting its manoeuvre-based, heavy armour combat skills. The new roles include humanitarian, peacekeeping, and operations other than war (OOTW).

Provide Comfort, Rwanda and others

Most of these operations have utilised the tactical mobility of aviation assets to great advantage. Beginning in April 1991, the Aviation Brigade (4th Brigade), 3rd Infantry Division (Mech.) plus supporting corps and special operations aviation units were deployed to northern Iraq and Turkey for Operation Provide Comfort, to conduct operations to aid the Kurdish refugees who had been driven from their residences. Other US Army Europe force packages have been deployed to Rwanda and Somalia, and detachments have supported Operation Southern Watch in Saudi Arabia. For years, a few UH-60s provided the only outside link to the American embassy in Lebanon, forming an air bridge from their staging location in Cyprus. Aircraft from the command have been used in humanitarian and peacekeeping operations in Rwanda and Somalia in recent years. A few Blackhawks have been painted white and given UN markings to support peacekeeping operations in northern Macedonia. These non-traditional operations are likely to become increasingly familiar to the aircrew and soldiers.

IFOR

The US Army's deployment of a substantial force during December 1995, as a major element of NATO's Implementation Force (IFOR), is a prime example of the service's doctrine that is known as operations other than war (OOTW). Under the name of Task Force Eagle, the command deployed a reinforced combat formation built around the entire 1st Armored Division. The massive fire power of the division gained additional forces, including more aviation elements. The division deployed a battalion of AH-64As (2-227 AVN), its general support aviation battalion (7-227 AVN), and its cavalry squadron (1-1 CAV) equipped with a unique mix of AH-1F and OH-58D aircraft; a second cavalry squadron, 3-4 CAV, was 'borrowed' from what is now the 1st Infantry Division. The units had begun training for just such a mission in January 1995, with units facing sophisticated simulations at CMTC in preparation for the anticipated peacekeeping role, planning for multiple scenarios. The 2-227 AVN took delivery of two specially equipped Apaches from the 1-24 AVN at Hunter AAF, just prior to the deployment. These aircraft were configured with SATCOM and modified sensor suites to allow the transmission of near real-time imagery to theatre and national commanders, thousands of miles away.

The 15,000-soldier division was supported by a theatre- and corps-level force package numbering about 5,000 more soldiers. Units assigned to the 21st TAACOM and 3rd COSCOM provided logistic support including AVIM and TA aviation elements. At least half-a-dozen air ambulance medical detachments (of three aircraft each) also deployed to the theatre from units assigned to the 421st Medical Evacuation Battalion.

Operations in Bosnia

Aircraft and aircrews assigned to the 12th Aviation Brigade also played an important role in the movement of materiel and soldiers to the designated American sector near Tuzla. CinCHawk-configured command and control Blackhawks proved vital for maintaining communication links between dispersed units when line-of-sight networks were impaired by mountainous terrain. Initial deployments of armoured columns through Croatia into Bosnia were hampered by the rain-swollen Sava River. CH-47Ds of A/5-159 AVN arrived one night at the river crossing, and by the next morning they were placing pontoon sections to allow the engineers to overcome the floods. After three days, the makeshift bridge, measuring nearly 3000 m (9,845 ft), was ready, allowing the heavy tanks and vehicles to complete their journey south to their designated postings under the cover of Apache and Kiowa Warriors.

Operations in Hungary

The 12th Aviation Brigade and 1st Armored Division were staged out of Taszar Air Base in Hungary, the Intermediate Staging Base (ISB) for US operations that is over 200 km (125 miles) from Tuzla. From the beginning of the operation, command and control, logistics, and the high tempo of operations were complicated by constant near-freezing weather, low cloud ceilings and mountainous terrain. In the first three months of operations over 1,900 flight hours were recorded. Support equipment and vehicles for all units, including aviation, were sent to Hungary by commercial trains which met repeated delays. The maintainers kept the fleet operating, and by March 1996 they had begun performing scheduled phase inspections in the field. Taszar also became home for the RC-12Ks of the 1st MIB(AE) deployed to support the operation. An air bridge of Air Force airlifters and US Army Europe C-12s, supplemented by US Army Reserve Command C-12Rs, has replenished the forces with high-priority cargo, perishables, staff and VIPs. Apaches from 6-6 CAV have made covering deployments as needed. Additional assets operated from Italy including MH-60As of the 3-160 SOAR, forward-deployed from Hunter AAF, Georgia.

J-STARS and ARL in the field

The Army and Air Force had planned to conduct the Multi-service Operational Test & Evaluation (MOT&E) of the E-8 J-STARS in southern Arizona in January 1996, but the deployment of US forces to Bosnia provided the opportunity to once again demonstrate the system's capabilities in a real-world combat environment. The test force was composed of personnel from the contractor (Northrop-Grumman), OPTEC and TEXCOM. One of the programme's prototype airframes (86-0417) and the EMD-tasked, full-scale development aircraft (90-0175) were forward-deployed to Rhein Main Air Base, Frankfurt, Germany on 15 December 1995 to participate in Operation Joint Endeavor. The aircraft operated around the disputed territory of the former Yugoslavia, tracking the movement of deployed NATO forces and those of the warring parties. The Army reportedly deployed nine ground station modules (GSMs) to forces on the ground in Bosnia and Hungary to receive data from the J-STARS platforms in a near real-time mode. An example of the system's use in a peace-keeping scenario was a 1st Armored Division Blackhawk making an emergency landing in an unsecured area in late December; the J-STARS aircraft tracked the surrounding area to ascertain whether vehicles or armour were attempting to intercept the aircraft and its crew. They were also used to observe the site preparations at Bosnian airfields and the building of the pontoon bridge by combat engineers over the Sava River that month. By March 1996 the J-STARS aircraft had been withdrawn to their test base at Melbourne, Florida to allow the aircraft to continue the development process. The gap in capability was partially filled by UAVs and the deployment of an Army DHC-7 Airborne Reconnaissance Low (ARL) aircraft.

The planned withdrawal of the 1st Armored Division would be replaced by a 'covering force' composed of a reinforced brigade task force from the 1st Infantry Division. Aviation elements assigned to this force include elements of 7-159 AVN and 2-6 CAV from the 12th Aviation Brigade, and 1-1 AVN, the Apache-equipped attack battalion assigned to the division's aviation brigade.

Bosnia repercussions

The objective aviation force for US Army Europe has been changed by events in Bosnia. It was planned that the 6th Aviation Det would become a theatre aviation (TA) company and be assigned eight C-12s, and that the 207th AVN CO would become a command aviation (CMD) company equipped with Blackhawk variants. Events have interceded and the two units have continued to operate a few remaining Hueys in support of their busy mission load. These aircraft and the CH-47Ds of E/502 AVN, based in Italy, are considered as echelons above corps (EAC) support units. 12th Aviation Brigade has been supplied for the near term to operate 16 CH-47Ds, 15 OH-58Cs, 38 UH-60A/Ls, 48 AH-64As and five C-12Fs. Remaining V Corps aviation will operate nearly 50 Blackhawks in medevac and AVIM units along with Intel-tasked RC-12s and UAVs that should be fielded by 1997. The two heavy divisions are expected to remain stable with 75 aircraft apiece, after one of the two remaining Apache battalions with the 1st Armored is inactivated. By late 1997, USAREUR/7A is expected to begin fielding the EH-60L Advanced Quickfix, followed by the UH-60C upgraded command and control variant, and then by the AH-64D Longbow Apache. The soldiers and aircrew assigned to US Army Europe/Seventh Army can expect a continued high operational tempo into the next century as the command continues to provide quality training in order to maintain optimal readiness.

Supreme Allied Commander, Europe/Supreme Headquarters Allied Powers, Europe, HQ Mons, Belgium; SACEUR/SHAPE

Flight Detachment, Chièvres AB, Belgium

UH-60A(C)	2	GS/VIP

US European Command, HQ Patch Barracks, Stuttgart, Germany; USEUCOM or EUCOM

Flight Operations Detachment, Echterdigen AAF, Stuttgart

C-12C		GS/VIP
UH-1H	2	GS/VIP

2 C-12C withdrawn 1995

US Army Europe/7th Army, Campbell Barracks, Heidelberg, Germany; USAREUR/7A

7th Army Training Command, Grafenwoehr, Germany; 7 ATC

Aviation Detachment, Grafenwoehr AAF

C-12C		GS
C-12F	1	GS
UH-1H	3	GS

1 C-12C replaced by C-12F in 1995

Combat Maneuver Training Center, Hohenfels, Germany; CMTC

Aviation Detachment, Hohenfels AAF

UH-1H	10	GS/OC & threat support
OH-58C		GS/OC

Unit replaced 6 OH-58C with 4 UH-1H in 1995

21st Theatre Army Area Command, Kaiserslautern, Germany; 21 TAACOM

207th AVN Company, Heidelberg AAF

C-12C		GS
C-12D		GS
C-12F	5	GS
UH-1H	5	GS
UH-60A	4	GS

Company replaced 8 C-12C, 1 C-12D with 8 C-12F by 1995, with some aircraft detached. 10 UH-1H to be replaced by 8 UH-60A/A(C) by 1996-97

70th Transportation Bn (AVIM), Coleman AAF, Mannheim, Germany; B Co./70 TRANS

UH-1H	2	AVIM/GS
UH-60A	2	AVIM/GS

Battalion responsible for the preparation and shipment of aircraft to and from Europe

Southern European Task Force, HQ Vicenza, Italy; SETAF

5th Theatre Army Area Command, Vicenza, Italy; 5 TAACOM

6th AVN Detachment

C-12C		GS
C-12F	2	GS
UH-1H	7	GS

2 C-12C replaced by C-12F by November, 1995. UH-1H to be retired or replaced by UH-60A by 1997

E Co./502nd Aviation Regt (MH), Aviano AB

CH-47D	16	MH

V Corps, Campbell Barracks, Heidelberg, Germany; VCORPS

3rd Corps Support Command, Wiesbaden AB, Germany; 3 COSCOM

7-159 AVN (AVIM), Illesheim AAF, Ansbach

UH-1H		AVIM
UH-60A	4	AVIM

Unit from 4 UH-1H to UH-60A, by 1994. One company detached to Wiesbaden AB

30th Medical Brigade, Heidelberg, Germany; 30 MEDBDE

421 Medical Evacuation Battalion, Wiesbaden AB; 421 MEB

45th Medical Co. (AA), Fliegerhorst AAF, Ansbach

UH-60A	15	AA

159th Medical Co. (AA), Darmstadt AHP

UH-60A	15	AA

236th Medical Co. (AA), Landstuhl AHP (Kaiserslautern)

UH-60A1	15	AA

Above left: White-painted UH-60s are deployed to the former Yugoslavian Republic of Macedonia, with the UN mission there.

Left: Airborne Army fire-power in Bosnia has been provided by the Apaches of several units, including 6 Squadron, 6th Cavalry 'The Killer Bees'.

Above: The major IFOR helicopter requirements have been for transport and Casevac (a contingency that never had to be faced).

12th Aviation Brigade, Illesheim AAF, Ansbach, Germany; 12 AVNBDE

11th Aviation (Group) Regiment, Illesheim AAF, Ansbach; 11 AVNGRP
2-6 CAV (AC), Illesheim AAF, Ansbach
OH-58C Scout
UH-60A CS/SAR
AH-64A 24 ATK/Scout
Battalion reassigned 13 OH-58C, 3 UH-60A and went from 18 to 24 AH-64A in 1994

6-6 CAV (AC), Illesheim AAF, Ansbach
OH-58C Scout
UH-60A CS/SAR
AH-64A 24 ATK/Scout
Battalion reassigned 13 OH-58C, 3 UH-60A and went from 18 to 24 AH-64A in 1994

166th Aviation (Group) Regiment, Illesheim AAF, Ansbach; 166 AVNGRP
A Co./5-159 AVN (MHB), Giebelstadt AAF, Mannheim
CH-47D 16 MH

C Co./6-159 AVN (ASLT), Giebelstadt AAF
UH-60L 15 ASLT
Company replaced 15 UH-60A with UH-60L in 1996

C Co./7-158 AVN (ASLT), Wiesbaden AAF
UH-60A ASLT
UH-60A(C) 2 C&C
UH-60L 15 ASLT
Company replaced 15 UH-60A with UH-60L in 1996-97

5-158 AVN (CMD), Wiesbaden AAF
C-12C GS
C-12F 3 GS
U-21A GS
UH-60A 4 CS
UH-60A(C) 4 C&C
4 U-21A replaced by C-12C/F in 1994. 3 C-12C replaced by C-12F in 1995 with some C-12s detached. USARC company of 15 OH-58C inactivated in 1996 in US

205th Military Intelligence Brigade, Wiesbaden AB; 205 MIBDE

1st MI Battalion (Aerial Exploitation), Wiesbaden AAF, Germany; 1 MIB (AE)
RC-12D 1 Training
RC-12K 8 Intel
RC-7B 1 ARL Intel
RC-7B ARL aircraft assigned to unit TDY as needed

4500th Joint STARS Sqn
(Y)E-8A 1 Intel
E-8C 1 Intel
USAF squadron with joint Army/Air Force mission crew, forward-deployed to Rhein Main AB, Frankfurt, Germany from December 1995 to March 1996

1st Armored Division, Bad Kreuznach, Germany; 1AD

Division Support Command, Bad Krueznach; 1AD DISCOM

A Co./127 DASB, Fliegerhorst AAF, Hanau
UH-60A 2 AVIM
Div. Aviation Support Bn

Aviation Brigade/4th Brigade, Fliegerhorst AAF, Hanau; 1AD AVNBDE

2-227 AVN (ATK), Fliegerhorst AAF, Hanau
OH-58C Scout
UH-60A CS/SAR
AH-64A 24 ATK/Scout
Battalion reassigned 13 OH-58C, 3 UH-60A and went from 18 to 24 AH-64A in 1994

3-227 AVN (ATK), Fliegerhorst AAF, Hanau
OH-58C Scout
UH-60A CS/SAR
AH-64A 24 ATK/Scout
Battalion reassigned 13 OH-58C, 3 UH-60A and went from 18 to 24 AH-64A in 1994. To inactivate by 1997

7-227 AVN (GSAB), Fliegerhorst AAF, Hanau
OH-58C 6 TAR
UH-60A GS/ASLT
UH-60A 4 CS
UH-60A(C) 4 C&C
EH-60A 3 Intel
UH-60L 16 GS/ASLT
Unit from replaced 16 UH-60A with UH-60L in 1996

1-1 CAV, Armstrong AHP, Budingen
AH-1F Air Cav
OH-58C Air Cav
OH-58D Air Cav
OH-58D(I) 16 Air Cav
Battalion replaced 12 OH-58C with 12 OH-58D in 1994. Replaced 8 AH-1F, 12 OH-58D with 16 OH-58D(I) in 1996

3-4 CAV, Schweinfurt AAF
AH-1F Air Cav
OH-58C Air Cav
OH-58D(I) Air Cav
Battalion replaced 8 AH-1F, 12 OH-58C with 16 OH-58D(I) in 1995 and reassigned to 1st AD to deploy to Bosnia in 1995. Reflagged as 1-4 AVN in 1996 returning to 1st ID(M)

1st Infantry Division, Wuerzburg, Germany; 1ID(M)
Division reflagged from 3ID(M) in January 1996

Division Support Command, Kitzingen, Germany; 1ID DISCOM
A Co./603 DASB, Katterbach AHP, Ansbach, Germany
UH-60A 2 AVIM
Div. Aviation Support Bn

Aviation Brigade/4th Brigade, Katterbach AHP, Ansbach; 1ID AVNBDE

1-1 AVN (ATK), Katterbach AHP, Ansbach
OH-58C Scout
UH-60A CS/SAR
AH-64A 24 ATK/Scout
Battalion reassigned 13 OH-58C, 3 UH-60A and went from 18 to 24 AH-64A in 1994. Reflagged from 3-1 AVN in 1996

2-1 AVN (GSAB), Katterbach AHP, Ansbach
OH-58C 6 TAR
UH-60A GS/ASLT
UH-60A 4 CS
UH-60A(C) 4 C&C
EH-60A 3 Intel
UH-60L 16 GS/ASLT
Battalion reflagged from 7-1 AVN and 16 UH-60A replaced by UH-60Ls in 1996

1-4 CAV, Schweinfurt AAF, Germany
OH-58D(I) 16 Air Cav
Battalion reflagged from 3-4 CAV in 1996 and returned from duty with 1AD

US Army Land Force Southeast, Cigli Airfield, Izmir, Turkey; USLANDSOUTHEAST/ALFSE

Flight Detachment
C-12F GS
C-12F 2 GS
UH-1H 3 GS
Unit replaced 2 C-12C with C-12F in 1996

Turkey US Logistics Group, Sinop, Turkey; TUSLOG
Flight Detachment
C-12F 1 GS

Eighth US Army (EUSA/8th Army) – South Korea

The Eighth Army (EUSA) is the numbered theatre command that controls US Army forces deployed to the Republic of Korea (RoK). The command and its assigned units are among the key military assets tasked to defend South Korea from aggression or invasion. The command is responsible for the control of all US land warfare assets and their preparation for all possible contingencies.

The 8th Army's headquarters staff oversees the readiness of deployed forces and the rapid reinforcement of US and RoK units if deterrence does not work and opposing forces engage. The operational plans for such reinforcement are highly classified but land warfare assets would be drawn principally from continental US (ConUS) based forces, deployed via air and sealift. Units based in Alaska and Hawaii, including elements of the 10th and 25th Infantry Divisions (Light), would be among the first to provide additional capability if required. I Corps, based at Ft Lewis, Washington is the designated Pacific war-fighting corps and XVIII Airborne Corps, based at Ft Bragg, North Carolina is the contingency corps with worldwide deployment capability. In 1996 III Corps, designated as the heavy reinforcement corps, also deployed units and conducted combat exercises in the theatre. Eighth Army is directly supported by Pacific Air Forces (PACAF) assets assigned to 5th Air Force, Yokota AB, Japan, 7th Air Force, Osan AB, Korea, 11th Air Force, Elmendorf AFB, Alaska and ConUS-based strategic airlift, bomber and strike aircraft assets.

Eighth Army is headquartered at Yongsan garrison in the capital of Seoul. The four-star commander of the theatre has multiple responsibilities, simultaneously acting as commander of the United Nations Command (UNC), US Forces Korea (USFK), and the RoK-US Combined Forces Command (RoK/US CFC, or commonly referred to just as CFC). All of the forces are trained and equipped to conduct and sustain land warfare under a variety of combat scenarios. CFC directly commands over 655,000 allied forces, nearly 95 per cent of them RoK male and female soldiers, with at least 37,000 US men and women in the command structure.

The war that never ended

EUSA became the theatre command for the Korean peninsula during the Korean War, which began on 25 June 1950. A ceasefire was signed in 1953 but an armistice has never been negotiated and even now, nearly 50 years on, the Demilitarized Zone still exists. At peak strength, over 325,000 US soldiers and airmen were assigned to the theatre, three corps commanded American and South Korean manoeuvre forces, and eight active and Army National Guard divisions had served in-theatre, although not all at once.

The Eighth Army units, and its aligned commands, remain faced with a North Korean army of about 1,000,000 soldiers, with roughly two-thirds positioned just north of the DMZ, between 15 and 30 miles (24 and 48 km) from what has to be the most heavily defended border in the world today. The North Koreans' systems are primarily of Soviet design, simple yet effective, and they are supported by a large air force and dense air defence network of radar-controlled missiles and guns. This well-trained and disciplined force suffers from a lack of funding for modernised equipment, along with the rest of the economically and politically isolated country. What it lacks in technology and sustaining power, it compensates with sheer numbers in such areas as soldiers, field artillery guns, theatre ballistic missiles, and an enormous special operations force, believed to number over 100,000 men. The country routinely trains for air, ground and seaborne insertion of its forces. It operates a large fleet of coastal patrol vessels, over 100 An-2 biplanes and at least 55 McDonnell Douglas 500 series helicopters, all utilised for co-ordinated, clandestine attacks.

Unstable nation

The North Korean economy has been described as being on the edge of collapse for most of the last decade and the country has suffered a severe drought since 1995, which has left it without adequate food production for its population. It may surprise Western observers that many people in South Korea regard reunification with North Korea to be a greater probability than an invasion. They point out that recent North Korean missile tests in the Sea of Japan are specifically targeted to impact in close proximity to the Japanese coastline, and proffer this as evidence that North Korea is trying to pick a fight with Japan or threaten its economic and industrial interests, perhaps to refight World War II.

The forces of 8th Army operate alongside the ground forces of the RoK units in the CFC Ground Component Command (CFC-GCC), formerly known as the Combined Field Army (CFA), composed of both US and Republic of Korea soldiers. The RoK army contributes a force structure of 540,000 soldiers operating in 21 divisions, and ample reservists could fill a total of 48 divisions if mobilised. The only US division-sized unit assigned directly to the CFC-GCC is the 2nd Infantry Division, a mechanised infantry and armour force. The 'Indianhead Division' is based north of Seoul, strategically positioned along the border with North Korea to be among the first units that would be engaged by the North if it attempted a potential invasion across the DMZ. Two brigades are based full-time in Korea, and a third has been relocated to Ft Lewis, Washington, prepared to return to the peninsula on short notice. A South Korean armoured brigade is directly assigned to the division, highlighting the close co-operation between the two countries' armies. The division's support command (DISCOM), field artillery (DIVARTY) and aviation brigades (AVNBDE) are also forward-deployed in Korea. Numerous other combat units are assigned at the theatre level, or echelons above corps (EAC), including the 8th Personnel Command, 8th Military Police Brigade, 17th Aviation Brigade, 18th Medical Command, 19th Support Command, 175th Theater Finance Command, 501st Military Intelligence Brigade, Special Operations Command-Korea (SOC-K), and numerous other units based in and outside the theatre.

For the last decade the principal Army aviation forces deployed with the command have been the aviation brigades assigned to 2nd Infantry Division and the 17th Aviation Brigade (17 AVN BDE). The 2nd Infantry's aviation brigade's attack battalion, 1-2 AVN, operated AH-1F HueyCobras until 1996, when they were replaced by AH-64As. 5-17 CAV, reflagged in 1996 as 4-7 CAV, is the division's cavalry battalion. It was among the first Army cavalry units to upgrade its air cavalry troops with the OH-58D(I), beginning training in the type in October 1993, replacing its OH-58As and C-Nite-equipped AH-1Fs. The unit completed its training at Ft Hood, Texas in July 1994 and redeployed to Korea. 2-2 AVN is the brigade's general support aviation battalion and has added UH-60Ls within the last two years. The 2nd's DISCOM commands the division aviation support battalion (DASB) and its assigned AVIM (aviation intermediate maintenance) and vehicle maintenance companies.

The 17th Aviation Brigade is part of the Combined Aviation Force (CAF), or Ground Component Aviation Force (GCAF), assigned to CFC. This joint RoK/US aviation command is composed of at least 14 aviation battalions with almost 400 aircraft assigned, roughly 150 from the US Army. This impressive aviation force is equivalent in size to that assigned to the 101st Airborne Division (Air Assault). RoK army aviation forces are organised along the lines of US Army aviation units and there is extensive symmetry in their doctrine, equipment, organisation and training. South Korean army aviation units operate the UH-1H, AH-1F/J, CH-47D and UH-60P (an indigenously assembled variant equivalent to the UH-60L) along with large numbers of MD 500/530 military variants optimised for gunship, observation, scout, target acquisition and special operations roles. As an example of the interoperability of the forces, in late 1995 a combat team of about 300 soldiers from the 1st Brigade, 1st Cavalry Division was deployed to the peninsula for Exercise Foal Eagle, conducting air assault training with RoK UH-60Ps.

Force improvements

This theatre aviation brigade has undergone significant upgrading and change in the last several years. AH-64A Apaches have only recently (by 1994) replaced the C-Nite-equipped AH-1Fs with the 4th and 5th Battalions of the 501st Aviation Regiment (4-501 & 5-501 AVN). These battalions are technically assigned to I Corps and are forward-deployed to augment the combat capabilities within the theatre. The theatre medium-lift helicopter battalion, 2-52 AVN, was redesignated in 1996 from 2-501 AVN, and operates two companies of Chinooks. They conduct a variety of missions, alongside the CH-47Ds acquired by South Korea in the early 1990s. The 1st Bn/52nd Aviation Regt, also redesignated in 1996 from 1-501 AVN, formerly operated a mixed fleet of fixed-wing transports, UH-1Hs and UH-60 Blackhawks. It has transferred its C-12s to the newly formed 6-52 AVN, a reserve theatre aviation (TA) battalion. The brigade is supported by an AVIM battalion, 3-52 AVN (formerly the 3-501st AVN), and is technically assigned to the 19th Support Command (19 SUPCOM).

Above: VIP Blackhawks detached to the 78th Bn, Zama, Japan have been painted in this high-visibility finish.

Right: Heavylift support for Army units worldwide is the responsibility of the CH-47D fleet.

Above: The Blackhawk is a tactical transport without equal that has also excelled in many special missions roles. US Army contracts for the H-60 currently stand at 1,692 until 2001.

In 1996 the Army began a reorganisation of its aviation assets in the theatre. The change of the regimental affiliation of the 17th Aviation Brigade's battalions from the 501st to the 52nd occurred early in the year. The 52nd is a unit designation with a distinguished history in the Vietnam conflict. In May 1996 the Army began to forward-deploy elements of the 6th Cavalry Brigade (Air Combat) to Korea. This involved the movement of headquarters elements and at least one battalion of Apaches from their base at Hood AAF, Ft Hood, Texas. The 5-501 AVN was redesignated as the 1-6 CAV and also reassigned to this brigade. This move gives 8th Army three aviation brigade formations for the foreseeable future and delineates the available assets to focus on their respective assignments to conduct division, theatre and deep strike missions. It also gives commanders the framework for rapid reinforcement of Army aviation units from ConUS, in case it may be required.

8th US Army, HQ Yongsan, Seoul, RoK; EUSA/8th Army

6th Cavalry Bde (Air Cbt), Desiderio AAF, Camp Humphreys, RoK; 6 ACCB/AVNBDE

Brigade forward-deployed from III Corps, Ft Hood, TX in 1996

1-6 CAV (Air Combat), Camp Eagle, Hoengsong, RoK

OH-58A	13	SCT
UH-60A	3	CS
AH-64A	18	ATK

Battalion activated 1996. Unit to lose OH-58A and UH-60A by 1997 and gain 6 AH-64As

3-6 CAV (Air Combat), Camp Humphreys, Pyongtaek, RoK

AH-64A	24	ATK/SCT

Battalion relocated from Hood AAF, Ft Hood, TX in 1996

17th Aviation Brigade, Seoul AB, Seoul, RoK; 17 AVNBDE

1-52 AVN (CMD), Seoul AB, Seoul, RoK

UH-60A(C)	12	C&C
UH-60A(E)	12	ASLT/CS
OH-58A	6	TAR

Battalion reflagged 1-501 AVN and changed from TA to CMD role in 1996

2-52 AVN (MHB), Camp Humphreys, Pyongtaek, RoK

CH-47D	32	MH

Battalion reflagged from 2-501 AVN (MHB) in 1996

6-52 AVN (TA), Seoul AB, Seoul, RoK

C-12F	8	TA/GS
C-23B/B+		TA/GS

USARC-assigned battalion activated in 1996; 8 C-12Fs assigned in-theatre with remaining 8 C-12Fs and 16 C-23B/B+s to be assigned to USARC units 1996-97

4-501 AVN (ATK), Camp Page, Chunchon, RoK

OH-58A		SCT
UH-60A		CS
AH-64A		ATK

Battalion reflagged to 1-2 AVN and reassigned to 2 ID(M) in 1996

5-501 AVN (ATK), Camp Eagle, Hoengsong, RoK

OH-58A		SCT
UH-60A		CS
AH-64A		ATK

Battalion reflagged to 1-6 CAV and reassigned to 6 ACCB in 1996.

18th Medical Command, Yongsan, Seoul, RoK; 18 MEDCOM

52nd Medical Evacuation Bn, Yongsan, Seoul, RoK; 52 MEB
377th Medical Co. (AA), Seoul AB, RoK

UH-60A	15	AA

542nd Medical Co. (AA), Camp Page, Chunchon, RoK

UH-60A	15	AA

Unit activated 1995

19th Support Command, Camp Henry, Taegu, RoK; 19 SUPCOM

3-52 AVN, (AVIM), Camp Humphreys, Pyongtaek, RoK

UH-60A	4	AVIM

Battalion reflagged from 3-501 AVN in January 1996

501st Military Intelligence Bde, Camp Humphreys, Pyongtaek, RoK; 501 MIBDE

3rd MI Battalion (Aerial Exploitation); 3 MIB (AE)

RC-12D	1	Training
RC-12H	6	Intel
OV-1D		Intel
RV-1D		Intel
RC-7B(ARL)	3	Intel

12 OV-1Ds, 6 RV-1Ds replaced by 3 RC-7B(ARL-M)s in 1996. RC-12D/H to be replaced by RC-12P in 1997

751st MI Battalion

UH-1H	3	Support

Battalion may retire UH-1H by 1997

2nd Infantry Division, Camp Casey, Tongduchon, RoK; 2ID(M)

Division Support Command, Camp Casey, Tongduchon, RoK; 2ID DISCOM
Division Aviation Support Bn (DASB), Camp Stanley, Uijongbu, RoK; C-2 AVN

UH-60A	2	AVIM

Company from 2 UH-1H in 1996

Aviation Brigade, Camp Stanley, Uijongbu, RoK; 2ID AVNBDE
1-2 AVN (ATK), Camp Page, Chunchon, RoK

OH-58A	13	SCT
UH-60A	3	CS
AH-1F(N)		ATK
AH-64A	18	ATK

Battalion reflagged from 4-501 AVN in 1996. Unit to lose 13 OH-58As, 3 UH-60As by 1997 and gain 6 AH-64As

2-2 AVN (GSAB), Camp Stanley, Uijongbu, RoK

OH-58C	6	TAR
UH-60L	16	GS
UH-60A	4	CS
UH-60A(C)	4	C&C
EH-60A	3	Intel

Battalion reformed to GSAB from ASLT role and gained 4 UH-60A(C)s in 1996

4-7 CAV, Camp Edwards, Yono-Re-Ti, RoK

OH-58D(I)	16	AIR CAV

Battalion reflagged from 5-17 CAV in 1996

US Army Pacific (USARPAC)

The US Army Pacific (USARPAC) is the Army component assigned to the US Pacific Command (USPACOM), which is the unified war-fighting command headquartered at Marine Corps Base Camp H. M. Smith, located on a hill overlooking Pearl Harbor, Hawaii. From this command headquarters, the commander-in-chief (CinCPAC) and his staff are assigned the responsibility of maintaining American interests in a territory covering one-third of the earth's surface, from the eastern coast of Africa, northeast to the Southeast Asian land mass, up to the waters bordering Russia, up to the North Pole (including Alaska), along the West Coast of the United States, to a line extending due south from the border of Mexico and Guatemala, to the waters of Antarctica, and everything in between. The distances are enormous and key areas of interest to the US, such as Japan and Korea, are halfway around the world from Washington, DC. The Asia-Pacific theatre of operations includes 100 million sq miles (260 million km^2) bordered by over 50 countries, is home to a population of almost 3 billion people (roughly three-fifths of the world's population), and nearly 40 per cent of all US trade is conducted there.

Stability in the Pacific Rim

The military stakes in the region are high. The seven largest armies in the world reside in this area, collectively with more than 12 million soldiers under arms. Eighty-five per cent of these are ground forces. Despite the occasional flare-ups of minor conflicts, and threatening gestures between long-time adversaries, the area has remained relatively free of large-scale conflict since the early 1970s. This *de facto* stability has led to tremendous international trade, which in turn has spurred internal economic growth among almost all the countries whose livelihood is conducted across or around the Pacific Ocean. Despite the great differences in culture, military affairs and political systems, prosperity continues; much of the credit has to be attributed to the commitment of the United States government, and to its powerful military forces in the region that have repeatedly proved to be able to deter regional warfare. Over 307,000 US soldiers, sailors and airmen were deployed with PACOM by early 1996.

Since the early 1990s the United States has shifted its attention from a basically stable Europe to strengthening its military capabilities in USPACOM in order to maintain the stability of the region. An area of considerable attention to CinCPAC and his staff is the Korean Peninsula, where the Eighth US Army remains ever-vigilant to the potential for conflict along the heavily defended Demilitarized Zone. USPACOM and USARPAC spend considerable resources and time working closely with EUSA elements in the Republic of Korea (RoK), ready to provide combat and support forces for contingency and reinforcement of war-fighting capabilities.

USArmy Pacific was known as the US Western Command (WESTCOM) until 1990, remaining headquartered at Ft Shafter, Hawaii. The command represents the land warfare component of USPACOM, charged with maintaining a flexible and responsive force posture that can deploy and fight anywhere in the region. The active-duty combat forces directly assigned to USARPAC are primarily light forces, capable of rapidly deploying to trouble spots with all their equipment loaded on US Air Force strategic and tactical airlifters. Most are based in the states of Alaska, Hawaii and Washington, and on several of the islands of Japan. USARPAC conducts numerous training and command post exercises (CPXs) with military elements from the countries throughout its area of responsibility, including Australia, Japan, Malaysia, Singapore and Thailand.

'Eye-Corps' spearhead

In 1995, the Army designated I Corps (pronounced eye-corps) as the manoeuvre corps for US Army Pacific, replacing IX Corps, which was realigned and became the 9th Theater Army Area Command (9th TAACOM). IX Corps had acted primarily as a reinforcement corps for US Army Pacific and the Eighth US Army in Korea. That role has been maintained with its redesignation. 9th TAACOM shares its headquarters with USArmy Japan (USARJ) at Camp Zama, outside the city of Tokyo. 9th TAACOM is responsible for maintaining the logistics, support and sustaining capabilities vital to combat forces from its forward location in the western Pacific. It operates facilities for war reserve stocks for use in potential contingencies and maintains a small aviation element to support those efforts. USArmy Japan is a major subordinate command of USARPAC that focuses its time and resources on building working relationships and planning for bilateral training operations with the Japan Ground Self-Defence Force through training and command post exercises. USARJ is also the Army component of the unified subordinate command of US Forces, Japan (USFJ). USAJ/9th TAACOM is staffed with 1,100 personnel on Honshu Island plus another 800 based at Torii Station on Okinawa.

I Corps, headquartered at Ft Lewis, Washington, is assigned to Forces Command (FORSCOM) for training and support during peacetime. In a major force structure reorganisation, the commander of USAPACOM delegated operational control of the I Corps headquarters to US Army Pacific in 1994, designating it as the Army's war-fighting headquarters in the Pacific theatre. The net effect is a closer working relationship between both commands and affirms the focus of the soldiers assigned to this geographically dispersed command. With the inactivation of IX Corps, I Corps has taken over the added responsibility for the land warfare defence of Japan, closely co-ordinating with the JGSDF. The corps trains and deploys to locations throughout the Pacific and is unique in that it constitutes most of its war-fighting capability from reserve component (RC) units, both Army National Guard and US Army Reserve Command (USARC). In the event of a contingency or major conflict, the command would be rapidly reinforced from units assigned to FORSCOM, primarily from XVIII Airborne Corps, and those assigned to US Army Special Operations Command (USASOC).

The principal active-duty war-fighting force available to USARPAC and ICORPS is the 25th Infantry Division (Light), based at Schofield Barracks near Hickam AFB, Hawaii. The division was established there in October 1941. The installation covers 14,000 acres (5670 ha) and soldiers from the division use training facilities on several of the islands, including the Pohakuloa Training Area covering 206,000 acres (83370 ha) northwest of Hilo. One of the division's three infantry brigades recently relocated to Ft Lewis, Washington, which borders McChord AFB; the Hawaii ArNG's 29th Infantry Brigade (Light) regularly trains with the unit.

The division headquarters and two brigades were deployed to Haiti in 1995 to replace units involved in the occupation during Operation Uphold Democracy. Also in that year, the 25th ID deployed a battalion-sized task force to the Multi-national Force and Observers (MFO) stationed between Egypt and Israel in the Sinai Desert. Aircrew of the division's aviation brigade get plenty of practice conducting overwater flights between the Hawaiian islands. Both its attack battalion, 1-25 AVN, and its cavalry squadron, 3-4 AVN (recently reflagged from the 5-9 CAV), made the transition to the OH-58D(I) Kiowa Warriors during 1995-96. The service took over the former Wheeler AFB on 1 November 1991, adding 1,300 acres (525 ha) to the Schofield Barracks reservation which it borders, and redesignating it as an army airfield (AAF).

An extensive logistics and support infrastructure is maintained under the command of US Army, Hawaii. It is enhanced by corps support elements of I Corps, the USARC 9th Army Reserve Command (9th ARCOM) and units of the Hawaii ArNG. The National Guard had operated 1-193 AVN (ATK), an attack battalion of HueyCobras, into the early 1990s when the unit transitioned to the Chinook. The unit initially took delivery of CH-47C aircraft formerly operated by Australia and acquired by the Army when the Royal Australian Army purchased D models. A Special Operations Theater Support Element supports deployments of SF and SOA assets.

US Army, Alaska

US Army, Alaska, a regional command, evolved from elements formerly assigned to the 6th Infantry Division (Light), which was activated in the 1980s and based at Ft Wainwright, Alaska. This division's aviation brigade was unique in that its resources attack unit was an Army Reserve unit, 2-123 AVN (ATK), based at St Paul Downtown Airport, Minnesota. The ASLT and CAV units were based with the division in Alaska and 2-123 AVN was deployed to Alaska a few times to exercise with the rest of the division. The division was inactivated in 1993, along with its aviation brigade, and a single infantry brigade remained in the state, realigning with the 10th Infantry Division in 1996. From the aviation brigade, a single battalion and several detachments remain to provide support.

The 207th Infantry Group (Scout) is an Alaska ArNG-assigned unit composed primarily of native Eskimo who are well adapted to living in the state's harsh and wild terrain. They act as a first-line unit that provides an indigenous defence capability over the barren Alaska wilderness. An organic aviation force operates to a series of

***Above:* Like the other US services Army Aviation has a large fleet of C-12s, which has been bolstered by the acquisition of ex-USAF C-12F/Js.**

***Right:* All Hawaii-based Army Aviation assets, like this 2-25 AVN UH-60A, are stationed at Schofield Barracks, Wheeler AAF.**

***Below:* These ski-equipped CH-47Ds are operated by 4-123 AVN (formerly C Co. /228 AVN), USAR ALASKA, based at Ft Wainright.**

***Above:* This UH-60, with hastily chalked-on exercise markings, is also carrying a door-mounted M60 machine-gun.**

widely dispersed detachments, enabling the unit to maintain its commitments. The assigned aircraft operate with skis in the winter, allowing their operation from glaciers and frozen lakes. It has been announced that one company of Hueys will inactivate in the near future and the unit's UV-18As will reform into a theatre aviation company, and be replaced by another fixed-wing aircraft, under an obscure programme known as the Alaska Support Aircraft (ASA). It is likely that remanufactured C-23B+ aircraft will fill the requirement, perhaps as soon as 1997.

Ft Richardson is adjacent to Elmendorf AFB, which would be a key airlift facility in case of any contingency movement throughout the theatre. The principal war-fighting training centre for Alaska, and allied units in the Pacific, is the Northern Warfare Training Center (NWTC) at Ft Greely. It is scheduled to relocate to Ft Wainwright in 1997.

US Pacific Command, HQ Camp H. M. Smith, Hawaii; USPACOM

(US Army Pacific, HQ Fort Shafter; USARPAC)

US Army Readiness Group, Pacific, Ft Shafter, HI; ARGPAC
USARPAC Flight Detachment, Hickam AFB, HI

C-12D		OSA
C-12F	1	OSA
C-20E	1	OSA/VIP

Unit gained C-20E in 1994 and replaced 1 C-12D with C-12F by November 1995

US Army, Japan/9th Theater Army Area Command, Camp Zama, Japan; USAJ/9 TAACOM

78th Aviation Battalion, Camp Zama, Japan

C-12C		GS
C-12F	2	GS
UH-1H	5	GS
UH-60A	3	GS/VIP

Fixed-wing aircraft based at NAF Atsugi, Japan. Unit replaced 2 C-12C with C-12F by 1996

US Army Alaska, Ft Richardson, AK; USAR ALASKA

Arctic Support Brigade, Ft Richardson, AK; ARTIC SUPBDE
4-123 AVN (TA), Wainwright AAF, Ft Wainwright, AK

CH-47D	16	MH
UH-60A	15	ASLT

Companies reflagged from A Co./123 AVN (ASLT) and C Co./228 AVN (MH) in 1995

F Co./228 AVN (AVIM), Wainwright AAF, Ft Wainwright, AK

UH-60A	1	AVIM

283rd Medical Det. (AA), Wainwright AAF, Ft Wainwright, AK

UH-1V	6	AA

TDY aircraft deployed to Ft Greely

207th Infantry Group (Scout), Anchorage, AK; 207 INFGRP
AK ArNG-assigned unit

1-207 AVN (SCT), Bryant AHP, Ft Richardson, AK

UV-18A	6	TA/GS
UH-1H	15	GS/CS
UH-60L	15	ASLT

AK ArNG-assigned unit with 15 UH-1H to retire by 1997

Detachment 1, Nome AP, AK

UV-18A	1	GS
UH-60L	1	SLT

Forward-deployed detachment

Detachment 2, Bethel AP, AK

UV-18A	1	GS
UH-60L	1	ASLT

Forward-deployed detachment

Detachment 3, Kotzebue AP, AK

UV-18A	1	GS
UH-60L	1	ASLT

Forward-deployed detachment

Detachment 4, Juneau AP, AK

UV-18A	1	GS
UH-60L	1	ASLT

Forward-deployed detachment

23rd AVN Det (AVIM), Bryant AHP, Ft Richardson, AK

UH-60L	1	AVIM

AK ArNG-assigned unit

Det 1, 1085th Medical Co. (AA), Bryant AHP, Ft Richardson, AK

UH-1V	6	AA

AK ArNG-assigned unit with rest of unit assigned to SD ArNG

US Army Garrison AVN Det, Wainwright AAF, Ft Wainwright, AK

C-12D	2	GS

US Army Garrison AVN Det., Allen AAF, Ft Greely, AK

UH-1H	3	GS

I Corps, HQ Ft Lewis, WA; ICORPS
FORSCOM-assigned unit

45th Corps Support Group (Forward), Schofield Barracks, HI; 45 COSGRP (FWD)
C Co./193rd AVN (MH), Wheeler AAF, Schofield Barracks, HI

CH-47C		MH
CH-47D	8	MH

HI ArNG-assigned unit replaced 8 CH-47C with CH-47D in 1996

B Co./214th AVN (MH), Wheeler AAF, Schofield Barracks, HI

CH-47D	8	MH

Unit relocated from NAS Barbers Point in 1996

E Co./214th AVN (AVIM), Wheeler AAF, Schofield Barracks, HI

UH-1H		AVIM
UH-60A	2	AVIM

Unit replaced 2 UH-1H with UH-60A in 1996

68th Medical Det (AA), Hickam AFB, HI

UH-1H/V		AA
UH-60A	6	AA

Unit replaced 6 UH-1H/V with UH-60A 1995

25th Infantry Division (Light), Schofield Barracks, HI; 25ID(L)

Division Support Command, Schofield Barracks, HI; 25ID DISCOM

C/25 AVN Co. (AVIM), Wheeler AAF, Schofield Barracks, HI

UH-60A	2	AVIM

Unit reflagged from H/25 AVN in 1996

Aviation Brigade, Schofield Barracks, HI; 25ID AVNBDE

1-25 AVN (ATK), Wheeler AAF, Schofield Barracks, HI

UH-1H		CS
AH-1F		ATK
OH-58C		SCT
OH-58D(I)	24	ATK/SCT

Replaced 21 AH-1F, 3 UH-1H, 13 OH-58C with 24 OH-58D(I) in 1995

2-25 AVN (ASLT), Wheeler AAF, Schofield Barracks, HI

UH-60A		ASLT
UH-60A	4	CS
UH-60A(C)	4	C&C
EH-60A	3	Intel
UH-60L	30	ASLT

Battalion replaced 30 UH-60A with UH-60L in 1995. Unit reflagged from 4-25 AVN in 1996

3-4 CAV (RECON), Wheeler AAF, Schofield Barracks, HI

UH-1H		CS
AH-1F		Air Cav
OH-58C		Air Cav
OH-58D(I)	16	Air Cav

Battalion replaced 1 UH-1H, 8 AH-1F, 12 OH-58C with 16 OH-58D(I) in October 1995. Unit reflagged from 5-9 CAV in 1996

US Army South (USARSO)

The US Army South (USARSO) is the Army command element of the US Southern Command (USSOUTHCOM or SOUTHCOM), responsible for US military operations in and around the countries of the Americas, specifically those of Central and South America. The area of interest includes a land area measuring 3,000 by 7,000 miles (4830 by 11265 km) and a population of over 350 million people. SOUTHCOM's geographic area of interest begins at the US/Mexico border, continues to the island nations of the Caribbean Sea basin and to the countries of Central and South America. This includes peripheral portions of both the Atlantic and Pacific Oceans. SOUTHCOM is making preparations to relocate to Miami, Florida in the next few years and USARSO will follow.

The Panama Canal

Historically, United States interests in the region were focused around the defence of the Panama Canal. Ulntil 1903 Panama was a province of Colombia and an uprising conducted with the tacit endorsement of then-President Theodore Roosevelt led to its independence. US economic interests quickly began to build the canal, and US Army troops were deployed to the country to provide security to construction crews. The US was granted rights to protect a 10-mile (16-km) buffer zone on either side of the canal after its completion by developers in 1914, and soldiers are still deployed to the country. During World War II the canal became the focal point for the defence of the western Caribbean Sea and the approaches along the coast of Central and South America. It was heavily reinforced by air and ground forces to guard against the threat of invasion by Germany or Japan. After the war, US military activity retrenched to the Canal Zone. The change of governments in Cuba in 1959 brought renewed interest in the region and for the next 30 years American forces based in Panama became heavily involved in supporting the governments of the region in their efforts to counter insurgencies and civil wars. In 1977 the United States agreed to a treaty with Panama to return the canal to that government, effective at noon on 31 December 1999.

US Army South (USARSO) is the smallest of the Army theatre commands, with barely 5,000 active-duty troops remaining in 1996. The command has always used active-duty and reserve component troops to perform temporary duty (TDY) missions of up to six months in length, to augment the assigned forces. This has been the case since the 1980s when SOUTHCOM broadened its mission from just guarding access to the Panama Canal, and it began to be used to actively support the governments in El Salvador and Honduras against internal insurgencies. The command has also been active in performing various counter-drug operations, in assistance to host countries and in interdiction missions across international borders. From 1993-95, more than 80,000 reserve component soldiers, from all the service branches, conducted training missions in Latin America. Combat reinforcement to USARSO would likely come from the contingency tasked units assigned to I Corps and XVIII Airborne Corps, both assigned to Forces Command (FORSCOM) during peacetime.

Operations in the Americas

USARSO is headquartered at Quarry Heights, Panama, near SOUTHCOM headquarters. Both headquarters are scheduled to be relocated to Miami, Florida by 1998 and some units have begun to relocate to continental US bases. The vast majority of USARSO assets have been based in Panama, and are routinely detached to serve in other Central and South American countries, when invited. The command was reinforced with soldiers from the 5th Infantry Division (Mechanized), 7th Infantry Division (Light), the 82nd Airborne Division and the 160th Special Operations Aviation Group in the invasion of Panama in December 1989, known as Operation Just Cause. The command has been involved in maintaining the feeding, shelter and medical treatment of tens of thousands of Cuban and Haitian political refugees that were detained at the Guantanamo Naval Station from 1994 to early in 1996. Recently, the command deployed several UH-60As to support Operation Safe Border, a multi-national observer force that operates along the disputed Ecuador-Peru border, tasked to keep the two countries from fighting over the territory.

The command theatre aviation brigade, the 128th Aviation Brigade, is reported to have inactivated in 1995. At its peak, the brigade controlled over 130 aircraft, in two battalions and a few detachments. Additional units that were formerly tasked to support the theatre were USARC-assigned 2-228 Aviation and the ArNG's 1-192 AVN, a theatre defence aviation battalion (TDAB). The remnants of the first and fourth battalions of 228 AVN remain available in-theatre. Less than 30 aircraft remain assigned and are expected to consolidate within the 4-228 AVN based at Soto Cano AB, Honduras, sometime by 1997. The units are also augmented with temporary duty (TDY) active and reserve components deployed from FORSCOM. An Army National Guard C-12F has been detached to the theatre over the last few years, flown by aircrews deployed from the numerous state ArNG flight dets. The main operating base for the 128th AVN BDE has been Ft Kobbe, Panama, which shares the ramp space with Howard AFB. The 4th Bn/228th Aviation Regt was activated in Honduras in the 1980s, with some of their aircraft operating in support of US military activities in El Salvador during that country's civil war.

Clandestine ops

The other remaining battalion-sized aviation unit assigned is the Military Intelligence Battalion (Low Intensity) (MI BN(LI)), based at Orlando International Airport, Florida. The unit has many of its assets forward-deployed throughout the USARSO geographic area of responsibility. The unit had operated RU-21H Guardrail V aircraft after their withdrawal from Europe through 1994. They were supplemented by the RU-21A/B/C aircraft assigned to the Army Reserve unit, the 138th Aviation Company. The battalion gained three specially modified RC-12G aircraft in a programme known as Crazyhorse in 1991, with these aircraft tasked to perform low-technology Sigint missions, probably against drug smugglers and indigenous guerrilla movements. By 1994 the command gained three Bombardier/de Havilland Canada DHC-7s specially configured for surveillance missions in a programme known as Airborne Reconnaissance Low. The aircraft are capable of operating at forward locations after self-deploying over long ranges. Two of the aircraft were originally configured with mission packages optimised for Comint and the third for Imint. By late 1995 the command may have received three additional aircraft, all configured with both sensor packages, which allowed the original aircraft to be withdrawn for retrofitting with the complete system packages, to perform as multi-purpose surveillance platforms. The sensor data can also be off-loaded directly to ground-based units. The type is reported to have gained the designation of RC-7B by 1995. (One source has indicated that the battalion has relocated to Patrick AFB, Florida, but that has not been confirmed to date.)

There has been little public discussion about the extensive involvement of US Army special forces and special operations aviation assets that have been used extensively. The 3rd Battalion/160th SOAR has a detached company of MH-60Ls assigned to the theatre and they are regularly supplemented by platoons of additional SOA aircraft on TDY missions from their Stateside bases. The aircraft support counter-drug missions, providing covert transportation of US

Above: Despite the dominance of the UH-60, substantial numbers of UH-1s continue to serve front-line units, in second-line roles.

Left: This Hawaii-based UH-60 takes advantage of Wheeler AAF's fresh-water spray system after low-level operations over the sea.

Above: UH-60As and UH-60Ls are widely used by the Army's medical evacuation units – in many cases still operating alongside the UH-1V.

and host nation military forces assisting law enforcement agencies such as the US Department of Justice's Drug Enforcement Agency. These aviation assets are often supported by AFSOC assets including AC-130E/U gunships and MC-130 transports and air refuelling assets.

US Southern Command, HQ Quarry Heights, Panama; USSOUTHCOM (US Army South, HQ Ft Clayton, Panama; USARSO)

Special Operations Command, South, Ft Kobbe, Panama; SOC-SOUTH
D/3-160 SOAR

MH-60L	10	SOA

Company redesignated from 617th SOA Det in 1995. Unit detached from 3-160 SOAR, Hunter AAF, GA

142nd Medical Evacuation Bn, Ft Clayton, Panama; 142 MEB
214 Medical Det. (AA), Albrook AFS, Ft Clayton, Panama

UH-60A	6	AA

128th Aviation Brigade, Ft Clayton, Panama; 128 AVNBDE
Brigade inactivated 199

1-228 AVN, (TA), Howard AFB, Ft Kobbe, Panama

C-12F	3	GS
CH-47D	8	MH
UH-60A	2	C&C
UH-60A	2	AVIM

1 C-12F detached from DC ArNG, Fixed Wing Det with TDY ArNG aircrews. ASLT company with 15 UH-60A inactivated in 1994. Remaining aircraft to reassign to 4-228 AVN by 1997

4-228 AVN (ASLT), Soto Cano AB, Comayagua, Honduras

UH-60A	15	ASLT
UH-60A	1	AVIM

Battalion to gain units from 1-228 AVN by 1997

Puerto Rico ArNG TARC Flight Detachment

C-12F	1	GS/OSA
C-23B	1	GS
UH-1H	2	GS

PR ArNG-assigned unit. Muniz ArNG, San Juan IAP, PR

Virgin Islands ArNG TARC Flight Detachment

C-23B	1	GS
UH-1H	2	GS

VI ArNG-assigned unit. Alexander Hamilton AP, St Croix, VI

470th Military Intelligence Brigade, Ft Clayton, Panama; 470 MIBDE

Military Intelligence Bn, (Low Intensity), Orlando IAP, FL; MIB(LI)

DHC-7	2	Training/GS
RC-7B	3	Intel
RC-12D		Training
C-12F	1	GS
RC-12G		Intel
RU-21H		Intel

Two active-duty companies inactivated by 1995 with 9 RU-21H, 1 RC-12D, 3 RC-12G reassigned or retired

138 MI Company

RU-21H		Intel
RC-12D	1	Training
RC-12G	3	Intel

USARC-assigned unit replaced 6 RU-21H with RC-12D/G in 1995

Forces Command (FORSCOM)

The Army's Forces Command (FORSCOM) is a major command of the Department of the Army tasked to train, mobilise and project strategic land forces worldwide. Its headquarters is at Ft McPherson, Georgia, located on the western periphery of Atlanta. FORSCOM is composed of all continental US (ConUS) active-duty, ArNG and USARC units and personnel not directly assigned to another unified command, such as those assigned to the US Special Operations Command (USSOCOM). FORSCOM is also tasked to plan for the land defence of the continental US and Canada, to provide military support to civil authorities during disasters and emergency situations and support federal law enforcement efforts as needed. The command controls nearly 80 per cent of the service's 495,000 active soldiers and nearly all of the reserve component (RC) force, expected to number 582,000 in FY97. Collectively, FORSCOM provides over two-thirds of the Army's total war-fighting capability. The command headquarters spends much of its time preparing these forces to deploy to potential battlefields and contingencies anywhere in the world, to deter aggression, to project power and to enforce political objectives, to conduct operations other than war, or to destroy adversarial military forces.

Forces Command was activated in the 1980s to establish a cadre of units that could be used to reinforce and sustain forward-deployed forces with the theatre commands. FORSCOM was redesignated from a separate DoD command to the land warfare element of the US Atlantic Command (USACOM, formerly USLANTCOM), the unified war-fighting command, on 1 October 1993. USACOM is headquartered in Norfolk, Virginia and during the Cold War was primarily tasked with keeping the sea lanes of the North and South Atlantic Ocean free from air, surface and submarine threats. Since its realignment, the command's mission has been broadened to provide US military forces where needed and to ensure that they have been trained to operate in joint forces assignments. FORSCOM focuses its resources in order to plan and execute land force operations within the USACOM area of responsibility and to protect US national security interests, an example of which is the drug war. The four-star general commanding FORSCOM also functions as the commander of the Army forces of USACOM.

FORSCOM maintained 17 major installations and at least as many smaller installations during 1995. The command is composed of at least 235,000 male and female active-duty soldiers and about 600,000 reserve component soldiers in strategic reserve, making it the largest Army command, with nearly two-thirds of the Army's total combat forces and a corresponding proportion of aviation assets. Several echelons of command are assigned to FORSCOM, any of which can be assigned and deployed to any designated theatre or unified command. During peacetime, FORSCOM commands the Third US Army (THREEUSA), also headquarted at Ft McPherson. During Operation Desert Shield/Storm, THREEUSA was mobilised to deploy to Saudi Arabia. Within five months, FORSCOM and THREEUSA deployed nearly 200,000 active and reserve soldiers, 2,000 tanks, 1,500 aircraft, and tens of thousands of vehicles, infantry fighting vehicles and large-calibre guns. Upon the cessation of hostilities, THREEUSA returned to Ft McPherson to prepare for any potential conflicts that could arise in the region in the future; all its forces are maintained on computers and paper, until they may be mobilised and requisitioned again.

Training at the NTC and JRTC

Combat training is the focal point of FORSCOM and among the premier assets of those efforts are the combat training centres (CTCs). The best known of the CTCs is the National Training Center (NTC) at Ft Irwin, California, which trains armour and mechanised infantry forces in manoeuvre warfare tactics in desert terrain that closely emulates that found in Southwest Asia. Brigade-sized task forces deploy for realistic and sophisticated training exercises against well-honed adversary forces that utilise the manoeuvre tactics of the former Soviet Union. A mechanised, land warfare aggressor force, the Opposing Force (OPFOR), is known as the Red Guards and closely follow the warfighting doctrine and tactics of massed armour formations developed by the former Soviet Union and still used by many military forces around the world. The Army unit, officially designated as the 11th Armored Cavalry Regiment, is equipped with actual and surrogate threat weapons and support systems including tanks, infantry fighting vehicles, communication systems and vehicles. The OPFOR utilises a company of 'Hueys', some of which have received rudimentary modifications so that they roughly resemble Mi-24/25s. Actual threat aircraft types assigned to OTSA/OPTEC routinely deploy to provide added threat realism. Fixed-wing, close air support sorties are provided by the Air Force which stages simultaneous Air Warrior exercises from Nellis AFB, Nevada to add to the complexity of the exercises. A small force of OH-58s, assigned to TRADOC, provides transportation for the observer/controllers who act as referees, safety co-ordinators and independent evaluators of the units being trained (see *World Air Power Journal* Volumes 26 and 27).

FORSCOM took command of the Joint Readiness Training Center (JRTC) from the Training and Doctrine Command (TRADOC) when the centre relocated from Little Rock AFB, Arkansas to Ft Polk, Louisiana in 1993. JRTC focuses on training light infantry and special operations forces in contingency operations that cover a variety of scenarios including those involving civilian and military hostages, disaster and humanitarian relief, military operations in urban terrain (MOUT) and peacekeeping assistance roles. The terrain consists primarily of thick pine forests. The centre offers unique training sites such as a mock airfield, a simulated military complex and a city complex covering 2.7 sq miles (7 km^2) that is used for urban warfare simulations; the latter was recently named the Shughart Gordon Main City Complex in honour of the heroism of two soldiers in the streets of Mogadishu, Somalia in October 1993, who were posthumous recipients of the Congressional Medal of Honor.

The OPFOR for JRTC is an airborne infantry unit (1-509 INF (ABN)) and is supported by TDY special forces and a permanent OTSA/OPTEC detachment of threat aircraft. It is known to conduct unexpected parachute and helicopter air assaults from these aircraft and a small force of Blackhawks that operates with the centre's flight detachment. The Air Force provides airlift. Air Warrior II exercises are co-ordinated with the rotations, with strike aircraft such as A-10s and F-16s providing close air support. These aircraft are based at locations away from JRTC, including Barksdale AFB, NAS New Orleans and Alexandria International Airport (formerly England AFB) in Louisiana, Little Rock AFB in Arkansas and civilian facilities such as Ellington Field at Houston, Texas. In the last few years, international participation has increased with NATO and Eastern Europe forces deployed under a combined political and military initiative called Partnership for Peace (PFP). The reputation of JRTC is such that other military forces have come from as far as Australia to test their skills against the technology, terrain and training in engagements at the centre. The value of such diverse training, to all sides, is incalcuable.

FORSCOM and Force XXI

Forces Command is also responsible for a series of Advanced Warfighting Experiments (AWEs) and Battle Command Training Programs (BCTPs). The experiments are usually wrapped around field exercises that are used to demonstrate and evaluate doctrine, technology and tactics. The command is one of several that is involved in the Force XXI programme, in which digital network technology will be used to link all elements on the battlefield from the individual infantry solider on the ground to the National Command Authority (NCA). The objective of this AWE is to send a brigade-sized task force to NTC in early 1997 to test the developments in the field. BCTP exercises are sophisticated command post exercises conducted in simulated tactical operations centres at Ft Leavenworth, Kansas. They involve little or no actual movement of combat forces in the field but are orientated to rotations of corps and division-level battle staffs. These exercises will increasingly use linked systems simulators that emulate all land warfare systems including armour, aviation, field artillery, infantry, intelligence and logistics, tied through data networks to other facilities in ConUS, and eventually around the world.

Among the better-known field exercises conducted by FORSCOM is Roving Sands, played out annually in thousands of square miles of the western US. This exercise is undertaken for the benefit of air defence artillery (ADA) forces which make their branch home at Ft Bliss, Texas. Opposing air forces from Air Force, Army, Marine Corps and Navy units deploy to several sites in New Mexico and Texas to conduct force-on-force air battles with the objective of allowing ADA units to influence the air battle and demonstrate ways of preventing fratricide, or 'friendly fire'. Roving Sands has also been used to integrate new or emerging technologies into these fluid engagements, and in recent years additional experiments in data communication interoperability, co-operative engagement, theatre missile defence (TMD), unmanned aerial vehicles (UAVs) and other classified systems have all participated in the exercise. FORSCOM units have been integral to another joint force exercise, All Source Combat Identification Evaluation Team, held over the Gulf of Mexico annually.

FORSCOM's armies

To co-ordinate and supervising the training of reserve component (RC) forces, the Army had operated five geographically dispersed, active-duty numbered ConUS armies into the early 1990s. The First US Army (ONEUSA) at Ft George G. Meade, Maryland, the Second US Army (TWOUSA) at Ft Gillem, Georgia, the Fourth US Army (FOURUSA) at Ft Sheridan, Illinois, the Fifth US Army (FIVEUSA) at Ft Sam Houston, Texas and the Sixth US Army (SIXUSA) which relocated from the Presidio of San Francisco, California to Ft Carson, Colorado before it was inactivated. ONEUSA and FOURUSA were also inactivated in recent years and ONEUSA reflagged the TWOUSA command headquarters element. Today, ONEUSA supervises units east of the Mississippi River and FIVEUSA supervises the units based to the west. These headquarters continue to report to FORSCOM. RC forces are more integral than ever to US Army plans and operations, and every operation since Operation Desert Storm has made use of RC personnel. The deployment of Army soldiers to the Multi-national Force and Observers to the Sinai desert in 1995 was executed with a battalion force with 21 per cent active component forces, 71 per cent ArNG and 8 percent Army Reserve.

The Army National Guard maintains a number of units that perform depot- or intermediate-level maintenance on active and reserve component aviation platforms. They report to the ConUS armies during peacetime but if they are activated they will usually be assigned at the theatre level. These units fall under several designations depending on their assigned roles and mission. They include Aviation Classification Repair Activity Depots (AVCRADs), Theatre Army Maintenance Companies (TAMC) and Aviation Intermediate Maintenance Companies (AVIMs). During peacetime they report to ONEUSA and FIVEUSA and are supervised by the Mobilization AVCRAD Control Element (MACE), which is a mobilisation headquarters for these maintenance units that have also been referred to as Aviation Depot Maintenance Roundout Units (ADMRUs).

FORSCOM commands reserve component forces that are designed to augment the capability of active component forces (AC) that are with

Above: This OH-58 was attached to the National Training Center at Fort Irwin and operated from Barstow-Daggett AP.

Below: C Co./3-159 AVN operates these much-modified 'Aggressor' JUH-1Hs to train armoured units during NTC exercises.

Right: Former-Soviet types, such as this Kamov Ka-28 Double Trouble, are flown by OPTEC/OPFOR to provide added realism during NTC and other exercises.

the command or deployed to theatre commands. The US Army Reserve Command (USARC) commands and sustains Army Reserve units in ConUS and overseas. Army Reserve forces are funded directly with federal US appropriations and can be called to active duty at short notice. USARC has been involved in a major reorganisation in the last few years and the component is now being orientated as the Army's primary provider of combat service support capability. A substantial aviation force has been inactivated. USARC is expected to maintain five aviation battalions, two fixed-wing theatre aviation units, two attack battalions and a CH-47D-equipped medium helicopter battalion.

The National Guard Bureau (NGB), through the Army National Guard (ArNG), has commands in all 50 states, the District of Columbia and the territories of Guam, Puerto Rico and the Virgin Islands. Its funding is separately appropriated by Congress and, while it is generated at the federal level, it is administered through the respective state governments by a series of legal agreements. The call-up of ArNG units to active duty is more structured towards short-term deployments, except in cases of extreme emergencies. The aviation units of ArNG are also in the middle of reorganising, with many units standing down only to be reconstituted with different aircraft types and roles. By the end of 1996, ArNG still operated nearly 2,500 aircraft, about 200 of which are fixed-wing, the remainder rotary-winged.

Forces Command, HQ Ft McPherson, Atlanta, GA; FORSCOM

US Army Garrison (USAG)
UH-1H 2 GS
Flight Detachment at Brown Field, Fulton County AP, Atlanta, GA

First US Army, HQ Ft Gillem, GA; ONEUSA
Aviation Readiness Group

Mobilization AVCRAD Control Element, Weide AAF, Aberdeen PG, MD; MACE
C-23B 1 GS
Flight Activity

1204th TAMC, Weide AAF, Aberdeen PG, MD
UH-1H 1 GS
UH-60L 1 GS
Flight Activity

1109th AVCRAD, Groton-New London AP, CT
C-23B 2 GS
UH-1H 2 GS
Flight Activity

1108th AVCRAD, Gulfport-Biloxi Regional AP, MS
C-23B 2 GS
UH-1H 2 GS
Flight Activity

US Army Garrison (USAG), Ft Buchanan, PR
UH-1H 2 GS
Flight Detachment

Fifth US Army, HQ Ft Sam Houston, San Antonio, TX; FIVEUSA

US Army Garrison (USAG)
UH-1H GS
Flight Detachment at Martindale AAF, San Antonio. Unit reassigned from FORSCOM to MEDCOM in October 1995 with 2 UH-1H

1106th AVCRAD, Fresno Air Terminal, CA
C-23B 2 GS
UH-1H 2 GS

1105th/1107th AVCRAD, Springfield MAP, MO
C-23B 2 GS
UH-1H 2 GS

National Training Center, HQ Ft Irwin, CA; NTC

11th Armored Cavalry Regiment/Opposing Force; 11 ACR/OPFOR

C Co./3-159 AVN (ASLT), Barstow-Daggett AP, CA
UH-1H 17 GS
JUH-1H 6 Aggressor

247th Medical Det. (AA), Barstow-Daggett AP, CA
UH-60A 6 AA

Joint Readiness Training Center, HQ Ft Polk, LA; JRTC

36th Medical Det. (AA), Polk AAF, Ft Polk, LA
UH-1V 6 AA

Multinational Force & Observers, El Gorah, Sinai Peninsula, Egypt

1st US Army Support Battalion, Opira Airfield
UH-1H 10 GS
UH-60A GS
10 UH-1H to be replaced by UH-60A in 1997

I Corps

I Corps, commonly known as 'Eye Corps', is a contingency corps that has undergone significant change in its force structure and roles. The corps had been assigned to Korea from 1950 until it was replaced by the US/Korea Combined Field Army in 1980. The command was reconstituted in 1981 at Ft Lewis, Washington, outside Tacoma, with a primary mission of reinforcing the Pacific theatre and a secondary mission of European reinforcement. From the 1980s the units of ICORPS have had to train for a wide variety of potential warfare scenarios including facing armour units in Europe, jungle warfare in Asia, desert warfare in the Middle East and urban warfare (which was actually conducted in Panama during Operation Just Cause in December 1989). At its peak in the late 1980s, the corps was organised with three active-duty light infantry divisions: the 6th, based at Ft Wainwright, Alaska, which was reassigned to US Army Pacific; the 7th, based and inactivated at Ft Ord, California in 1990; and the Ft Lewis-based 9th, also known as a motorised division, equipped with a unique variety of vehicles to manoeuvre over open terrain features such as desert or tundra.

I Corps supports two individual manoeuvre brigades at Ft Lewis that are directly assigned to the 2nd Infantry and the 25th Infantry Divisions, one constituted from the remnants of the 9th Infantry and the other relocated from Schofield Barracks, Hawaii. On paper, the combat power of ICORPS is composed of several ArNG divisions and enhanced armour and infantry brigades that train with and are supported by I Corps. If called to active duty, most of these units would undergo a brief 30-90-day training period before being classified as combat ready. If the corps had to forward-deploy to the Pacific theatre in an emergency, it would likely constitute much of its war-fighting force from active component units drawn from III Corps and XVIII Airborne Corps. The corps aviation brigade and most of its support elements are also assigned to RC units, which have begun a process of change owing to the ongoing reorganisation of the Army National Guard and Army Reserves.

The corps is unique in that its principal combat aviation force, the 66th Aviation Brigade, is assigned to the Washington ArNG. This brigade is composed of active-duty, ArNG and USARC units scattered over at least a dozen states. With the changes brought about by ARI, the brigade is undergoing a major reorganisation of its assigned units. The 185th Aviation Group, Mississippi ArNG, has assumed command of the assault, command, combat support, light utility and medium lift battalions. The 540th Aviation Group, also assigned to the Washington ArNG, was to have commanded the attack helicopter battalions, but it now appears that the 211th Aviation Group (Utah ArNG) will be the unit designation. The brigade has commanded two active-duty Apache battalions, the 4th and 5th Battalions/501st Aviation Regiment (Attack) that were forward deployed to Korea, serving with 17th Aviation Brigade. Both 4-501 and 5-501 AVN were redesignated in 1996, one taking over as the attack battalion with 2nd Infantry Division and the other being reassigned to the 6th Cavalry Brigade, with both units being reflagged in the process. Some of the attack units assigned to the brigade are also believed to have a European reinforcement role. The ArNG units assigned to 66th Aviation Brigade may continue to change designations and flags for the next year or two as the force makes adjustments to its structure under the ARI programme, which is expected to be completed by 1999.

The 103rd Corps Support Command (103 COSCOM) oversees numerous combat support and combat service support units attached to the corps. The brigade-sized unit maintains AVIM and medical evacuation aviation units for I Corps. The air ambulance/medical evacuation companies attached have remained relatively stable, so far, as the ArNG reorganises its assets. Several of the assigned detachments have changed alignments.

ICORPS has assigned several armoured cavalry regiments in the last 10 years. The 116th ACR, assigned to the Idaho ArNG, with its aviation element based at Camp Murray, Washington, was assigned with the corps until at least 1990 when it was redesignated as the 116th Cavalry Brigade. It was replaced by the 2nd ACR which inactivated in Germany in January 1992 but was reactivated later that year at Ft Lewis as a LIGHT ACR. By October 1993 that brigade-sized unit was relocated to Ft Polk and reassigned to XVIII Airborne Corps. It was replaced with the Tennessee ArNG's 278th ACR and its aviation element, 4-278 ACR. This ACR is now likely to be equipped with the Bell OH-58D(I) from 1997, allowing its aviation element greater capability and deployability.

I Corps, HQ Ft Lewis, WA; ICORPS

103rd Corps Support Command, Des Moines, IA; 103 COSCOM
USARC-assigned unit

1-109 AVN (AVIM), Boone MAP, IA
IA ArNG-assigned unit

E Co./106 AVN (AVIM), Midway AP, Chicago, IL

UH-1H		AVIM
UH-60A	2	AVIM

IL ArNG-assigned unit replaced 2 UH-1H with UH-60A in 1996

D Co./109 AVN (AVIM), Boone MAP, IA

UH-1H		AVIM
UH-60A	2	AVIM

IA ArNG-assigned unit replaced 2 UH-1H with UH-60A in 1996

D Co./137 AVN (AVIM), Akron-Canton AP, N. Canton, OH

UH-1H		AVIM
UH-60A	2	AVIM

OH ArNG-assigned unit replaced 2 UH-1H with UH-60A in 1996

F Co./228 AVN (AVIM), St Paul Downtown AP, MN

UH-1H		AVIM

USARC-assigned unit in activated in 1996

62nd Medical Group, Ft Lewis, WA; 62 MEDGRP

85th Medical Evacuation Bn; 85MEB

54th Medical Co. (AA), Gray AAF, Ft Lewis

UH-1V	15	AA

Active-duty unit

126th Medical Co. (AA), Mather AP, Sacramento, CA

UH-1V	15	AA

CA ArNG-assigned unit

717th Medical Co. (AA), Santa Fe MAP, NM

UH-1V	15	AA

NM ArNG-assigned unit with 6 UH-1V with Det 1 (NV ArNG) at Reno-Stead AP, NV

1022nd Medical Co. (AA), Cheyenne MAP, WY

UH-1V	15	AA

WY ArNG-assigned unit with 6 UV-1V with Det 1 (CO ArNG) at Buckley ANGB, Aurora, CO

1042nd Medical Co. (AA), McNary Field, Salem, OR

UH-1V	15	AA

OR ArNG-assigned unit

1085th Medical Co. (AA), Rapid City RAP, SD

UH-1V	15	AA

UT ArNG-assigned unit with 6 UH-1V with Det 1 (MT ArNG) at Helena RAP, MT

1187th Medical Co. (AA), Boone MAP, IA

UH-1V	15	AA

IA ArNG assigned unit with 6 UH-1V with Det 1 (MN ArNG) at St Paul Downtown AP, MN

1250th Medical Co. (AA), West Jordan AP, UT

UH-1V	15	AA

UT ArNG-assigned unit

66th Aviation Brigade, Camp Murray, Tacoma, WA; 66 AVNBDE
WA ArNG-assigned unit

185th Aviation Group, Jackson MAP, MS; 185AVNGRP
MS ArNG-assigned unit

1-108 AVN (ASLT), Forbes Field, Topeka, KS

UH-1H		ASLT
UH-60A	30	ASLT

KS ArNG-assigned unit replaced 45 UH-1H with UH-60A in 1996 with a company in OK ArNG

2-135 AVN (CSAB), Buckley ANGB, Aurora, CO

UH-1H		ASLT
UH-60A	30	ASLT

CO ArNG-assigned unit activated in 1995 to replace UH-1H with 32 UH-60A in 1997-98

2-126 AVN (LUH), Otis ANGB, Falmouth, MA

UH-1H	32	LUH

MA ArNG-assigned unit with companies in CT, MA and VT ArNG

3-140 AVN (MHB), Stockton MAP, CA
CA ArNG-assigned unit replaced 6-158 AVN(MH) in 1995

G Co./3-140 AVN, Stockton MAP, CA

CH-47D	16	MH

CA ArNG-assigned unit with 8 CH-47D at Det 1 (NV ArNG) at Reno-Stead AP, NV

C Co./193 AVN (MH), Wheeler AAF, Schofield Barracks, HI

CH-47D	8	MH

HI ArNG-assigned unit

B Co./214 AVN (MH), Wheeler AAF, Schofield Barracks, HI

CH-47D	8	MH

USARPAC-assigned unit relocated from NAS Barbers Pt in 1995

C Co./214 AVN (MH), Lewis AAF, Ft Lewis, WA

CH-47D	16 MH	

Active-duty unit

1-185 AVN (CMD), Jackson MAP, MS

C-12F	5	GS
U-21A		GS
UH-1H		CS/C&C
UH-60A	24	CS/C&C
OH-58D(I)	15	TARC

MS ArNG-assigned unit replaced 30 UH-1H with UH-60A and 5 U-21A with C-12F in 1996

1-214 AVN (ASLT), AFRC Los Alamitos, CA

UH-1H		ASLT

USARC-assigned unit inactivated in 1996, 46 UH-1H retired

211th Aviation Group (Regiment), W. Jordan, UT; 211 AVNGRP
UT ArNG-assigned unit

1-168 AVN (ATK), Gray AAF, Ft Lewis, WA

AH-1F	21	ATK
UH-1H	3	CS
OH-58A	13	SCT

Above: This UH-60, on strength with the 101st Airborne Division, is seen waiting in a clearing from another Blackhawk operating in the same tiny area.

Right: In standard configuration the Blackhawk can carry 15 fully-armed troops, but this load can be boosted to 20 with minimally-equipped personnel.

Below: Surviving AH-1s have largely been relegated to Army National Guard service.

Below right: Basic OH-58As have been largely, but not completely, withdrawn.

WA ArNG-assigned unit to replace OH-58A and UH-60A with 3 AH-1F by 1998

1-183 AVN, (ATK), Boise Air Terminal, ID

OH-58A	13	SCOUT
UH-60A	3	CS
AH-64A	18	ATK

ID ArNG-assigned unit to replace OH-58A and UH-60A with 6 AH-64A by 1998

1-189 AVN (ATK), Helena RAP, MT

AH-1F	21	ATK
UH-1H	3	CS
OH-58A	13	SCT

MT ArNG-assigned unit to replace OH-58A and UH-1H with 3 AH-1F by 1998

1-211 AVN (ATK), West Jordan, UT

OH-58A	13	Scout
UH-60A	3	CS
AH-64A	18	ATK

UT ArNG-assigned unit to replace OH-58A and UH-60A with 6 AH-64A by 1998

278th Armored Cavalry Regt, Knoxville, TN; 278 ACR

TN ArNG-assigned unit

D Co./107th AVN (AVIM), Smyrna AP, TN

UH-1H		AVIM
UH-60A	2	AVIM

TN ArNG-assigned unit replaced 2 UH-1H with UH-60A in 1995

4-278 ACR (RAS), Smyrna AP, TN

UH-1H		ASLT/CS
AH-1F	26	ATK/AIR CAV
OH-58A	27	AIR CAV/Scout
UH-60A	15	ASLT
UH-60A	3	CS
EH-60A	3	CEWI

TN ArNG-assigned unit replaced 26 UH-1H with UH-60A in 1995. To replace 26 AH-1F, 27 OH-58A with 40 OH-58D(I) in 1997

III Corps

III Corps is a mobile armour corps, heavy in armour and mechanised infantry units. The command, also known as the 'Phantom Corps', is equipped with substantial armour and mechanised infantry units and is currently assigned to prepare its units for possible deployment to support contingency operations with any of the unified commands. During the 1980s and through the early 1990s, IIICORPS was tasked primarily to reinforce Europe and some of the command's units were forward-deployed to bases in northern Germany. The Army has shrunk its active-duty, heavy armour and mechanised infantry units through the recent drawdown of forces, and III Corps will be the focal point for these forces for the foreseeable future.

The corps headquarters is at Ft Hood, Texas and the manoeuvre force is composed of heavy armour and mechanised units. Since the 1960s the command has been tasked primarily with reinforcement of US Army and NATO forces in Europe. Several exercises, known as Return of Forces to Germany (REFORGER), were conducted in the 1980s, some on a massive scale involving the deployment and airlift of hundreds of aircraft, thousands of vehicles and nearly 100,000 soldiers at a time. The combat strength of the corps has been reduced significantly from the late 1980s when, at its peak, it consisted of five active-duty divisions, an ACR and numerous brigades and smaller units. Two ArNG divisions were attached to the corps for training and, including them, IIICORPS operated the equivalent of nine aviation brigades, nearly 1,000 aircraft.

The corps deployed numerous units to participate in Operation Desert Storm, being assigned to VIICORPS, XVIIIABNCORPS and Marine Forces, Central Command during the conflict. The 3rd Armored Cavalry Regiment (3ACR) was assigned to support XVIIIABNCORPS and the 1st Brigade/2nd Armored Division (2AD) provided the heavy armour to reinforce the 1st and 2nd Marine Divisions. The 2nd Armored Division's aviation brigade was deployed as the theatre aviation brigade, reporting directly to 3rd Army. The 1st Cavalry Division and the 1st Infantry Division (Mech.) were both assigned to VII Corps. Aviation units of 13th COSCOM, 504th MI BDE and the CH-47D battalion assigned to 6th Cavalry Brigade, 2-158 AVN, were also deployed to Southwest Asia, along with a few ArNG and USARC aviation units, mostly air ambulance medevac units. Over 400 aircraft assigned or attached to III Corps participated in the conflict, with others remaining Stateside, prepared to deploy on very short notice.

IIICORPS remains tasked to provide reinforcing armoured forces; it also plans extensively for a variety of scenarios including assisting contingency deployments to Europe and Korea. The force is now composed of two armoured divisions, 1st Cavalry, 4th Infantry (Mech.), which reflagged the 2nd Armored Division at Ft Hood in December 1995. The 3rd ACR, 3rd COSCOM, 6th ACCB and 504th MIBDE are deployable units with substantial aviation capabilities. The former 1st Infantry Division (Mech.) was inactivated in 1995 at Ft Riley, Kansas, losing its aviation brigade, and its flag designation was transferred to Europe to reflag what used to be the 3rd Infantry Division. One of this division's manoeuvre brigades remains at Ft Riley, supported by III Corps in peacetime, using active-duty, ArNG and USARC aviation assets during training exercises. The former 4th Infantry Division (Mech.) was inactivated in 1995 at Ft Carson, Colorado, also using its aviation brigade.

The corps is supported by a number of other major units, including III Corps Artillery which supports four active-duty, and several ArNG, field artillery brigades from its headquarters at Ft Sill, Oklahoma. The 3rd Finance Group, 3rd Personnel Group, 31st Air Defence Artillery Brigade and the 89th Military Police Brigade are units without aviation missions that provide vital support to the corps, along with numerous smaller unit formations. The ArNG has reorganised many of its armour and infantry brigade formations into 15 enhanced brigades. Although these units can be tasked to contingency operations in any theatre, they have reinforcement roles and are aligned with III Corps for training and support. The Army National Guard's 35th Infantry (KS ArNG) and 49th Armored Divisions (TX ArNG) are considered as part of the strategic reserve forces and are supported by III Corps in their training efforts.

The 21st century cavalry

The Army has placed one of its more unusual aviation units under the control of III Corps. The 21st Cavalry Brigade (Aviation) is responsible for the training and fielding of the service's attack and cavalry battalions and squadrons. A common doctrine is used in a number of programmes, including the unit training and fielding programme (UFTP), the reserve-component unit fielding and training programme (RCUFTP), and unit sustainment training (UST). The brigade was redesignated in 1996 from the Combat Aviation Training Brigade (CATB), which was originally activated in the mid-1980s as the Apache Training Brigade (ATB). The change in designation reflects the evolving role of the unit, from just fielding the AH-64A, adding the OH-58D(I) Kiowa Warrior in 1992, and, by 1997, beginning to train its first AH-64D Longbow Apache battalions and squadrons. The designation of 21st Cavalry is an effective marketing slogan, reflecting the unit's role in advancing Army aviation into the next century.

The 13th Corps Support Command (13 COSCOM) is the command element for the combat support and combat service support units assigned to III Corps. With a strength of over 6,000 soldiers, it is the largest of the component units assigned directly to the corps. The command comprises several groups, each assigned a number of battalions. This unit has participated in disaster relief within many states in the US and has deployed overseas to many countries including Haiti, Mexico, Nicaragua and Somalia, rendering personnel and capabilities to host country authorities. Corps-level AVIM units assigned to 13 COSCOM include I Company/158th Aviation Regiment which supports the aircraft of 6th Cavalry Brigade (Air Combat) based at Ft Hood. An Army Reserve AVIM unit, I/158 AVN was inactivated in 1996 at its base at NAS Dallas, Texas. Its assets would likely be assigned to an Illinois ArNG unit, 1-106 AVN (AVIM), if that unit were called to active duty. The 1st Medical Group directly supports III Corps and reports to a reserve component brigade. The unit supports active and reserve component, air and ground ambulance units in several states. The first UH-60A Blackhawks assigned to 36 MEB were assigned to the 571st Medical Company at Ft Carson, Colorado in 1995. The unit operates in hot-and-high environments and the useful load of the UH-1H/V is constrained in those conditions.

The 6th Cavalry Brigade (Air Combat) is the corps-level aviation brigade assigned to III Corps. It was established after the Vietnam War to give the Army a formidable, deployable deep strike aviation force. For many years the brigade trained to reinforce Europe in the event of a conflict and until the 1980s it operated over 300 active-duty helicopters. The unit was the first to field the AH-64A Apache in 1986 when 7-17 CAV, later redesignated 3-6 CAV, became the first unit to transition from the AH-1 HueyCobra. By the time of Operation Desert Storm, the brigade was assigned three active-duty Apache squadrons tasked for deep strike missions and other active and reserve component battalions and companies. The brigade began the conversion to the ARI force structure in late 1994 and completed the programme in 1996. This reorganisation led to the loss of 1-6 CAV, 4-6 CAV and 2-158 AVN, the active-duty CH-47D battalion that had served the brigade since 1987. The remaining force structure for the brigade (at least on paper) are ArNG and USARC units which continue to undergo significant change into 1997. By summer 1996, the brigade headquarters was forward-deployed to South Korea to serve alongside units of the Eight US Army (EUSA), taking 3-6 CAV with it and gaining another Apache unit already stationed in the theatre, which was then redesignated as 1-6 CAV.

New intelligence assets

The 504th Military Intelligence Brigade operates aviation assets in its 15th MI Battalion. This was the first FORSCOM unit to field Hunter UAVs in early 1996. The brigade's 15th MIB(AE) has not operated OV/RV-1s since 1993, and has since lacked an airborne reconnaissance and optical surveillance capability. 3rd Armored Cavalry Regiment was based at Ft Bliss, Texas during the 1980s when it received the call in late 1990 to deploy to Southwest Asia. During Operation Desert Storm the unit distinguished itself while serving as a principal armour element assigned to XVIII Airborne Corps. The brigade-sized unit was upgraded with additional brigades and battalions until it was nearly the size of a division during the conflict. The unit returned to Ft Bliss, where it resided until late 1995 when it was relocated to Ft Carson, Colorado. The reinforced brigade has been proposed to upgrade to a mixed fleet of AH-64s and OH-58D(I)s, but those plans have been pushed back a number of times and it continues to operate AH-1F HueyCobras with its regimental aviation squadron, 4-3 ACR.

The 1st Cavalry Division (1CD) is a heavy armoured division that carries the cavalry designation to honour the tradition and heraldry stretching to the horse soldiers of the 19th century. This division pioneered the airmobile concept during the Vietnam War and the Triple Capability (TRICAP) programme which integrated attack aviation, armour and mechanised infantry as a direct predecessor to today's integrated manoeuvre formations. It converted to a standard armour division in the 1970s when it redeployed to Ft Hood. Since Operation Desert Storm, the division has been extremely busy augmenting the XVIII Airborne Corps and redeploying armoured task forces with aviation assets to the Persian Gulf several times since the war to deter further Iraqi aggression. The division has three manoeuvre brigades based at Ft Hood and its aviation brigade is the last among the active-duty divisions to operate the AH-1F. It is scheduled to transition to the OH-58D(I)s and AH-64D in 1997.

The 4th Infantry Division (Mechanized) reflagged the 60-year-old 2nd Armored Division in late 1995 and has been assigned as the Army's Experimentation Force (EXFOR) to test and evaluate the systems and tactics that will lead the Army into the 21st century under a concept known as Force XXI. The division is preparing to deploy a brigade-sized task force to NTC to field validate the systems in 1997 and determine which technologies will best suite the future needs of the service's combined arms, manoeuvre forces. Some of the aircraft assigned to its aviation brigade have been modified with improved data systems for this exercise, including CH-47Ds of the Texas ArNG's 3-140 AVN which will participate alongside its active-duty counterparts. The brigade will evaluate other emerging aviation programmes including the upgraded UH-60C and Longbow Apache during these trials.

III Corps, HQ Ft Hood, Texas; IIICORPS

6th Cavalry Brigade (Air Combat), Hood AAF, Ft Hood, TX; 6 ACCB
Brigade forward-deployed with Eighth US Army (EUSA) and relocated to Republic of Korea in 1996

28th Aviation Group (Regiment), Arlington, TX; 28 AVNGRP
USARC-assigned group to be inactivated in 1996 and replaced with ArNG group

1-106 AVN (LUH), Decatur AP, IL

UH-1H	32	LUH

IL ArNG-assigned unit with companies in IA, IL and IN

1-158 AVN (CMD), NAS Dallas, TX

C-12C		GS
C-12F	5	GS
U-21A		GS
UH-1H		CS/C&C

USARC-assigned unit replaced 2 C-12C, 3 U-21A with C-12F in 1995. 30 UH-1H, 15 OH-58A retired in 1995 with active-duty company B/1-158 AVN(CMD) to 8 UH-60A unit based at Hood AAF, Ft Hood

2-158 AVN (MH), Hood AAF, Ft Hood, TX

CH-47D		MH

Unit replaced by 3-149 AVN in 1996. 2 active-duty companies inactivated with 32 CH-47D reassigned

3-149 AVN (MHB), NAS Dallas, Grand Prairie, TX
TX ArNG-assigned unit

G Co./104 AVN (MH), Mid-State AP, Philipsburg, PA

CH-47D	16	MH

PA ArNG-assigned unit with Det 1 assigned 8 CH-47D of CT ArNG, Bradley IAP, Windsor Locks, CT

Above: The Army's trials fleet of AH-64Ds is still in the hands of McDonnell Douglas Helicopters, at Mesa, Arizona.

Right: Troops of the 10th Mountain Division, aboard the USS Eisenhower during Operation Restore Democracy in 1994.

Below: Note the AGM-114 Hellfire training rounds on this Ft Hood, based AH-64A.

Below right: The Army currently operates over 450 CH-47Ds.

G Co./3-149 AVN (MH), NAS Dallas, Grand Prairie, TX
CH-47D 16 MH
TX ArNG-assigned unit with 8 CH-47D with Det 1, OK ArNG, Muldrow AHP, Lexington, OK

G/185 AVN (MH), Key Field, Meridian, MS
CH-47D 16 MH
MS ArNG-assigned unit with Det 1 assigned 8 CH-47D of IL ArNG, Greater Peoria Regional AP, IL

4-158 AVN (CSAB), Moore AAF, Ft Devens, MA
UH-1H 45 CS
USARC-assigned unit to inactivate in 1996, to be replaced by ArNG unit with 32 UH-60A

7-158 AVN (ASLT), Scott AFB, IL
UH-60A 30 ASLT
USARC-assigned unit replaced by ArNG unit 1996

385th Aviation Group, Papago AAF, Phoenix, AZ; 385 AVNGRP
AZ ArNG-assigned unit

1-6 CAV (AC), Hood AAF, Ft Hood, TX
OH-58C SCT
UH-60A CS
AH-64A ATK
Unit inactivated in 1996 and reassigned 13 OH-58C, 3 UH-60A and 18 AH-64A. Unit designation reflagged 5-501 AVN(ATK) in Korea/EUSA

3-6 CAV (AC), Hood AAF, Ft Hood, TX
OH-58C SCT
UH-60A CS
AH-64A ATK/SCT
Unit replaced 13 OH-58C, 3 UH-60A with 6 AH-64A in 1995. Unit forward-deployed with 6 ACCB to Korea/EUSA 1996 with 24 AH-64A

4-6 CAV (AC), Hood AAF, Ft Hood, TX
OH-58C SCT
UH-60A CS
AH-64A ATK
Unit inactivated in 1996 and reassigned 13 OH-58C, 3 UH-60A and 18 AH-64A

1-285 AVN (ATK), Pinal County Airpark, Marana, AZ
OH-58A 13 SCT
UH-60A 3 CS
AH-64A 18 ATK
AZ ArNG-assigned unit to replace 13 OH-58A, 3 UH-60A with 6 AH-64A by 1997

13th Corps Support Command, Ft Hood, TX; 13 COSCOM

3-135 AVN (AVIM), Springfield MAP, MO
MO ArNG-assigned unit

F Co./135th AVN (AVIM), Frankfort MAP, KY
UH-1H AVIM
UH-60A 2 AVIM
KY ArNG assigned unit replaced 2 UH-1H with UH-60A in 1994

K Co./158th AVN (AVIM), Hood AAF, Ft Hood, TX
UH-1H AVIM
UH-60A 2 AVIM
Unit replaced 2 UH-H with UH-60A in 1995

L Co./158th AVN (AVIM), NAS Dallas, Grand Prairie, TX
UH-1H AVIM
OH-58A AVIM
USARC-assigned unit inactivated in 1995. 2 UH-1H, 1 OH-58A reassigned

1st Medical Group, Ft Hood, TX; 1 MEDGRP

36th Medical Evacuation Bn, Ft Hood, TX; 36MEB

24th Medical Co. (AA), Lincoln MAP, NE
UH-1V 15 AA
NE ANG-assigned unit with 6 UH-1V with Det 1 (KS ArNG), Forbes Field, Topeka, KS

82nd Medical Co. (AA), Marshall AAF, Ft Riley, KS
UH-1V 15 AA

172nd Medical Co. (AA), Robinson AAF, N. Little Rock, AR
UH-1V 15 AA
AR ANG-assigned unit activated in 1996

507th Medical Co. (AA), Ft Sam Houston, TX
UH-1V 15 AA
3rd Platoon located at Hood AAF, Ft Hood with 6 UH-1V

571st Medical Co. (AA), Butts AAF, Ft Carson, CO
UH-60A 15 AA
Unit replaced 15 UH-1H/V with UH-60A in 1995

812th Medical Co. (AA), Lakefront AP, New Orleans, LA
UH-1V 15 AA
LA ANG-assigned unit

832nd Medical Co. (AA), West Bend AP, WI
UH-1V 15 AA
WI ANG-assigned unit

1267th Medical Co. (AA), Jefferson City MAP, MO
UH-1V 15 AA
MO ANG-assigned unit

21st Cavalry Brigade (Aviation), Hood AAF, Ft Hood, TX; 21 CAVBDE

Brigade formerly known as Combat Aviation Training Brigade (CATB) and previous to that as Apache Training Brigade (ATB)
OH-58D(I) 6 AIR CAV Training
AH-64A 6 ATK/SCT Training
AH-64D ATK/SCT Training
UH-60A 3 CS
Instructor cadre, AH-64D training to begin in 1997

504th Military Intelligence Bde, W. Ft Hood, TX; 504 MIBDE
15th MI BN(AE), Robert Gray AAF, W. Ft Hood, TX
RC-12D 6 Intel
UAV 6 Intel

1st Cavalry Division, Ft Hood, TX; 1CD

Division Support Command, Ft Hood, TX; 1CD DISCOM
C Co./227 AVN (AVIM), Robert Gray AAF, W. Ft Hood, TX
UH-60A 2 AVIM
Unit reflagged from F/227 and replaced 2 UH-1H with 2 UH-60A in 1996

Aviation Brigade/4th Brigade, Ft Hood, TX; 1CD AVNBDE

1-227 AVN (ATK), Robert Gray AAF, W. Ft Hood, TX
AH-64A 24 ATK/SCT
Unit replaced 13 OH-58A, 3 UH-60A with 6 AH-64A in 1996

7-6 CAV (AC), Montgomery County AP, Conroe, TX
AH-64A 24 ATK/SCT
USARC-assigned unit replaced 13 OH-58C, 3 UH-60A with 6 AH-64A in 1996

2-227 AVN (GSAB), Robert Gray AAF, W. Ft Hood, TX
UH-1H GS
OH-58C 6 TARP/GS
OH-58D TAR
EH-60A 3 CEWI
UH-60A 4 C&C
UH-60L 16 ASLT/GS
UH-60L(C) 4 C&C
Unit replaced 6 OH-58D with OH-58C and 9 UH-1H, 15 UH-60A with UH-60L in 1995-96. Unit reflagged from 4-227 AVN in 1996

1-7 CAV, Robert Gray AAF, W. Ft Hood, TX
AH-1F 16 AIR CAV
UH-1H CS
OH-58C AIR CAV
Unit replaced 1 UH-1H, 12 OH-58C with 8 AH-1F in 1996

1st Infantry Division (Mechanized), Ft Riley, KS; 1ID(M)
ivision inactivated in 1996. 1st ID(M) flag relocated to Wuerzburg, Germany to reflag 3ID(M).

Division Support Command, Ft Riley, KS; 1ID DISCOM
601st Aviation Support Bn, Marshall AAF, Ft Riley, KS
UH-1H
A Co. reflagged from F/1 AVN(AVIM) in 1994, inactivated in 1995

Aviation Brigade, Ft Riley, KS; 1ID AVNBDE

1-1 AVN (ATK), Marshall AAF, Ft Riley, KS
OH-58C SCT
UH-60A C
AH-64A ATK
Unit inactivated in 1995 and reassigned 13 OH-58A, 3 UH-60A, 18 AH-64A

4-1 AVN (CMD), Marshall AAF, Ft Riley, KS
UH-1H GS
OH-58D TAR
EH-60A Intel
UH-60A ASLT
Unit inactivated in 1995 and reassigned 6 UH-1H, 6 OH-58D, 3 EH-60A, 15 UH-60A

1-4 CAV, Marshall AAF, Ft Riley, KS
UH-1H CS
AH-1F AIR CAV
OH-58C AIR CAV
Unit inactivated in 1995 and reassigned less 1 UH-1H, 8 AH-1F, 12 OH-58C

2nd Armored Division, Ft Hood, TX; 2AD
Division inactivated in 1995 and assets reflagged as 4ID(M)

Division Support Command, Ft Hood, TX; 2AD DISCOM

F Co./502 AVN (AVIM), Hood AAF, Ft Hood, TX
UH-60A AVIM
Company reflagged as F/4 AVN (AVIM) in 1995 with 2 UH-60A

Aviation Brigade, Ft Hood, TX; 2AD AVNBDE
1-502 AVN (ATK), Hood AAF, Ft Hood, TX
AH-64A ATK/SCT
Unit inactivated in 1995 and to 4ID(M) with 24 AH-64A

2-502 AVN (GSAB), Hood AAF, Ft Hood, TX
UH-60A CS
UH-60A(C) C&C
EH-60A Intel
UH-60L ASLT/GS
Unit inactivated in 1995 and reflagged as 2-4 AVN (GSAB) to 4ID(M) with 4 UH-60A, 4 UH-60A(C), 3 EH-60A and 16 UH-60L

2-1 CAV, Hood AAF, Ft Hood, TX
OH-58D(I) AIR CAV
Unit inactivated in 1995 and reflagged as 1-10 CAV to 4ID(M) with 16 OH-58D(I)

4th Infantry Division (Mechanized), Ft Hood, TX; 4ID(M)
Division flag relocated from Ft Carson, CO to reflag assets of 2AD in 1995

Division Support Command, Ft Hood, TX; 4ID(M) DISCOM

F Co./4th AVN (AVIM), Hood AAF, Ft Hood, TX
UH-60A 2 AVIM
Unit reflagged from F/502 AVN in 1995 with 2 UH-60A

Aviation Brigade, Ft Hood, TX; 4ID AVNBDE
1-4 AVN (ATK), Hood AAF, Ft Hood, TX
AH-64A 24 ATK/SCOUT
Unit reflagged from 1-502 AVN in 1995

2-4 AVN (CMD), Hood AAF, Ft Hood, TX
UH-60L 16 GS
UH-60A(C) 2 C&C
EH-60A 3 CEWI
UH-60C 2 C&C
UH-60L 4 CS
Unit reflagged from 2-502 AVN in 1995. 2 UH-60A(C) replaced by UH-60C in 1996-97

1-10 CAV, Hood AAF, Ft Hood, TX
OH-58D(I) 16 AIR CAV
Unit reflagged from 2-1 CAV in 1995

3rd Armored Cavalry Regt, Ft Carson, CO; 3 ACR
Brigade-sized unit relocated from Ft Bliss, TX in 1995

I Co./158th AVN (AVIM), Butts AAF, Ft Carson, CO
UH-60A 2 AVIM
Unit relocated from Biggs AAF, Ft Bliss, TX in 1995

4-3 ACR(RAS), Butts AAF, Ft Carson, CO
AH-1F 40 ATK/AIR CAV
OH-58C AIR CAV/SCOUT
EH-60A 3 INTEL
UH-60L 15 ASLT/GS/CS
Unit relocated with 3ACR in 1995, 27 OH-58C replaced by 14 AH-1F. From 18 to 15 UH-60L in 1996

XVIII Airborne Corps (XVIIIABNCORPS)

XVIII Airborne Corps is the Army's contingency corps, tasked to prepare its assigned units for a wide variety of conflicts, anywhere in the world. Some of the corps's units – including the 18th Aviation Brigade, 82nd Airborne Division and 101st Airborne Division (Air Assault) – have large portions of their personnel and assets ready to deploy on less than 18 hours' notice. The corps has a primary mission to support USCENTCOM and USSOUTHCOM, and its units are trained and supplied for rapid deployment to these two diverse regions. The command also prepares and plans for potential conflicts in the European and Pacific theatres, if the need arises. Known as the 'Dragon Corps', it is assigned a variety of unique light infantry, mechanised infantry, armour and support units which give commanders and planners the ability to customise force packages and task forces for a wide variety of scenarios. The traditional home for the corps has been Ft Bragg, near Fayetteville, North Carolina.

The corps is the first to receive the latest equipment and it has been among the most active in the US Army since the Vietnam War. The HQ and most of its assigned units were deployed to Saudi Arabia during Operation Desert Shield/Storm. XVIII Airborne Corps was one of two corps assigned to Third US Army (THREEUSA), leading the 24th Infantry Division (Mech.), 82nd Airborne Division, 101st Airborne Division (Air Assault), 18th Aviation Brigade and many support units during the conflict. The corps was reinforced with the 3rd Armored Cavalry Regiment from IIICORPS, 12th Aviation Brigade from VIICORPS and the French 6th Light Armored Division. At peak strength, the force consisted of over 115,000 soldiers, 21,000 wheeled vehicles, 4,300 tracked and armour vehicles and nearly 1,100 Army aircraft from its six aviation brigades. Since the end of the war, XVIIIABNCORPS has maintained a presence in Kuwait, pre-positioning the equivalent armour, vehicles and war-fighting stocks necessary to support an armour brigade. The personnel to man the equipment would be deployed on short notice from their bases in the US. The 24th Infantry Division, now the 3rd Infantry Division, has been the primary unit tasked to fulfil this mission in any potential contingency, and since at least 1993 the 1st Cavalry Division, assigned to III Corps, has supplemented this mission. Both units have repeatedly sent task force-sized units to the theatre to operate the equipment for short periods, both in training exercises and to deter any potential Iraqi military aggression.

Major combat support and combat service support elements of XVIIIABNCORPS are assigned to the 1st Corps Support Command (1 COSCOM). This reinforced brigade-sized unit commands the combat support and combat service support units, including the 56th MEB which commands medical companies and detachments, some assigned to ArNG units. A new battalion, 4-159 AVN, was activated in 1996 to consolidate the aviation intermediate maintenance (AVIM) units dispersed to several bases assigned to the corps. The 224th Military Intelligence Bn (AE) is assigned to an MI brigade which supports the corps, most recently operating RC-12Ns and OV/RV-1Ds until the latter was retired from service with the unit in September 1996.

The 18th Aviation Brigade (Corps) (Airborne) is the corps aviation brigade and was activated in 1987 at Simmons Army Airfield, Ft Bragg, North Carolina, where it continues to be based. It is currently assigned nine battalions with about 150 aircraft. The brigade was among the first ConUS units to transition from the AOE to ARI structure at its Ft Bragg base. With the drawdown of units in Europe from 1992, two Apache units, 1-229 and 3-229 AVN (ATK), were activated from units relocated from Germany. Two ArNG Apache battalions in North and South Carolina are also available to the brigade and they routinely train with the unit. Another active-duty Apache battalion is technically assigned to the 1st Aviation Brigade, a TRADOC command, at Ft Rucker in peacetime. This unit has performed as a battalion-level aviation experimentation force (EXFOR) and was the first to operate the OH-58D(I) alongside the Apache. It operated prototype AH-64Ds against AH-64As in a force-on-force exercise known as the Force Development Test and Evaluation (FDT&E), and also validated the tactics for the RAH-66, even though the aircraft is still in prototype development.

Above: This UH-60L is operated by the 82nd Airborne Division which has two air assault units equipped with Blackhawks, based at Ft Bragg.

Above: The 10th Infantry Division (Light), also known as the 10th Mountain Division, was one of the last front-line AH-1F users.

Left: Troops of the 101st Airborne deplane from a UH-60. The 101st is entirely dependent on helicopters for its battlefield mobility.

Right: The load-carrying ability of the UH-60L Blackhawk is demonstrated by this HUMVEE-toting example.

The brigade bases some of its units at Hunter AAF, in Savannah, Georgia. Among the other units assigned to the brigade is the 4-2 Light Regimental Aviation Squadron (4-2 LRAS), which is detached from its parent unit, the Ft Polk, Louisiana-based 2nd Armored Cavalry Regiment (Light). This facilitates the training for the unit alongside other XVIII Airborne Corps assets as the unit prepares for deployment. Its aircrews all receive deck landing qualification (DLQ) to permit operation from naval surface warfare combatants and auxiliary ships.

The changes in the composition of the aviation units in XVIII Airborne Corps has been dramatic. The corps aviation brigade, 18th AVNBDE, and the aviation brigades of the four divisions assigned full-time to the corps have undergone a major change, from 1,208 aircraft assigned in FY94 to a projected force of 914 in FY97, composed of fewer – but more capable – combat aircraft. The following chart illustrates the transition of force levels that has taken place over the last four years.

Inventory Levels

Aircraft	*FY94*	*FY97*
UH-1H	235	32
AH-1F	70	0
CH-47D	112	96
OH-58A/C	238	21
OH-58D	58	-
OH-58D(I)	-	168
UH-60A/L	243	357
AH-64A	252	240

The 10th Infantry Division (Light), known as the 10th Mountain Division, is one of only a handful of light infantry divisions remaining in active-duty service. The aviation brigade was based at Griffiss AFB, 80 miles (130 km) from Ft Drum, from 1988-92 when the unit was able to finally consolidate its aviation force at Wheeler Sack AAF. Elements of the brigade were employed to support the relief of southern Florida after Hurricane Andrew devastated the area in August 1992, and they were a primary force in support of Operation Restore Hope in Somalia from December of that year. Elements of 3-17 CAV, 2-25 AVN (ATK), 3-25 AVN (ASLT) and E/25 AVN (AVIM) provided a formidable cover force for UN famine relief assistance. The brigade's AH-1Fs proved well suited to the cover mission, in what may be the last combat role for the type in US Army service. Additional Army air assets were deployed with the unit from the US Army Europe/7th Army assigned 12th Aviation Brigade and the 101st Airborne Division under Task Force Falcon. Much of the aviation brigade was deployed onboard the USS *George Washington* (CVN-73) in September 1994 in anticipation of the invasion of Haiti in Operation Restore Democracy. The brigade reflagged many of its units in early 1996 and has replaced its Cobras with OH-58D(I)s in both its attack and cavalry battalions. One of its manoeuvre brigades was inactivated in 1995 and replaced with the 1st Brigade/6th Infantry in Alaska.

The 24th Infantry Division (Mechanized) has been the XVIIIABN's primary armoured and mechanised infantry force since the 1980s. The division, garrisoned at Ft Stewart, GA, served with distinction in Operation Desert Storm and is the armoured cornerstone of 18th Airborne. Since 1993 the Air Force has directly assigned the 347th Wing at Moody AFB, Georgia to support the division. It was redesignated as the 3rd Infantry Division (Mechanized) in 1996 and most of its aviation units were reflagged at that time. The division's aviation brigade is configured to the standards of other heavy divisions but is supplied with two attack helicopter battalions, gaining the 1-111 AVN of the Florida ArNG in 1995.

The 'All Americans'

The 82nd Airborne Division, the 'All Americans', continues to be one of the Army's premier rapid-response units. It is tasked with a forced entry mission to seize high-priority targets such as airfields, ports and other transportation hubs that would be required to allow reinforcement US and allied units to assemble and prepare for action against potential adversaries. It trains constantly to deploy anywhere in the world with no notice and to be ready to fight once it arrives. The elite unit is the only US division that is completely outfitted and trained to deploy entirely by parachute, and its soldiers routinely train with Air Force C-130s, C-141s, C-5s and C-17s. Its main strike force is three light infantry brigades, one of which is on alert status to deploy anywhere in the world on 18 hours' notice. Its division support command (DISCOM), division artillery brigade and supporting units are also equipped and structured to parachute from Air Force airlifters. Elements of the division have recently participated in the invasions of Grenada, Panama, the liberation of Kuwait, and in the occupation of Haiti during September 1994. The 82nd was initially planning for a large-scale, airborne and parachute assault which was cancelled at the last minute, while many of their soldiers were in C-130s *en route* to the attack. Its aviation brigade had been pre-positioned in the Bahamas, prepared to transit the Caribbean Sea to meet up with the soldiers who would parachute in. When the invasion was cancelled, the troops were airlifted into the country to maintain a relatively peaceful occupation in order to restore Haiti's elected government.

The 82nd's aviation brigade is uniquely equipped, transitioning its attack and cavalry units entirely to OH-58D(I) Kiowa Warrior aircraft in recent years, replacing more heavily armed Apaches in its attack battalion with the smaller and more easily deployed Bell design. The division is expected to receive a further enhanced variant of the OH-58D(I), known as the Multi-Purpose Light Helicopter (MPLH), which is capable of being used for additional roles including medical evacuation, air assault and some cargo lift. Planners continue to argue the merits of not supporting the division directly with Apaches, and the possibility remains that a battalion will be assigned in the future, perhaps an ArNG unit. The ASLT battalion fields EH-60A and UH-60L variants, and the unit is expected to be among the first to field the upgraded EH-60L Advanced QuickFix variant now in development. The brigade works very closely with the 18th Aviation Brigade, Army Special Forces and the US Air Force's 23rd Wing, based at co-located Pope AFB. The 23rd, also known as the 'Flying Tigers', is assigned directly to support the 82nd.

The 101st: Airmobile

The 101st Airborne Division (Air Assault) is another light infantry division, configured for heliborne assault. The division is based at Ft Campbell, Kentucky which straddles the Kentucky and Tennessee state lines. The 101st operates enough helicopters to provide simultaneous lift to one of the division's three combat infantry brigades, so has the largest aviation brigade assigned at the division level. It is the only division with its own organic CH-47D battalion, its own assigned medevac air ambulance company of UH-60s, and the only one with three attack battalions, along with its AIR CAV unit. The division represents the ultimate in air mobility and its unique capabilities were developed and validated in the Vietnam War, owing its airmobile heritage to the 11th Air Assault Division, later redesignated as the 1st Cavalry Division (Airmobile). These units proved the helicopter's role on the modern battlefield and the 101st took on the mission. The 101st maintains a ready brigade, with an aviation task force, on alert status for worldwide deployment.

The division was mobilised in August 1990 to deploy to Southwest Asia during Operation Desert Shield, becoming one of the first units to arrive in Saudi Arabia to deter further conflict. Apaches of the 1st Battalion/101st Aviation Regiment (1-101 AVN) fired the first shots of the war. Escorted by Air Force MH-53Js, nine aircraft conducted a deep strike against an Iraqi radar installation located under a major corridor for strike aircraft heading into targets on the first night of the air war. During the ground war, the division moved 100 km (62 miles) over one night to set up a support base for a forward-deployed brigade, deep in Iraqi territory. Attack and cavalry units were heavily engaged against Iraqi armour units, including the elite Republican Guard. The aviation brigade was also assigned to support US forces in Somalia from December 1992 and into late 1993. A UH-60A assigned to 9-101 AVN was lost to ground fire in September 1993 with the loss of a crew member and a passenger. Aviators of the unit were crucial in supporting the evacuation of casualties from the ill-fated Task Force Ranger mission on 3-4 October 1993, which resulted in the loss of several special operations MH-60Ls and 18 aircrew and special forces soldiers, after a fire-fight reminiscent of battles of the 19th century.

The ground elements of the 2nd Armored Cavalry Regiment (Light), or 2ACR(L), have relocated to Ft Polk, Louisiana. This reinforced brigade owes its heritage to the unit which maintained its presence along the borders of East Germany during much of the Cold War, prepared to slow down the expected Soviet armour invasion that never came. The unit was originally inactivated in January 1992 but the flag was transferred to redesignate the 199th Infantry Brigade (Motorized) at Ft Lewis, Washington, later that year. By late 1993 the unit relocated to Ft Polk, near Leesville, Louisiana and it is now the primary combat unit assigned to this post.

The XVIIIABNCORPS has been assigned a select few ArNG and USARC units. They are maintained and trained in accordance with the corps's rapid-deployment contingency roles. These units have also recently undergone transition to the ARI-specified inventory and equipment levels, undergoing realignment in the process. The total force of the units assigned to the 18th Airborne Corps will remain at the forefront of land warfare capabilities, as its soldiers maintain it as one of the premier war-fighting formations.

XVIII Airborne Corps, HQ Ft Bragg, North Carolina; XVIIIABNCORPS

1st Corps Support Command, Ft Bragg, NC; 1 COSCOM
4-159 AVN (AVIM), Simmons AAF, Ft Bragg, NC
UH-60A 6 AVIM
Unit with active and ArNG companies in AL, GA, and NC

44th Medical Brigade, FT Bragg, NC; 44 MEDBDE

56th Medical Evacuation Battalion, Ft Bragg, NC; 56 MEB
57th Medical Co. (AA), Simmons AAF, Ft Bragg, NC
UH-60A 15 AA

229th Medical Det (AA), Wheeler Sack AAF, Ft Drum, NY
UH-1V 6 AA

498th Medical Co. (AA), Lawson AAF, Ft Benning, GA
UH-60A 15 AA

Medical CECAT (AA), Lovell Field, Chattanooga, TN
UH-60A 3 AA
YUH-60Q 1 AA
TN ArNG-assigned unit with 2 UH-60A to upgrade to UH-60Q 1997

151st Medical Evacuation Battalion, Dobbins AFB, Marietta, GA; 151 MEB
U-21A 3 AA

104th Medical Co., (AA), Weide AAF, Aberdeen Proving Ground, MD
UH-1V 15 AA
MD ArNG-assigned unit activated in 1996

121st Medical Co., (AA), Davison AAF, Ft Belvoir, VA
UH-1V 15 AA
DC ArNG-assigned unit with 6 UH-1V with Det 1 (WV ArNG) at Wood County AP, Parkersburg, WV; both units activated in 1995

198th Medical Co., (AA), Wilmington-New Castle AP, DE
UH-1V 15 AA
DE ArNG-assigned unit with 6 UH-1V with Det 1 (PA ArNG) at Muir AAF, Annville, PA; both activated in 1996

1059th Medical Co., (AA), Otis ANGB, Falmouth, MA
UH-1V 15 AA
MA ArNG-assigned unit activated in 1996

1159th Medical Co., (AA), Concord MAP, NH
UH-1V 15 AA
NH ArNG-assigned unit with 6 UH-1V with Det 1 (NJ ArNG) at Mercer County AP, W. Trenton, NJ activated in 1996

429th Medical Evacuation Battalion, Hunter AAF, Savannah, GA; 429 MEB
U-21A 3 AA
GA ArNG-assigned unit activated in 1995

107th Medical Co., (AA), Akron-Canton Reg. AP, N. Canton, OH
UH-1V 15 AA
OH ArNG-assigned unit activated in 1996

148th Medical Co., (AA), Winder AP, GA
UH-1V 15 AA
GA ArNG-assigned unit relocated from Dobbins AFB in1995

681st Medical Co., (AA), Shelbyville MAP, IN
UH-1V 15 AA
IN ArNG-assigned unit activated in1996

1241st Medical Co., (AA), Richmond IAP, Sandston, VA
UH-1V 15 AA
VA ArNG-assigned unit

1255th Medical Co., (AA), Hawkins Field, Jackson, MS
UH-1V 15 AA
MS ArNG-assigned unit

18th Aviation Brigade, Simmons AAF, Ft Bragg, NC; 18 AVNBDE

'Golden Knights', US Army Parachute Team, Simmons AAF, Ft Bragg
C-12C 1
C-31A 2
UV-20A 2
Unit replaced 1 U-21A with C-12C 1996

4-2 ACR(L), Simmons AAF, Ft Bragg, NC; 2 LRAS
OH-58D(I) 32 AIR CAV
UH-60L 15 ASLT/CS
Unit forward-deployed from 2ACR, Ft Polk, LA

159th Aviation Group, Simmons AAF, Ft Bragg, NC; 159 AVNGRP
1-58 AVN (ATS), Simmons AAF, Ft Bragg, NC
PA-31T 1 GS/OSA
UH-1H 4 GS
Unit provides air traffic services for FORSCOM. PA-31T to be replaced by C-12 and UH-1H to be retired by 1997

1-131 AVN (CSAB), Birmingham MAP, Alabama
UH-60A 32 CS
AL ArNG-assigned unit with companies in AL and FL

1-159 AVN (CMD), Simmons AAF, Ft Bragg, NC
C-12F 5 GS
OH-58C 15 TAR
UH-60L 12 CS
UH-60L(C) 12 C&C
Unit gained 8 UH-60L, 8 UH-60L(C) in 1996

2-159 AVN (MHB), Simmons AAF, Ft Bragg, NC
Active-duty unit

A/2-159 AVN (MH), Simmons AAF, Ft Bragg, NC
CH-47D 16 MH
Active-duty company

B/2-159 AVN (MH), Hunter AAF, Savannah, GA
CH-47D 16 MH
Active-duty company

F/131 AVN (MH), Birmingham IAP, AL
CH-47D 16 MH
AL ArNG-assigned unit with 8 CH-47D of Det 1 (GA ArNG) at Hunter AAF, Savannah, GA

6-159 AVN (ASLT), Lawson AAF, Ft Benning, GA
UH-60A 30 ASLT

Above: AH-1s are widely distributed among National Guard units, which operate a mix of AH-1F/AH-1Ss.

Below: C-23s are being transferred to Reserve units to provide wartime contingency logistics support.

Above: National Guard RAID units operate FLIR-equipped OH-58A(R)s on drug interdiction tasks.

Below: The substantial numbers of UH-1s still in the ArNG may yet be re-engined to further prolong their lives.

USARC-assigned unit to be inactivated by 1996 and replaced with ArNG ASLT unit

1-169 AVN (LUH), Bradley IAP, Windsor Locks, CT
UH-1H 32 LUH
Unit activated 1996 with companies in CT, DE, ME and WV

1-244 AVN (GSAB), Lakefront AP, New Orleans, LA
UH-60A 32 GS
LA ArNG-assigned unit from ASLT to GSAB role and replaced 46 UH-1H with 32 UH-60A in 1996-97

229th Aviation Group (Regiment), Simmons AAF, Ft Bragg, NC; 229 AVNGRP
1-229 AVN (ATK), Simmons AAF, Ft Bragg, NC
AH-64A 24 ATK/SCT

2-229 AVN (ATK), Guthrie AHP, Ft Rucker, AL
AH-64A 24 ATK/SCT
Battalion assigned to 1st AVNBDE at USAAVNC, supporting TRADOC in peacetime

3-229 AVN (ATK), Simmons AAF, Ft Bragg, NC
AH-64A 24 ATK/SCT

449th Aviation Group (Regiment), Salisbury, NC; 449 AVN GRP
NC ArNG-assigned unit

1-130 AVN (ATK), Raleigh-Durham AP, NC
OH-58A 13 SCT
UH-60L 3 CS
AH-64A 18 ATK
NC ArNG-assigned unit to replace OH-58A, UH-60L with 6 AH-64A in 1996-97

1-151 AVN (ATK), McEntire ANGB, SC
OH-58A 13 SCT
UH-60L 13 CS
AH-64A 18 ATK
SC ArNG-assigned unit to replace OH-58A, UH-60L with 6 AH-64A in 1996-97

525th Military Intelligence Brigade, Ft Bragg, NC; 525 MIBDE
224th MI Bn., Hunter AAF, Savannah, GA
RC-12N 13 Intel
UAV 12 Intel
Unit replaced 20 OV/RV-1D with UAVs in 1996

3rd Infantry Division (Mechanized), Ft Stewart, GA; 3ID(M)
Division reflagged assets of 24ID(M) and relocated from Wuerzburg, Germany in 1996

Division Support Command, Ft Stewart, GA; 3ID DISCOM
603 Aviation Support Bn, Hunter AAF, Savannah, GA; 603 ASB
UH-60A 2 AVIM

Aviation Brigade, Hunter AAF, Savannah, GA; 3ID AVNBDE
1-3 AVN (ATK), Hunter AAF, Savannah, GA
AH-64A 24 ATK/SCT
Unit reflagged from 1-24 AVN (ATK) in 1996

1-111 AVN (ATK), Craig Field, Jacksonville, FL
AH-64A 24 ATK/SCT
FL ArNG-assigned unit

2-3 AVN (GSAB), Hunter AAF, Savannah, GA
OH-58C 6 TAR
UH-60A 4 CS
UH-60A(C) 4 C&C
EH-60A 3 Intel
UH-60L 16 ASLT/GS
Unit reflagged from 4-24 AVN (GSAB) in 1996

3-7 CAV, Hunter AAF, Savannah, GA
UH-1H CS
AH-1F AIR CAV
OH-58C AIR CAV
OH-58D(I) 16 AIR CAV
Unit replaced 1 UH-1H, 8 AH-1F and 12 OH-58C with OH-58D(I) and reflagged from 2-4 CAV in 1996

10th Infantry Division (Light), Ft Drum, NY; 1ID(L)
also known as 10th Mountain Division

Division Support Command, Ft Drum, NY; 10ID DISCOM
C Co./10th AVN (AVIM), Wheeler Sack AAF, Ft Drum, NY
UH-1H AVIM
UH-60A 2 AVIM
Unit replaced 2 UH-1H with UH-60A and reflagged from C/24 AVN (AVIM) 1996

Aviation Brigade, Wheeler Sack AAF, Ft Drum, NY; 10ID AVNBDE
1-10 AVN (ATK), Wheeler Sack AAF, Ft Drum, NY
OH-58D(I) 24 ATK/SCT
Unit replaced 18 AH-1F, 13 OH-58C, and 3 UH-60L with OH-58D(I) in 1995. Reflagged from 2-25 AVN (ATK) in 1996

2-10 AVN (ASLT), Wheeler Sack AAF, Ft Drum, NY
UH-60A 4 CS
UH-60A(C) 4 C&C
EH-60A 3 Intel
UH-60L 30 ASLT
Unit replaced 6 OH-58C, 9 UH-1H with UH-60A/A(C) in 1995. Reflagged from 3-25 AVN (ASLT) in 1996

3-17 CAV, Wheeler Sack AAF, Ft Drum, NY
AH-1F AIR CAV
UH-1H CS
OH-58C AIR CAV
OH-58D(I) 16 AIR CAV
Unit replaced 1 UH-1H, 8 AH-1F, and 12 OH-58C with OH-58D(I) in 1995

82nd Airborne Division, Ft Bragg, NC; 82AD

Division Support Command, Ft Bragg, NC; 82ABN DISCOM
D Co./82 AVN (AVIM), Simmons AAF, Ft Bragg, NC
UH-60L 2 AVIM

Aviation Brigade, Ft Bragg, TX; 82ABN AVNBDE
1-82 AVN (ATK), Simmons AAF, Ft Bragg, NC
OH-58D(I) 24 ATK/Scout
Replaced 13 OH-58C, 3 UH-60L, 18 AH-64A with OH-58D(I) in 1994

2-82 AVN (ASLT), Simmons AAF, Ft Bragg, NC
EH-60A 3 CEWI
UH-60L 34 ASLT/CS
UH-60L(C) 4 C&C
Unit replaced 12 OH-58C with 8 UH-60L/L(C) in 1994

1-17 CAV, Simmons AAF, Ft Bragg, NC
OH-58D(I) 24 AIR CAV

101st Airborne Division (Air Assault), Ft Campbell, KY; 101AD(AASLT)

Division Support Command, Ft Campbell, KY; 101ABN DISCOM
8-101 AVN (AVIM), Campbell AAF, Ft Campbell, KY
UH-60A 6 AVIM
Unit has 3 AVIM companies

326th Medical Evacuation Bn, Ft Campbell, KY; 326 MEB

50th Medical Co. (AA), Campbell AAF, Ft Campbell, KY
UH-60A 15 AA

Aviation Brigade, Campbell AAF, Ft Campbell, KY; 101AD AVNBDE
1-101 AVN (ATK), Campbell AAF, Ft Campbell, KY
AH-64A 24 ATK/SCT
Unit replaced 13 OH-58C, 3 UH-60A with 6 AH-64A in 1995

2-101 AVN (ATK), Campbell AAF, Ft Campbell, KY
AH-64A 24 ATK/SCT
Unit replaced 13 OH-58C, 3 UH-60A with 6 AH-64A in 1995

3-101 AVN (ATK), Campbell AAF, Ft Campbell, KY
Unit inactivated in 1995 with 13 OH-58C, 3 UH-60A, 18 AH-64A reassigned

8-229 AVN (ATK), Goodman AAF, Ft Knox, KY
AH-64A 24 ATK/Scout
USARC-assigned unit replaced 3-101 AVN (ATK) 1995

3-101 AVN (ASLT), Campbell AAF, Ft Campbell, KY
UH-60L 30 ASLT
Unit reflagged from 9-101 AVN (ASLT) in 1995

4-101 AVN (ASLT), Campbell AAF, Ft Campbell, KY
UH-60L 30 ASLT

5-101 AVN (ASLT), Campbell AAF, Ft Campbell, KY
UH-60L 30 ASLT

6-101 AVN (CMD) Campbell AAF, Ft Campbell, KY
UH-60A 16 GS/CS
EH-60A 3 Intel
UH-60L(C) 8 C&C
Unit replaced 30 UH-1H with UH-60A, UH-60L/L(C) in 1995

7-101 AVN (MHB), Campbell AAF, Ft Campbell, KY
CH-47D 48 Medium Heli
Unit replaced 3 UH-1H with 3 CH-47D in 1995

9-101 AVN (ASLT), Campbell AAF, Ft Campbell, KY
UH-60L ASLT
Unit inactivated in 1995 with assets reflagged to 3-101 AVN

2-17 CAV, Sabre AHP, Ft Campbell, KY
OH-58D(I) 32 AIR CAV

2nd Armored Cavalry Regt (Light), Ft Polk, LA; 2 ACR(L)

4-2 ACR(L), Simmons AAF, Ft Bragg, NC; 2 LRAS
OH-58D(I) 32 ATK/AIR CAV
UH-60L 15 ASLT/GS/C&C
Aviation battalion forward-deployed with 18th AVNBDE (Corps)

US Army National Guard (ArNG)

The Army National Guard operates aviation units in all 50 states, the District of Columbia and the territories of Guam, Puerto Rico and the Virgin Islands. The Air Force and Army Guard are represented at the Pentagon by the National Guard Bureau (NGB), which acts as their advocate within the political process in Washington, DC. Funding for the ArNG comes from Congress and is separate from federal Army Reserve forces; it is managed through the separate state governments by a series of legal agreements. Much of the ArNG's equipment was purchased through the federal government, but the funds for its operation and staffing are run at the state level. The ArNG units are available to be called at the discretion of the President, or through federal requests by Congress, in times of extreme emergencies. The use of ArNG forces on active duty is usually for periods of less than six months, but there have been exceptions.

To active duty

If an ArNG unit has an assignment to an active-duty command, it will train and prepare for service like the AC units, but, unless activated, it is technically commanded by the governor of each respective state or territory through the military representative, The Adjutant General (TAG). The TAG, or AG as they are sometimes referred to, is usually a one- or two-star general with active-duty experience who has spent several years in the ArNG organisation. The troop command of each state is formed under a State Area Command (STARC), or in the case of the District of Columbia and the trust territories (Guam, Puerto Rico, and Virgin Islands), a DARC or TARC.

ArNG forces have been undergoing significant reorganisation and upgrading since the 1980s. By the end of FY97, many ArNG units will have inactivated, including aviation ones. In many cases, attack or assault units will be replaced by newly reconstituted units with different aircraft types and missions. Many are air ambulance, medical companies that will make up for the shortfall created when USARC air ambulance units were lost. The Army National Guard now provides FORSCOM and the forward-deployed theatre commands with over half of their available air ambulance units and personnel. Some separate infantry brigades had been assigned their own flight detachments of up to six UH-1Hs and OH-58As for support roles until 1995, when these units were inactivated. The 207th Infantry Group (Scout) of the Alaska ArNG is assigned to US Army Pacific (USARPAC), operating a composite theatre battalion of fixed- and rotary-wing aircraft that supports the defence of the huge territory and is available for deployment.

Force re-equipment

The Army National Guard accepted its first AH-64A in 1987 and now fields seven battalions. The UH-60A/L fleet has continued to expand and over 300 are scheduled to be in service by 2000. The Mississippi ArNG fielded the first and only RC-assigned OH-58D(I) Kiowa Warrior company in late 1993 and, with the value attached to these aircraft, it is almost assured that this unit could see combat deployment in future years. Numerous ArNG aviation assets were called up during Operation Desert Shield/Storm, including the C-23B fleet just entering the inventory and several units of medical evacuation Hueys. No ArNG attack helicopter assets were called up or deployed, leaving some to question the Army's commitment to its Total Force concept of integrated active/reserve component force packages that was used in the 1980s to justify the assignment of sophisticated aviation systems to Guard units. With the ARI programme just beginning to be implemented in the Guard, and with numerous aircraft entering the command from inactivated active-duty units, ArNG units are replacing their AH-1E/P/S aircraft with the very capable AH-1F. The ArNG has assumed management responsibility for upgrading the remaining HueyCobras with the Night Targeting System (NTS) upgrades. The Guard Chinook units have recently reorganised and they are now at full strength, representing a large portion of corps-assigned medium lift forces. The ArNG continues to replace assault/GS-tasked UH-1Hs with UH-60As at a steady pace, but hundreds of Hueys are likely to remain flying with the National Guard for years to come. UH-1Vs will still be the primary air ambulance until a replacement can be found, or more Blackhawks are procured. The branch has been the lead organisation in the development of the YUH-60Q, but funding for upgrading only two additional aircraft had been approved by 1996. At the end of 1996, ArNG aviation still operated nearly 2,500 aircraft, about 200 of which are fixed-wing.

The ArNG will provide FORSCOM with an augmentation force of about 367,000 soldiers. The largest combat formations administered by the ArNG are eight combat divisions, each with its own aviation brigade assigned. These divisions are considered a strategic reserve force, and their modernisation follows that of higher priority units. The Army National Guard is in the process of equipping and training 15 enhanced-readiness brigades that are separate from the divisions, including a single armoured cavalry regiment assigned to the Tennessee ArNG, which is unique in having its own regimental aviation squadron (RAS). These brigades, a force equal to five additional divisions, will be maintained at a level of readiness that allows them the training and first-line equipment needed to make an overseas deployment within 90 days. Three additional separate brigades are structured to support specific objectives, including specific theatre deployments. Numerous other aviation units are assigned to active-duty corps-level aviation brigades, and those operating air ambulance/medical evacuation and intermediate maintenance units are assigned to corps support commands (and are listed with those commands).

'Drug war' RAIDs

Eleven combat enhancement capability detachments (CECATs) were used for a variety of roles including supporting law enforcement agencies LEAs in the drug war. These units were inactivated in FY96 with a net loss of 66 UH-1Hs that were retired or redistributed, and their mission has been largely replaced by reconnaissance air interdiction detachments (RAIDs). At least 84 OH-58As were upgraded for this role with the addition of lengthened 'bush skids' facilitating the ventral mounting of FLIR Systems AAQ-21 turrets and communication systems that allow the passengers and aircrew to talk directly with LEAs. The original programme was set up to provide at least 26 with flights of three aircraft each, to be operated throughout their respective states. In 1996 the programme was restructured to concentrate these assets along the southern states that border Mexico and the Gulf of Mexico, or states such as Arkansas, Kentucky, Oklahoma and Oregon that offer optimal growth environments for marijuana cultivation. The remaining detachments will be strengthened to six aircraft each in 14 states, with aircraft deploying as needed away from their bases. Those states that are losing RAID activities will likely be supplemented by aircraft operated directly by federal/state LEAs.

National Guard Bureau, HQ Pentagon, Washington, DC; NGB

Army National Guard Readiness Center, Arlington, VA

Reconnaissance Air Interdiction Detachments (RAIDs)

AL ArNG RAID Flight Activity, Dannelly Field, Montgomery
OH-58A(R) 3 RECON/OBS

AZ ArNG RAID Flight Activity, Pinal Air Park, Marana
OH-58A(R) 5 RECON/OBS/TRAINING

AR ArNG RAID Flight Activity, Camp Robinson AAF
OH-58A(R) 3 RECON/OBS

CA ArNG RAID Flight Activity, Mather AP, Sacramento
OH-58A(R) 3 RECON/OBS

FL ArNG RAID Flight Activity, Craig Field, Jacksonville
OH-58A(R) 3 RECON/OBS

GA ArNG RAID Flight Activity, Winder AP
OH-58A(R) 3 RECON/OBS

HI ArNG RAID Flight Activity, General Lyman Field, Hilo
OH-58A(R) 3 RECON/OBS

IN ArNG RAID Flight Activity, Shelbyville Municipal AP
OH-58A(R) 3 RECON/OBS

KY ArNG RAID Flight Activity, Daniel Boone AHP, Frankfort
OH-58A(R) 3 RECON/OBS

LA ArNG RAID Flight Activity, Camp Beauregard, Pineville
OH-58A(R) 3 RECON/OBS

MI ArNG RAID Flight Activity, Grand Ledge AP
OH-58A(R) 3 RECON/OBS

MO ArNG RAID Flight Activity, Memorial AP, Jefferson City
OH-58A(R) 3 RECON/OBS

MS ArNG RAID Flight Activity, Hawkins Field, Jackson
OH-58A(R) 3 RECON/OBS

NJ ArNG RAID Flt Activity, Mercer County AP, West Trenton AP
OH-58A(R) 3 RECON/OBS

NM ArNG RAID Flight Activity, Las Cruces
OH-58A(R) 3 RECON/OBS

OK ArNG RAID Flight Activity, Muldrow AHP, Lexington
OH-58A(R) 3 RECON/OBS

OR ArNG RAID Flight Activity, McNary Field, Salem
OH-58A(R) 3 RECON/OBS

PA ArNG RAID Flight Activity, Muir AAF, Ft Indiantown Gap
OH-58A(R) 3 RECON/OBS

TN ArNG RAID Flight Activity, Smyrna AP
OH-58A(R) 3 RECON/OBS

TX ArNG RAID Flight Activity, Muellar MAP, Austin
OH-58A(R) 3 RECON/OBS

VA ArNG RAID Flight Activity, Richmond IAP, Sandston
OH-58A(R) 3 RECON/OBS

WA ArNG RAID Flight Activity, Camp Murray, Tacoma
OH-58A(R) 3 RECON/OBS

28th Infantry Division (Mech.), Ft Indiantown Gap, Annville, PA; 28ID(M)
PA ArNG-assigned command with units in PA, VA and WV

Division Support Command, Ft Indiantown Gap, Annville, PA; 28ID DISCOM
F Co./104 AVN (AVIM), Muir AAF, Ft Indiantown Gap, Annville, PA
UH-1H 2 AVIM
PA ArNG-assigned unit

Aviation Brigade, Muir AAF, Ft Indiantown Gap, Annville, PA; 28ID AVNBDE
PA ArNG-assigned unit

1-104 AVN (ATK), Washington County AP, PA
UH-1H 3 CS
AH-1F 18 ATK
OH-58A 13 SCT
PA ArNG-assigned unit to replace 3 UH-1H, 13 OH-58A with 6 AH-1F in 1996-97

2-104 AVN (GSAB), Muir AAF, Ft Indiantown Gap, Annville, PA
UH-1H 39 ASLT/GS/C&C
OH-58C 6 TAR
PA ArNG-assigned unit from ASLT to GSAB role 1995 with UH-1H to be replaced by 24 UH-60A IN 1996-97

1-104 CAV, Muir AAF, Ft Indiantown Gap, PA
AH-1F 16 AIR CAV
PA ArNG-assigned battalion replaced 1 UH-1H, 8 AH-1S and 12 OH-58A with AH-1F in 1996

29th Infantry Division (Light), Ft Belvoir, VA; 29ID(L)
VA ArNG-assigned command with units in MD, NJ and VA

Division Support Command, Ft Belvoir, VA; 29ID DISCOM
VA ArNG-assigned unit
F Co./104 AVN (AVIM), Weide AAF, Aberdeen Proving Grounds, MD
UH-60A 2 AVIM

Aviation Brigade, Weide AAF, Aberdeen PG, MD; 29ID AVNBDE
MD ArNG-assigned unit
1-150 AVN, (ATK), Mercer County AP, W. Trenton, NJ
AH-1F 24 ATK/SCT
NJ ArNG-assigned battalion assigned to brigade in 1995

1-224 AVN (ATK), Weide AAF, Aberdeen PG, MD
MD ArNG-assigned unit inactivated in 1995 and 3 UH-1H, 18 AH-1F and 13 OH-58A reassigned

2-224 AVN (ASLT), Byrd Field, Richmond IAP, Sandston, VA
OH-58C 6 TAR
UH-60A 38 ASLT/CS/C&C
VA ArNG-assigned unit with 31 UH-1H replaced by 23 UH-60A in 1996. Companies in MD and VA ArNGs

1-158 CAV, Weide AAF, Aberdeen PG, MD
AH-1F 16 AIR CAV
MD ArNG-assigned unit with 1 UH-1H, 12 OH-58A replaced by 8 AH-1F by 1995

34th Infantry Division, St Paul, MN; 34ID
MN ArNG-assigned command, formerly designated as 47ID with units in IL, IA, MN and WI

Division Support Command, St Paul, MN; 34ID DISCOM
MN ArNG-assigned unit, formerly designated 47ID DISCOM
F Co./147 AVN (AVIM), St Paul Downtown AP, MN
UH-1H 2 AVIM
MN ArNG-assigned unit

Aviation Brigade, St Paul Downtown AP, MN; 34ID AVNBDE
MN ArNG-assigned unit, formerly designated 47ID AVNBDE
1-147 AVN (ATK), Truax Field, Dane County AP, Madison County AP, WI
WI ArNG-assigned unit went from ATK to CMD role and reassigned to 3 ARMY 1995. UH-1H, 18 AH-1S and 13 OH-58A reassigned

2-147 AVN, (ASLT), St Paul Downtown AP, MN
UH-1H 55 ASLT/CS/C&C
OH-58A 6 TAR
MN ArNG-assigned unit to replace UH-1H with 38 UH-60A by 1998

3-134 AVN, (ATK), St Paul Downtown AP, MN
AH-1F 24 ATK/SCT
MN ArNG-assigned unit activated 1995

1-194 CAV, Waterloo MAP, IA
AH-1F 16 AIR CAV
IA ArNG-assigned unit with 1 UH-1H, 8 AH-1S and 12 OH-58A replaced by AH-1F in 1996.

35th Infantry Division (Mechanized), Ft Leavenworth, KS; 35ID(M)
KS ArNG-assigned command with units in CO, IA, KS, ME and MO

Division Support Command, Ft Leavenworth, KS; 35ID DISCOM
E Co./135th AVN (AVIM), Buckley ANGB, Aurora, CO
UH-1H 2 AVIM
CO ArNG-assigned unit

Aviation Brigade, Jefferson City, MO; 35ID AVNBDE
MO ArNG-assigned unit relocated from Capital City AP, KY in 1996

1-135 AVN, (ATK), Whiteman AFB, MO
AH-1F 24 ATK/SCT
MO ArNG-assigned unit replaced 3 UH-1H, 13 OH-58A with 6 AH-1F in 1996

2-135 AVN, (GSAB), Buckley ANGB, Aurora, CO
UH-1H 39 CS
OH-58A 6 SCT
CO ArNG-assigned unit went from ATK to GSAB role and replaced 18 AH-1F, 7 OH-58A with 36 UH-1H in 1996 and to replace with 24 UH-60A by 1997. Companies in CO, IA and KS ArNG

1-167 CAV, Lincoln MAP, NE
AH-1F 16 AIR CAV
NE ArNG-assigned unit replaced 1 UH-1H, 8 AH-1P and 12 OH-58A with AH-1F in 1996

38th Infantry Division, Indianapolis, IN; 38ID
IN ArNG-assigned command with units in IN, KY, MI and OH

Division Support Command, Indianapolis, IN; 38ID DISCOM
IN ArNG-assigned unit
F Co./238 AVN (AVIM), Shelby County AP, Shelbyville, IN
UH-1H 2 AVIM
IN ArNG-assigned unit to replace UH-1H with 2 UH-60A in 1997

Aviation Brigade, Grand Ledge AP, MI; 38ID AVNBDE
MI ArNG-assigned unit
1-238 AVN (ATK), Grand Ledge AP, MI
UH-1H 3 CS
AH-1F 18 ATK
OH-58A 13 SCT
MI ArNG-assigned unit to replace UH-1H, OH-58A with 6 AH-1F in 1997

2-238 AVN, (ASLT), Shelby County AP, Shelbyville AP, IN
UH-1H 32 ASLT/GS/C&C
OH-58A 6 TAR
UH-60A 15 ASLT
IN ArNG-assigned unit to replace UH-1H with 9 UH-60A in 1996-97. Companies with IN, KY and MI ArNGs

1-238 CAV, Rickenbacker ANGB, OH
AH-1F 16 AIR CAV
OH ArNG-assigned unit relocated from Shelbyville, IN in 1996 and replaced 1 UH-1H, 8 AH-1P and 13 OH-58A with AH-1F

40th Infantry Division (Mechanized), AFRC Los Alamitos, CA; 40ID(M)
CA ArNG-assigned command with units in CA and NV

Division Support Command, AFRC Los Alamitos, CA; 40ID DISCOM
F Co./140 AVN (AVIM), Los Alamitos AAF, CA
UH-1H AVIM
Unit to replace UH-1H with UH-60A by 1997

Aviation Brigade, Fresno, CA; 40ID AVNBDE
CA ArNG-assigned unit
1-140 AVN, (ATK), Stockton MAP, CA
UH-1H 3 CS
AH-1S 21 ATK
OH-58A 13 SCT
CA ArNG-assigned unit to replace UH-1H, AH-1S, and OH-58A with 24 AH-1F by 1998

2-140 AVN, (GSAB), Los Alamitos AAF, CA
UH-1H 9 GS/C&C
OH-58A 6 TAR
UH-60A 15 ASLT
CA ArNG-activated in 1996 to replace 9 UH-1H with UH-60A by 1997 and reorganise

1-18 CAV, Los Alamitos AAF, CA
UH-1H 1 CS
AH-1P 8 AIR CAV
OH-58A 12 AIR CAV
CA ArNG-assigned unit to replace UH-1H, AH-1P and OH-58A with 16 AH-1F by 1998

42nd Infantry Division (Mechanized), Troy, NY; 42ID(M)
NY ArNG-assigned command with units in CT, MA, NY and RI

Division Support Command, Albany, NY; 42ID DISCOM
NY ArNG-assigned unit
F Co./142 AVN (AVIM), Albany County AP, Latham, NY
UH-1H AVIM
UH-60A 2 AVIM
NY ArNG-assigned unit replaced 2 UH-1H with UH-60A in 1996

Aviation Brigade, Patchogue, NY; 42ID AVNBDE
NY ArNG-assigned unit

1-122 AVN (ATK), Quonset Pt AP, Providence, RI
AH-1F 24 ATK/SCT
RI ArNG-assigned unit replaced 3 UH-1H, 21 AH-1S and 13 OH-58A with 24 AH-1F in 1996

1-142 AVN (ATK), Albany County AP, Latham, NY
NY ArNG-assigned unit inactivated 1996 with 3 UH-1H, 18 AH-1F and 13 OH-58A reassigned

2-142 AVN, (GSAB), Albany County AP, Latham, NY
OH-58C 6 TAR
UH-60A 24 ASLT/GS/CS/C&C
NY ArNG-assigned unit activated 1996

2-126 AVN (ASLT), Otis ANGB, Falmouth, MA
MA ArNG-assigned unit reassigned to ICORPS in 1996 with 32 UH-1H, 6 OH-58A

1-101 CAV, Rochester-Monroe County AP, Rochester, NY
AH-1F 16 AIR CAV
NY ArNG-assigned unit reflagged assets of 1-142 AVN in 1966 with 16 AH-1F

5-117 CAV, Picatinny Arsenal, Dover, NJ
NJ ArNG-assigned unit inactivated in 1996 with 16 AH-1F reassigned

49th Armored Division, Camp Mabry, Austin, TX; 49AD
TX ArNG-assigned command with units in NM and TX

Division Support Command, Camp Mabry, Austin, TX; 49AD DISCOM

F Co./149 AVN (AVIM), Mueller AP, Austin, TX
UH-1H 2 AVIM
TX ArNG-assigned unit replacing UH-1H with UH-60A by 1997

Aviation Brigade, Mueller AP, Austin, TX; 49AD AVNBDE
TX ArNG-assigned unit

1-149 AVN (ATK), Ellington Field, Houston, TX
OH-58A 13 SCT
UH-60L 3 CS
AH-64A 18 ATK
TX ArNG-assigned unit to replace 13 OH-58A, 3 UH-60L with 6 more AH-64A by 1998

2-149 AVN (GSAB), Martindale AAF, San Antonio, TX
OH-58C 6 TAR
UH-60A 8 CS/C&C
EH-60A 3 Intel
UH-60L 16 ASLT/GS
TX ArNG-assigned unit activated in 1996

1-124 CAV, Mueller AP, Austin, TX
AH-1F 16 AIR CAV
TX ArNG-assigned unit replaced 1 UH-1H, 12 OH-58A with 8 AH-1F in 1996

Operational Support Airlift Command (OSACOM)

OSACOM was redesignated and realigned on 2 October 1995 from the assets of the former OSAC – which, coincidentally, was also called the Operational Support Airlift Command. The difference was the realignment of the command from a component command of the Military District of Washington to a field operating agency of the US Army, assigned to the National Guard Bureau. The command now manages all OSA aircraft, in four categories: long-range jets, medium-range jets, short-range turbines and cargo aircraft. OSACOM headquarters is at Davison Army Airfield, Ft Belvoir, Virginia. The rotary-wing assets formerly assigned to OSAC, still based at Davison AAF, were reassigned to the newly activated 12th Aviation Battalion (12 AVN) and remained assigned to MDW.

The previous incarnation of OSAC was an active-duty unit activated on 1 October 1992 at Davison AAF. The core of the command was the former Davison Aviation Command (DAC). The Army inactivated its Installation Flight Detachments (IFDs) assigned to US Army Garrisons (USAGs) at various bases and reassigned them to flight detachments at different hub locations.

The OSA aircraft assigned to the Army National Guard (ArNG) state area commands (STARCs) were organised as ArNG OSA state flight detachments on 1 September 1994. This change made better use of OSAC scheduling to incorporate the Guard aircraft into a system that allows greater availability and flexibility to meet transportation requirements. These state flight detachments became affiliated with OSACOM upon its activation.

OSACOM has a requirement for 15 long-range jet aircraft and currently operates a mix of C-20E/F/J variants, adapted from the Gulfstream II/III/IV family. It currently operates only three aircraft in this class, with one C-20E, supported by OSACOM, assigned to US Army Pacific (USARPAC). The command has also increased its fleet of medium-range jets, acquiring two C-21As from the Air Force to join a single aircraft of the type, acquired as a Learjet 35 in 1987. The service has a requirement for between 29 and 35 aircraft of this type, put to bid in 1994 in a programme known as C-XX (Medium Range). This will provide the Army with a non-developmental jet aircraft design already in production to fill a mission requirement of 600-1,800 nm (1110-3330 km), positioned between the short-range C-12/U-21 fleet and the long-range Gulfstream types. The Cessna Ultra was selected as the winner in 1996 and the aircraft will be designated as UC-35A, with first deliveries expected by 1997.

The last U-21 Ute was retired by 1996. They were replaced by additional C-12C/D/F/L aircraft made available by the delivery of at least 38 surplus Air Force C-12Fs taken over by the Army in September 1995. Several C-12Rs with upgraded EFIS cockpits have also been delivered. The Army had previously flown nine C-26Bs. They were accepted by the Army but by late 1996 some sources indicated that they would be turned over to South American services to assist their efforts in the drug war.

By the end of 1996 a new joint command was established at Scott AFB, Illinois: JOSAC, Joint Operational Support Airlift Command. This unit is an element of the US Transportation Command (USTRANSCOM) headquartered at Scott. Its function will be to provide better utilisation of the OSA fleet assigned to the different services. As a result of this reorganisation and the preparation of OSACOM staff, that unit will play a greater role in the movement of material and personnel with their fleet. As a direct result of the changes, the Navy put most of its fleet of UC-12s into storage at Davis-Monthan, Arizona.

(National Guard Bureau, HQ Pentagon, Washington, DC)

Operational Support Airlift Command, Davison AAF, Ft Belvoir, VA; OSACOM

US Army Priority Air Transport Detachment, Andrews AFB, Maryland; USAPAT
C-20E 1 OSA/VIP
C-20F 1 OSA/VIP
C-20J 1 OSA/VIP
C-21A 3 OSA/VIP
UC-35A 2 OSA/VIP
Unit from 1 to 3 C-21A in 1995. 2 UC-35A gained in 1996-97

OSACOM Eastern Region, Fulton County AP, Atlanta, Georgia

Rucker Regional Flight Center, Cairns AAF, Ft Rucker, AL
C-12C OSA
C-12L 3 OSA
2 U-21A replaced by C-12C by 1996

Ft Belvoir Regional Flight Center, Davison AAF, Ft Belvoir, VA
C-12C 4 OSA
C-12D 4 OSA

Georgia RFC, Brown Field, Fulton County
C-12C OSA
3 U-21A replaced by C-12C in 1996

Illinois RFC, Quad Cities MAP, Milan, IL
C-12C OSA
2 U-21A replaced by C-12C in 1996, plus more C-12s by 1996

Kentucky RFC, Goodman AAF, Ft Knox, KY
C-12C 5+ OSA
2 U-21A replaced by C-12C in 1996

North Carolina RFC, Simmons AAF, Ft Bragg, NC
C-12C 5 OSA

Langley RFC, Langley AFB, Hampton, VA
C-12C OSA
3 U-21A replaced by U-21H July 1995, replaced by C-12C in 1996

OSACOM Western Region, Robert Gray AAF, Ft Hood, TX

Arizona Regional Flight Center, Libby AAF, Ft Huachuca, AZ
C-12C 4 OSA

California RFC, Mather AP, Sacramento, CA
C-12C 3 OSA
Relocated from Bicycle Lake AAF, Ft Irwin, CA in 1994. 1 U-21A replaced by C-12C in 1996

Colorado RFC, Peterson AFB, CO
C-12C 4 OSA

Kansas RFC, Sherman AAF, Ft Leavenworth, KS
C-12C OSA
3 U-21A replaced by C-12C by 1996

Oklahoma RFC, Henry Post AAF, Ft Sill, OK
C-12C OSA
5 U-21F replaced by C-12Cs in 1996

Texas RFC, Robert Gray AAF, Ft Hood, TX
C-12C OSA
2 U-21A replaced by C-12C by 1996

Utah RFC, SLC No. 2 AP, West Jordan, UT
C-12C 3 OSA

Lewis RFCr, Gray AAF, Ft Lewis, WA
C-12C OSA
2 U-21A replaced by C-12C by 1996

ArNG State Area Command (STARC) assigned detachments

Alabama ArNG STARC Flight Det, Dannelly Field, Montgomery
C-12F 1 OSA
C-23B 1 GS/TA

Alaska ArNG STARC Flight Det, Bryant AHP, Ft Richardson
C-12F 1 OSA

Arkansas ArNG STARC Flt Det, Robinson AAF, Camp Robinson
C-26B 1 OSA

Arizona ArNG STARC Flight Detachment, Phoenix IAP
C-12R OSA
1 C-12D replaced by C-12R in 1996

California ArNG STARC Flight Det, Mather AP, Sacramento
C-12F 1 OSA

Colorado ArNG STARC Flight Detachment, Buckley ANGB
C-26B 1 OSA

Connecticut ArNG STARC Flt Det, Bradley IAP, Windsor Locks
C-12 2 OSA
1 U-21A replaced by C-12 in 1996

Delaware ArNG STARC, Wilmington-New Castle AP
C-12 2 OSA
U-21A replaced by C-12 in 1996

District of Columbia ArNG DARC Flight Det, Davison AAF, Ft Belvoir
C-12F 1 OSA
C-26B 1 OSA
UH-60A 2 GS/VIP
1 C-12F deployed to USARSO, Ft Kobbe, Panama

Florida ArNG STARC Flight Det, St Augustine Mun. AP
C-12F 1 OSA

Georgia ArNG STARC, Dobbins AFB, Marietta
C-26B 1 OSA

Hawaii ArNG STARC Flight Det, Wheeler AAF, Oahu
C-26B 1 OSA

Idaho ArNG STARC Flight Detachment, Gowen Field, Boise
C-12F 1 OSA

Illinois ArNG STARC Flight Detachment, Decatur AP
C-12F 1 OSA

Indiana ArNG STARC Flight Det, Shelby County AP, Shelbyville
C-12 2 OSA
1 U-21A replaced by C-12 in 1996

Iowa ArNG STARC Flight Detachment, Boone MAP
C-12 1 OSA
U-21A OSA
1 U-21A replaced by C-12 in 1996

Kansas ArNG STARC Flt Det, Forbes Field, Topeka
C-12D 1 OSA

Kentucky ArNG STARC Flt Det, Capitol City AP, Frankfort
C-12 2 OSA
1 U-21A replaced by C-12 in 1996

Louisiana ArNG STARC Flt Det, Lakefront AP, New Orleans
C-12D 1 OSA

Massachusetts ArNG STARC Flt Det, Hanscom State AP
C-26B 1 OSA

Maine ArNG STARC Flight Detachment, Bangor IAP, ME
C-12 2 OSA
1 U-21A replaced by C-12 in 1996

Michigan ArNG STARC Flight Det, Abrams Mun, Grand Ledge
C-12D 1 OSA

Minnesota ArNG STARC Flt Det, St Paul Downtown AP
C-12 2 OSA
1 U-21A replaced by C-12 in 1996

Mississippi ArNG STARC Flt Det, Hawkins Field, Jackson
C-12D 1 OSA

Missouri ArNG STARC Flt Det, Memorial AP, Jefferson City
C-12D 1 OSA

Montana ArNG STARC Flight Det, Helena County AP
C-12R 2 OSA
1 C-12D replaced by C-12R in 1996

Nevada ArNG STARC Flight Det, Reno Stead AP, Reno
C-12 1 OSA
U-21A OSA
1 U-21A replaced by C-12 in 1996

Nebraska ArNG STARC Flight Det, Lincoln Mun. AP
C-12 2 OSA
1 U-21A replaced by C-12 in 1996

New Hampshire ArNG STARC Flt Det, Concord Mun. AP
C-12 2 OSA
1 U-21A replaced by C-12 by 1996

New Jersey ArNG STARC Flight Det, Mercer County AP, W. Trenton
C-12 2 OSA
1 U-21A replaced by C-12 in 1996

New Mexico ArNG STARC Flight Det, Santa Fe Mun. AP
C-12D 1 OSA

New York ArNG STARC Flt Det, Albany County AP, Latham
C-12F 1 OSA

North Carolina ArNG STARC Flt Det, Rowan County AP, Salisbury
C-26B 1 OSA

North Dakota ArNG STARC Flight Det, Bismarck Mun. AP
C-12D 1 OSA

Ohio ArNG STARC Flt Det, Rickenbacker ANGB, Columbus
C-26B 1 OSA

Oklahoma ArNG STARC Flt Det, Westheimer AP, Norman
C-12D 1 OSA

Oregon ArNG STARC Flight Det, McNary Field, Salem
C-12 2 GS/TA
C-23B GS/TA
1 U-21A replaced by C-12 in 1996

Pennsylvania ArNG STARC Flight Det, Muir AAF, Annville
C-12F 1 OSA

Rhode Island ArNG STARC Flight Det, Quonset State AP
C-12 2 OSA
1 U-21A replaced by C-12 in 1996

Sth Carolina ArNG STARC Flt Det, McEntire ANGB, Eastover
C-26B 1 OSA

South Dakota ArNG STARC Flight Det, Rapid City Reg. AP
C-12F 2 OSA
1 C-12C replaced by C-12F in 1995

Tennessee ArNG STARC Flight Det, Smyrna AP
C-12F 1 OSA

Texas ArNG STARC Flight Det, Mueller AP, Austin
C-12F 1 OSA

Utah ArNG STARC Flt Det, SLC Mun. AP, No. 2, West Jordan
C-23B 1 GS/TA
C-12F 1 OSA

Vermont ArNG STARG Flight Det, Burlington Mun. AP
C-12 2 OSA
1 U-21A replaced by C-12 in 1996

Virginia ArNG STARC Flight Det, Richmond IAP, Sandston
C-12F 1 OSA

Washington ArNG STARC Flight Det, Gray AAF, Tacoma
C-12D 1 OSA

W Virginia ArNG STARC Flt Det, Benedum AP, Bridgeport
C-12 1 OSA
1 U-21A replaced by C-12 in 1996

Wisconsin ArNG STARC Flt Det, Dane County AP, Madison
C-26B 1 OSA

Wyoming ArNG STARC Flight Det, Cheyenne Mun. AP
C-12 1 OSA
1 U-21A replaced by C-12 in 1996

US Army Reserve Command (USARC)

Army Reserve aviation began in the 1970s with a handful of aircraft and units assigned. It grew significantly during the 1980s, along with the other Army active and reserve component force structure. In October 1990 the US Army Reserve Command (USARC) was established to increase the role of the Chief of Army Reserve (CAR) in the command and control of Army Reserve forces. On 18 October 1991 the command was formally activated with its headquarters at Ft Gillem, Atlanta, Georgia. The command has since presided over a massive restructuring and realignment with the Army National Guard (ArNG) that has focused USARC on combat service support missions. The command operates 10 Regional Support Commands (RESCOMs), which recently replaced 21 Army Reserve Commands (ARCOMs) that administer and co-ordinate reserve units in several states each. These are aligned with First US Army (ONEUSA) at Ft Gillem, Georgia and Fifth US Army (FIVEUSA) at Ft Sam Houston, TX. USARC also maintains a few division-sized training units, equipped as cadre units that can constitute replacement combat formations in a matter of months. The Army Reserve has been reduced from 319,000 soldiers in 1989 to an estimated force of 215,000 by the end of FY97.

New aviation organisation

The new command gained a sizeable aviation force when it was first organised in 1990. It had over 600 aircraft on inventory, about 40 fixed-wing, and of the remainder 400 were Bell UH-1H/Vs. The command was organised during the build-up for Operation Desert Shield, and many of its units were involved in the activation of RC units. Although it is a numerically smaller aviation force than the ArNG, the Army Reserves sent a larger number of aircraft and units, a much greater figure proportionally. The two Blackhawk-equipped assault battalions were activated, 7-158 AVN actually being deployed to Southwest Asia. One theatre aviation, one AVIM and one military intelligence company were deployed to Saudi Arabia to work beside their active-duty counterparts, along with nine air ambulance medevac detachments. Another three MED DETs were activated for service at ConUS locations.

By 1995 the substantial aviation force began to be inactivated. By the end of 1996, USARC was down to five aviation battalions, two fixed-wing theatre aviation units, two attack battalions and a CH-47D-equipped medium helicopter battalion, and a single military intelligence aviation company. These units are assigned to corps- and theatre-level aviation commands and are included with those command overviews.

This *World Air Power Journal* US Army Air Power Analysis was compiled by Thomas M. Ring, a Dallas-based computer consultant, to whom we extend our appreciation

INDEX

Page numbers in **bold** refer to an illustration

INDEX

Picture acknowledgments

Front cover: Ted Carlson/Fotodynamics. **4:** Christian Hauser, Alexander Mladenov. **5:** Chris Lofting, Michel Fournier, Chris Ryan. **6:** Marcus Fulber, Ton van Dreumel. **7:** Aldo Ciarini, Achille Vigna, Jelle Sjoerdsma. **8:** Yefim Gordon, Ottogalli/Marchetti. **9:** Alan Key, M. Knight, Tieme Festner. **10:** British Aerospace, Terry Senior. **11:** Paul Jackson, Terry Senior, Yaso Niwa. **12:** Yaso Niwa, Boeing, Kawasaki. **13:** Carl Richards, Nigel Pittaway. **14:** Terry Panopalis, McDonnell Douglas. **15:** Lockheed Martin, Northrop Grumman. **16:** Regent Dansereau, Danielle Leong. **17:** McDonnell Douglas (two). **18:** Chris Knott/API, McDonnell Douglas. **19:** Carl Richards (two), Mark Munzel. **20:** Jonathan Chuck (two), Robert F. Dorr. **21:** Robert F. Dorr, RNZAF. **22:** Jim Winchester, Yefim Gordon (two). **23:** Yefim Gordon, US Navy. **25-27:** Marco Pennings. **28-37:** Baldur Sveinsson. **38:** Jim Hooper. **39:** Werner Luddick/Executive Outcomes (two), Jim Hooper. **40:** Aerospace (two), Jim Hooper. **41:** Werner Luddick/Executive Outcomes (two), Aerospace. **42:** Aerospace. **43:** Aerospace (four). **44:** Jim Hooper (three). **45:** Jim Hooper (two). **46** Jim Hooper (three). **47:** Jim Hooper (two). **48:** Jim Hooper (two), Aerospace. **49:** Jim Hooper (two). **50-51:** Lockheed Martin, via Chris Pocock. **52:** Lockheed Martin (two). **53:** Lockheed Martin (two), LADC via Chris Pocock. **54:** via Chris Pocock, Lockheed Martin. **55:** Lockheed Martin (three). **56:** Lockheed Martin (four). **57:** Lockheed Martin, via Chris Pocock, LADC via Chris Pocock (two). **58:** 100th SRW via David Donald (two), Bruce Bailey via David Donald. **59:** Chris Pocock (two), Bob Archer via Chris Pocock. **60:** LADC via Chris Pocock, USAF, Lockheed Martin. **61:** Lockheed Martin (two), USAF. **62:** Lockheed Martin, NARA via Chris Pocock (two). **63:** Aerospace, Lockheed Martin, MAP. **64:** NASA via Chris Pocock, Lockheed Martin. **65:** Lockheed Martin (two). **66:** Lockheed Martin (two). **67:** Peter R. Foster, Randy Jolly, Chris Pocock. **68:** Robert E. Kling, John Gourley (three). **69:** John Gourley, Doug Youngblood (two), Robert E. Kling, Bob Burns. **70:** Ted Carlson (two). **75:** Steven D. Eisner, Ted Carlson. **76:** Randy Jolly, Lockheed Martin (two), Ted Carlson (two), Joe Cupido. **77:** Lockheed Martin, Ted Carlson (four), Steven D. Eisner (three). **78:** Ted Carlson, Steven D. Eisner, Randy Jolly. **79:** Lockheed Martin, Steven D. Eisner. **80:** Peter R. Foster, Chris Ryan. **81:** David Donald, Robert E. Kling. **82:** Peter R. Foster, Lockheed Martin. **83:** Lockheed Martin via Chris Pocock (three), Hughes Radar Systems Group via Chris Pocock (two), via Chris Pocock, USAF via Chris Pocock, Lockheed Martin. **84:** Peter R. Foster, Richard Gennis. **85:** Lockheed Martin via Chris Pocock, Richard Gennis. **86:** via Chris Pocock, Joe Cupido, Randy Jolly. **87:** Randy Jolly, via Chris Pocock. **88-89:** Ted Carlson (four). **90:** Lockheed Martin, Ted Carlson. **91:** Lockheed Martin (three). **92:** Jeremy Flack/API, Frederic Lert. **93:** Frederic Lert (three). **94:** Lockheed Martin. **95:** Ted Carlson (two). **96:** John Gourley, Dana Bell, Robert E. Kling, Hendrik J. van Broekhuizen, Chris Wheatley via Chris Pocock, Richard Gennis, David Donald (four). **97:** via Chris Pocock, Randy Jolly (six), David Donald (two). **98:** Ted Carlson (three), Steven D. Eisner (two). **99:** Randy Jolly, Stephen Kill, via Chris Pocock (three). **100:** Sergei Skrynnikov, Yefim Gordon Archive. **101:** Yefim Gordon Archive (two), Sukhoi Design Bureau. **102:** Ian Black, Hans Nijhuis. **103:** Hans Nijhuis, Sukhoi Design Bureau, Yefim Gordon Archive. **104:** Hans Nijhuis (two). **105:** Yefim Gordon, Dennis Thomsen, Hans Nijhuis. **106:** Tieme Festner, Yefim Gordon. **107:** Sukhoi Design Bureau, Yefim Gordon. **108:** Yefim Gordon Archive (two). **109:** Roman Kondrat'yev via Yefim Gordon, Yefim Gordon. **110:** Sukhoi (two). **111:** Robert Hewson, Gordon Upton. **112:** Yefim Gordon (three), Mike Badrocke (two). **113:** Yefim Gordon (two). **114:** Yefim Gordon (two). **115:** Yefim Gordon Archive (three). **116:** Yefim Gordon, Chris Ryan, Paul Duffy via Jon Lake (two). **117:** Yefim Gordon Archive, Sukhoi Design Bureau. **118:** Hans Nijhuis, Tim Senior. **119:** Dennis Thomsen. **120:** Yefim Gordon, Hans Nijhuis, Alexander Mladenov. **122:** Sukhoi Design Bureau (two). **123:** via Jon Lake, Hans Nijhuis. **124:** Yefim Gordon, Hans Nijhuis. **125:** Yefim Gordon (two), Hans Nijhuis. **126-131:** David Donald. **133:** Ted Carlson/Fotodynamics (two), USAF, Tieme Festner. **135:** Giani Gianandrea, Robin Polderman, Timm Ziegenthaler. **137:** F. Widdershoven/ASA, Randy Jolly, Tim Ripley. **139:** Peter R. Foster (two), Robbie Shaw. **141:** F. Widdershoven/ASA, Jonathan Chuck, Peter R. Foster, Barry D. Smith. **143:** F. Widdershoven/ASA, Robbie Shaw, Barry D. Smith. **145:** Mal Gault (two), Carl Richards (two). **147:** Patrick Allen, Robbie Shaw (two), Neil Dunridge. **149:** Ted Carlson/Fotodynamics, Neil Dunridge, Robert L. Lawson, Peter R. Foster. **151:** Robert E. Kling, Tony Cassanova, Patrick Allen (two). **153:** René J. Francillion, Graham Robson, Neil Dundridge (two).